2005
NCAA MEN'S WOMEN'S TRACK AND FIELD AND CROSS COUNTRY RULES

NATIONAL COLLEGIATE ATHLETIC ASSOCIATION

[ISSN 0736-511X]

THE NATIONAL COLLEGIATE ATHLETIC ASSOCIATION

P.O. Box 6222
Indianapolis, Indiana 42606-6222
317/917-6222
ncaa.org
December 2004

Manuscript Prepared By: The NCAA Men's and Women's Track and Field Committee.

Edited By: Crissy Schluep, *Assistant Director of Media Coordination for Championships.*

Contents

NCAA Men's and Women's Track and Field Committee

Russ Jewett

Bob Podkaminer

Linda Barley

Roger Blalock

Karen Boen

Jennifer Breuer

D. Elton
Cochran-Fikes

Tracy Cumming

Div.		Term Expires
II	**Chair:** Russ Jewett	9-1-06 *
	Pittsburg State University, Pittsburg, Kansas 66762	
	Secretary-Rules Editor: Bob Podkaminer	9-1-08
	P.O. Box 9221, Santa Rosa, California 95405	
III	Linda Barley	9-1-07 *
	York College (New York), Jamaica, New York 11451	
I	Roger Blalock	9-1-08 *
	Purdue University, West Lafayette, Indiana 47907-1031	

* Not eligible for reappointment.

4

Troy Engle   Joe Franklin   Greg Gilbert   Mark Guthrie

DeTrease Harrison   Jim Jones   Sue McGrath-Powell   Craig McPhail

Div.		Term Expires
II	Karen Boen	9-1-06 *
	Stonehill College, Easton, Massachusetts 02357	
III	Jennifer Breuer	9-1-08 *
	Trinity University (Texas), San Antonio, Texas 78212	
I	D. Elton Cochran-Fikes	9-1-07 *
	University of Pennsylvania, Philadelphia, Pennsylvania 19104-6322	
II	Tracy Cumming	9-1-07 *
	San Francisco State University, San Francisco, California 94132-1722	
III	Troy Engle	9-1-06 *
	Occidental College, Los Angeles, California 90041	
I	Joe Franklin	9-1-08 *
	Butler University, Indianapolis, Indiana 46208-3443	
II	Greg Gilbert	9-1-07 *
	University of Findlay, Findlay, Ohio 45840	
III	Mark Guthrie	9-1-07 *
	University of Wisconsin, La Crosse, La Crosse, Wisconsin 54601	

*Not eligible for reappointment.

Darlene Moore   David Nielsen   Roberta Page   Benjamin Paxton

Josh Payne   Jim Pennington   R. Craig Poole   Connie
                                                                    Price-Smith

Div.		Term Expires
I	DeTrease Harrison	9-1-07 *
	Virginia Commonwealth University, Richmond, Virginia 23284-3013	
III	Jim Jones	9-1-05 *
	Salisbury University, Salisbury, Maryland 21801	
I	Sue McGrath-Powell	9-1-06 *
	University of Delaware, Newark, Delaware 19716	
II	Craig McPhail	9-1-08 *
	Lees-McRae College, Banner Elk, North Carolina 28604	
II	Darlene Moore	9-1-05
	Fort Valley State University, Fort Valley, Georgia 31030	
I	David Nielsen	9-1-06
	Idaho State University, Pocatello, Idaho 83209-001	
II	Roberta Page	9-1-05 *
	Shippensburg University of Pennsylvania, Shippensburg, Pennsylvania 17257	
I	Benjamin Paxton	9-1-05 *
	Winthrop University, Rock Hill, South Carolina 29733	
III	Josh Payne	9-1-07 *
	Hanover College, Hanover, Indiana 47243	
III	Jim Pennington	9-1-05 *
	Springfield College, Springfield, Massachusetts 01109-3707	

*Not eligible for reappointment.

Vanessa
Seljeskog

LaVerne Sweat

Donna Thomas

Matt Utesch

Dennis Weber

Div.		Term Expires
I	R. Craig Poole	9-1-08 *
	Brigham Young University, Provo, Utah 84602-2241	
I	Connie Price-Smith	9-1-06 *
	Southern Illinois University at Carbondale, Carbondale, Illinois 62901-6620	
III	Vanessa Seljeskog	9-1-08 *
	Macalester College, St. Paul, Minnesota 55105	
I	LaVerne Sweat	9-1-05 *
	Norfolk State University, Norfolk, Virginia 23504-3907	
I	Donna Thomas	9-1-07 *
	University of Tennessee, Knoxville, Knoxville, Tennessee 37996	
I	Matt Utesch	9-1-05 *
	Lehigh University, Bethlehem, Pennsylvania 18015-3089	
II	Dennis Weber	9-1-08 *
	Fort Hays State University, Hays, Kansas 67601	

*Not eligible for reappointment.

Members whose terms expired after the 2004 annual meeting or resigned from committee:
    Richard D. Clay, University of North Dakota
    John Kane, Boston College
    Ron Mann, Northern Arizona University
    Finn Pincus, Roanoke College
    Annie Schweitzer-Bennett, Wake Forest University
    Monica Severson, Wartburg College

Track and field committee members are selected by division and by geographical location. Questions or suggestions regarding the material in this publication should be directed to a committee person in your area.

For rules interpretations, contact members of the rules subcommittee:
    Bob Podkaminer (secretary-rules editor;
        e-mail: RPodkam@aol.com) 707/545-1781
    Troy Engle 323/259-2715
    Greg Gilbert..419/434-6788
    Sue McGrath-Powell 302/831-8738
    R. Craig Poole 801/422-7508

Major Rules Changes for 2004-05

The figures below refer to rule, section and article, respectively.

The administrative procedures for regional and national championships, which are contained in the administrative handbooks, amy be obtained online at ncaa.org.

Each changed or altered segment is identified in the rules by a screened background.

Rules Organization

The rules have been designated as either administrative rules or conduct rules. Typically, administrative rules are those dealing with preparation for the competition. The conduct rules are those that have to do directly with the competition.

Rules may not be altered, unless flexibility is indicated in a specific rule.

NCAA member institutions are required to conduct their intercollegiate contests according to these rules. Violations will be subject to NCAA enforcement procedures.

The administrative rules indicated in this book are listed below. All other rules deal with the conduct of track and field competition.

Points of Emphasis

Construction of New Facilities

Final track measurements to verify compliance with NCAA rules must be metric. It is possible for imperial measurements to be used during the construction process. (See Rule 1 Introduction)

Hammer Cage Placement

It is recommended that the hammer cage panel on the right side be set parallel to the sector line or 2.85 meters off the sector line, whichever is less. (See Rule 1-10-1, Note 1)

Meet Referee Duties

Meet management is reminded that the meet referee may not serve as a member of the games committee. (See Rule 3-5-1)

Uniform Rule

Relay team members may wear pants, shorts, briefs or any combination thereof, that are of an identical primary color. (See Rule 4-2-3)

Starting Violation Defined

If a competitor commences the starting motion after assuming a full and final set position and before the report of the pistol/starting device, it shall be considered a false start. (See Rule 5-2c)

Qualifying and Drawing Lanes

In an event where no preliminary round is contested, the games committee may assign preferred lanes by entry performance. (See Rule 5-11-4)

Absence from Competition

In events other than the vertical jumps, if a competitor is not present for an attempt in the finals, it shall be deemed that the competitor is passing, once the allowable time period for the attempt has elapsed. (See Rule 6-1-5)

Order of Competition – High Jump-Pole Vault Five-Alive Procedure

The current interpretation and use of the five-alive procedure is as follows: Five-alive is used when there are large fields in the high jump or pole vault (i.e., nine or more at a given height). Five-alive will be abandoned when the number of competitors remaining at a given height is fewer than nine; the five-alive system is abandoned and replaced by a continuous flight until the next height change. (See Rule 6-4-3)

Tapping in the Pole Vault

The practice of tapping in the pole vault is prohibited during warm-ups and competition. Failure to adhere to this prohibition will result in immediate disqualification of the assisted athlete from the competition. (See Rule 6-6-4)

Javelin

Flat throws will not be considered a legal throw in the javelin. (See Rule 6-10-1)

Part I:
THE RULES

Position Statement

The rules contained in the following pages are intended to help avoid problems in track and field meets. The track and field committee responsible for these rules recognizes that they are neither perfect nor complete. They are not intended to cover all unusual situations. They are intended to be simple and concise.

Decisions made by applying these rules and those situations not covered by these rules must be reached consistent with the spirit of fair play and safety, specifically:

Officials—Knowing rules and being just, objective and courteous, while firm in enforcing rules. Acts of dishonesty, unsporting conduct or unprofessional behavior are unacceptable in the sport of track and field and subject to reprimand and/or removal by meet management.

Spectators—Acting in a sporting manner at all times. A spectator who acts in an unsporting manner may be removed from the premises. Meet management shall be responsible for any removal.

Coaches and Institutional Representatives—Doing the utmost within the rules to help athletes perform their best, placing honor and team welfare above victory. Acts of dishonesty, unsporting conduct or unprofessional behavior are unacceptable in the sport of track and field and subject to reprimand and/or removal by meet management.

Athletes—Asking no unfair advantage, resorting to no questionable practices and doing nothing small or mean to gain an end. Athletes should be sportsmen in the finest sense, always honoring teammates and opponents with their best effort, accepting victory with pride and humility, while accepting defeat with goodwill. Acts of dishonesty, unsporting conduct or unprofessional behavior are unacceptable in the sport of track and field and subject to warning, disqualification and/or removal by the referee.

NCAA Tobacco Policy

In accordance with NCAA Bylaws 11.1.5 and 17.1.7 (Division I), 11.1.5 and 17.1.8 (Division II), and 11.1.3 and 17.1.10 (Division III), the use of tobacco by student-athletes or meet personnel (e.g., coaches, trainers, managers and officials) is prohibited during practice and competition.

Any student-athlete or meet personnel who uses tobacco during practice or competition shall be disqualified for the remainder of that practice or competition.

During regular-season competition, it is the responsibility of each institution to enforce the rule for its own student-athletes and meet personnel. During championships competition, the games committee shall enforce the rule.

Call for Rules Changes Proposals

In an effort to include coaches in the rules process, the NCAA Men's and Women's Track and Field rules subcommittee invites all NCAA head coaches or other interested parties to submit rules proposals for discussion at the subcommittee's annual meeting in June. The subcommittee is interested in your ideas and concerns relative to these rules – those you think need to be changed, reinterpreted, added, deleted, etc.

Authors of rules proposals are required to secure signatures of support from head coaches at two different NCAA institutions. Any proposal failing to meet this requirement will not be considered by the committee.

Submit your rules proposal via mail or fax with the exact language you would like to see in the rules book. Please include your name, institution, mailing address, phone number and e-mail address, if applicable. The final rules changes are at the discretion of the committee.

All completed proposals are due to Heather Perry at the NCAA national office (P.O. Box 6222, Indianapolis, Indiana 46206-6222 or fax to 317/917-6800) by May 1. If you have any questions about the proposal process, please contact Ms. Perry (317/917-6141; hperry@ncaa.org). The committee looks forward to reviewing your proposals and will make every attempt to contact you after the June meeting about the status of your proposal.

[Editor's Note: Reference is made in the following rules to certain publications of the International Association of Athletics Federations (IAAF). Information on IAAF publications may be obtained by accessing its Web site at www.iaaf.org.]

RULE 1

Construction of Facilities

Final track measurements to verify compliance with NCAA rules must be metric. It is possible for imperial measurements to be used when constructing track and field facilities.

Note: Figures are not drawn to scale.

SECTION 1. The Track

The Area

ARTICLE 1. The construction of track and field areas shall follow the International Association of Athletics Federations' rules with respect to grade or slope: "The maximum inclination permitted for tracks, runways, circles, and landing areas for throwing events shall not exceed 1:100 (1%) in a lateral direction and 1:1,000 (0.1%) in the running or throwing direction." In the high jump, the maximum inclination of the approach and takeoff area shall not exceed 1:250 (0.4%) in the direction of the center of the crossbar. Prevailing wind conditions should be considered when constructing field-event areas.

ARTICLE 2. The standard outdoor running track shall be 400 meters in length and not less than 6.40 meters (21 ft.) in width. Lanes shall have the same width with a recommended minimum of 1.07 meters (42 in.) and a maximum of 1.25 meters (48 in.) including the white line to the right. Lanes shall be marked on both sides by white lines 5.08 centimeters (2 in.) wide. The lanes shall be numbered with lane one on the left when facing the finish line.

The track may be bordered on the inside by a curb of concrete, wood or suitable material a minimum of 5.08 centimeters (2 in.) in height and width (see Figure 1). The edges of the curb shall be rounded.

Prevailing wind conditions should be considered when constructing running tracks.

Note: For larger meets, nine lanes of 1.07 meters (42 in.) are desirable.

Track Surveying

ARTICLE 3. Tracks shall be surveyed following initial construction and after resurfacing.

Track Markings

ARTICLE 4. It is recommended that the following color code be used when marking the track:

a. Starting line (white)—55/60 meters, 55-/60-meter hurdles, 100 meters, 100-/110-meter hurdles, 200 meters, 300 meters, 400 meters, 1,500 meters, mile, 3,000 meters, steeplechase, 5,000 meters, 10,000 meters;

b. Starting line (green)—800 meters;

c. Starting line (red)—800-meter relay;

d. Starting line (blue)—1,600-meter relay;

e. Multiple waterfall starting lines (white with green dashes);

f. Finish line (white)—all;

g. Relay exchange zones—400-meter relay (yellow), 800-meter relay (red), 1,600-meter relay (blue), 3,200-meter relay (green);

h. Hurdle locations—100 (yellow), 110 (blue), 300 (red), 400 (green), steeplechase (white);

i. Break line (green).

Note: It is recommended that this color code be used indoors.

Measuring Distances

ARTICLE 5. The distance to be run in any race shall be measured from start to finish between two theoretical hairlines. All distances not run in lanes shall be measured 30 centimeters (11.81 in.) outward from the inner edge of the track if a regulation curb is in place. If a curb is not used, lane one shall be measured 20 centimeters (7.87 in.) from the left-lane line as in other lanes. For world, American, collegiate and NCAA meet records, a regulation curb must be in place. In races run on straightaway courses, the distance shall be measured in a straight line from the starting line to the finish line.

For all races in lanes around one or more curves, the distance to be run in each lane shall be measured 20 centimeters (7.87 in.) from the outer edge of the lane line that is on the runner's left, except that the distance for the lane next to the curb shall be measured 30 centimeters (11.81 in.) from the curb. If a curb is not used, lane one shall be measured 20 centimeters (7.87 in.) from the left-hand line as in other lanes.

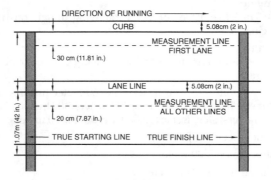

Figure 1—Track Measurements

Note: The following table may be applied to any track with semicircular turns, regardless of radius, for the purpose of determining the points for starts and exchange zones, but only where such points fall on a straightaway.

The table does not apply in determining those points which fall on a curve. In these cases, it will be necessary to locate such points by measuring each lane separately. This should be done by a competent engineer.

Lane Staggers for Races Around Turns

Number of turns to be run	4	3	2	1
For 30-inch Lanes				
Handicaps for Lane 2 over 1	27'2½"	20'4⅞"	13'7¼"	6'9⅝"
Handicaps for Lanes 3, 4, 5, 6, 7, 8 over next lanes to the inside	31'5"	23'6¾"	15'8½"	7'10¼"
For 36-inch Lanes				
Handicaps for Lane 2 over 1	33'6"	25'1½"	16'9"	8'4½"
Handicaps for Lanes 3, 4, 5, 6, 7, 8 over next lanes to the inside	37'8⅜"	28'3¼"	18'10¼"	9'5⅛"
For 42-inch Lanes				
Handicaps for Lane 2 over 1	39'9½"	29'10⅛"	19'10¾"	9'11⅜"
Handicaps for Lanes 3, 4, 5, 6, 7, 8 over next lanes to the inside	43'11¾"	32'11⅞"	21'11⅞"	11'
For 48-inch Lanes				
Handicaps for Lane 2 over 1	46'	34'6"	23'	11'6"
Handicaps for Lanes 3, 4, 5, 6, 7, 8 over next lanes to the inside	50'	37'6"	25'	12'6"

If Lane No. 1 is laid out 4 inches wider than the other lanes, the staggered schedule for Lane Nos. 3, 4, 5, 6, 7 and 8 can be applied to Lane No. 2.

Visible Starting Line

ARTICLE 6. a. The visible starting line, 5.08 centimeters (2 in.) wide, shall be marked on the track just within the measured distance so that its near edge is identical with the exactly measured and true starting line (see Figure 1).

b. The starting line for all races not run in lanes (including the 800 meters, when alleys are used) shall be curved so that all competitors run the same distance going into the curve (see Figure 2).

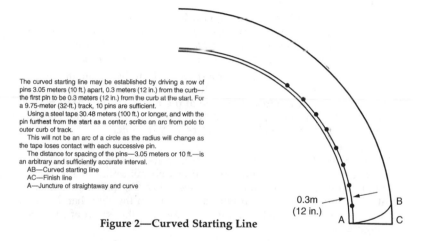

The curved starting line may be established by driving a row of pins 3.05 meters (10 ft.) apart, 0.3 meters (12 in.) from the curb—the first pin to be 0.3 meters (12 in.) from the curb at the start. For a 9.75-meter (32-ft.) track, 10 pins are sufficient.

Using a steel tape 30.48 meters (100 ft.) or longer, and with the pin furthest from the start as a center, scribe an arc from pole to outer curb of track.

This will not be an arc of a circle as the radius will change as the tape loses contact with each successive pin.

The distance for spacing of the pins—3.05 meters or 10 ft.—is an arbitrary and sufficiently accurate interval.

AB—Curved starting line
AC—Finish line
A—Juncture of straightaway and curve

0.3m
(12 in.)

B
A
C

Figure 2—Curved Starting Line

Visible Finish Line

ARTICLE 7. The visible finish line, 5.08 centimeters (2 in.) wide, shall be marked on the track just outside the measured distance so that its edge nearer the start is identical with the exactly measured and true finish line (see Figure 1).

Lane numbers of reasonable size shall be placed at least 15.24 centimeters (6 in.) beyond the common finish line. They shall be positioned facing the timing device.

The intersection of each lane line and the finish line shall be painted black in accordance with Figure 3.

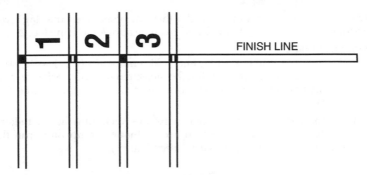

Figure 3—Finish-Line Intersections

Note: A common finish line is recommended for all races. Lines in the finish area should be kept to a minimum. If additional lines are necessary, they should be of a less conspicuous color than the finish line, so as not to cause confusion.

Except where their use may interfere with fully automatic timing devices, two white posts may denote the finish line and be placed at least 30 centimeters (11.81 in.) from the edge of the track. The finish posts shall be of rigid construction, approximately 1.4 meters (4.59 ft.) high, 80 millimeters (3.15 in.) wide and 20 millimeters (0.79 in.) thick.

Running Lanes
ARTICLE 8. In all races up to and including 400 meters, each contestant shall have a separate lane with a recommended minimum of 1.07 meters (42 in.) in width to be marked by white lines of chalk, similar substance or paint 5.08 centimeters (2 in.) in width. The line on the right-hand side of each lane shall be included in the measurement of the width of each lane (see Figure 1).

Break Line
ARTICLE 9. A visible break line 5.08 centimeters (2 in.) wide shall be an arc across the track at the entry of the back straight, showing the position at which competitors in the 800 meters and the second leg of the 1,600-meter relay are permitted to leave their respective lanes.

The arc of the break line should reflect an adjustment in each lane for the competitors in outside lanes having farther to travel than the competitors in the inside lanes to reach an inside position.

Note: To assist competitors in identifying the break line, small cones may be placed at the intersection of the lane line and the break line.

Relay Zones

ARTICLE 10. In all relays around the track, the baton exchange must be made within a 20-meter (65.62-ft.) zone, formed by lines drawn 10 meters (32.81 ft.) on each side of the measured centerline. All lines and/or boxes or triangles shall be inclusive within the zone.

International Zones

ARTICLE 11. A distinctive short mark not more than 10 meters (32.81 ft.) outside the passing zone shall indicate the starting point of the international zone. All lines and/or boxes or triangles shall be inclusive within the zone. Outgoing runners, while waiting to receive the baton, may take a position and begin running anywhere within the zone (see Rule 5-8-4).

SECTION 2. The Hurdles

Placement of Hurdles

ARTICLE 1. The placement of hurdles shall be done in accordance with the following table:

PLACEMENT OF HURDLES

	No. of Hurdles	Distance Start to 1st Hurdle	Distance Between Hurdles	Distance Last Hurdle to Finish
55-Meter Hurdles (men)	5	13.72m	9.14m	4.72m
55-Meter Hurdles (women)	5	13m	8.5m	8m
60-Meter Hurdles (men)	5	13.72m	9.14m	9.72m
60-Meter Hurdles (women)	5	13m	8.5m	13m
100-Meter Hurdles	10	13m	8.5m	10.5m
110-Meter Hurdles	10	13.72m	9.14m	14.02m
400-Meter Hurdles	10	45m	35m	40m

Lanes

ARTICLE 2. Hurdle lanes shall be at least 1.07 meters (42 in.) in width. If hurdle lanes are not marked on the track, they shall be judged as equivalent to 2.54 centimeters (1 in.) wider than the total width of the hurdles.

SECTION 3. The Steeplechase

Distance

ARTICLE 1. The standard distance for the steeplechase shall be 3,000 meters.

Jumps

ARTICLE 2. There shall be 28 hurdle jumps and seven water jumps included in the 3,000-meter event.

Note: Specifications on hurdle height can be found in Rule 2-3-3.

Water Jump

ARTICLE 3. The water jump shall be the fourth jump in each lap. If necessary, the finish line shall be moved to accommodate this rule.

Measuring Course

ARTICLE 4. The following measurements are given as a guide, and any adjustments necessary shall be made by lengthening or shortening the distance at the starting point of the race. In this chart, it is assumed that a lap of 400 meters or 440 yards has been shortened 10 meters (32.81 ft.) by constructing the water jump inside the track. If possible, the approach to and exit from the water-jump hurdle should be straight for approximately seven meters.

POSSIBLE STEEPLECHASE MEASUREMENTS

Lap of 390 meters

Distance from starting point to commencement of 1st lap, to be run without jumps	270 meters
Distance from start of 1st full lap to 1st hurdle	10m
From 1st to 2nd hurdle	78m
From 2nd to 3rd hurdle	78m
From 3rd hurdle to water jump	78m
From water jump to 4th hurdle	78m
From 4th hurdle to finish line	68m

390m x 7 laps = 2,730m

3,000m

Note: Since the water jump is constructed on the area inside or outside the track, thereby lessening or lengthening the normal distance of the laps, it is not possible to prescribe any rule specifying the exact length of the laps or to state precisely the position of the water jump. It should be borne in mind that there must be enough distance from the starting line to the first hurdle to prevent the competitors from overcrowding, and there should be approximately 68 meters (75 yds.) from the last hurdle to the finish line.

Jumps During First Lap

ARTICLE 5. The distance from the starting point to the finish line on the first lap shall not include any jumps.

Placement of Hurdles on Track

ARTICLE 6. The hurdles, including the water jump, shall be placed on the track so that 30 centimeters (11.81 in.) of the top bar, measured from the inside edge of the track, will be inside the track (see Figure 4).

Note: For dimensions of hurdles, see Rule 2-3-3. For weight of hurdles, see Rule 2-3-4.

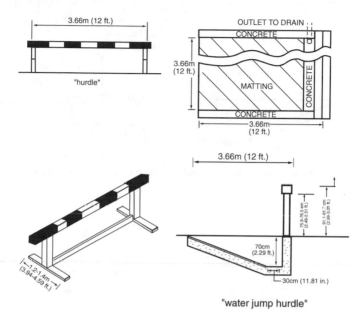

Figure 4—Water-Jump and Hurdle Measurements

Water-Jump Construction

ARTICLE 7. The water jump shall be 3.66 meters (12 ft.) in length and width. The water shall be a minimum of 70 centimeters (2.29 ft.) in depth immediately after the hurdle, and the pit shall have a constant upward slope from a point 30 centimeters (11.81 in.) past the water-jump hurdle to the level of the track at the far end (see Figure 4). It is recommended that the water jump be placed on the inside of the track. The landing surface inside the water jump should be composed of a nonskid, shock-absorbent material. A suitable material between the vertical uprights of the water-jump hurdle is recommended to aid the athlete with depth perception (see Figure 4).

  a. (Men and women) The hurdle at the water jump shall be firmly fixed in front of the water and be of the same height as the other hurdles in the competition.

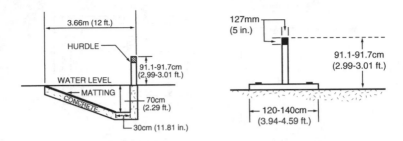

Figure 5—Water Jump and Hurdle Measurements (Men)

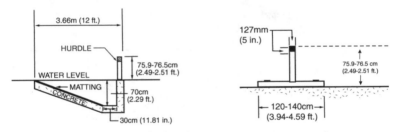

Figure 6—Water Jump and Hurdle Measurements (Women)

SECTION 4. The High Jump

Approach

ARTICLE 1. It is recommended that the approach be an octagon or square with a surface of at least 21 meters (68.90 ft.). The minimum length provided shall be 15 meters (49.21 ft.). The length of the approach run is unlimited.

Takeoff Area

ARTICLE 2. The takeoff area is the semicircle enclosed by a 3-meter (9.83-ft.) radius whose center point is directly under the center of the crossbar. For a record to be approved officially, any point within this area may not be higher than the tolerances (see Rule 1-1-1).

SECTION 5. The Pole Vault

Vaulting Box

ARTICLE 1. The vaulting box in which the vaulting pole is planted shall be constructed of suitable rigid materials. Its dimensions and shape shall be those shown in the accompanying diagram (see Figure 7).

The box shall be of a contrasting color from the runway and shall be immovably fixed in the ground so that all of its upper edges are flush with the takeoff area.

The angle between the bottom of the box and the stopboard (see Figure 7) shall be 105 degrees.

Runway

ARTICLE 2. The vaulting runway shall have a minimum length of 38.1 meters (125 ft.) (see Rule 1-1-1). It is recommended that the width of the runway be 1.22 meters (4 ft.).

The runway may be marked by a maximum of seven permanent lines at 30-centimeter (1-ft.) increments from the plant box back toward the start of the runway. These lines shall be a maximum of 90 centimeters (3 ft.) in length and 5.08 centimeters (2 in.) in width (see Figure 8).

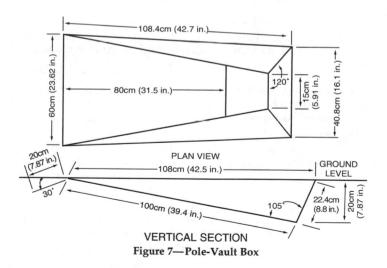

PLAN VIEW

VERTICAL SECTION

Figure 7—Pole-Vault Box

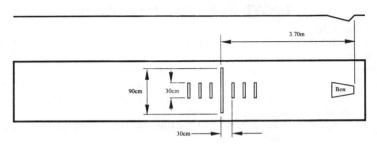

Figure 8—Pole Vault Runway Markings

SECTION 6. The Long Jump and Triple Jump

Runway

ARTICLE 1. The minimum length of the runway for the long jump and triple jump shall be 39.62 meters (130 ft.) from the edge nearest the pit of **each event's takeoff board.** It is recommended that the width of the runway be 1.22 meters (4 ft.) (see Rule 1-1-1). The construction and material of the runway shall be extended beyond the takeoff board to the nearer edge of the landing pit.

> For new construction, the minimum length of the runway should be 40 meters (131 ft., 3 in.) from the edge nearest the pit of each event's takeoff board.

When the runway is not distinguishable from the adjacent surface, it is recommended that it be bordered by lines 5.08 centimeters (2 in.) in width from the start of the nearer edge of the landing pit.

Landing Area

ARTICLE 2. The landing area shall be not less than 2.74 meters (9 ft.) in width and identical in elevation with the takeoff board. The area shall be filled with damp sand to an elevation identical with the takeoff board. Figure 9 shows an approved device for ensuring proper sand level.

a. In the long jump, the distance between the takeoff board and the nearer edge of the landing area shall be not less than 1 meter (3.28 ft.) or greater than 3.66 meters (12 ft.). The distance between the foul line and the farther edge of the landing area shall be at least 10 meters (32.81 ft.).

b. (Men) In the triple jump, the nearer edge of the landing area shall be at least 10.97 meters (36 ft.) (**12.5 meters or 41 feet is recommended**) from the foul line.

c. (Women) In the triple jump, the nearer edge of the landing area shall be at least 8.53 meters (28 ft.) (**10.97 meters or 36 feet is recommended**) from the foul line.

Takeoff

ARTICLE 3. The takeoff shall be a board made of wood or other suitable rigid material 19.8 to 20.32 centimeters (7.8 to 8 in.) wide, at least 1.22 meters (4 ft.) long and not more than 10 centimeters (3.94 in.) thick. The upper surface of the board must be level with the runway surface. This board shall be painted white and be firmly fixed in the runway.

In the absence of a takeoff board, the triple-jump takeoff area shall be 19.8 to 20.32 centimeters (7.8 to 8 in.) wide and at least 1.22 meters (4 ft.) long and shall be painted white or firmly affixed (e.g., tape) on the all-weather runway.

Foul Line

ARTICLE 4. The edge of the takeoff board nearest the landing pit shall be the foul line.

Foul-Indicator Aid

ARTICLE 5. For the purpose of aiding the calling of fouls, the area immediately beyond the foul line may be prepared as shown in Figure 10. A tray 10.2 centimeters (4 in.) wide filled with plasticene or other suitable material may be used.

The plasticene or other suitable material used should be of a contrasting color to, and level with, the takeoff board.

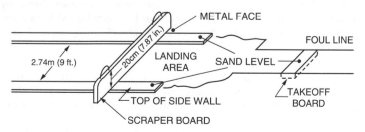

Figure 9—Control of Sand Level in Long Jump and Triple Jump

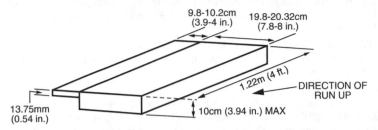

Figure 10—Long-Jump and Triple-Jump Takeoff Board and Foul Marker

SECTION 7. The Throwing Circles

Materials

ARTICLE 1. The circles in throwing events shall be made of a band of metal or suitable rigid material, as described in Figures 12, 15 and 17, the top of which shall be flush with the concrete outside the circle.

The interior surface should be of concrete or similar material and shall be 19.05 millimeters (0.75 in.), plus or minus 6 millimeters (0.24 in.), lower than the surface outside the circle.

Establishing the Sector

ARTICLE 2. The 34.92-degree sector may be laid out accurately by using the chart in Figure 11.

The level of the surface within the landing area (see specifications for each event) shall be the same as the level of the surface of the throwing circle (see Rule 1-1-1).

Diameters

ARTICLE 3. The inside diameters of the shot-put and hammer-throw circles shall be 2.135 meters (7 ft.), plus or minus 5 millimeters (0.20 in.), and the diameter of the discus circle shall be 2.5 meters (8.20 ft.), plus or minus 5 millimeters.

Circle

ARTICLE 4. The circle shall be made of metal or suitable rigid material 6 millimeters (0.24 in.) in thickness and 19.05 millimeters (0.75 in.) in height, plus or minus 6 millimeters, and be firmly secured flush with the throwing surface.

Note: The IAAF stipulates a flanged circle 76 millimeters (2.99 in.) in height, imbedded below the throwing surface to provide rigidity.

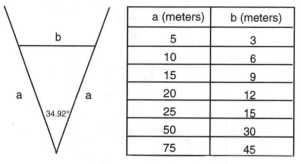

a (meters)	b (meters)
5	3
10	6
15	9
20	12
25	15
50	30
75	45

Figure 11—Establishing the Sector

Insert

ARTICLE 5. The insert shall be made of metal or suitable rigid material (rubber is not suitable) and be flush with the throwing surface. The height of the insert shall be 19.05 millimeters (0.75 in.), plus or minus 6 millimeters.

Dividing Line

ARTICLE 6. All circles shall be divided in half by a 5.08-centimeter (2-in.) line extending from the outer edge of the circle to the end of the throwing pad and measured at right angles to the imaginary center of the throwing sector. Lines shall not be painted within any throwing circle.

SECTION 8. The Shot-Put Area

Circle

ARTICLE 1. The circle shall be constructed in accordance with Figure 12.

Stopboard

ARTICLE 2. The stopboard shall be an arc of wood, or other suitable materials, painted white and firmly fixed so that its inner edge coincides with the inner edge of the shot-put circle. It shall measure 1.22 meters (4 ft.) in length along its inside edge, 112 to 116 millimeters (4.41 to 4.57 in.) in width and 98 to 102 millimeters (3.86 to 4.02 in.) in height (see Figure 12).

Sector

ARTICLE 3. Radial lines 5.08 centimeters (2 in.) wide shall form a 34.92-degree angle extended from the center of the circle. The inside edges of these lines shall mark the sector. The surface within the landing area shall be on the same level as the throwing surface (see Rule 1-1-1).

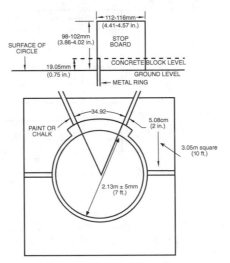

Figure 12—Shot-Put Circle
Note: Lines shall not be inside the circle.

SECTION 9. The Discus Area

Enclosure

ARTICLE 1. All discus throws shall be made from an enclosure or cage that shall be centered on the circle (see Figure 13).

Note 1: The height of the discus cage shall be at least 4 meters (13 ft., 1.5 in.).

Note 2: A discus cage is designed to provide limited protection for spectators, officials and competitors. It does not ensure the safety of the aforementioned personnel.

Note 3: A discus cage should be arranged in such a way to reduce the possibility of the implement ricocheting or rebounding back towards the competitor or over the top of the cage.

Circle

ARTICLE 2. The circle shall be constructed in accordance with Figure 15.

Sector

ARTICLE 3. The throwing sector for the discus shall be marked by two radial lines 5.08 centimeters (2 in.) wide that form a 34.92-degree angle, extended from the center of the circle. The inside edges of these lines shall

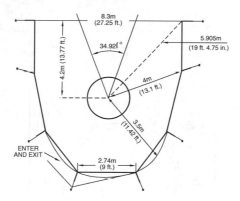

Figure 13—Construction for Discus Cage

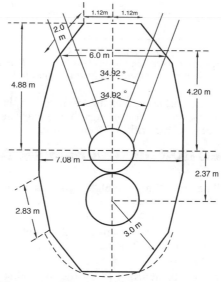

Figure 14—Cage for Hammer and Discus

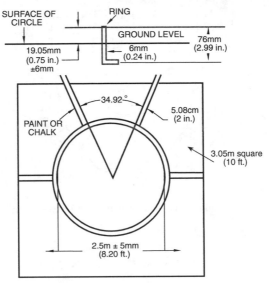

Figure 15—Discus Circle
Hammer requires an insert in the circle (see Figure 17 and Rule 1-7-5).
Note: Lines shall not be inside the circle.

mark the sector. The surface within the landing area shall be on the same level as the throwing surface. Sector flags should mark the ends of the lines. The sector shall be centered within the enclosure.

SECTION 10. The Hammer Area

Enclosure

ARTICLE 1. All hammer throws shall be made from an enclosure or cage that shall be centered on the circle (see Figure 16).

The cage shall be constructed as follows:

a. There shall be two movable panels at the front of the screen. These panels shall be at least 4.20 meters (13.78 ft.) but not more than 4.35 meters (14.27 ft.) in width.

b. These panels shall be attached to a fixed vertical support that is 2.85 meters (9.35 ft.) away from the sector line and 6.086 meters (20.08 ft.) out from the center of the circle.

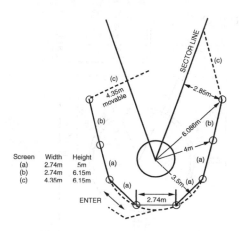

Figure 16—Construction for Hammer Cage

c. The height of the movable panels shall be 6.15 meters (20.18 ft.).

Note 1: When these panels are in place for a right-handed thrower, the panel on the left side shall extend inside the sector line by 1.5 meters (4.92 ft.). If this panel is shorter than this distance, then the panel shall be perpendicular to the sector line. It is recommended that the panel on the right side be set parallel to the sector line, or 2.85 meters off the sector line, depending on which is less. The panels shall be alternated for left-handed throwers.

Note 2: A hammer cage is designed to provide limited protection for spectators, officials and competitors. It does not ensure the safety of the aforementioned personnel. *Any flagged area should not be based on the reduced sector area.*

Note 3: A hammer cage should be arranged in such a way to reduce the possibility of the implement ricocheting or rebounding back towards the competitor or over the top of the cage. Precautions should also be taken to prevent the implement from going through any joints in the cage or the netting, or underneath the netting panels.

Note 4: The opening of the NCAA cage is different from the IAAF opening.

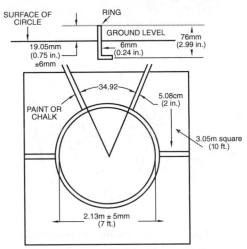

Figure 17—Hammer/Weight-Throw Circle
Note: Lines shall not be inside the circle.

Circle

ARTICLE 2. The circle shall be constructed in accordance with Figure 17 and Rule 1-7-4.

Sector

ARTICLE 3. The throwing sector for the hammer shall be marked by two radial lines 5.08 centimeters (2 in.) wide that form a 34.92-degree angle, extended from the center of the circle. The inside edges of these lines shall mark the sector. The surface within the landing area shall be on the same level as the throwing surface. Sector flags should mark the ends of the lines. The sector shall be centered within the enclosure.

SECTION 11. The Weight-Throw Area

This is an indoor event that may be contested outdoors. For construction of facilities, see Figures 17 and 25.

SECTION 12. The Javelin Area

Runway
ARTICLE 1. It is recommended that the runway be constructed of an artificial surface for a width of 4 meters (13.12 ft.) for the entire length of the runway. The minimum length of the runway for the javelin shall be 36.58 meters (120 ft.). If an artificial surface is used, it is recommended that the runway be extended 1 meter (3.28 ft.) beyond the foul line for safety reasons. The runway shall be marked by two parallel lines 5.08 centimeters (2 in.) in width and a minimum of 1.22 meters (4 ft.) apart for 36.58 meters (120 ft.).

For new construction, the minimum length of the runway for the javelin shall be 36.5 meters (119 ft., 9 in.).

Foul Line
ARTICLE 2. The foul line shall be 7 centimeters (2.76 in.) wide and painted white and shall be made in the shape of an arc with a radius of 8 meters (26.25 ft.). The distance between its extremities shall be 4 meters (13.12 ft.) measured straight across from end to end. Lines shall be drawn from the extremities of the arc at right angles to the parallel lines marking the runway. These lines should be 75 centimeters (2.46 ft.) in length and 7 centimeters (2.76 in.) wide.

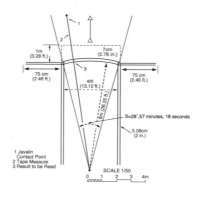

Figure 18—Javelin-Throwing Area

Sector
ARTICLE 3. Radial lines 5.08 centimeters (2 in.) wide shall be extended from the center of the circle of which the arc of the foul board is a part through the extremities of the arc. The inside edges of these lines shall mark the sector. The surface within the landing area shall be on the same level as the throwing surface (see Rule 1-1-1). Sector flags should mark the ends of the lines (see Figure 18).

Engineer's Diagram of Track and Field Layout
Blueprints of an NCAA-commissioned 400-meter track and field layout may be purchased for $7.50 each from NCAA Publishing, P.O. Box 361147, Indianapolis, Indiana 46236-5323.

RULE 2

Equipment

Note: Imperial distances are conversions from metric measurements and are approximate and less accurate.

SECTION 1. Starting Blocks

Starting blocks must be made without devices that could provide artificial aid in starting. They may be adjustable but must be constructed entirely of rigid materials. They should be set in place easily and quickly and be removed without damage to the track.

SECTION 2. Hurdles

Material
ARTICLE 1. Hurdles shall be constructed of metal, wood or other suitable material.

Design
ARTICLE 2. The hurdles shall consist of a base and two uprights supporting a rectangular frame, with a single crossbar. The crossbar shall be of wood or other suitable material, with beveled edges, and have a height of 70 millimeters (2.76 in.). The center of the crossbar shall be directly over the end

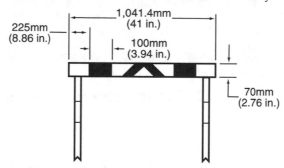

Figure 19—Hurdle Measurements

35

of the base. The surface facing the starting line shall be white in color with two vertical or diagonal stripes. A center chevron should be added to help contestants determine the center of the lane.

Measurements

ARTICLE 3. The following table provides hurdle measurements and pull-over force:

HURDLE MEASUREMENTS

	Minimum	Maximum
Width	1,041.4mm (41 in.)	1,200mm (47.24 in.)
Length of Bases	....	700mm (27.56 in.)
Weight of Hurdles	10kg (22 lbs., 2.5 ozs.)	....
Pull-Over Force at Each Height	3.6kg (8 lbs.)	4kg (8 lbs., 13 ozs.)

HEIGHT	MEN	WOMEN
55/60 Hurdles	106.7cm (42 in.)	84cm (33 in.)
110/100 Hurdles	106.7cm (42 in.)	84cm (33 in.)
400 Hurdles	91.4cm (36 in.)	76.2cm (30 in.)

Pull-Over Force

ARTICLE 4. Pull-over force refers to the 3.6 kilograms (8 lbs.) of steady pulling force required to overturn a hurdle when applied to the center of the uppermost edge of the top crossbar and in the direction of the finish line. If the weights cannot be adjusted to the required overturning force, it is recommended that the next greater setting be used, since records will not be allowed when the overturning force or the weight of the hurdle is less than the required minimum.

When a definite counterweight setting for intermediate hurdles has not been made by the manufacturer, it may be possible to attain the correct adjustment by setting one weight as for the 106.7-centimeter (42-in.) height and the other weight as for the 76.2-centimeter (30-in.) height.

Height Tolerance

ARTICLE 5. A difference of 3 millimeters (0.12 in.) above or below the required height will be tolerated.

SECTION 3. Steeplechase Hurdles

Material

ARTICLE 1. Hurdles shall be constructed of metal, wood or other suitable material.

Design

ARTICLE 2. The hurdles shall consist of a base and two uprights supporting a rectangular frame, with a single crossbar. The crossbar shall be of wood or other suitable material, without sharp edges or with a 6.35-millimeter (0.25-in.) bevel, and have a height of 127 millimeters (5 in.) square (see Figure 4). The crossbar shall be white in color with stripes of one distinctive contrasting color.

Dimensions

ARTICLE 3. Steeplechase and water-jump hurdles shall be at least 3.66 meters (12 ft.) in width. It is recommended that the first hurdle be at least 5 meters (16.40 ft.) in width.

a. (Men) The hurdles shall be not less than 91.1 centimeters (2.99 ft.) nor more than 91.7 centimeters (3.01 ft.) high.

b. (Women) The hurdles shall be not less than 75.9 centimeters (2.49 ft.) nor more than 76.5 centimeters (2.51 ft.) high.

Weight

ARTICLE 4. The weight of each hurdle shall be at least 80 kilograms (176.4 lbs.).

Base

ARTICLE 5. Each hurdle shall have on either side a base between 1.2 meters (3.94 ft.) and 1.4 meters (4.59 ft.) long (see Figure 4).

SECTION 4. The Relay Baton

Dimensions

ARTICLE 1. The relay baton shall be not less than 280 millimeters (11.02 in.) or more than 300 millimeters (11.81 in.) in length; its circumference shall be 11.43 to 12.7 centimeters (4.5 to 5 in.).

Material, Shape

ARTICLE 2. The baton shall be a smooth, hollow tube; of wood, metal or other rigid material, and made in one piece. The use of tape or other material on the baton is prohibited.

SECTION 5. The High Jump

Landing Pad

ARTICLE 1. The high-jump pad shall have a minimum dimension of 4.88 meters wide by 2.44 meters deep (16 ft. by 8 ft.). It should be high enough and of a composition that will provide a safe and comfortable landing. A minimum height of 66.04 centimeters (26 in.), including the top pad unit, is preferred. The landing-pad sections must be fastened together and covered with a common top cover. The landing pit may not extend into the plane of the crossbar.

Distance Between Standards

ARTICLE 2. The distance between the vertical uprights (standards) shall be 4 to 4.04 meters (13.12 to 13.25 ft.).

Crossbar Supports

ARTICLE 3. The horizontal supports of the crossbar shall be flat and rectangular, 4 centimeters (1.6 in.) wide and 6 centimeters (2.4 in.) long, and friction-free. Each support shall point toward the opposite upright so that the crossbar will rest between the uprights along the narrow dimension [3.81 centimeters (1.5 in.)] of the support.

Extended Height

ARTICLE 4. The uprights shall extend at least 100 millimeters (3.94 in.) above the support of the crossbar.

Crossbar Shape, Composition

ARTICLE 5. The crossbar shall be circular and made of suitable material. The ends of the crossbar shall be smooth and shall not be covered with rubber or any other material that has the effect of increasing the friction between the surface of the crossbar and the supports.

Crossbar Dimensions

ARTICLE 6. The diameter of the bar must be at least 25 millimeters but not more than 30 millimeters (0.98 to 1.18 in.).

The crossbar shall be 4 meters (13.12 ft.) in length and shall have a maximum weight of 2.2 kilograms (4.85 lbs.).

The ends of the crossbar shall be constructed in such a way that a flat surface of 25 to 30 millimeters (0.98 to 1.18 in.) by 150 to 200 millimeters (5.91 to 7.87 in.) is designed for the purpose of placing the bar on the supports of the uprights.

SECTION 6. The Pole Vault

Landing Pad

ARTICLE 1. The pole-vault pad measurement beyond the vertical plane of the stopboard shall be a minimum of **6 meters wide by 5 meters deep (19 ft., 8 in. by 16 ft., 5 in.).**

The front portion of the pad **is to be the same width as the back units, 6 meters (19 ft., 8 in.), and shall extend a minimum of 1.53 meters (5 ft.) forward from the top of the back of the vaulting box (toward the runway).** The maximum cutout for the vaulting box shall be 91.44 centimeters (36 in.), measured across the bottom of the cutout. The back of the cutout shall be placed so that the pit does not affect the bend of the pole. For pads with an angled cutout, the recommended maximum distance from the stopboard to the beginning of the pad is 15 centimeters (6 in.). The back of the cutout shall be placed no farther than 36 centimeters (14.17 in.) from the vertical plane of the stopboard.

If the landing pad does not extend to the area immediately around the vaulting box, a collar of 2 to 4 inches of padding of uniform thickness shall cover the area behind and to the sides of the vaulting box that are not protected by the landing pad. Such padding shall be semi-permanent and shall not affect the bend of the pole.

A height of 81.28 centimeters (32 in.), including the top pad unit, is required. The landing-pad sections must be fastened together with a common top cover. Suitable padding **shall** be placed around the base of the standards.

Standards

ARTICLE 2. Any style of uprights or posts may be used for the pole vault, provided the style is rigid and supported by a base not to exceed 10.16 centimeters (4 in.) in height above the ground. Cantilevered uprights are recommended.

The distance between the vertical uprights or between the extension arms where such are used shall be 4.32 meters (14 ft., 2.04 in.).

Upright Pegs

ARTICLE 3. The crossbar shall rest on round metal pegs that project not more than 55 millimeters (2.17 in.) at right angles from the uprights and have diameters of not more than 13 millimeters (0.512 in.). The upper surfaces of these pegs shall be smooth, without indentations or aids of any kind that might help to hold the crossbar in place.

Crossbar Shape, Composition

ARTICLE 4. The crossbar shall be circular and made of suitable material. The ends of the crossbar shall be smooth and shall not be covered with rubber or any other material that has the effect of increasing the friction between the surface of the crossbar and the supports.

Crossbar Dimensions

ARTICLE 5. The diameter of the crossbar must be at least 29 millimeters but not more than 31 millimeters (1.14 to 1.22 in.).

The crossbar shall be between 4.48 and 4.52 meters (14.7 to 14.83 ft.) in length. The maximum weight shall be 2.25 kilograms (4.96 lbs.).

For the purpose of placing the bar on the supports of the uprights, the ends of the crossbar shall be constructed in such a way that a flat surface of 29 to 35 millimeters (1.14 to 1.38 in.) by 200 millimeters (7.87 in.) is provided.

SECTION 7. The Vaulting Pole

The vaulting pole may be of any material or combination of materials. It may be of unlimited size and weight.

SECTION 8. The Shot

Outdoor Shot Material

ARTICLE 1. The shot shall be constructed of solid iron, brass or any metal not softer than brass, or of a shell of such metal completely filled with lead or other material. Movement within the shot is permitted.

Shape

ARTICLE 2. The shot must be spherical in shape, and the surface must be smooth without indentations so that an advantage is not gained by grip.

Specifications

ARTICLE 3. The shot shall conform to the following specifications:

	MEN'S	WOMEN'S
Weight (Minimum)	7.26kg (16 lbs.)	4kg (8 lbs., 13 ozs.)
Diameter (Minimum)	110mm (4.331 in.)	95mm (3.740 in.)
(Maximum)	130mm (5.118 in.)	110mm (4.331 in.)

SECTION 9. The Discus

Composition

ARTICLE 1. The discus shall be composed of a smooth metal rim permanently attached to a wood or synthetic body. Metal plates may be set flush into the sides of the wood or synthetic body, provided that the equivalent area is flat and that the total weight of the implement meets the specifications.

Shape

ARTICLE 2. The two sides of the discus shall be identical and shall be made without indentations, projecting points or sharp edges. The sides shall taper in a straight line from the beginning of the curve of the rim to a circle that is a distance of 25 millimeters (0.98 in.) from the center of the discus. The edge of the metal rim shall be rounded in a true circle.

Specifications

ARTICLE 3. The discus must conform to the following specifications:

	MEN'S	WOMEN'S
Weight (Minimum)	2kg (4 lbs., 6.548 ozs.)	1kg (2 lbs., 3.274 ozs.)

Metal Rim		
Outer Diameter		
(Minimum)	219mm (8.622 in.)	180mm (7.087 in.)
(Maximum)	221mm (8.701 in.)	182mm (7.165 in.)
Thickness at 6mm		
(.236 in.) from outer		
edge (Minimum)	12mm (.472 in.)	12mm (.472 in.)
Metal Plates		
Diameter		
(Minimum)	50mm (1.969 in.)	50mm (1.969 in.)
(Maximum)	57mm (2.244 in.)	57mm (2.244 in.)
Thickness at center		
and within	25mm (.984 in.)	25mm (.984 in.)
	from center	from center
(Minimum)	44mm (1.732 in.)	37mm (1.456 in.)
(Maximum)	46mm (1.811 in.)	39mm (1.535 in.)

SECTION 10. The Hammer

Head

ARTICLE 1. The head of the hammer shall be made of solid iron or other metal not softer than brass or of a shell of such metal filled with lead or other solid material. It must be spherical in shape.

If a filling is used, it must be inserted in such a manner that it is immovable. The center of gravity shall be not more than 6 millimeters (0.236 in.) from the center of the sphere.

Wire

ARTICLE 2. The wire shall be a single, unbroken and straight length of spring-steel wire not less than 3 millimeters (0.118 in.) in diameter and shall be such that it cannot stretch appreciably while the hammer is being thrown. The wire should be looped at both ends as a means of attachment.

Grip

ARTICLE 3. The grip may be either of single- or double-loop construction, but it must be rigid and without hinging joints of any kind and made so that it cannot stretch appreciably while being thrown. It must be attached to the wire in such a manner that it cannot be turned within the loop of the wire to increase the overall length of the hammer.

It shall be in the shape of an isosceles triangle or a sector of a circle (see Figure 20).

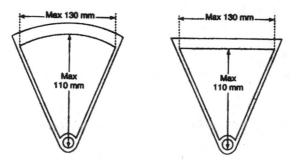

Figure 20—Hammer Grips

Connection
ARTICLE 4. The wire shall be connected to the head by means of a functioning swivel that may be either plain or ball-bearing. The grip shall be connected to the wire by means of a loop. A swivel may not be used.

Specifications
ARTICLE 5. The hammer shall conform to the following specifications:

	MEN'S	WOMEN'S
Weight (Minimum)	7.260kg (16 lbs.)	4kg (8 lbs., 13 ozs.)
Diameter of Head		
(Minimum)	110mm (4.331 in.)	95mm (3.740 in.)
(Maximum)	130mm (5.118 in.)	110mm (4.331 in.)

Length (complete as thrown, measured from inside of the grip)

	MEN'S	WOMEN'S
(Minimum)	117.5cm (3.85 ft.)	116cm (3.81 ft.)
(Maximum)	121.5cm (3.99 ft.)	119.5cm (3.92 ft.)

SECTION 11. The Javelin

Material
ARTICLE 1. The javelin shall consist of three parts: a metal head, a shaft and a cord grip. The shaft may be constructed of metal, and shall have fixed to it a metal head terminating in a sharp point.

Cord Grip
ARTICLE 2. The cord should be about the center of gravity without thongs, notches or indentations of any kind on the shaft and shall not exceed the diameter of the shaft by more than 8 millimeters (0.315 in.).

Cross Section

ARTICLE 3. The cross section shall be regularly circular throughout, although a maximum difference of two percent between the largest and the smallest diameter is permitted. The maximum diameter of the shaft shall be immediately in front of the grip. The central portion of the shaft, including the part under the grip, may be cylindrical or slightly tapered toward the rear; but the reduction in diameter, from immediately in front of the grip to immediately behind, may not exceed 0.25 millimeters. From the grip, the javelin shall taper regularly to the tip at the front and the tail at the rear. The longitudinal profile from the grip to the front tip and to the tail shall be straight or slightly convex (see Note); and there must not be an abrupt alteration in the overall diameter, except immediately behind the head and at the front and rear of the grip, throughout the length of the javelin. At the rear of the head, the reduction in the diameter may not exceed 2.5 millimeters (0.098 in.); and this departure from the longitudinal profile may not extend more than 30 centimeters (11.81 in.) behind the head.

Note: The shape of the longitudinal profile may be checked quickly and easily using a metal straight edge at least 50 centimeters (19.69 in.) long and two feeler gauges 0.20 millimeters and 1.25 millimeters thick. For slightly convex sections of the profile, the straight edge will rock while in firm contact with a short section of the javelin. For straight sections of the profile with the straight edge in firm contact, it must be impossible to insert the 0.20-millimeter gauge between the javelin and the straight edge anywhere over the length of contact. This shall not apply immediately behind the joint between the head and the shaft. At this point, it must be impossible to insert the 1.25-millimeter gauge.

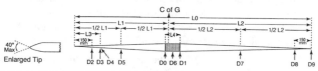

INTERNATIONAL JAVELIN

Lengths (all dimensions mm)						Diameters (all dimensions mm)				
		Men		Women				Men		Women
Serial	Detail	Max	Min	Max	Min	Serial	Detail	Max	Min	Max	Min
L0	Overall	2700	2600	2300	2200	D0	In front of grip	30	25	25	20
L1	Tip to C of G	1060	900	920	800	D1	At rear of grip	–	D0-0.25	-	D0-0.25
1/2L1	Half L1	530	450	460	400	D2	150mm from tip	0.8 D0	–	0.8 D0	–
L2	Tail to C of G	1800	1540	1500	1280	D3	At rear of head	–	–	–	–
1/2L2	Half L2	900	770	750	640	D4	Immediately behind head	–	D3-2.5	–	D3-2.5
L3	Head	330	250	330	250	D5	Half way tip to C of G	0.9- D0	–	0.9 D0	–
L4	Grip	160	150	150	140	D6	Over grip	D0 + 8	–	D0 + 8	–
						D7	Half way tail to C of G	–	0.9 D0	–	0.9 D0
						D8	150mm from tail	–	0.4 D0	–	0.4 D0
						D9	At tail	–	3.5	–	3.5

Mobile Parts

ARTICLE 4. The javelin shall not have mobile parts or other apparatus that, during the throw, could change its center of gravity or throwing characteristics.

Taper of Shaft

ARTICLE 5. The tapering of the shaft to the tip of the metal head shall be such that the diameter, at the midpoint between the center of gravity and the tip of the metal head, shall not exceed 90 percent of the maximum diameter of the shaft and, at a point 150 millimeters (5.91 in.) from the tip of the metal head, 80 percent of the maximum diameter. The tapering of the shaft to the tail at the rear shall be such that the diameter, at the midpoint between the center of gravity and the tail, shall be not less than 90 percent of the maximum diameter of the shaft. At a point 150 millimeters (5.91 in.) from the tail, the diameter shall be not less than 40 percent of the maximum diameter of the shaft.

Specifications

ARTICLE 6. The javelin shall conform to the following specifications:

	MEN'S	WOMEN'S
Overall Weight (inclusive of cord grip)		
(Minimum)	800g (1 lb., 12.25 ozs.)	600g (1 lb., 5.16 ozs.)

SECTION 12. Calibration of Measuring Devices

It is recommended that all equipment used for timing, measuring wind, weighing and measuring implements, and measuring performance be certified for accuracy before the first competition each year and preferably before each major competition (see Rules 5-12-1a-3, 5-12-2, 6-1-11, 6-1-14 and 7-2-1).

Note: Certification methods shall be obtained from the manufacturer of the device.

RULE 3

Meet Personnel

SECTION 1. Officials

Number, Types

ARTICLE 1. The number of officials necessary to conduct a track and field meet varies with the size and type of meet being conducted. The following officials are recommended for a large meet:

a. *General officials*

Games committee	Medical doctor and/or certified
Meet director	trainer
Meet referees	Marshals
Juries	Announcers
Scorers	Press steward
Custodian of awards	Surveyor

b. *Track-events officials*

Clerks of course	Umpires
Judges of finish	Hurdle setters and block setters
Manual timers	Wind-gauge operator(s)
Starters	Records coordinator
Lap counter(s)	Running referee

Head finish evaluator—(fully automatic timing)
Timing-device operator(s)—(fully automatic timing)

c. *Field-events officials*

Head field judge	Implement inspector
Field judges	Wind-gauge operator(s)
Markers	Throwing referee
Measurers	Jumping referee

Additional Officials

ARTICLE 2. The games committee shall have authority to make such additions to the above list as it deems advisable.

Selection of Officials

ARTICLE 3. Officials should be individuals who have followed track closely over a period of years. They must know what rules violations are, and how and where they tend to occur.

SECTION 2. The Surveyor

The meet director shall possess a surveyor's written certification listing the exact measurements as given in these rules for the following:

a. Levels of the track, runway, approach and landing surfaces;

b. Permanent track measurements;

c. Start and finish lines;

d. Track lanes;

e. Baton-passing zones;

f. Steeplechase water-jump pit;

g. Hurdle placements; and

h. Throwing surfaces—the shot, hammer and discus circles, and the javelin runway—and all sectors.

SECTION 3. The Games Committee

The primary purpose of the games committee is to give specialized assistance and guidance to the meet director such as:

a. Determine the number and assignments of officials (see Rules 3-1-2, 8-5-2);

b. Assist the meet director with meet administration (see Rules 3-4-2, 8-6-1);

c. Serve as the final authority on appeals of referees' decisions (jury of appeals);

d. Authorize all fully automatic timing devices (see Rules 3-11-3-Note, 5-12);

e. Determine the number of competitors an institution is allowed in each event (see Rule 4-1-3);

f. Determine the use and placement of competitors' numbers (see Rule 4-2-4);

g. Approve the time schedule and changes in order of events (see Rules 4-3-1, 4-3-4);

h. Verify that all events are held at the main meet venue (**Exception:** Conference championships).

Note: Institutions may request a waiver to hold events elsewhere by petitioning the appropriate divisional chair by December 1 for indoor meets and March 1 for outdoor meets.

i. Determine the number of lapped runners who shall remain in the competition (see Rule 5-4-2-Note);

j. Determine the structure for running timed-section finals (see Rule 5-10);

k. Determine qualifying procedures and drawing for lanes (see Rule 5-11);

l. Decide procedures to resolve ties for the last qualifying position in subsequent rounds (see Rules 5-11-8, 6-2-2);

m. Set the relay substitution policy (see Rule 5-8-2);

n. Approve the timing equipment to be used (see Rule 5-12);

o. Determine the use of implements for the meet (see Rule 6-1-12);

p. Set the time and place for inspecting, weighing and measuring all implements to be used in the meet (see Rule 6-1-12);

q. Approve measuring apparatus (see Rule 6-1-15);

r. Designate field-event site or runway at least one hour before competition begins (see Rule 6-1-18);

s. Determine the number of field-event competitors who will advance to the final round (see Rule 6-2-1);

t. Establish a time by which all preliminaries in a field event must be completed (see Rule 6-2-3);

u. Group field-event competitors (see Rule 6-4-1);

v. Set starting heights and increments (see Rules 6-4-2, 6-5-1, 9-2-2j);

w. Determine the length of the cross country course (see Rule 8-2-1); and

x. Determine the use of facilities for combined events (see Rule 9-2-2g).

Note: The games committee duties apply to the combined events.

SECTION 4. The Meet Director

Primary Role

ARTICLE 1. The meet director is the central person behind the success of a track and field meet. The meet director shall stimulate the enthusiasm and

coordinate the promotional efforts of the organizing and games committees. The meet director is responsible to these committees for all aspects of
the meet. This person must foresee all the needs of competitors, officials
and spectators and ensure that all the technical details of the meet have
been taken care of within the requirements of the rules.

Duties

ARTICLE 2. With the help and guidance of the games committee, the meet
director shall:

a. Organize and conduct meet promotion;

b. Provide and prepare the track and field grounds;

c. Provide facilities and equipment (e.g., batons, steel tape measures);

d. Provide full and early information to all competing schools;

e. Appoint and inform officials and prepare officials' materials;

f. Arrange meetings;

g. Inform competing schools of suitable lodging, dining and ground trans-
    portation;

h. Inform competing teams of acceptable materials for making marks on
    the track, runways or approaches;

i. Arrange for certification of all calibrated measuring and timing devices
    (see Rules 2-12, 5-12-1a-3);

j. Establish reporting times for athletes in all events;

k. Verify team scores and meet results within 24 hours after the comple-
    tion of the meet; and

l. Retain photos, hand times and field-event results through July 1, 2005.

SECTION 5. The Referee(s)

Primary Role

ARTICLE 1. The referee(s) shall be knowledgeable and qualified to inter-
pret the NCAA track and field rules, above all other officials, ensuring fair
and safe competition for all competitors and disqualifying those whose
acts violate the rules of fair and safe competition. The referee shall not
serve as any other official or as a member of the games committee.

Duties

ARTICLE 2. The powers and duties of the referee(s) shall be:

a. After consulting with the appropriate officials, to take such actions and make such decisions that provide each contestant a fair and equal opportunity (see Rule 10-4-7-Note 2);

b. To have the authority to act upon all apparent violations of the rules that are observed in meets in which a games committee has been established;

c. To decide all questions for which the rules make no provisions;

d. To have sole power to warn and/or disqualify contestants as provided by these rules (exception, see Rule 3-8-1).

　　The referee shall indicate a warning to the athlete verbally and by showing a yellow card. A second violation constitutes disqualification, which shall be indicated to the athlete verbally and by showing a red card.

　　If, in the opinion of the referee, the violation is severe, disqualification will occur without warning.

　　The referee shall disqualify contestants for violation of the honest-effort rule.

　　Warnings and disqualifications shall be noted in writing by the referee(s) on appropriate meet results and shall identify the rule that applies;

e. To decide place winners in track events when the judges of the finish cannot reach a decision and when official films of the finish are available;

f. In the event of record performances, the running referee shall verify the results of the place and time and shall check all related conditions;

g. In the event of record performances, the throwing and jumping referees, or three field judges, shall verify all measurements and all related conditions;

h. To oversee the inspecting, checking, weighing and measuring of all implements and apparatus to be used by competitors in the meet;

i. To make certain that field events begin when scheduled, are properly organized and continue without delays; and

j. To enforce uniform, relay uniform, number, shoe and logo rules.

Finality of Decisions

ARTICLE 3. The referee's decisions in all matters shall be final and without appeal, except in those meets where a games committee has been established for that special purpose. The games committee then will have the final authority.

SECTION 6. The Umpires

Duties of Head Umpire

ARTICLE 1. The duties of the head umpire shall be:

a. To instruct umpires as to the rules and violations in general and as to the special track conditions and special regulations established for the meet by the games committee or appropriate referee (see Rule 10-4);

b. To place umpires where they can best judge possible violations;

c. To secure from the umpires, and clarify, the facts of all apparent violations of track rules;

d. To report apparent violations to the appropriate referee; and

e. To check the proper placement, height and weight of the hurdles when a hurdles inspector is not provided by the games committee.

Duties of Umpires

ARTICLE 2. The duties of the umpires are to detect and report, in writing, without waiting for a protest, all apparent violations of the rules to the head umpire. In so doing, they do not assume responsibility for disqualification—only the referee can make a disqualification. A flag, yellow or white, shall be made visible as soon as the umpire's area is cleared to indicate the umpire's judgment. Each umpire shall use a yellow signal flag to indicate apparent violations. A white flag should be raised to indicate that a violation has not occurred. In races of 5,000 meters and longer, the use of white flags is not necessary.

Before the start of relay races, a yellow flag shall be held aloft in each zone until the competitors in each zone are ready, at which time a white flag shall be raised.

Note: Umpires should be highly qualified and available in sufficient numbers to carry out their duties properly.

Placement of Umpires

ARTICLE 3. a. The head umpire shall be stationed, or move from place to place, during a race so that all possible violations may be seen and thus augment umpires' reports with personal information.

b. The following plan is recommended for placement of umpires:

(1) Umpires shall be given a chart of the track on which each umpire's number and station is located for each track event, and a flag to indicate possible violations. Each umpire must cover the assigned station for each race.

(2) During races around the track, one or more umpires should be stationed so as to observe violations on the turns, on the backstretch and at the finish. Although it is not the responsibility of timers or judges of the finish to report violations, the referee may, with propriety, seek and weigh their observations in making a decision.

(3) During straightaway dashes and hurdle races, at least two umpires shall stand behind the starting line while the others are at intervals along the track.

(4) In order to judge baton passes in relay races, four umpires shall be assigned to each passing zone. Two shall stand on the inside of the track and two on the outside and sight along the staggered zone lines to ensure that the baton is exchanged within the passing zone.

SECTION 7. The Clerk(s) of the Course

The clerk of the course, with the help of assistant clerks as the meet may require, shall be responsible for:

a. Maintaining the track time schedule;

b. Calling together and placing athletes in their proper positions with needed instructions related to their event (including advancement procedures) before the start of each race;

c. Placing all relay team members, especially sprint relays, in their proper positions on the track;

d. Enforcing competitors' uniform, relay uniform, competitors' number, shoes and logo rules at time of check-in; and

e. Related duties as requested by the starter and the games committee.

SECTION 8. The Starter

Duties

ARTICLE 1. The starter shall have entire control of the competitors when on their marks and during the start; and, along with the assistant starter(s), the starter shall decide, without appeal, whether a start is fair and legal, or which athlete(s) shall be charged with a false start. The starter shall be responsible for:

a. Starting races promptly after the athletes have been turned over to the starter by the clerk of the course;

b. Answering questions on the rules and conditions governing the start of each race;

c. Signaling by a bell or pistol the start of the last lap of each race, if a lap counter is not available;

d. Determining if a false start was intentional; and

e. Ensuring that starting blocks are set up within the competitor's lane.

In staggered starts, the starter is to take a position and remain stationary so that the distance between the starter and all the competitors is approximately the same. If a speaker system is used, it must be positioned so that each competitor can hear the commands simultaneously.

Assistant Starters

ARTICLE 2. The meet director shall appoint assistant starters with power of recall in the case of an unfair start. Such assistants are of special value when the starter has difficulty seeing the entire field.

SECTION 9. The Fully Automatic Timing Officials

Operator(s) Duties

ARTICLE 1. There shall be appointed officials who shall operate the fully automatic timing system used for the competition. Where more than one picture-taking device is used, one device should use color film (see Rule 5-12-3-7).

The timing-device operator shall have direct communication with the starting judge and head finish judge.

If the timing device fails to start, the operator shall recall the race by firing a pistol.

After the race is over, the timing-device operator shall forward the photograph to the head finish evaluator.

If a malfunction should occur, the timing-device operator shall notify the proper official(s) immediately and the predetermined back-up system shall be designated the official result.

Photo Evaluator(s) Duties

ARTICLE 2. It is recommended that the head finish evaluator be removed from the finish-line area and isolated from all competitors, officials and coaches so that this person is free from distraction while performing the duties.

The head finish evaluator shall, by utilizing the official picture of the finish, be responsible for the evaluation and interpretation of finish places and times.

In the event a protest is filed or additional assistance is required (as in ruling on close finishes), the referee shall be called to render a decision.

Official Pictures

ARTICLE 3. Fully automatic timing systems have priority over manual times and judges' picks.

SECTION 10. Manual Judges of the Finish

Number, Duties

ARTICLE 1. When two or more fully automatic timing devices are used, there should be a head judge of the finish plus additional judges as deemed necessary by the head judge and meet management.

When one fully automatic timing device is used, there shall be a head judge plus one judge for each scoring place.

When fully automatic timing devices are not used, there shall be a head judge of the finish plus two judges, assigned by the head judge, for each scoring place.

The judges' decision as to the order of finish shall be final, except for possible action taken by the head judge or referee.

Placement of Judges

ARTICLE 2. Judges of the finish for each place shall serve on opposite sides on elevated stands at a minimum distance of 3.05 meters (10 ft.) from the edge of the track.

Procedure for Picking Places

ARTICLE 3. The finish judges shall watch the race until the competitors are within 9.14 meters (10 yds.) of the finish line, then should concentrate on the finish line (see Rule 5-3).

Without consulting other judges, each judge shall write the place selection on a card and hand it to the head judge. The decisions of judges picking higher-scoring places shall overrule those of judges picking lower-scoring places.

The head judge shall view the finish as a whole. Should the head judge see a place winner who is overlooked by all finish judges, and whose proper place cannot be decided in the manner described above, the head judge shall rule on the finish.

Note: When official pictures from the fully automatic timing device(s) are not available, those from another system (e.g., videotape) authorized by the games committee before the start of the competition may be used to verify the results reported by the judges of the finish.

SECTION 11. The Manual Timers

Number, Duties

ARTICLE 1. When two or more fully automatic timing devices are used, there should be a head timer plus additional timers as deemed necessary by the head timer and meet management.

When one fully automatic timing device is used, there shall be a head timer plus one timer for each scoring place.

When fully automatic timing devices are not used, there must be three official timers of first place, one of whom shall be the head timer. When possible, there shall be two timers, assigned by the head timer, for each scoring place. Times for all place winners and the wind reading must be recorded. The head timer shall assign one of the timers to give intermediate times.

After each race, the head timer shall be responsible for recording the results from the manual timers in tenths of seconds.

Note: For methods of timing and equipment requirements, see Rule 5-12.

Placement of Timers

ARTICLE 2. Timers for each place shall serve from opposite sides on elevated stands at a minimum distance of 3.05 meters (10 ft.) from the edge of the track.

Procedure for Timing

ARTICLE 3. The watch will be started with the index finger upon the sight of the flash or smoke of the gun or starting apparatus. The timer stops the watch with the index finger when any part of the competitor's torso crosses the perpendicular plane of the near edge of the finish line. The torso is defined as any part of the body other than the head, neck, arms, legs, hands or feet.

Without consulting with other timers, each timer shall report the results to the head timer. The head timer shall decide the official time for each competitor.

SECTION 12. The Field Judges

Number

ARTICLE 1. There shall be one head field judge and such other judges or measurers as each event may require.

Head Judges of Field Events

ARTICLE 2. The head judge of each field event shall serve under the field referee with the help of assistant judges and measurers and shall:

a. Conduct the event in accordance with the rules;

b. Ensure that field events begin when scheduled, are properly organized and continue without delays;

c. Judge the competitors' efforts as being fair or foul by displaying the respective white (fair) or red (foul) flag immediately after the trial is completed. When flags are not used, verbal decisions shall not be given until the performance is completed;

d. Judge the high jump and pole vault as success or failure;

e. Read and record all attempts (two separate judges when possible);

f. Certify the results for each completed event and turn them over to the announcer and scorer;

g. Enforce uniform, number, shoe and logo rules at the time of check-in;

h. Ensure that all measuring devices are in working order (see Rule 6-1-14); and

i. Report all apparent violations to the appropriate referee.

SECTION 13. The Implement Inspector

The implement inspector, under the supervision of the field referee, shall weigh and measure, and then certify with an identifying mark, all implements to be used in competition. Illegal implements shall be impounded until competition in that event is concluded.

SECTION 14. The Scorer

The scorer and such assistants as are necessary, shall keep a record for the chair of the games committee and/or meet director of the complete results in all events: team scores, individual place winners and their performances, and such additional information as may be available.

SECTION 15. The Announcer

Duties
ARTICLE 1. The announcer and any assistants shall give meet information to the spectators using available auditory and visual aids. The announcer's job is to give relevant information in the fewest words possible with minimum disruption of attention from the competition.

Relevant Information
ARTICLE 2. Relevant information shall include:

a. Names, numbers and affiliations of competitors;

b. Lane assignments or order of competition (field events);

c. Past performances of outstanding competitors;

d. Outstanding contestants before they perform;

e. In track events, intermediate times and, occasionally, the order of competitors;

f. Results—placings, times, distances, heights, records—at the earliest possible moment. Field-event results shall be announced imperially. If the performances are measured for record consideration, the results shall be announced imperially and then metrically; and

g. Current cumulative team scores.

Supplementary Visual Aids
ARTICLE 3. Successful meet promotion has demonstrated that announcing should be supplemented by numerous and varied visual aids. Among these are:

a. Electrically lighted scoreboards on which entries, results and brief messages can be displayed;

b. Rotating signboards for field events on which a competitor's number and performance are placed manually;

c. Posters that give the name of the next competitor in a field event before the athlete performs;

d. Crossbar height indicators;

e. Distance indicators for field events, located outside landing areas; and

f. Lane numbers for sprints and hurdles.

SECTION 16. The Marshal
The duty of the marshal and assistants shall be to keep all areas of the track and the field clear and unobstructed so as best to meet the needs of contestants, officials and spectators. Unauthorized persons shall not be allowed on the track or field. Coaches, inactive officials, noncompeting athletes, photographers, public-communications representatives, etc., shall be assigned special areas or seating where they do not interfere with the proper conduct of the meet.

SECTION 17. The Press Steward
The press steward shall inform the representatives of the press as to all occurrences on the track and the field, and to such related facts as may

interest them. Specifically, the press steward shall obtain the names and teams of all competitors, full names of all place winners, the time or distance of each winning or record performance, and desired information concerning past performances.

SECTION 18. The Wind-Gauge Operator(s)

The wind-gauge operator(s) shall ensure that the wind-measuring instrument is installed and operated in accordance with Rule 7-2-1. The operator shall ascertain the velocity of the wind in the running direction of the appropriate events (100 meters, 200 meters, 100- or 110-meter hurdles, long jump and triple jump). This information shall be recorded for each race or attempt and be included in the final results.

SECTION 19. The Lap Counter(s)

A lap counter(s) shall be appointed to notify each competitor of the number of laps that still need to be completed. Adequate lap counters must be provided to accurately count laps for all runners in distance races. The start of the final lap shall be signaled by the firing of a gun or the ringing of a bell.

SECTION 20. The Medical Doctor/ Certified Trainer

ARTICLE 1. The medical doctor/certified trainer shall examine injured athletes and make recommendations to the athlete, the athlete's coach and the representative of any sponsoring organization as to the advisability of continued participation by the athlete in the meet. Such recommendations shall be considered in the application of the honest-effort rule.

ARTICLE 2. Should the decision be made to withdraw the athlete from the current event, the athlete shall be scratched from any subsequent event(s) in the meet, unless otherwise approved to continue participation by the medical doctor/certified trainer.

SECTION 21. Medical Personnel

It is the responsibility of medical personnel whenever an athletics participant suffers a laceration or wound where oozing or bleeding occurs, to stop the practice or event at the earliest possible time and provide the athlete with appropriate medical treatment. The athlete should leave the event or practice, and not return until the oozing or bleeding stops.

RULE 4

The Meet

SECTION 1. The Competitors

Responsibility of Competitor

ARTICLE 1. Before competition, a competitor shall be responsible for checking implements and equipment with officials, wearing the proper uniform according to Rule 4-2-1, displaying the correct number as described by meet management, and reporting on time.

Competitors are to abide by the letter and spirit of the rules and shall be responsible for conducting themselves in an honest and sporting fashion at all times towards opponents, officials and spectators.

Competitors who conduct themselves in an unsporting manner, or who are offensive by action or language, shall be warned and/or disqualified by the referee from the event and from the remainder of the meet (see Rule 3-5-2d).

Honest Effort

ARTICLE 2. a. Athletes must participate honestly in all trials and finals of all track or field events in which they legally are declared or they shall be barred from all remaining events in the current meet. Athletes must compete with maximum effort and/or qualify from trials into the finals.

b. Athletes must participate honestly in the finals of all events in which they are legally declared and qualified, and in which such participation is a criteria for entry in a subsequent meet.

Note 1: It is understood that passing on attempts in field events is a strategy available in those events and is not considered a question of honest effort, provided at least one attempt has been made.

Note 2: Failure to complete a combined-event competition shall not affect subsequent participation in an open event.

Number of Entries

ARTICLE 3. The meet director or games committee shall determine the number of entries an institution is allowed in each event.

SECTION 2. The Competition

Uniform

ARTICLE 1. When engaged in competition, each competitor must wear an official team uniform or be disqualified.

A uniform should consist of school-issued shorts or briefs, top, or one-piece body suit. However, any outer garment (e.g., sweat pants, tights) that is school-issued becomes the official uniform. Clothing worn in addition must be worn under the uniform. It is recommended that such clothing be of a solid color (for cross country, see Rule 8-8).

The uniform must be clean and of a material and design as not to be objectionable.

Bare midriff tops are not acceptable. (Note: The uniform top must meet or hang below the waist band when the competitor is standing.) Uniforms must allow for competitors' numbers to be placed above the waist (front and back) and for hip numbers to be placed on the hip, not on the leg or thigh. Uniform tops must not obscure hip numbers.

Wearing any part of the official team competition uniform illegally (e.g., top off or intentionally shortened, shoulder straps lowered) while in the area of competition shall lead to a warning by the nearest official and, if repeated, to disqualification by the meet referee (see Rule 3-5-2d).

The use of, or wearing of, artificial noisemakers by competitors is prohibited.

Logos

ARTICLE 2. An institution's official uniform and all other items of apparel (e.g., team jersey, socks) that are worn by student-athletes in competition may bear a single manufacturer's or distributor's normal trademark, not to exceed 2¼ square inches, including any additional material (e.g., patch) surrounding the normal trademark or logo. The logo or trademark must be contained within a four-sided geometrical figure (i.e., rectangle, square, parallelogram).

In addition, an institution's official uniform cannot bear a design element similar to the manufacturer's that is in addition to another logo or that is contrary to the size restriction.

A student-athlete representing an institution in intercollegiate competition is limited to wearing apparel items that include only the logo (not to exceed 2¼ square inches) of an apparel manufacturer or distributor. The student-athlete may not wear apparel that identifies any other entity, other than the student-athlete's institution.

These restrictions apply to all apparel worn by student-athletes during the conduct of competition, including premeet or postmeet activities.

Relay Uniforms

ARTICLE 3. The primary color of any one-piece body suits worn by members of a relay team must be the same as the primary color of the top of those members not wearing one-piece body suits. The members may wear pants, shorts or briefs, or a combination thereof that are of an identical primary color. The length of one-piece body suits, if worn, may vary.

Any visible garment worn under the tops shall be of an identical color as those worn by other members of the relay team. Any visible garment worn under the pants, shorts, briefs or one-piece body suits shall be of an identical color as those worn by other members of the relay team.

Numbers

ARTICLE 4. a. Unless decided otherwise by the games committee, a competitor shall not be allowed to start and compete without a competitor's number. In meets where competitors' numbers are prescribed officially, the competitor must wear the competitor's number assigned by meet management; the number must be visible without alterations when the athlete is competing.

b. The use of additional numbers affixed to the uniform to aid in the placing of competitors in a race shall be at the direction of the clerk of the course so that proper logos are not obscured and uniform requirements are observed.

Shoes

ARTICLE 5. Athletes may compete in bare feet or with shoes on one or both feet. The number of spike positions per shoe shall not exceed 11.

Features on the sole and/or heel (grooves, ridges, indentations, or protrudances) are permissible if constructed of the same or similar material as the sole.

When a competition is conducted on a synthetic surface, that part of each spike which projects from the sole or heel must not exceed 9 millimeters, except in the high jump or javelin throw, in which it must not exceed 12 millimeters. Facility considerations may further limit the type and length of spikes allowed.

Note: Before the competition, competitors' uniform, relay uniform, number and shoe rules shall be enforced by the clerk, referee and the head event officials. Violations after notification by these officials are subject to disqualification.

Protests

ARTICLE 6. Protests relating to matters that develop during the conduct of the meet should be made at once and not later than 30 minutes after the results have been announced officially. Any such protests must be submitted in writing by a coach to the protest table. The protest shall be submitted to the referee, who shall render a decision. Protests relating to Articles 1, 2 and 3 shall not interrupt an event once it begins (see Rule 5-2-Note 5).

Visual Aids

ARTICLE 7. In cases other than the review of official photo-timing pictures, visual aids (videotape, photos) may not be used to determine the outcome of a protest or appeal.

Appeals

ARTICLE 8. The decision of the referees may be appealed through the games committee.

Correctable Error

ARTICLE 9. Within 72 hours after the last event of a meet, or before the subsequent round, results can be corrected if administrative errors are detected (e.g., incorrect calculation of team, individual or combined-event scores, timing error).

SECTION 3. Order of Events

Time Schedule

ARTICLE 1. The games committee shall approve a definite time schedule well in advance of the meet.

Intervals

ARTICLE 2. The interval between the starting times of track events shall not exceed 10 minutes, except that after the 3,000 meters and steeplechase the interval shall be 15 minutes; the 5,000 meters interval 20 minutes and the 10,000 meters interval 40 minutes. Field events shall be scheduled so that:

a. They shall be completed before the last track event, and

b. They permit the combined-events participation of some athletes.

Two-Session Meets

ARTICLE 3. In two-session meets (either two days or two sessions in one day), it is recommended that trial heats be held in the same order and with the same time interval as in finals.

Order of Events

ARTICLE 4. The order of events for outdoor meets should be:

With Preliminary Heats

10,000 Meters
60 minutes before track events—Hammer,
    Pole Vault and Long Jump
Triple Jump (immediately after Long Jump)
30 minutes before track events—Shot Put,
    High Jump and Javelin
Discus (immediately after Shot Put)
400-Meter (440-Yard) Relay
3,000 Meters/Steeplechase
400 Meters—Preliminaries
100/110-Meter Hurdles—Preliminaries
100 Meters—Preliminaries

1,500 Meters
400 Meters—Finals
100 Meters—Finals
100/110-Meter Hurdles—Finals
200 Meters—Preliminaries
400-Meter Hurdles—Preliminaries
800 Meters
200 Meters—Finals
400-Meter Hurdles—Finals
5,000 Meters
1,600-Meter (Mile) Relay

Without Preliminary Heats

10,000 Meters
60 minutes before track events—Hammer
45 minutes before track events—Pole Vault
    and Long Jump
Triple Jump (immediately after Long Jump)
30 minutes before track events—Shot Put and
    Javelin
Discus (immediately after the Shot Put)
15 minutes before first track event—High Jump
3,000 Meters/Steeplechase

400-Meter (440-Yard) Relay
1,500 Meters
100/110-Meter Hurdles
400 Meters
100 Meters
800 Meters
400-Meter Hurdles
200 Meters
5,000 Meters
1,600-Meter (Mile) Relay

*Note 1: Changes from this order can be made by the games
committee or by mutual agreement of the competing teams. For example, blocking events by gender or specialty is permitted.*

Note 2: See Rule 10-3 for indoor order of events.

RULE 5

Track Events

SECTION 1. The Start

Control of Start

ARTICLE 1. The starter has sole control over all aspects of the start. The starter's decisions shall be final (see Rule 3-8-1). A starting-area marshal shall be assigned to assist in keeping the starting area clear and quiet.

Practice starts are not allowed in conjunction with the starter's commands (see Rule 3-5-2d).

Start

ARTICLE 2. All races shall be started as a result of the starter activating a simultaneous audible and visible signal. The report of a pistol that can be cocked, not less than .32 caliber, or an electron tone of at least 112dB at 15 feet, together with the flash/smoke generated by the pistol, or an electronic flash/strobe, clearly visible to the timers, shall be used. A misfire shall not be a start. A .22 caliber pistol may be used at indoor events.

Starting Blocks

ARTICLE 3. The starting blocks must be set within each competitor's assigned lane. Starting blocks must conform to legal requirements (see Rule 2-1). Hand grips or body supports are prohibited.

Starting Races—600 Meters or Shorter

ARTICLE 4. The starter, after receiving a "ready" signal from the head finish judge and alerting all competitors, shall direct the runners to "On your marks."

The runners shall take the "On your marks" position (either crouched or standing) promptly and in such a way that any part of the body does not touch the track on or beyond the starting line.

The starter then shall direct them to "Set." At this command, all competitors **shall at once and without delay** assume their full and final set positions. Then, when all are motionless, the starter shall discharge the pistol (see Rule 5-2-Notes).

Starting Races—800 Meters and Longer
ARTICLE 5. Where appropriate, the starter shall have the runners take a position approximately 3 meters behind the starting line. On the command "On your marks," runners shall, without delay, advance to the starting line and, when all competitors are steady, the pistol shall be fired.

Recall Point
ARTICLE 6. a. Outdoor track. If, in a race not run in lanes, a runner falls during approximately the first 100 meters due to contact with another runner, the race shall be recalled.

b. Indoor track. The point for recall shall be not later than the end of the first turn (see Rule 10-4-6).

Staggers
ARTICLE 7. In races run in lanes around at least one turn, the starts and relay exchange zones must be staggered so that competitors or teams run the same distance. If the number of competitors exceeds the number of lanes on the track, all groups shall use a waterfall or alley start, which may be staggered. If there are two or more heats, all heats must use the same starting procedure.

The first leg of the 1,600-meter relay (mile relay) shall be run with a three-turn stagger. The 800-meter run shall be run in lanes around the first curve using a one-turn stagger. The staggers for each lane shall be measured by a certified engineer.

SECTION 2. Starting Violations

Violations at the start of a race include:

a. If a competitor at the start of a race uses tactics obviously intended to disconcert an opponent, the competitor shall be warned by the starter and, if such action is repeated, shall be disqualified.

b. A false start may be charged against a runner who fails to comply promptly with the command "On your marks" or with the various requirements of the command "Set."

c. If a competitor commences the starting motion after assuming a full and final set position and before the report of the pistol/starting device, it shall be considered a false start. If the start was not fair in the judgment of the starter, the starter must recall the competitors with a second shot. If the unfair start was due to one or more competitors "beating the pistol," it shall be considered a false start and the starter must charge the offender(s), who shall be disqualified. If the unfair start is not due to any competitor, a false start shall not be charged.

d. A competitor who cuts in front of another runner without proper clearance or one full stride on the curved line start shall be disqualified (see Rule 5-5-3a).

Note 1: The starter usually finds it necessary to disqualify only one runner for a false start. By quickly saying "Stand up" after a break, the starter can release the other runners from their marks. Runners who, in the starter's judgment, have been led off their marks by a false starter shall not be disqualified. However, if two or more runners break together, the starter must disqualify all of them.

Note 2: For any reason, either before or after the word "Set," the starter may cancel a start by directing all runners to stand up. After allowing the runners a brief time for adjustments, a new start shall be made. Starters must conform to the prescribed commands as set forth in the rules.

Note 3: When using a stand-up start, after the command "On your marks," all competitors shall move to the starting line and assume a steady and motionless position.

Note 4: The starter shall confer only with the officials assigned to the starting line [assistant starter(s) and starting-area marshal] in cases when there are questions regarding the start.

Note 5: The starter shall rule on intentional-false-start protests.

SECTION 3. The Finish

Placing Finishers
ARTICLE 1. The runners shall be placed in the order in which any part of their torso (as distinguished from the head, neck, arms, legs, hands or feet) reached the perpendicular plane of the nearer edge of the finish line.

Finish Tape
ARTICLE 2. When fully automatic timing is used, finish tape shall not be used.

Returning in Lanes
ARTICLE 3. To help the judges identify the place winners of races run in lanes, finish runners must return in their lanes to the finish line.

SECTION 4. Legal Running

Legal Running in Lanes

ARTICLE 1. In all races run in lanes, competitors shall start and finish within their assigned lanes.

Note: If a runner runs outside the assigned lane in the straightaway or runs outside the outer line on the curve, without material advantage gained and no other runner obstructed, a disqualification shall not take place.

Legal Running Without Lanes

ARTICLE 2. The following situations shall constitute legal running in non-lane events:

a. A competitor may run anywhere on the track at any pace or any change of pace as long as the competitor does not impede or obstruct by any body or arm action the progress of another runner.

b. A competitor may pass another runner legally on either the right or left side.

c. A competitor may cut in front of another runner, provided that the overtaking runner has one full stride (this rule also applies to the curved line start).

d. A competitor who is lapped in a distance race shall run a normal course.

Note: If the runner is required to withdraw, the runner shall exit to the inside of the track. The games committee has the authority to determine the number of lapped runners who shall remain in the competition.

SECTION 5. Running Violations

All Races

ARTICLE 1. When an athlete commits a flagrant foul in a race to aid a teammate, all persons from the offending team in that event shall be disqualified. Such an infraction shall be reported by the umpire and ruled on by the referee.

In Lanes

ARTICLE 2. The referee, after consulting with the appropriate officials, shall disqualify a competitor who:

a. Impedes another runner;

b. In a race run on a curve, steps on or over the lane line to the left with two consecutive steps of the left foot;

c. Does not start and finish within the assigned lane; or

d. In a race starting but not finishing in lanes, does not cross the break line within the assigned lane.

Note: The referee, after consulting with the appropriate officials, shall not disqualify a competitor who:

1. *Is pushed or forced by another runner to step on or over the lane line to the left without material advantage gained, or*

2. *Steps out of his or her lane on the straightaway.*

Not in Lanes

ARTICLE 3. The referee, after consulting with the appropriate officials, shall disqualify a competitor who:

a. Jostles, cuts across or obstructs another competitor so as to impede the other runner's progress. Direct contact is not necessary; any action that causes another runner to break stride or lose momentum is grounds for disqualification;

b. Veers to the right or to the left so as to impede a challenging runner or forces the challenging runner to run a greater distance;

c. Voluntarily leaves the track or abandons the race, then returns later to continue the race;

d. Tries to force a way between two leading runners and makes direct contact so as to impede the progress of either;

e. Steps on or over the curb with two consecutive steps of the left foot;

f. Is paced or assisted by a competitor of the opposite gender in the same race; or

g. Is paced or assisted by lapped competitors or those about to be lapped.

Note: The referee, after consulting with the appropriate officials, shall not disqualify a competitor who:

1. *Is pushed or forced by another runner to step on or over the curb without material advantage gained, or*

2. *Steps on or over the curb on the straightaway unless an advantage is gained by improving position.*

Illegal Assistance

ARTICLE 4. a. On the report of an official, a warning or disqualification shall be ruled by the referee when a competitor has been aided (see Rule 3-5-2d). This includes aid provided by a coach, a teammate not in the race or a noncompetitor connected with the competitor's team, directly or indirectly, who is on the track or within the infield track area.

b. The viewing of a videotape or photos, or the use of any wireless communication device, by a competitor during event competition is prohibited.

c. The use by competitors of video or audio devices, radio transmitters or receivers, mobile phones, computers, or any similar devices in the competition area is prohibited.

SECTION 6. Hurdling Violations

The referee, after consulting with the appropriate officials, shall disqualify a competitor who:

a. Advances or trails a leg or foot below the top horizontal plane or plane extended of the hurdle;

b. Runs around or under a hurdle;

c. Runs over a hurdle not in the hurdler's lane;

d. Impedes another hurdler; or

e. Knocks down any hurdle by hand.

SECTION 7. The Steeplechase

The referee, after consulting with the appropriate officials, shall disqualify a competitor who:

a. Advances or trails a leg or foot below the top horizontal plane of the hurdle;

b. Runs around a hurdle;

c. Does not attempt every hurdle; or

d. Does not go over or through the water.

SECTION 8. The Relays

Relay Racing

ARTICLE 1. Four competitors constitute a relay team, each of whom, except in shuttle relays, carries a baton.

Relay Substitution

ARTICLE 2. The games committee shall set the relay substitution rule policy.

Common Relay Events

ARTICLE 3. Relays commonly run include:

a. 400-Meter Relay (4 x 100 meters) or
    440-Yard Relay (4 x 110 yards).

b. 800-Meter Relay (4 x 200 meters) or
    880-Yard Relay (4 x 220 yards), a four-turn stagger is recommended.

c. 1,600-Meter Relay (4 x 400 meters) or
    Mile Relay (4 x 440 yards), a three-turn stagger shall be used.

d. 3,200-Meter Relay (4 x 800 meters) or
    Two-Mile Relay (4 x 880 yards).

e. 6,000-Meter Relay (4 x 1,500 meters),
    6,400-Meter Relay (4 x 1,600 meters) or
    Four-Mile Relay (4 x 1 mile).

f. Sprint Medley Relay (100, 100, 200, 400 meters or 110, 110, 220, 440 yards), a three-turn stagger is recommended.

g. Sprint Medley Relay (200, 200, 400, 800 meters or 220, 220, 440, 880 yards), a three-turn stagger is recommended.

h. Distance Medley Relay (1,200, 400, 800, 1,600 meters or 1,320, 440, 880, 1,760 yards).

i. (Men) Shuttle Hurdle Relay (4 x 110-meter or 4 x 120-yard hurdles).

j. (Women) Shuttle Hurdle Relay (4 x 100-meter hurdles).

Positions for Receiving the Baton

ARTICLE 4. In the sprint relays, outgoing runners, while waiting for the baton, may use the international zone if the incoming runner is running a leg of 200 meters (220 yards) or less. If the runner elects to use the international zone, the runner must be positioned entirely inside that zone within the runner's lane. Outgoing runners may place two separate pieces of tape or suitable material as determined by meet management on the track. These pieces of tape or material may not be longer than the width of the lane nor wider than 2 inches, and may be placed anywhere within the outgoing runner's lane. (The takeoff point may be marked outside the international zone.)

In all other relays around the track, outgoing runners, while waiting for the baton, must take preparatory positions entirely within the 20-meter (65.62-ft.) passing zone. Outgoing runners may not place any markings on the track.

Receivers for relay exchanges that do not occur in assigned lanes shall line up in the same relative position as their incoming teammates; the leaders shall pass in the first position, the second-place holders in the second position, etc. When interference is not possible, receivers may move to the inside.

Passing the Baton

ARTICLE 5. In all relays around the track, the baton must be passed between teammates within a 20-meter zone. The zone lines are inclusive in the measurement and are drawn 10 meters on each side of the measured centerline. The baton must be passed—not thrown—by each runner to the succeeding runner. If, in a genuine attempt to pass the baton, it is **dropped within** the passing zone, either runner may retrieve it. A baton **dropped outside** the passing zone must be recovered by the person who dropped it. A member of a relay team may not run outside the passing zone for the purpose of taking the baton from a faltering or fallen teammate.

After Passing the Baton

ARTICLE 6. Competitors, after exchanging the baton, must remain in their lanes or established paths until the course is clear in order to avoid contact with the other competitors.

Shuttle Hurdle Relay

ARTICLE 7. In the shuttle hurdle relay, the passing zone is 1.22 meters (4 ft.). The outgoing runner must be motionless and may not leave the starting line until the incoming runner's torso breaks the plane of the 1.22-meter (4-ft.) passing zone.

SECTION 9. Relay Racing Violations

The same rules and penalties with reference to fouling or illegal assistance that apply to other running events also shall apply to relay racing. In addition, the referee, after consulting with the appropriate officials, shall disqualify a relay team when:

a. During a relay race, any member of that team is disqualified;

b. Any member of a team uses a device or substance on either hand that enhances contact with the baton (e.g., gloves or adhesive substances);

c. The baton is passed outside the 20-meter (65.62-ft.) passing zone;

d. The baton is recovered illegally after being dropped;

e. While running, a team member transports the baton in a manner other than in the hand;

f. The last runner of the team finishes the race without a baton;

g. After passing the baton, a runner veers out of the passing lane or from a straight course and impedes an opposing runner;

h. Assuming a preparatory position in any race run in lanes, any part of the outgoing runner breaks the plane of the adjacent lane lines so as to interfere with another runner;

i. The outgoing runner waiting for the baton does not take a position entirely within the 20-meter (65.62-ft.) passing zone (**exception**, see Rule 5-8-4); or

j. A team member runs more than one leg.

SECTION 10. Timed-Section Finals

If the limits of time or facilities require, to ensure safety and equity of competition, races (including relays) shall be run as a final in timed sections. The structure for running finals as timed sections shall be determined by the games committee and must be consistent throughout the meet.

SECTION 11. Qualifying and Drawing for Lanes

Purpose of Qualifying

ARTICLE 1. The games committee of any large meet may reduce the number of contestants to a workable size by establishing qualifying standards or by requiring qualifying heats, conducted under specified conditions and preceding the competition proper.

In cases where an athlete has qualified for the final and is unable to compete, another athlete shall not be moved into the final.

Responsibility

ARTICLE 2. The games committee shall be responsible for the drawing of lanes.

Regulations for Forming Heats

ARTICLE 3. The heats in running events shall be formed according to the following regulations, unless otherwise determined by the games committee:

a. The declared competitors shall be assigned to first-round heats in the order their names are listed on the ranked performance list, working alternately from left to right and right to left. This procedure could cause two or more teammates to be assigned to the same heat. These heats shall not be altered. Draw heat order by lot.

Examples to form heats:

2 Heats			3 Heats	
Heat 1	*Heat 2*	*Heat 1*	*Heat 2*	*Heat 3*
1	2	1	2	3
4	3	6	5	4
5	6	7	8	9
8	7	12	11	10
9	10	13	14	15
12	11	18	17	16

(Numbers represent runners ranked in order of performance.)

b. The following table shall be used in forming preliminary heats for the 100, 200, 400 and 800 meters, 100/110 hurdles, 400 hurdles and corresponding yard events:

No. of Entries	No. of Preliminary Heats	No. of Semifinal Heats	No. in Final
For six lanes:			
1 to 6	0	0	6
7 to 12	2	0	6
13 to 18	3	2	6
19 to 24	4	2	6
25 or more requires quarterfinals following above pattern.			
For seven lanes:			
1 to 7	0	0	7
8 to 14	2	0	6
15 to 21	3	2	6
22 to 28	4	2	6
29 or more requires quarterfinals following above pattern.			
For eight lanes:			
1 to 8	0	0	8
9 to 16	2	0	8
17 to 24	3	2	8
25 to 32	4	2	8
33 to 40	5	2	8
41 or more requires quarterfinals following above pattern.			
For nine lanes:			
1 to 9	0	0	9
10 to 18	2	0	8
19 to 27	3	0	9
28 to 36	4	3	9
37 to 45	5	3	9
46 to 54	6	3	9

55 or more requires quarterfinals following above pattern.

c. In those events in which more than two rounds are contested, it is preferred that at least two qualifiers from each heat advance to the next round.

d. Principles of forming heats for second and subsequent rounds of competition are as follows:

(1) Weigh *place* first.

(2) Weigh *time* second.

Note: If fully automatic timing malfunctions, see Rule 5-12-5.

(3) Seed each group of place winners as a unit by their times. Seed winners, then seed second-place runners, etc. Work from left to right, and from right to left and then all qualifiers on time in descending order.

(4) Draw heat order by lot.

3 Heats, 4 Qualifiers		4 Heats, 4 Qualifiers		5 Heats, 3 Qualifiers	
Heat 1	Heat 2	Heat 1	Heat 2	Heat 1	Heat 2
1-1	1-2	1-1	1-2	1-1	1-2
2-1	1-3	1-4	1-3	1-4	I-3
2-2	2-3	2-1	2-2	1-5	2-1
3-2	3-1	2-4	2-3	2-3	2-2
3-3	4-1	3-1	3-2	2-4	2-5
4-3	4-2	3-4	3-3	3-2	3-1
		4-1	4-2	3-3	3-4
		4-4	4-3	3-5	(draw for heat by lot)

Legend:
1-1 = Fastest first-place runner.   2-1 = Fastest second-place runner.
1-2 = Second fastest first-place runner.   2-2 = Second fastest second-place runner.

Regulations for Assigning Lanes

ARTICLE 4. The following procedures shall be used in drawing/assigning lanes:

a. In the first round of competition, lanes shall be drawn by lot. In an event in which no preliminary round is contested, the games committee may assign preferred lane by entry performance.

b. For competition other than first round, lane assignments shall be made as follows:

(1) Races not starting in lanes shall be drawn by lot.

(2) In races that start but do not finish in lanes (including the 800 meters and the 1,600-meter relay), the preferred lanes shall be assigned first

to the heat winners in descending order by time and then to all qualifiers by time in descending order.

(3) Races run completely in lanes, assign to preferred lanes as follows:

    (a) Advancement determined by place:

        (1) Weigh place first.

        (2) Weigh time second.

    (b) Advancement determined by time:

        Weigh by time in descending order.

Note: Before the start of competition, the games committee shall decide the ranked order of preferred lanes one at a time and event by event. The best available lanes shall be used. It is recommended that the athlete seeded No. 1 be placed inside the athlete seeded No. 2. When unusual conditions make the original drawings unfair to one or more runners, the games committee or referee may make such changes as will produce greater fairness.

Alternating Lanes for Duals, Triangulars

ARTICLE 5. When track conditions permit, lanes shall be drawn and alternated by schools for each individual event. School A might draw lanes 1-4-7; school B, 2-5-8; and school C, 3-6-9. Each school then shall place its runners in its lanes.

Canceling Heats

ARTICLE 6. If heats are drawn for a race but the number of competitors who report to run is small enough to be run in one race, the heats shall be canceled and the race shall be run as a final only at the originally scheduled final time.

Redrawing Heats

ARTICLE 7. Whenever the number of entries or scratches reduces the number of competitors in any heat so as to eliminate the element of competition, the games committee shall redraw the heats, reduce the number of qualifiers from each heat to a number that will guarantee competition and select any additional qualifiers on a time basis.

Tie for Last Qualifying Position

ARTICLE 8. In the event of a tie for the last qualifying place for a subsequent race, and assuming positions on the track are available, the tying runners all shall qualify. If enough lanes are not available, the position(s) shall be determined by reading the phototiming devices to the 1/1,000th of a second or lesser fraction, by a runoff or drawn by lot, based on a decision before the meet by the games committee.

Qualifying for Finals

ARTICLE 9. The following procedures shall be used to form all finals, unless otherwise determined by the games committee (see Rule 5-10):

a. A maximum of nine runners or teams shall run in any heat or final of the 100, 200, 400 and 800 meters, 100/110 hurdles, 400 hurdles, 400 and 1,600 relays.

b. In all races started in lanes, if there are the same number of or fewer entries than there are lanes on the track, the event shall be run as a final.

c. In races run entirely in lanes, the heat winners shall advance to the final. All other qualifiers shall advance on the basis of time in the preliminary heats. Finals shall include eight or nine qualifiers, of which eight may score (100-200-400-400 relays-hurdles). When more than one qualifying round is run, see Rule 5-11-3c.

d. In races that start in lanes but do not finish in lanes, the first two places in each heat shall advance and all other qualifiers shall advance on the basis of time. If there are four or more heats, the heat winner shall advance and all other qualifiers shall advance on the basis of time.

e. If 15 or fewer competitors report for the 1,500 meters, the event shall be run as a final.

f. If 18 or fewer competitors report for the 3,000 or 5,000 meters, or steeplechase, the events shall be run as finals.

g. If preliminaries are run in the 1,500, 3,000 or 5,000 meters, or steeplechase, the maximum number that may qualify for finals would be 12 in the 1,500, 14 in the 3,000 and steeplechase, and 16 in the 5,000. It is recommended that at least four places from each heat advance; however, at least two qualifiers must advance on the basis of time. If there are three heats, at least three competitors advance on place and at least two must advance on the basis of time.

SECTION 12. Timing

Methods of Timing

ARTICLE 1. The following methods of timing are listed in the order of preference, depending on availability:

a. Fully automatic timing (FAT).

   (1) Photoelectric timing:

      (a) Must utilize equipment that is started automatically by the energy of the shell exploding in the starter's gun.

(b) Must, by an electronic or optical device, determine the instant the first part of each runner's torso reaches the finish line, and record the finish time automatically on film or print out which is synchronized with a time scale graduated in 1/100ths of a second.

(c) Should determine times and places by the use of equipment that guarantees perpendicularity between the time scale and the precise point of finish for each runner.

(d) Times should be read to the next highest 1/100th of a second.

(2) Videotape. Videotape may be used as long as it complies with the provisions of Rule 5-12-1a and:

(a) It uses a camera aligned with the finish line.

(b) It uses videotape that produces 50 (fifty) frames/second.

(c) The official time is read from the time of the frame where the runner is positioned at, or immediately after, the finish line.

(d) Is capable of producing a printed picture that shows a time for each runner and whether the timing device has started automatically by the starter's gun.

(3) Certification. Each fully automatic timing device must be certified and guaranteed by the manufacturer to meet the requirements for certification (see Rule 2-12).

b. Manual timing (MT). All other methods of timing are manual timing.

Methods of Recording Time

ARTICLE 2. a. When fully automatic timing (FAT) is used, results must be recorded in 1/100th of a second.

b. When fully automatic timing (FAT) is used, and the timing system allows, ties will be broken by reading the film to the 1/1,000th of a second.

c. When manual timing (MT) is used, times must be rounded to the slower 1/10th of a second. Watches recording in hundredths of a second must be rounded up to the next tenth. After each race, the head timer shall be responsible for recording the results from the timers. If two timers agree, their time shall be the official time. If all three watches disagree, the middle watch shall be the official time. If only two timers record the time, the slower time shall be official.

d. Final results must indicate method of timing (FAT-10.33 or MT-10.4) and wind velocity in miles per hour (e.g., 4.473 mph) or meters per second (e.g., 2.0 mps).

e. Wind velocity in miles per hour (e.g., 4.473 mph) or meters per second (e.g., 2.0 mps) should be recorded for the 100 and 200 meters, and 100 and 110 hurdles.

Championships Equipment Requirements

ARTICLE 3. The following are minimum requirements, unless otherwise agreed upon by the games committee:

(1) Equipment must be fully automatic.

(2) Equipment must be capable of monitoring the adequacy of the power source.

(3) Equipment must have an automatic battery-power takeover system in the event of line system power failure.

(4) Equipment must have protection of the time base accuracy from surges in the power source.

(5) Equipment must produce a photo-finish photograph with read-out times.

(6) An alternate finish-line crew shall operate to judge and provide manually operated timing results to supplement the fully automatic timing system.

(7) Three fully automatic timing devices must be used, **one of which can distinguish color.** The fully automatic timing devices must be positioned on opposite sides of the track. It is understood that lighting requirements may not be sufficient at night to properly distinguish color. There shall be a minimum of two independent power circuits for these timing devices.

Fully Automatic Conversions

ARTICLE 4. Hand times must be rounded up (see Rule 5-12-2c) before adding a conversion factor. The conversion factor of .24 seconds between fully automatic timing (FAT) and manual timing (MT) must be used when conversions are desired (i.e., MT + .24 = FAT). In championships meets, .24 shall be used in all events to determine seed times.

Malfunction of Fully Automatic Timing

ARTICLE 5. In the event of a malfunction of fully automatic timing in one or more of several heats or sections, the following procedure shall apply: Hand times must be used for all heats or sections to determine advancement (heats) or final placings (sections).

Note: Times for those heats or sections in which automatic timing functioned properly shall be listed on the final results.

RULE 6

Field Events

SECTION 1. General Rules for Field Events

Time Limit

ARTICLE 1. In the throwing events, a competitor shall be charged with an unsuccessful attempt if the competitor does not initiate a trial within one minute after the competitor's name has been called by the event judge.

ARTICLE 2. In the jumping events, a competitor shall be charged with an unsuccessful attempt if the competitor does not initiate a trial within one minute after the pit, crossbar or standards have been prepared or set, and after the competitor's name has been called by the event judge.

ARTICLE 3. In the high jump and pole vault, when there are two or three competitors remaining in the competition at the start of a round, or when a competitor is taking consecutive attempts while other competitors remain in the competition, high jumpers shall have two minutes and pole vaulters three minutes to initiate an attempt.

After all other competitors have failed, a competitor who has won the event has the right to continue vaulting or jumping at a height the competitor chooses until elimination by three consecutive failures. The competitor shall be allowed four minutes for the high jump and five minutes for the pole vault to initiate an attempt.

ARTICLE 4. Visible time indicators should be stationed at each field event so that they can be seen by competitors, officials and fans. If visible time indicators are not used, the event timer shall give a 30-second warning. The warning signal (a yellow flag) must be raised and held in position for the remaining 30 seconds.

Absence From Competition

ARTICLE 5. If a competitor is competing in another event that requires a long absence, the head judge of an event may allow that competitor to take qualifying or preliminary attempts out of the official order, within the competitor's designated flight, which may or may not be in succession. Excused competitors must not delay the start of the finals.

Should a competitor miss a turn in the finals, the head judge shall refuse permission for that competitor to take that turn.

In the vertical jumps, competition must continue in the excused competitor's absence; the athlete shall compete at the existing height upon return. The head judge of the event may allow the competitor to take attempts out of the official order, which may or may not be in succession.

In events other than the vertical jumps, if a competitor is not present for an attempt in the finals, it shall be deemed that the competitor is passing once the allowable time period for the attempt has elapsed.

Completion of Preliminaries

ARTICLE 6. Each flight in the preliminaries is completed when the last competitor in the flight has either taken the final attempt or the time limit for the attempt has expired.

Illegal Assistance

ARTICLE 7. a. On the report of an official, a warning or disqualification, shall be ruled by the referee when a competitor has been aided (see Rule 3-5-2d). This includes aid provided by a coach, a teammate who is not in the event or by any noncompetitor connected with the competitor's team, directly or indirectly, and who is stationed in the field-event areas (see Rule 5-5-4).

b. The viewing of a videotape or photos, or the use of any wireless communication device, by a competitor during event competition is prohibited.

c. The use by competitors of video or audio devices, radio transmitters or receivers, mobile phones, computers, or any similar devices in the competition area is prohibited.

Note: In meets involving five or fewer teams, meet management may allow coaches to confer with athletes in the field of competition.

Jumping Aids

ARTICLE 8. Weights or artificial aids shall not be allowed in the jumping events except a wind sock to help the competitor determine wind direction and velocity, and a foot pattern to indicate placement of takeoff mark in the jumping events.

Taping Aids

ARTICLE 9. Restrictions are detailed in sections pertaining to the pole vault (see Rule 6-6-4), shot put (see Rule 6-8-2), discus (see Rule 6-9-2), javelin (see

Rule 6-10-2), hammer (see Rule 6-11-2) and 35-pound weight (see Rule 10-9-6).

Shoe Restrictions

ARTICLE 10. Competitors are not permitted to wear shoes that incorporate any device that aids performance or shoes in which the sole and inner sole, including grooves, ridges or cleats, have an overall total thickness in excess of 13 millimeters (0.51 in.). Competitors may not use any appliance either inside or outside the shoe that will have the effect of increasing the thickness of the sole and inner sole above the permitted 13-millimeter maximum.

The decision of the head judge as to the legality of shoes may be appealed by a contestant to the referee who shall render a decision.

Warm-Up Restrictions

ARTICLE 11. Once competition begins, it shall be a foul or missed attempt if a competitor uses the runway, ring or takeoff area for practice purposes.

In vertical jumps, an athlete who has not taken an attempt in at least one hour may use the runway and landing areas without the crossbar at a height change with the permission of the event official.

A high jumper has a maximum of one and one-half minutes and a pole vaulter has a maximum of two minutes to warm up. Such warm-up must occur at height changes.

Field-Event Implements

ARTICLE 12. The games committee may limit the use of implements in a meet (exception: vaulting poles) to those provided by the games committee. If this is not done, the games committee shall allow each competitor to use a personal implement, provided it meets legal specifications. To determine this, the games committee shall set a time and place, before the start of the event, for inspecting, weighing and measuring of all implements to be used in the meet (warm-up and competition). Weighing and measuring devices must be capable of certifying the implements within the allowable event specifications.

In the event an implement should become damaged during the course of the competition, its use shall be permitted only after it has been reinspected and approved.

A competitor may use another competitor's implement, with the other competitor's permission, during competition.

Competitors are not allowed in the impact area during warm-up or competition. Implements shall be carried (not thrown) out of the sector by an official.

Illegal Implements

ARTICLE 13. A field-event competitor shall be disqualified if that competitor:

a. Uses an implement (shot, discus, javelin, hammer, weight, vaulting pole or jumping shoe) that has been altered illegally after having been inspected officially, or

b. Uses an implement that was not certified before competition or an illegal implement in competition.

All records and/or points scored with the use of such illegal implements or shoes shall be canceled.

Throwing Events From Circles

ARTICLE 14. In all throwing events from circles, a competitor must start from a stationary position inside the circle. A competitor is allowed to touch the inside of the iron band marking the circumference of the circle or the inside of the stopboard.

It shall be a foul throw if, after stepping into the circle and starting a throw, a competitor:

a. Touches the top of the iron band;

b. Touches the top of the stopboard;

c. Touches the outside of the circle with any part of the body;

d. Improperly releases the shot, discus, hammer or weight;

e. Exits the circle improperly (see related sections of this rule for each event); or

f. Does not initiate an attempt within one minute after his or her name has been called by the event judge (see Rule 6-1-1).

Note: A throw will be considered valid if it lands within the sector, even though it may have touched the cage.

Competitors may not apply any substance on the throwing surface of the circle.

In order to obtain a better grip, competitors may use any suitable substance only on their hands (exceptions: see Rules 6-8-2, 6-9-2, 6-10-2, 6-11-2).

Taking Measurements

ARTICLE 15. All measurements of height or distance may be made with a steel tape, certified fiberglass tape or bar (steel tapes are recommended). Of these three devices, only the steel tape is acceptable for record purposes.

A scientific measuring apparatus, the accuracy of which is certified by the IAAF, also may be used if approved by the games committee and/or the NCAA Men's and Women's Track and Field Committee. For record purposes, a certified scientific measuring apparatus also is acceptable.

When measuring the throwing events, long jump or triple jump, that part of the tape that records distance shall be held by the official at the circle, scratch line or takeoff board.

In the pole vault and high jump, measurement of the official height shall be from a point on the same level as the takeoff to the lowest point on the upper side of the crossbar.

Efforts judged to be foul shall not be measured.

Recording Performances

ARTICLE 16. a. Performances that result in a pass or foul shall be recorded as: P=Pass, F=Foul.

b. Metrics is the preferred system of measurement. Distances measured metrically shall be recorded to the nearest lesser centimeter (i.e., fractions less than one centimeter must be ignored).

c. Imperial measurement is an acceptable alternative. Distances shall be recorded to the lesser quarter-inch for the horizontal jumps, shot put and weight throw, and to the lesser inch for the discus, hammer and javelin.

d. When performances are measured metrically, it is recommended that they are recorded, displayed and announced metrically and imperially.

e. **For world, American, collegiate and NCAA championships records, marks must be measured and recorded metrically.**

Measuring Height of Bar

ARTICLE 17. An accurate measurement of the height of the high-jump or pole-vault crossbar shall be taken each time it is raised to a new height (or lowered to determine first place); each time a new crossbar replaces a broken one; **each time a standard(s) has been displaced**; and for record attempts, each time the bar is touched (see Rule 7-2-5).

Wind Considerations

ARTICLE 18. The games committee shall designate the official site or runway to be used at least one hour before the competition begins. It is the responsibility of the field-event judge and meet referee to ensure fair and safe competition. In the event of unsafe wind conditions once competition has begun, competition may be suspended, but the event venue (e.g., direction of jumping) shall not be changed.

Safety Considerations

ARTICLE 19. It is the responsibility of the field-event judge and meet refer-ee to ensure fair and safe competition. In the event of unsafe conditions once competition has begun (e.g., weather or facility concerns), competition may be suspended, but the event venue (e.g., direction of jumping) shall not be changed.

Safety Measures

ARTICLE 20. All throwing areas shall be roped and flagged. Officials should maintain visual contact with the throwing circle or runway when in the impact area. Competitors should maintain visual contact with the throwing circle or runway when retrieving implements. A competitor should not be in the impact area to retrieve those implements.

An official should be present at all field events to monitor all warm-ups.

SECTION 2. Preliminary Procedures

Purpose of Preliminaries

ARTICLE 1. The games committee must determine the number of com-petitors who shall advance from preliminary rounds to the final round.

To be in the finals, a competitor must make at least one legal mark in the preliminaries.

When an athlete who has advanced to a subsequent round is unable to compete, another athlete shall not advance.

Preliminary Attempts

ARTICLE 2. Field-event contestants who first report after the first compet-itive attempt has been made shall not be allowed to compete in the event. In the preliminaries of the throwing events, long jump and triple jump, each contestant shall be allowed three attempts. Competitors tying for the last position shall advance to the finals, unless otherwise ruled by the games committee before the competition.

In scored meets with four or fewer teams, it is recommended that the top eight performances advance to the finals, plus a minimum representation of two competitors (if entered) from each institution in conformance with Rule 6-2-1.

It is recommended in scoring meets with five or more teams that one more competitor than the number of scoring places should advance to the finals, and in nonscoring meets that the number qualifying for the finals should be consistent with the number that qualify in straightaway laned races.

All performances made in field-event preliminaries shall be counted with performances in the finals to determine final place-winners. Competitors shall be credited with the best of all their efforts.

Time Limit
ARTICLE 3. The games committee may establish a time by which all preliminaries in a field event (especially the long jump and triple jump) must be completed. Preliminaries not taken before this time shall be forfeited.

SECTION 3. Alternative Procedures

Four-Attempt Competition
ARTICLE 1. If the limits of time or facilities require, to ensure safety and equity of competition, horizontal jumps and throws shall be contested as a four-attempt competition.

Time Limit
ARTICLE 2. The games committee may establish a time by which all preliminaries in a field event (especially the long jump and triple jump) must be completed. Preliminaries not taken before this time shall be forfeited.

Guaranteed Measurement
ARTICLE 3. The games committee may establish a minimum distance that must be reached to guarantee a measurement of an attempt. All attempts that meet or exceed the minimum distance must be measured.

SECTION 4. Order of Competition

Grouping Competitors

ARTICLE 1. It is recommended that competitors be arranged in flights not larger than 12 and not smaller than five.

Assignment to flights may be random or based on entry performances. The games committee shall determine the order in which flights are contested.

If weather or ground conditions render this method unfair to some competitors, the referee may require that all attempts be taken one at a time in the order drawn.

A **maximum** of 15 minutes for warm-up attempts shall be permitted before each flight. Between preliminaries and finals there can be a general warm-up by all competitors, but the same warm-up period shall be allowed for competitors of each flight.

Determining Order of Competition

ARTICLE 2. In the throwing events, long jump and triple jump, the order of competition within a flight shall be drawn by lot. Each competitor in a flight shall complete three attempts in the order drawn. In the finals of these events, competition shall be in reverse order of performance in the preliminaries. For the final three attempts, the finalists shall compete in one flight.

High-Jump, Pole-Vault Procedure

ARTICLE 3. In the high jump and pole vault, each competitor is allowed an attempt in the order in which the competitor's name has been drawn by lot. The competitor is granted a maximum of three attempts at any one height. The competitor may accept all three attempts or may choose to pass any of them. (For warm-up restrictions, see Rule 6-1-11.)

Those who fail and choose to take a second attempt at the same height shall take this second attempt in the order drawn and, similarly, for their third attempts. Competitors may, likewise, pass their second and/or third attempts. (Any "pass" is for a single attempt only. To pass all attempts at a given height, competitors must indicate that they are passing all three of their attempts at that height and the official should so record.) Passes must be indicated before the start of the clock.

When there are large fields in the high jump or pole vault (i.e., nine or more at a given height), it is advisable to establish continuing flights of five competitors. Once an athlete has cleared or missed three attempts at a height, another athlete shall be added, moving down the order of competition until all athletes have completed attempts at each height. Therefore, jumps attempted by athletes would not be separated by more than four attempts from other athletes at any height.

When the number of competitors remaining at a given height is fewer than nine, the five-alive system is abandoned and replaced by a continuous flight until the next height change.

The following is a sample performance record for a high-jump/pole-vault competition:

(Key: O Cleared; X Failed)

	1.78		
A	X1	X1	X1
B	X2	X2	X2
C	X3	O3	
D	X4	X4	O4
E	X5	X5	O5
F	O3		

Explanation of example:
Jumper A (1) failed trial one X1
Jumper B (2) failed trial one X2
Jumper C (3) failed trial one X3

Jumper D (4) failed trial one X4
Jumper E (5) failed trail one X5
Jumper A (1) failed trial two X1
Jumper B (2) failed trial two X2
Jumper C (3) cleared trial two O3
Jumper D (4) failed trial two X4
Jumper E (5) failed trial two X5
Jumper A (1) failed trial three X1
Jumper B (2) failed trial three X2
Jumper F (3) cleared trial one O3
Jumper D (4) cleared trial three O4
Jumper E (5) cleared trial three O5

The competitor is permitted to continue jumping or vaulting at subsequent heights but is disqualified as soon as three consecutive unsuccessful attempts have been made, regardless of the heights at which the unsuccessful attempts are made.

The crossbar shall not be lowered after the competition has started, except as provided in Rule 7-1-5a-(3) to determine a first-place winner.

SECTION 5. The High Jump

Legal Jump
ARTICLE 1. A legal high jump is one in which a competitor jumps from one foot.

Starting Height
ARTICLE 2. The starting height of the crossbar and each successive height shall be determined by the games committee and/or jury. It is recommended that the crossbar be raised in increments of 5 centimeters (2 in.).

Attention should be paid to national standards and/or records when determining starting heights and increments.

There shall be a space at least 10 millimeters (0.39 in.) between the ends of the crossbar and the uprights. The standards shall not be moved once the competition has been started. For safety reasons, the landing area may be adjusted.

One face of each crossbar shall be marked so that the crossbar always is placed with the same surface up.

Failed Attempt
ARTICLE 3. A failed attempt shall be called:

a. When the crossbar is displaced in an attempt to clear it;

b. When a competitor touches the ground or landing area beyond the plane of the crossbar or the crossbar extended without clearing the bar;

c. If a competitor fails to initiate an attempt within one minute after his or her name has been called by the event judge and time is indicated (see Rules 6-1-2, 6-1-3); or

d. If a competitor violates the warm-up restrictions (see Rule 6-1-11).

Accidental Displacement

ARTICLE 4. a. If the crossbar is displaced by a force disassociated with the competitor, and if it is after the competitor clearly is over, the jump is successful. If the crossbar is displaced before the competitor is over, the competitor shall be given another attempt.

b. It is not considered a failed attempt if a competitor clears the crossbar, lands in the pit and, while exiting under control, accidentally displaces the crossbar.

Jumping Aids

ARTICLE 5. Two marks may be used each with a single piece of tape not longer than 15 centimeters (6 in.). The mark(s) cannot be located within two meters of either standard and must be made with tape as approved by meet management. The use of unacceptable material shall lead to the disqualification of the competitor. After warm-up and before competition, the high-jump official shall ask all competitors to identify their designated mark(s). All other marks shall be removed.

Improperly Fastened Supports

ARTICLE 6. If improperly fastened supports slip downward when a jumper hits the crossbar without displacing it, the head judge of the event shall rule "no jump" and allow the jumper another trial. Should the bar be displaced, it shall be a failed attempt.

SECTION 6. The Pole Vault

Starting Height

ARTICLE 1. The starting height of the bar and each successive height shall be determined by the games committee and/or jury. It is recommended that the bar be raised in increments of 15 centimeters (6 in.).

It is suggested that attention be paid to national standards and/or records when determining starting heights and increments.

One face of each crossbar shall be marked so that the crossbar always is placed with the same surface up.

Note: For placement of the pole-vault landing pad, see Rule 2-6-1.

Failed Attempt
ARTICLE 2. A failed attempt shall be called when:

a. After the vault, the bar does not remain on the pegs because of the action of the competitor while vaulting;

b. A competitor steadies the bar during an attempt;

c. A competitor leaves the ground in an attempt to vault and fails to clear the crossbar;

d. Without clearing the bar, any part of the competitor's body or the pole touches the ground or the landing area beyond the vertical plane of the inside edge of the top of the box;

e. During a vault, a competitor moves the upper hand higher on the pole or raises the lower hand above the upper hand;

f. A competitor fails to initiate an attempt within one minute after the bar and standard have been set and the competitor's name has been called by the event judge (see Rules 6-1-2, 6-1-3); or

g. A competitor violates the warm-up restrictions (see Rule 6-1-11).

Note: It shall not be counted as a trial or failure if a competitor's pole breaks during an attempt to clear the bar.

Accidental Displacement
ARTICLE 3. a. If the crossbar is displaced by a force disassociated with the competitor, after the competitor clearly is over, the vault is successful. If the crossbar is displaced before the competitor is over, the competitor shall be given another attempt.

b. If the wind is of such intensity that the pole is forced against the crossbar so as to displace it, the vault is successful.

c. It is not considered a failed attempt if a competitor clears the crossbar, lands in the pit and, while exiting under control, accidentally displaces the crossbar.

Jumping Aids
ARTICLE 4. A maximum of two markers may be placed adjacent to the runway, but not on the runway. These markers must be made with a material that is approved by meet management. **(Note: Shoes as a marker are not acceptable.)** The use of unacceptable material shall lead to the disqualification of the competitor. This restriction applies to practice, warm-up and competition. A competitor may not place foreign material in the vaulting box.

The vaulting pole shall have no assisting device other than two layers of adhesive tape applied with uniform thickness above the bottom of the hand hold.

Competitors may use a glove or an adhesive substance on their hands or on the pole in order to obtain a better grip. The use of a forearm cover to prevent injuries also shall be allowed.

The practice of tapping (i.e., assisting the competitor at takeoff) is prohibited during warm-ups and competition by anyone (i.e., coach, teammate, other competitors, official). Failure to adhere to this prohibition will result in immediate disqualification from the competition for the assisted athlete.

Catching the Pole
ARTICLE 5. The pole may be caught by an assigned official when circumstances warrant.

Moving Uprights
ARTICLE 6. Competitors may have the uprights moved toward the landing area not less than 45 centimeters (18 in.) and not more than 80 centimeters (31.5 in.) from the extension of the inside edge of the top of the box.

Improperly Fastened Supports
ARTICLE 7. If improperly fastened supports slip downward when a vaulter hits the crossbar without displacing it, the head judge of the event shall rule "no vault" and allow the vaulter another attempt. Should the bar be displaced, it shall be a failed attempt.

SECTION 7. The Long Jump and Triple Jump

Method of Triple Jump
ARTICLE 1. In the triple jump, a competitor shall make the first jump (sometimes called the hop) by landing on the takeoff foot; the second jump (sometimes called the step) by landing on the non-takeoff foot, and the third jump into the landing area.

Multiple Takeoff Boards
ARTICLE 2. In the triple jump, a maximum of two boards per gender may be used. Before the start of the event, the competitors must declare the board they will use throughout the competition. There must be an identifying mark placed next to the board being used.

Jumping Aids
ARTICLE 3. The use of weights or grips of any kind is forbidden. Markers may not be placed in the landing area or on the runway, but a maximum of

two markers may be placed adjacent to the landing area or runway. These markers must be made with a material that is approved by meet management. **(Note: Shoes as a marker are not acceptable.)** The use of unacceptable material shall lead to the disqualification of the competitor. This restriction applies to practice, warm-up and competition.

Foul Jump
ARTICLE 4. It shall be a foul jump and not measured if:

a. The takeoff foot (shoe) extends beyond the foul line;

b. In attempting a jump, a competitor runs beyond the foul line extended;

c. In the course of landing, the competitor touches the ground outside the landing area nearer to the takeoff than the nearest break in the landing area made by the jump;

d. After completing a jump, the competitor walks back through the landing area; or

e. The competitor does not initiate an attempt within one minute after the pit has been prepared and his or her name has been called by the event judge (see Rule 6-1-2).

Note: It is not a foul, however, if a competitor walks back through the landing area after the official has ruled the attempt fair.

Measuring Legal Jump
ARTICLE 5. Each legal jump shall be measured at right angles to the foul line from (a) the nearest break in the ground, inside the landing area, made by any part of the competitor's feet, hands, body or uniform, to (b) the foul line extended.

SECTION 8. The Shot Put

Legal Put
ARTICLE 1. A legal put shall be made from within the circle without touching the top edge of the circle or the top surface of the stopboard and shall land within the prescribed sector.

A legal put must be made from the shoulder with one hand only so that, during the attempt, the shot does not drop behind or below the shoulder. A competitor must start from a stationary position inside the circle (see Rule 6-1-14).

Throwing Aids

ARTICLE 2. Taping of any part of the hand, thumb or fingers shall not be acceptable in the shot put, except to cover or protect an open wound. Such taping must be shown to the head event judge before the event starts.

In order to obtain a better grip, competitors may use any suitable substance only on their hands and neck. Only chalk may be applied directly to the implement. A support belt may be worn.

Foul Put

ARTICLE 3. It shall be a foul put and not measured if, after entering the circle and starting the put, the competitor:

a. Uses any method contrary to the definition of a legal put;

b. Causes the shot **to fall on or outside the lines** marking the sector;

c. Touches with any part of the body, before the shot hits the ground:

  (1) Any surface of the metal band except the inside surface,

  (2) Any surface of the stopboard except its inside surface, or

  (3) The area outside the circle;

d. Puts a shot that does not conform to the legal requirements (see Rules 2-8, 6-1-13);

e. Wears any illegal device or illegal taping on the putting hand, thumb or fingers (see Rule 6-8-2);

f. Leaves the circle before the shot hits the ground;

g. Leaves the circle from the front half; or

h. Fails to initiate an attempt within one minute after his or her name has been called by the event judge (see Rule 6-1-1).

Note: It is not a foul if any part of the competitor's body swings outside the circle without touching.

Measuring Legal Put

ARTICLE 4. The measurement of a put shall be from the nearest edge of the first mark made by the shot to the inside edge of the stopboard nearest such mark, measured along an extended radius of the circle (see Rule 6-1-15).

SECTION 9. The Discus Throw

Legal Throw

ARTICLE 1. A legal throw in the discus is one that is thrown from the circle into the legal sector. A competitor must start from a stationary position inside the circle (see Rule 6-1-14).

Throwing Aids

ARTICLE 2. Taping of any part of the hand, thumb or fingers shall not be acceptable in the discus, except to cover or protect an open wound. Such taping must be shown to the head event judge before the event starts.

In order to obtain a better grip, competitors may use any suitable substance only on their hands. Only chalk may be applied directly to the implement. A support belt may be worn.

Foul Throw

ARTICLE 3. It shall be a foul throw and not measured if, after entering the circle and starting the throw, the competitor:

a. Uses any method contrary to the definition of a legal throw;

b. Causes the discus to fall on or outside the lines marking the sector;

c. Touches with any part of the body, before the discus hits the ground:

   (1) Any surface of the metal band except the inside surface, or

   (2) The area outside the circle;

d. Leaves the circle before the discus hits the ground;

e. Leaves the circle from the front half;

f. Throws an implement that does not conform to the legal requirements (see Rules 2-9, 6-1-13);

g. Drops the discus outside the circle during the preliminary swings that precede the turn and throw;

h. Fails to initiate an attempt within one minute after his or her name has been called by the event judge (see Rule 6-1-1); or

i. Wears any illegal device or illegal taping on the throwing hand, thumb or fingers (see Rule 6-9-2).

Note: It is not a foul if any part of the competitor's body (to include the heel) swings outside the circle without touching.

Measuring Legal Throw

ARTICLE 4. The measurement of a legal throw shall be from the nearest edge of the first point of contact made by the discus to the inside edge of the circle nearest such mark along an extended radius of the circle (see Rule 6-1-15).

SECTION 10. The Javelin Throw

Legal Throw

ARTICLE 1. The javelin must be held by the grip and the throw made from behind the arc. The javelin must fall metal head-first within the sector.

If the metal head of the javelin makes the first contact within the legal sector, the throw shall be legal and shall be measured even though the shaft of the javelin then swings and makes contact with the ground outside the sector.

The thrower must not permit the body to rotate through a full turn at any time during the approach or delivery. (If an athlete aborts a throw, the approach ends and the thrower may return to the starting position.) The delivery of the javelin must be made with a distinct, above-the-shoulder motion of the throwing arm, and the thrower's last contact with the javelin during its release shall be with the cord grip.

Throwing Aids

ARTICLE 2. Taping of any part of the hand, thumb or fingers shall not be acceptable in the javelin, except to cover or protect an open wound. Such taping must be shown to the head event judge before the event starts.

In order to obtain a better grip, competitors may use any suitable substance only on their hands. Only chalk may be applied directly to the implement. A support belt may be worn.

Marks or markers may be placed adjacent to the runway or landing surface, but may not be placed on the runway or landing surface. These marks must be made with a material that is approved by meet management. **(Note: Shoes as a marker are not acceptable.)** The use of unacceptable material shall lead to the disqualification of the competitor. This restriction applies to practice, warm-up and competition.

Judge Rules on Throws

ARTICLE 3. One judge shall rule on the legality of the landing of the throw. The judge shall be perpendicular with the landing and low enough to determine the first legal point of contact with the ground.

Foul Throw

ARTICLE 4. It shall be a foul throw and not measured if, during an attempt to throw, the competitor:

a. Uses any method contrary to the definition of a legal throw;

b. Touches with any part of the body, before the javelin hits the ground:

  (1) Any surface of the foul line extended,

    (2) The run-up lines, or

    (3) The area outside the foul line or the run-up lines;

c. Fails to hold the javelin by the cord grip;

Note: A competitor may hold the javelin at the end of the cord grip even though one or more fingers and thumb touch the javelin shaft.

d. Throws a javelin that does not conform to the legal requirements (see Rules 2-11, 6-1-13);

e. Leaves the runway before the javelin hits the ground;

f. Exits the runway ahead of the foul-line arc and the lines drawn from its extremities;

g. Causes the javelin **to land on or outside the lines** marking the sector;

h. Fails to initiate an attempt within one minute after his or her name has been called by the event judge (see Rule 6-1-1); or

i. Wears any illegal device or illegal taping on the throwing hand, thumb or fingers (see Rule 6-10-2).

If the javelin breaks during the release or while in the air, it shall not count as a trial, provided the throw was made in accordance with the rules. If the javelin breaks upon contact with the ground, a substitute throw shall not be permitted and the throw shall be measured, provided it was made in accordance with the rules.

Note: A competitor may steady or guide the javelin with the nonthrowing hand during the run-up.

Measuring Legal Throw

ARTICLE 5. The measurement of the throw shall be made from the nearest edge of the first legal point of contact made by the javelin to the inside circumference of the arc or foul line, measured along a line from the contact point to the center of the circle of which the arc is a part (see Rule 6-1-15).

SECTION 11. The Hammer Throw

Legal Throw

ARTICLE 1. A legal hammer throw shall be made from the circle and shall land within the legal sector. There are no restrictions on the positions and actions of the thrower. A competitor may interrupt an attempt once started and lay the head of the hammer inside or outside of the circle and start again from a stationary position inside the circle.

When the competitor is in a starting position before the preliminary swings or turns, the competitor is allowed to put the head of the hammer on the ground inside or outside the circle.

When throwing the hammer, gloves for the protection of the hands are permitted. The gloves must be smooth on the back and the front and the fingertips must be exposed (i.e., the tips of the fingers on the gloves must not be closed). An additional layer of leather may be affixed to the palm of the glove to protect the hand further.

Throwing Aids

ARTICLE 2. The use of tape on the hand shall not be acceptable in the hammer, except to cover or protect an open wound. However, taping of individual fingers is permissible. Any taping must be shown to the head event judge before the event starts.

In order to obtain a better grip, competitors may use any suitable substance only on their hands and/or gloves. Only chalk may be applied directly to the implement. A support belt may be worn.

Foul Throw

ARTICLE 3. It shall be a foul throw and not measured if, after entering the circle and starting a throw, the competitor:

a. Uses any method contrary to the definition of a legal throw;

b. Touches with any part of the body, before the hammer hits the ground:

   (1) Any surface of the metal band except the inside surface, or

   (2) The area outside the circle;

c. Leaves the circle before the hammer has made contact with the ground as a result of the throw;

d. Leaves the circle from the front half;

e. Throws an implement that does not conform to the legal requirements (see Rules 2-10, 6-1-13);

f. Causes the hammer **to fall on or outside the lines** marking the sector; or

g. Fails to initiate an attempt within one minute after his or her name has been called by the event judge (see Rule 6-1-1).

If the head of the hammer falls within the legal sector, the throw shall be legal and shall be measured, even though the wire and handle contact the ground outside the sector. It shall not be a foul throw if the hammer, when released, touches any part of the cage and lands within the legal sector.

It shall not be considered a foul throw if the head of the hammer touches the ground when the competitor makes the preliminary swings or turns. However, if the head of the hammer touches either the inside or outside of the circle after the throw begins, the thrower must continue the throw or a foul throw shall be charged.

A competitor may interrupt an attempt once started, return to a stationary position, lay the head of the hammer inside or outside of the circle, and begin again.

If the hammer breaks during a throw or while in the air, it shall not count as a throw provided it was made in accordance with the rules. If a competitor thereby loses his equilibrium and commits a foul, it shall not count against him or her.

Measuring Legal Throw

ARTICLE 4. The measurement of a throw shall be from the nearest edge of the first mark made by the head of the hammer to the inside edge of the circle along an extended radius of the circle (see Rule 6-1-15).

RULE 7

Scoring, Records

SECTION 1. Scoring

Meet Scoring

ARTICLE 1. Scoring in meets with four or fewer teams shall be recorded as follows:

No. of Teams in Meet	Individual Events								Relay Events			
2	5	3	2	1					5	3		
3	7	5	4	3	2	1			7	5	4	
4	9	7	6	5	4	3	2	1	9	7	6	5

The number of entries per event shall be determined by meet management. Only two individual entries per institution shall score. One relay entry per institution shall score.

ARTICLE 2. Scoring in meets with five or more teams, and all championships meets regardless of the number of teams, shall be recorded as follows:

No. of Teams in Meet	Individual Events								Relay Events						
5 or fewer	10	8	6	4	2	1			10	8	6	4	2		
6 or more (6 scoring)	10	8	6	4	2	1			10	8	6	4	2	1	
6 or more (8 scoring)	10	8	6	5	4	3	2	1	10	8	6	5	4	3	2	1

The number of entries per event shall be determined by meet management. All individual entries shall have the ability to score in the competition. One relay entry per institution shall score.

Ties—Track Events

ARTICLE 3. If two or more competitors are judged as having tied for a place, points for the places involved shall be equally divided between these competitors. *Example:* If, in a triangular meet, there is a two-way tie for second place, the two competitors each shall be given four and one-half points, and the next competitor shall receive three points for fourth place.

Ties—Throws and Horizontal Jumps

ARTICLE 4. In those events in which places are decided by measurement (the throwing events, long jump and triple jump), ties produced by identical measurements shall be separated by the second-best performances of the tying competitors; if a tie still remains, by the third-best performances, and so forth. Therefore, it is mandatory to measure every attempt.

Ties—Vertical Jumps

ARTICLE 5. a. In the high jump and pole vault, ties shall be separated as follows (see also accompanying example):

(1) The competitor with the lowest number of jumps at the height at which the tie occurs shall be awarded the higher place.

(2) If the tie still remains, the competitor with the lowest total of failures throughout the competition up to and including the height last cleared shall be awarded the higher place.

(3) If the tie still remains:

(a) If it concerns first place, the competitors tying shall have one more jump at the lowest height attempted by any of the tied competitors above the tying height and, if a decision is not reached, the bar shall be lowered (if both fail to clear the height) or raised (if both clear the height) 3 centimeters (approximately 1 in.) in the high jump and 8 centimeters (approximately 3 in.) in the pole vault. There shall be one jump at each height until the tie is broken. Competitors so tying must jump on each occasion when breaking the tie.

> Withdrawal from competition in a jump-off shall not affect participation in subsequent events or negate a competitor's performance in that event.

(b) If it concerns a place other than first, the competitors shall be awarded the same place in the competition.

Note: In the high jump and pole vault, each competitor shall be credited with the best of all his or her jumps in the competition proper, including performances made in the jump-off of a first-place tie.

b. The following is a sample performance record for a high-jump competition:

(Key: P Passed; O Cleared; X Failed)

	1.78	1.83	1.88	1.93	1.98	2.03	2.08	TOTAL FAILURES	PLACE
A	P	XO	O	XO	P	XXO	XXX	4	2
B	O	O	O	X	XO	XXO	XXX	4	2
C	O	O	X	O	XXO	XXO	XXX	5	4
D	O	P	P	XXO	XXO	XO	XXX	5	1

It will be noted that competitors A, B, C and D all have cleared 2.03 and all have failed at 2.08. The apparent tie is separated as follows:

(1) Since D cleared 2.03 on the second attempt, while the others cleared on their third attempts, D is declared the winner.

(2) Since C has more failures than either A or B, C is given fourth place.

(3) Since A and B cleared the height on the same jump and both have the same number of failures, they tie for second place.

SECTION 2. Records

Acceptable Wind Velocity
ARTICLE 1. Official acceptance of a world, American, collegiate or NCAA championships record in the long jump, in the triple jump or in any race that is not run around the complete oval of the track requires that a reliable wind instrument shall record that any assisting wind does not exceed an average velocity of 2 meters per second (4.474 mph). An assisting wind is one that blows at a runner's back, either directly or in a slanting direction.

The length of time that shall be averaged for each event shall be as follows: long jump and triple jump—five seconds; 100 meters—10 seconds; 100 or 110 hurdles—13 seconds; 200 meters—10 seconds. When the 200 meters is run around one curve, the length of time shall be 10 seconds, beginning as the runners enter the straightaway. The wind velocity measurement shall be initiated when the competitor passes a mark 40 meters from the takeoff board in the long jump and 35 meters from the takeoff board in the triple jump. If the competitor runs fewer than 40 meters in the long jump or fewer than 35 meters in the triple jump, the wind velocity shall be measured from the start of the run.

A reliable wind instrument is one that employs the use of a directional tube and measures meters per second or miles per hour. The wind-measuring instrument shall be placed beside the sprint track, adjacent to lane one, preferably 50 meters from the finish line. In the long jump and triple jump, the wind-measuring instrument shall be 20 meters from the takeoff board. The instrument shall not be more than 2 meters from the track or runway, and shall be approximately 1.22 meters (4 ft.) above the competition surface.

The wind gauge shall be read in meters per second, rounded and recorded to the next higher tenth of a meter per second in the positive direction (i.e., a reading of 2.03 meters per second shall be recorded as 2.1; a reading of -2.03 meters per second shall be recorded as -2.0).

Records in Hurdles
ARTICLE 2. When hurdles do not conform to official specifications, a record shall not be allowed.

Records in Preliminaries
ARTICLE 3. Records made in track or field preliminaries, or in qualifying trials, may be accepted even though the athlete does not place in the final.

Records in Field Events
ARTICLE 4. To be accepted as records, performances in field events must occur within the number of attempts officially permitted, must be measured with a steel tape or an IAAF-certified scientific measuring device, and must be measured metrically. Additional trials for records shall not be recognized.

Throwing implements must be verified by the referee or implement inspector that they were certified before competition (i.e., check for the identifying mark), and recertified after record performances.

Records in High Jump, Pole Vault
ARTICLE 5. In the high jump and pole vault, the crossbar height shall be measured before record attempts or if the bar had been touched by an athlete before another athlete also jumping at the record height.

Records in Combined Events
ARTICLE 6. The conditions imposed for recognizing records in individual events shall have been compiled within each of the events where wind speed is measured. The speed shall not exceed 4 meters per second.

NCAA Championships Records
ARTICLE 7. NCAA regionals and championships records shall be the only records maintained by the NCAA.

The chair of the Men's and Women's Track and Field Committee shall appoint records chairs for each of the three NCAA divisions. It shall be the responsibility of each chair to obtain certification of records set at their respective championships. For further information, refer to the NCAA championships handbook for indoor or outdoor track. These records forms should be given to the respective NCAA liaison and kept on file at the NCAA national office.

RULE 8

Cross Country

SECTION 1. General Rules

There are varying circumstances encompassing the sport of cross country. Due to the variance in seasons, climatic conditions and distances, it is difficult to standardize all facets of the sport. The following rules shall set forth the standards for use in collegiate programs in the sport.

SECTION 2. The Course

Course Lengths

ARTICLE 1. The variances of course lengths shall be:

a. Men—The length of a cross country race shall be from 8,000 to 10,000 meters, unless otherwise mutually agreed upon by coaches or determined by the games committee.

b. Women—The length of a cross country race shall be from 5,000 to 8,000 meters, unless otherwise mutually agreed upon by the coaches or determined by the games committee.

Course Layout

ARTICLE 2. The course shall be confined, as far as possible, to fields, woods and grasslands. Parks, golf courses or specially designed courses are recommended. The turf should be of a quality to promote safety and freedom from injury to the runners, keeping the following in mind:

a. Dangerous ascents or descents, undergrowth, deep ditches, and in general any hindrance detrimental to the contestants must be avoided.

b. Narrow gaps shall be not less than 2 and preferably 5 meters in width for nonchampionships courses and not less than 10 meters in width for championships courses. Obstacles and other hindrances shall be avoided throughout the course; and any narrowing of the course must be avoided for the first 600 to 800 meters and the last 200 to 300 meters of the race.

c. Continuous traversing of roadways should be avoided.

d. The direction and path of the course shall be defined clearly for the runners.

e. Turns must be gradual.

Course Markings

ARTICLE 3. The course shall be properly measured along the shortest possible route that a runner may take; and it must be marked clearly by at least two of the following methods, presented in order of preference:

a. Sign posts not less than 7 feet high, with large directional arrows on boards fastened to the tops of the posts so that the arrows shall be visible plainly at a distance to competitors approaching the posts. The posts shall be placed at every point where the course turns, on the side of the direction of the turn and wherever there is any doubt as to the direction of travel;

b. A single white or colored line for directional purposes only—not to be assumed as the measured line—or two lines that mark the outside borders of the course, one on the measured course marking its shortest perimeter and the second such that runners cannot vary from the proper course. In addition, these two lines serve as restraining lines for spectators. Lines on the turns must vary in color from the color of lines approaching the turn.

c. Marked by flags, sign posts or stakes, which meet the following conditions:

   (1) At least 7 feet above ground level;

   (2) A turn to the left is marked by a red flag or arrow of direction on a sign post or stake;

   (3) A turn to the right is marked by a yellow flag or arrow of direction on a sign post or stake;

   (4) A course continuing straight is marked by a blue flag or arrow of direction on a sign post or stake; and

   (5) All flags, sign posts or stakes used shall mark the shortest perimeter of the course.

Note: All of the above course-marking devices must be placed on the edge of the measured line when lines and flags, sign posts or stakes are used to mark the course.

SECTION 3. The Start

The start should be surveyed to permit each competitor to line up equidistant from the first turn. It is recommended further that:

a. The middle of the starting arc should be marked with a perpendicular line. The arc should be described so that all starting positions are equal distance from the focal point not less than 400 meters from the starting line that marks the most desirable route.

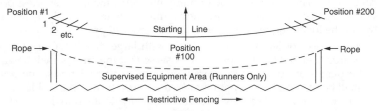

Figure 21—Starting Area

b. The start shall be located so as to provide a long straight route from the starting line. The first turn shall be not less than 200 meters, preferably not less than 400 meters, from the start on nonchampionships courses and not less than 600 meters, preferably not less than 800 meters, from the start on championships courses.

c. The starting line shall be wide enough to provide a 50-centimeter (19.69-in.) space for five front-line starters.

d. Lane positions or boxes shall be numbered from left to right facing the running area and shall be drawn by lot.

Note: It is recommended that the start and finish be within close proximity; however, confusion with each other must be avoided.

SECTION 4. The Finish

Finish Area
ARTICLE 1. It is recommended strongly that the finish area be relatively close to the start of the race. It also shall be on fairly level ground and have a finish area to include a straightaway finish of at least 200 to 300 meters.

Placing Finishers
ARTICLE 2. In addition to the approved fully automatic timing system, an officially designated video or photograph may be used to determine the order of finish.

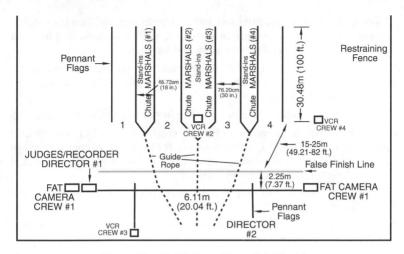

Figure 22—Finish Area (Funnel & Chute)

Finish Line

ARTICLE 3. The finish line shall be at least 10 meters (32 ft., 9.72 in.) wide and located at right angles to the course line. It shall be marked brightly and be visible from a distance. The finish line is at the mouth of the finish chute or finish corral.

Note 1. Stand-ins (Chute Assistants). Located near ropes to take competitors' position in chute area.

Note 2. Directors 1 & 2 (Gate Controllers). Coordinate rope changes.

Note 3. Gate Controllers 1-6. Use ropes attached to various posts off finish chutes to direct runners into chute.

Note 4. Judges/Recorder Stand. Should be at a height and distance enabling identification of runners as they cross the line. It also should not obstruct the FAT camera.

Note 5. Guide rope(s) for chute change shall extend five meters (16. ft., 4.8 in.) in front of the finish line.

Note 6. Worker area at back of chute accommodates computers, quick scores, etc.

Finish Chute

ARTICLE 4. The use of a finish chute is recommended at all cross country meets that do not use the transponder (chip) system to aid in meet administration and to provide accuracy and fairness to the competitors (see Figure 22).

a. The chute shall be constructed with suitable materials such as stakes joined with rope, snow fence or firm posts with streamers. Sturdiness of material is recommended for safety and longevity.

b. The chute begins at the width of the finish line and narrows to a single or multiple-chute funnel between 15 and 25 meters (49 ft., 2.4 in. and 82 ft.) from the finish line.

c. The posts at the narrow funnel shall be firm and padded for safety.

d. The chute shall be approximately 76.20 centimeters (30 in.) in width and the length shall be 30.48 centimeters (1 ft.) for every runner entered in the competition. It is recommended that the chute be 30.48 meters (100 ft.) in length for championships meets.

e. The guide rope(s) shall extend five meters (16 ft., 4.8 in.) in front of the finish line.

f. No officials shall stand in the area between the finish line and false-finish line at the beginning of the chute rope.

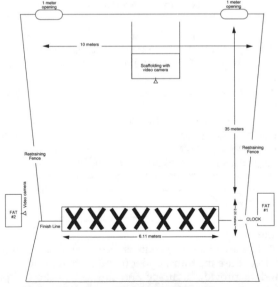

Figure 23—Finish Area (Corral)

g. It is recommended that the area between the finish line and the false-finish line be painted in a checkerboard pattern. This pattern shall begin two inches beyond the finish line.

Finish Corral

ARTICLE 5. The use of a finish corral to aid in meet administration is recommended at all cross country meets in which the transponder (chip) system is used (see Figure 23).

SECTION 5. Officials

Number and Types

ARTICLE 1. The number of officials necessary to conduct a cross country meet varies with the size and type of meet being conducted. The following officials are recommended for a large meet:

a. *General officials*

Organizing committee
Games committee
Referee
Jury of appeals
Course inspection committee
Headquarters organizations
Custodian of awards
Announcers and assistants
Marshal and assistants

Petitions committee
Meet director
Press steward and assistants
Surveyor
Medical doctors and/or certified
    trainers
Team attendants
Traffic control
Film crews

b. *Course Officials*

Clerks of course
Starters
Umpires
Timers
Judges of finish

Time recorders
Finish place recorders
Gate controllers
Finish area marshals
Scorer and quick scorers

Additional Officials

ARTICLE 2. The games committee shall have authority to make such additions to the above list as it deems advisable.

Note: The duties of appropriate officials are described in Rule 3. Exceptions pertaining specifically to cross country are described in the following section.

SECTION 6. Duties of Meet Officials

Meet Director

ARTICLE 1. The meet director is the central person behind the success of a cross country meet. The meet director shall stimulate enthusiasm and coordinate the promotional efforts of the organizing and games committees. The meet director is responsible to these committees for all aspects of the actual conduct of the meet on the course. This person must foresee all the needs of competitors, officials and spectators and ensure that all the technical details of the meet have been taken care of within the requirements of the rules.

With the help and guidance of the games committee, the meet director shall:

a. Organize and conduct meet promotion;

b. Provide and prepare the cross country running course;

c. Provide facilities and equipment (e.g., stopwatches, flags);

d. Provide full and early information to all competing schools;

e. Appoint and inform officials and prepare officials' materials;

f. Arrange meetings;

g. Inform competing schools of suitable lodging, dining and ground transportation; and

h. Arrange for certification of all calibrated measuring devices (see Rule 2-12).

Referee

ARTICLE 2. The referee shall have the following responsibilities:

a. Oversee the inspection of the course, start and finish (see Rules 5-2, 5-3, 5-4);

b. Confer with all head officials before the meet to ensure that all are aware of their responsibilities;

c. Ensure that all rules are observed and render decisions on all technical aspects of the meet (see Rule 5-5);

d. Have the authority to disqualify any competitor for improper conduct or apparel and decide on any protests rendered; and

e. Review all final meet results.

Head Course Umpire and Umpires

ARTICLE 3. The head course umpire and the umpires shall have the following responsibilities:

a. Observe the conduct and the course of the runners during the race;

b. Record the numbers of the competitors who are in violation of the rules and report all violations to the referee; and

c. Position marshals at various points on the course in order to observe all areas, specifically at points where confusion may occur.

Announcers

ARTICLE 4. The announcer shall have the following responsibilities:

a. Inform the competitors and spectators of special information related to the course and meet procedures;

b. Call the runners to the start;

c. Inform the spectators of the name, position and time of the leading runners during the progress of the race at each 1,000-meter or mile mark;

d. Announce the leading two or three runners as they approach the finish; however, announcements should not be made while runners actually are crossing the finish line, since this would create confusion for the recorders;

e. Announce the unofficial quick scores and follow up with the official scores if ascertained in a reasonable length of time; and

f. Assist with the presentation of awards.

Clerks of Course

ARTICLE 5. There shall be clerks to line up the runners (who compete in large meets). The clerks shall have the following responsibilities:

a. Obtain the official list of teams that identifies team members and their numbers. Using the official list, clear the starting and equipment area of everyone except the clerks, equipment marshals and runners on the official list;

b. Begin in the middle of the starting line and line up the runners in consecutive order on either side of the middle, progressing to the outside starting position;

c. Enforce competitors' uniform, number and logo rules at time of check-in; and

d. Related duties as may be requested by the starter and the games committee.

Note: To ensure a fair and equal start, every runner should be, if at all possible, placed on the front line. All starting positions or boxes are numbered for ease in locating for the runners and the clerks.

Starters

ARTICLE 6. The head starter shall be responsible for starting the race in a prescribed manner that ensures an equal and fair start to all participants. With the cooperation of the assistant starters, the following procedures shall be followed:

a. When all runners are lined up ready for the start, the head starter shall have a flag, pistol and whistle and take a position in the middle of and a minimum of 50 meters in front of the starting line.

b. Give a brief and concise review of the starting commands and procedures to be used for the start with all competitors immediately before the race.

    (1) One whistle blast indicates "Runners to the line" position. Both arms of the starter, with a pistol in one hand and a red flag in the other, shall be held straight out from the shoulder at shoulder height. The position is to be held until all runners are on the line and steady.

    (2) In the "Runner set" position, the pistol and flag are raised slowly to straight overhead.

    (3) When all runners are steady, the pistol shall be fired. The start is a simultaneous act of firing the gun and pulling the flag down, providing both visual and auditory starting commands.

    (4) The recall is indicated with the head starter or assistant starters firing the pistol and the head starter waving the flag up and down vigorously. If a runner falls within the first 100 meters due to contact

Figure 24—Starters' Signals

with another runner, the race shall be recalled by a shot. Competitors shall be disqualified for a second false start.

c. The assistant starter should be stationed on an elevated platform located at one end of the starting line so the following duties can be performed:

(1) Have a complete view of the length of the starting line;

(2) Via access to the public-address system, turn over the runners to the head starter when the runners are ready; and

(3) Fire the pistol in case of a false start.

Note: If more than one assistant starter is used, they shall be stationed at each end of the starting line.

Judges of the Finish

ARTICLE 7. There shall be a head judge of the finish plus a designated number of additional judges as assistants, depending upon the size of the meet. The judges shall be assigned the following specific duties:

a. The head judge shall be placed on an elevated stand opposite the film crew and shall remain in that position and inform the assistant judges of finish-order placement of the participants as they cross the finish line.

b. The ground judges shall be responsible for the actual placing of the runners in their appropriate order of finish as they enter the narrowing funnel into the chute as indicated by the head finish judge.

Gate Controllers

ARTICLE 8. In races in which a chute is used, there shall be one person assigned to control each rope, and he or she shall be located where the finish funnel meets the narrow chutes. The gate controllers shall have the following responsibilities:

a. Watch both the chute in use and the incoming runner;

b. Switch the finished runners to other chutes by changing rope positions in a smooth operation before congestion in the filling chute;

c. Make sure the switch is coordinated with the judges of the finish and that the person who makes the tie stands outside the route when securing the ropes; and

d. Keep the finish area uncongested so the runner's finish position can be determined accurately.

Head Finish Area Marshal and Assistants

ARTICLE 9. The head finish area marshal and assistants shall have the following responsibilities:

a. Supervise the runners' progress through the finish area (i.e., chute or corral);

b. Assist in every way possible to ensure each runner's proper order of finish, if a chute is used;

c. Properly position the finish area marshals in order to assist in the finish procedures; and

d. Make sure that unauthorized individuals do not interfere at the finish.

Course Marshals

ARTICLE 10. Marshals should be attired so as to be easily identified. The duties of the head course marshal and the assistants shall be to keep all areas of the course clear and unobstructed so as to best meet the needs of the runners, officials and spectators. The course marshals shall have the following responsibilities:

a. Keep unauthorized persons away from restricted areas;

b. Keep spectators off the actual running course;

c. Prevent spectators from cutting across the course if they might impede a runner's progress;

d. Keep everyone except the appropriate officials and runners out of the finish area; and

e. Provide assistance in any aspect of the conduct of the meet to ensure safety and security for the participants and officials.

Timers

ARTICLE 11. The head timer shall be responsible for all phases of the finish times and results that require accurate timing. The head timer shall coordinate all timers, the timing of first place and the overall timing system (or systems) used in the competition. Other specific duties of the timers shall be:

a. First place—Use three official watches.

b. Other finish times—One time caller shall call out finish times loudly and clearly on a full-second basis as each runner crosses the finish line.

c. Time stations—One timer shall be assigned to call out times for all runners at every 1,000-meter or mile point throughout the competition.

d. Fully automatic timing (FAT) system—When this system is being used for the official meet results, time of all competitors shall be determined by viewing the official film from the FAT camera and reproduced on an official print-out. Times shall be recorded to the slower 10th.

e. Transponder (chip) system—When this system is being used for the official meet results, a ranked order list of times of all competitors shall be determined by reading the printout produced by the system.

Time Recorders

ARTICLE 12. The time recorder shall be responsible for recording the time of each runner at the finish as called out by the head timer. Methods of obtaining accurate times for each runner are as follows:

a. As each runner finishes, the assigned number can be recorded on a form sheet that has predetermined continuous and consecutive time columns.

b. If time does not permit the recording of contestants' numbers, then the recorder should place the appropriate number of checks of finishers at the appropriate time space.

Place-Finish Recorders

ARTICLE 13. There shall be two teams working independently of each other that shall record the runners' places. Their responsibilities are:

a. Team One of three persons shall be stationed opposite the time recorders at the finish line. A place recorder shall speak the assigned number worn by the runner as each crosses the finish line. One person records the announced numbers on a continuous numbering form. One person should use an audio tape recorder to record the finishers verbally with their assigned number.

b. Team Two of two to four persons, starting from the outlet end of the finish chute, shall progress from the first finisher to the last finisher.

   (1) One official shall check the individual runner's number (assigned).

   (2) A second official shall record the runner's number on a finish-place form (1-50, etc.) as called out by the head official.

   (3) A third official shall mark the contestant's finish place on the section of the perforated assigned number of the participant.

   (4) A fourth official shall remove the bottom section of the contestant's number and place the removed section on a spindle in the proper order of finish, when the chute system is used.

(5) An assistant shall give the contestant an order-of-finish card upon exiting the chute. This card is used by the coach to obtain a quick score for the team to be turned in to the quick-score area, if this method of scoring is being used for compilation of team scores. These scores are unofficial until verified for accuracy.

Film Crew and/or Fully Automatic Timing System

ARTICLE 14. For meets where congestion may arise and there is a definite need for complete accuracy of the finish, films are necessary. The use of four film crews shall ensure accuracy. Their duties are as follows:

a. Crew No. 1—The fully automatic timing system should be located on an elevated platform in line with and at the side of the finish line and perpendicular to the finish of the runners. (Two systems are recommended.) For championships meets, two systems are required.

   (1) Shoot directly down the line without any camera movement.

   (2) The use of color film would help in distinguishing uniform colors.

   (3) The system is enhanced when runners wear numbers attached to the side of the pant.

b. Crew No. 2—A videotape recorder should be located on an elevated platform at the point where the chute narrows to form the multiple chutes.

   (1) The system should be 15 to 25 meters (49.20 to 98.41 ft.) from the finish line.

   (2) Shoot directly at the front of the runners as they finish. The contestants' numbers should be visible.

   (3) The use of color film is recommended for all systems.

c. Crew No. 3—A videotape recorder should be located at a distance and height in front of the finish line enabling identification of runners as they cross the line.

d. Crew No. 4—A videotape recorder should be located at a distance and height behind the finish line enabling identification of runners as they enter the chute.

Note: See Figures 22 and 23 for crew placement.

Medical Doctors and/or Certified Trainers

ARTICLE 15. Provisions shall be made to provide medical aid to runners on the course.

SECTION 7. Scoring

Team Composition

ARTICLE 1. A cross country team may consist of 12 runners, or more if otherwise agreed upon.

Team Scoring

ARTICLE 2. a. All runners who finish a race shall be given an **overall-finish place.** However, only the first seven runners on any one team may be used in scoring places. An order for **team-finish placing** is established by removing all runners behind the top seven finishers on each team. Those teams not finishing at least five runners likewise shall not be included in the order of team finish.

b. The score shall be determined by totaling the points of the first five runners of each team to finish. The team scoring the lower number of points shall be the winner.

c. Although the sixth and seventh runners of a team to finish do not score points toward their team's total, their places, if better than those of any of the first five of an opposing team, serve to increase the team score of the opponents.

d. Ties in team scoring shall not be broken, except for advancement to the championships finals.

Note: Advancement criteria will be in the 2005 NCAA Men's and Women's Cross Country Championships Handbooks.

SECTION 8. The Uniform

Uniforms

ARTICLE 1. Uniforms for all cross country team members must meet the following criteria:

a. School issued;

b. Tops shall be identical;

c. Pants may be of any length but must have identical color; and

d. Visible undergarments must be of an identical solid color.

The uniform must be clean and of a material and design so as not to be objectionable.

Bare midriff tops are not acceptable. (Note: The uniform top must meet or hang below the waist band when the competitor is standing.) Uniforms must allow for competitors' numbers to be placed above the waist (front and back) and for hip numbers to be placed on the hip, not on the leg or thigh. Uniform tops must not obscure hip numbers.

Wearing any part of the official team competition uniform illegally (e.g., top off or intentionally shortened, shoulder straps lowered) while in the area of competition shall lead to a warning by the nearest official and, if repeated, to disqualification by the meet referee (see Rule 3-5-2d). The use of, or wearing of, artificial noisemakers by competitors is prohibited.

Logos
ARTICLE 2. An institution's official uniform and all other items of apparel (e.g., team jersey, socks) that are worn by student-athletes in competition may bear a single manufacturer's or distributor's normal trademark, not to exceed 2¼ square inches, including any additional material (e.g., patch) surrounding the normal trademark or logo. The logo or trademark must be contained within a four-sided geometrical figure (i.e., rectangle, square, parallelogram).

In addition, an institution's official uniform cannot bear a design element similar to the manufacturer's that is in addition to another logo or that is contrary to the size restriction.

A student-athlete representing an institution in intercollegiate competition is limited to wearing apparel items that include only the logo (not to exceed 2¼ square inches) of an apparel manufacturer or distributor. The student-athlete may not wear apparel that identifies any other entity, other than the student-athlete's institution.

These restrictions apply to all apparel worn by student-athletes during the conduct of competition, including premeet or postmeet activities.

SECTION 9. Disqualification

Competitors who fail to complete the prescribed course that is defined by a legal marking system shall be disqualified.

The referee, after consulting with the appropriate officials, shall disqualify a competitor who:

a. Gains an advantage by failing to complete the prescribed course that is defined by a legal marking system;

b. Jostles, cuts across or obstructs another competitor so as to impede the other runner's progress. Direct contact is not necessary; any action that causes another runner to break stride or lose momentum is grounds for disqualification;

c. Veers to the right or to the left so as to impede a challenging runner or forces the challenging runner to run a greater distance;

d. Tries to force a way between two leading runners and makes direct contact so as to impede the progress of either;

e. Commits a flagrant foul; or

f. Is unduly aided by a coach, a teammate not in the race or a noncompetitor associated with the team.

RULE 9

Combined Events

SECTION 1. Order of Events

Decathlon
ARTICLE 1. The decathlon consists of 10 events that shall be held on two consecutive days in the following order:

First Day	*Second Day*
100 Meters	110-Meter Hurdles
Long Jump	Discus Throw
Shot Put	Pole Vault
High Jump	Javelin Throw
400 Meters	1,500 Meters

Heptathlon—Women (Outdoor)
ARTICLE 2. The heptathlon consists of seven events that shall be held on two consecutive days in the following order:

First Day	*Second Day*
100-Meter Hurdles	Long Jump
High Jump	Javelin Throw
Shot Put	800 Meters
200 Meters	

Heptathlon—Men (Indoor)
ARTICLE 3. The heptathlon consists of seven events that shall be held on two consecutive days in the following order:

First Day	*Second Day*
55/60 Meters	55-/60-Meter Hurdles
Long Jump	Pole Vault
Shot Put	1,000 Meters
High Jump	

Note: 60 meters is the recommended distance for the dash and hurdles.

Pentathlon—Men (Indoor and Outdoor)

ARTICLE 4. The pentathlon consists of five events that shall be held on the same day in the following order:

Indoor	*Outdoor*
55-/60-Meter Hurdles	Long Jump
Long Jump	Javelin Throw
Shot Put	200 Meters
High Jump	Discus Throw
1,000 Meters	1,500 Meters

Pentathlon—Women (Indoor and Outdoor)

ARTICLE 5. The pentathlon consists of five events that shall be held on the same day in the following order:

Indoor	*Outdoor*
55-/60-Meter Hurdles	100-Meter Hurdles
High Jump	High Jump
Shot Put	Shot Put
Long Jump	Long Jump
800 Meters	800 Meters

SECTION 2. Officials and Administration

Officials

ARTICLE 1. The officials for the combined events shall be the following, plus any other officials that the meet director deems necessary:

Games committee	Timers
Combined-events jury	Announcer
Referee	Scorer
Starter	Combined-events director
Clerk of the course	FAT operators
Field judges	Markers
Marshals	Medical doctor and/or
Umpires (track)	certified trainer

Applicable Rules

ARTICLE 2. The rules for each of the events constituting the competition shall apply, except:

a. Each competitor shall be allowed only three attempts in the long jump and throwing events. These attempts must be taken in order.

b. In the running events and hurdles, competitors shall be disqualified in any event in which they have made two false starts.

c. Each competitor shall be independently timed by at least three timers,
    and the times shall be recorded in accordance with track and field rules.
    If FAT is used, it is suggested that two timing systems be utilized
    throughout the competition.

d. If both FAT systems fail, hand times for all competitors in that event
    shall be used.

e. If both FAT systems fail in the 800 and 1,500 meters, a conversion is not
    necessary. The results for competitions timed electronically and timed
    manually for these events are strictly comparable.

f. Altitude adjustment is not applicable to the 1,500 meters.

g. If separate but equal facilities are available for the decathlon events (pole
    vault, high jump and long jump) or pentathlon/heptathlon events (high
    jump and long jump), the games committee shall make the final deter-
    mination for use of the facilities.

h. In the high jump, each competitor shall be allowed two minutes
    between consecutive attempts;

i. In the pole vault, each competitor shall be allowed three minutes
    between consecutive attempts;

j. In the high jump and pole vault, the starting height of the crossbar shall
    be determined by the competitors. Each increment rise shall be deter-
    mined by the games committee and such increment raises shall be fol-
    lowed throughout the competition regardless of the number of competi-
    tors. The recommended increment for the high jump shall be 3 centime-
    ters and for the pole vault shall be 10 centimeters. When one competitor
    remains, only multiples of 3 centimeters in the high jump and 10 cen-
    timeters in the pole vault may be used.

k. The javelin and discus shall be measured to the lesser centimeter.

l. The shot put shall be measured to the lesser centimeter.

Note: It is recommended that all performances be measured with a steel tape.

Administration
ARTICLE 3. The administration of combined events always should provide
fair and equal competition for all events. The recommended number of
competitors for championships meets is 12 to 18.

Grouping Field-Event Competitors
ARTICLE 4. All competitors shall compete in field events in one continuous flight drawn by lot. (Example: If there are 16 entries, all 16 shall take one

attempt, or pass, before the initial competitor takes a second attempt.) In the vertical jumps, the five-alive method of competition shall be used (see Rule 6-4-3).

The exception to this would be if the host institution has two facilities where all conditions are equal. In this event, the 16 competitors could be split by lot, with eight at each facility, except in the vertical jumps, where competitors may be split based on past performance.

Forming Sections
ARTICLE 5. If sections and lane assignments are necessary in any running event, they shall be determined by lot.

a. It is recommended that not fewer than three competitors start in any section.

b. When possible and practical, all competitors in the 800, 1,000 and 1,500 meters should run in one section. If the number of competitors in the 800 or 1,000 meters exceed the number of lanes on the track, all groups shall use a waterfall start, which may be staggered (i.e., alleys). When using alleys, two-thirds of the competitors should be placed on the inside and one-third on the outside. The referee shall designate competitors for these groups. The current points leaders shall run in the final section.

c. Lanes shall be drawn by the games committee by lot for the 100 meters, 200 meters, 400 meters and hurdle events.

Hurdle Placement
ARTICLE 6. In order to assure equitable competition:

a. Hurdles may be run in alternate or consecutive lanes, as determined by the games committee.

b. Hurdles must be placed in all lanes.

Competitors Fouling Another Competitor
ARTICLE 7. A competitor who fouls another competitor in any event shall lose all the points gained in that event but shall be permitted to compete in the remaining event(s), unless the referee shall rule that the loss of points is not sufficient penalty.

Scoring
ARTICLE 8. An athlete failing to report and start in any events of the combined-event competition shall be considered to have abandoned the competition and shall not be allowed to participate in any following event of the combined-event competition. The competitor shall be listed in the final results as having abandoned the competition with no marks recorded.

The winner of the combined-events competition shall be the competitor who has scored the highest number of points in all events awarded on the basis of the International Association of Athletics Federations (IAAF) scoring tables. (See Part II)

Ties shall not be broken.

SECTION 3. Time Schedule

Intervals

ARTICLE 1. An interval of at least 30 minutes should be allowed between the time one event ends and the next event begins. Should circumstances dictate and at the discretion of the games committee, this interval may be altered.

Schedule

ARTICLE 2. a. The following guidelines should be used in preparing the combined-events time schedule (this is not to be confused with the official time allowable between events):

   (1) Forty-five seconds per shot put;

   (2) One minute per discus and javelin throw;

   (3) One minute per high jump (average 10 jumps per competitor);

   (4) One minute and 30 seconds per long jump;

   (5) Two minutes per pole vault (average eight vaults per competitor);

   (6) Eight minutes for one heat of any running event less than 800 meters; and

   (7) Ten minutes for one heat of the 800, 1,000 and 1,500 meters.

b. The referee shall have the power to designate an approximate starting time for all combined-events competition.

c. Due to the nature of combined-events competition, it is advisable to take temperature and humidity into consideration when determining the appropriate starting time.

d. Whenever both men's and women's combined events are conducted together, it is advisable to start the decathlon at least one hour before the heptathlon on both days.

RULE 10

Indoor Track: Facilities and Conduct

SECTION 1. General Statement

Where not provided in this section, please refer to the appropriate area of this rules book. Procedures for indoor championships are established by divisional games committees.

SECTION 2. The Indoor Facility

The Area

ARTICLE 1. Tracks, runways and takeoff areas should be covered with synthetic material or have a wooden surface. These surfaces should be able to accept 6 millimeter (0.25 in.) spikes for synthetic surfaces and 3 millimeter spikes (0.13 in.) for wood.

Where technically possible, runways shall have a uniform resilience.

Where possible, all events should be unobstructed by facility limitations (e.g., shortened runways, bleacher seats, overhead beams, etc.).

The Straightaways

ARTICLE 2. The lateral maximum inclination of the track shall not exceed 1:100 (1%) and the inclination in the running direction shall not exceed 1:250 (0.4%) at any point and 1:1,000 (0.1%) overall.

Lanes shall have the same width with a recommended minimum of 1.07 meters (42 in.) and a maximum of 1.25 meters (48 in.) including the white line to the right. Lanes shall be marked on both sides by lines 5.08 centimeters (2 in.) wide. The lanes shall be numbered with lane one on the left when facing the finish line.

There should be a minimum of 3 meters (9 ft., 9.96 in.) behind the start line and 10 meters (32 ft., 9.72 in.) beyond the finish line free of any obstruction. It is recommended that clearance beyond the finish line be at least 20 meters (65 ft., 7.44 in.).

Oval Track and Lanes

ARTICLE 3. The standard indoor running track shall be 200 meters or 220 yards in length. Furthermore, running tracks that are equal to or exceed the standard outdoor running track length, as defined by Rule 1-1-2, shall not be considered an indoor track. The length of any indoor track constructed after January 1, 2004, shall not exceed 300 meters.

The track shall consist of two horizontal straights and two curves with consistent radii, which may be banked. The curves may be bordered with a curb of suitable material approximately 5.08 centimeters (2 in.) in height and width.

The inside edge of the curb or lane line shall be horizontal throughout the length of the track with a maximum slope of 1:1,000 (0.1%). Any facility that exceeds this slope shall be defined as banked.

Where the inside edge of the track is bordered with a white line, it shall be marked additionally with cones. The cones shall be at least 20 centimeters (7.87 in.) high. The cones shall be placed on the track so that the outward face of the cone coincides with the edge of the white line closest to the track. The cones shall be placed at distances not exceeding 2 meters (6 ft., 6.72 in.) on the curves and 10 meters (32 ft., 9.72 in.) on the straightaways.

The track should have a minimum of six lanes. Lanes should have a recommended minimum of 91.44 centimeters (36 in.), including the lane line to the right. Lanes shall be marked by lines 5.08 centimeters (2 in.) wide. The intersection of each lane line and the finish line shall be painted black in accordance with Figure 3.

It is recommended that a maximum angle of banking should not be more than 18 degrees for a 200-meter track. This angle may vary based upon the size of a track. The angle of banking in all lanes should be the same at any cross section.

It is recommended that the inside radius of the curves on a 200-meter track should be not less than 18 meters (59 ft., 0.72 in.) and not more than 21 meters (68 ft., 10.8 in.).

Portable indoor tracks shall be surveyed before the first competition each year. Permanent indoor tracks shall be surveyed following initial construction and after resurfacing.

Track Markings

ARTICLE 4. See Rule 1-1-3.

Measuring Distances

ARTICLE 5. See Rule 1-1-4.

Overhead Clearance

ARTICLE 6. It is recommended that a minimum of 9.14 meters (30 ft.) overhead clearance be provided without obstruction (lights, beams, ceiling, etc.).

SECTION 3. Order of Events

Order of Events

The order of events for indoor meets should be:

One-Day Meet

With Preliminary Heats in Dashes and Hurdles

60 minutes before track events—Weight Throw	Dash Finals
30 minutes before track events—Pole Vault,	800 Meters/880 Yards
High Jump, Long Jump and Shot Put	1,000 Meters/1,000 Yards
Triple Jump (immediately after Long Jump)	200 Meters/300 Meters/300 Yards
Hurdle Preliminaries	3,000 Meters/Two Miles or 5,000 Meters/
Dash Preliminaries	Three Miles
Mile/1,500 Meters	1,600-Meter Relay/Mile Relay
Hurdles Finals	3,200-Meter Relay/Two-Mile Relay or
400 Meters/440 Yards	Distance Medley Relay
500 Meters/600 Yards	

One-Day Meet

Without Preliminary Heats

(If running a two-day meet, this order of events should be followed as closely as possible.)

60 minutes before track events—Weight Throw	800 Meters/880 Yards
30 minutes before track events—Pole Vault,	1,000 Meters/1,000 Yards
High Jump, Long Jump and Shot Put	200 Meters/300 Meters/300 Yards
Triple Jump (immediately after Long Jump)	3,000 Meters/Two Miles or 5,000 Meters/
Mile/1,500 Meters	Three Miles
Hurdles Finals	1,600-Meter Relay/Mile Relay
400 Meters/440 Yards	3,200-Meter Relay/Two-Mile Relay or
500 Meters/600 Yards	Distance Medley Relay
Dash Finals	

Note 1: Changes from this order can be made by the games committee or by mutual agreement of the competing teams. For example, blocking events by gender or specialty is permitted.

Note 2: Due to variances in facilities and events in indoor track, the games committee shall make decisions concerning the conduct of meets.

SECTION 4. Race Conduct

ARTICLE 1. Races less than 800 meters shall:

a. Have a separate lane at the start;

b. Start and continue in lanes at least until the end of the second turn (on a track of more than 200 meters/220 yards, a one-turn stagger shall be used).

ARTICLE 2. The 800 meters, 1,000 meters and 3,200-meter relay shall start and continue in lanes or alleys until at least the end of the first turn, if the number of competitors or teams exceeds the number of lanes on the track. On tracks of more than 200 meters/220 yards, a one-turn stagger shall be used.

ARTICLE 3. The 800 meters shall have not more than eight competitors per heat in the preliminaries or finals.

ARTICLE 4. In individual races longer than 1,000 meters, and the distance medley relay, all groups shall use a waterfall or alley start, which may be staggered, if the number of competitors or teams exceeds the number of lanes on the track.

Relay Order
ARTICLE 5. The order of the distance medley relay shall be: 1,200, 400, 800 and 1,600 meters (1,320, 440, 880 and 1,760 yards).

Recall Point
ARTICLE 6. The point for recall shall be not later than the end of the first turn.

Legal Running and Violations
ARTICLE 7. See Rules 5-4, 5-5, 5-6 and 5-9.

Note 1: Due to the narrow lanes, competitors in races with staggered starts may place their hands outside their lanes, but not beyond the starting line extended.

Note 2: Due to the narrow lanes, indoor races are more subject to collisions and unintended obstructions than outdoor races. Umpire and referee discretion is advised.

SECTION 5. Regulations for Meets With Preliminaries (Including Championships)

In all meets with preliminary rounds (including championships meets), the procedures in Rule 5-11 shall be used to form all finals, except for the following or **unless otherwise determined by the games committee**:

ARTICLE 1. Races that may be run in single-round timed-section finals or with preliminaries and finals with advancement based on time only (200, 300, 400, 500 and 600 meters, and 800- and 1,600-meter relays).

a. Preliminary rounds that have advancement to finals based on time only shall be formed by seeding competitors from the performance list, left to right throughout the heats.

Note: This seeding differs from seeding procedures in Rule 5-11 because advancement to the finals is based on time.

Heat 1	Heat 2	Heat 3
1	2	3
4	5	6
7	8	9
10	11	12

b. When eight competitors advance to the finals, the competitors shall qualify on the basis of time from preliminary rounds. The competitors with the four slowest times shall run in the first heat and the competitors with the four fastest times shall run in the second heat.

c. In single-round timed-section finals, the sections shall be seeded slow to fast, and shall compete in the same order.

d. In races that are run entirely in lanes (i.e., 55 meters, 60 meters, 55-meter hurdles, 60-meter hurdles), the heat winners shall advance to the final. All other qualifiers shall advance on the basis of time in the preliminary heats.

ARTICLE 2. If preliminaries are contested in the 400-, 500- and 600-meter dashes, and six competitors advance to the finals, the heat winners plus the next fastest times shall qualify.

ARTICLE 3. a. If preliminaries are contested in the 800 meters, 1,000 meters, and the 3,200-meter relay, eight competitors/teams shall qualify for the finals. It is recommended that the top two from each heat advance; however, at least two must advance on the basis of time.

b. Assignment to preliminaries will use the serpentine seeding procedure (see Rule 5-11-3a).

c. Finals shall be run in alleys with qualifiers assigned to preferred alleys as determined by the games committee.

ARTICLE 4. a. If preliminaries are run in the 1,500 meters/mile, 10 competitors shall qualify for the finals. It is recommended that the top three from each heat advance; however, at least two must advance on the basis of time.

b. If 12 or fewer competitors report for the 1,500 meters/mile, it is recommended that the event be run as a final.

ARTICLE 5. If preliminaries are run in the 3,000 meters, 12 competitors shall qualify for the final. It is recommended that the top four from each heat advance; however, at least two must advance on the basis of time.

SECTION 6. The Shot-Put Area

Circle
ARTICLE 1. See Figure 12.

Stopboard
ARTICLE 2. See Rule 1-8-2.

Sector
ARTICLE 3. See Rule 1-8-3.

Stop Barrier
ARTICLE 4. A stop barrier shall be used to contain the shot within the shot-put area.

SECTION 7. The Shot

Indoor Shot Material
ARTICLE 1. Where indoor facilities dictate, synthetic-covered implements with internal movement may be used.

Note 1: If the indoor shot breaks during the release or while in the air, the throw shall not count as an attempt, provided the attempt was made in accordance with the rules.

Note 2: If the indoor shot breaks upon contact with the impact area, a substitute attempt shall not be permitted and the attempt shall be measured, provided it was made in accordance with the rules.

Shape
ARTICLE 2. The shot must be spherical in shape, and the surface must be smooth so that an advantage is not gained by grip.

Specifications
ARTICLE 3. The shot shall conform to the following specifications:

	MEN'S	WOMEN'S
Weight (Minimum)	7.260kg (16 lbs.)	4kg (8 lbs., 13 ozs.)
Diameter (Minimum)	110mm (4.331 in.)	95mm (3.740 in.)
(Maximum)	145mm (5.709 in.)	130mm (5.118 in.)

SECTION 8. The Weight-Throw Area

Enclosure
ARTICLE 1. All weight throws shall be made from an enclosure or cage that shall be centered on the circle.

It is recommended that the cage be constructed as follows (see Figure 25):

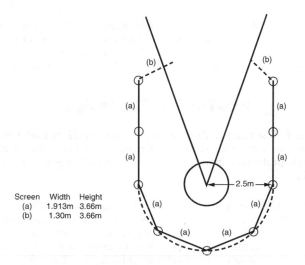

Screen	Width	Height
(a)	1.913m	3.66m
(b)	1.30m	3.66m

Figure 25—Construction of Weight Cage

a. There shall be two moveable panels at the front of the screen. These panels shall be 1.30 meters (4 ft., 3.24 in.) in width (see Note 1).

b. The height of the cage shall be at least 3.66 meters (12 ft.).

Note 1: When these panels are in place for a right-handed thrower, the panel on the left side shall extend inside the sector line by 1.5 meters (4.92 ft.). If this panel is shorter than this distance, then the panel shall be perpendicular to the sector line. The panel on the right side shall be opened such that the end of the gate will intersect and contact the sector line at a point approximately 9 meters (29 ft., 6.5 in.) from the center of the hammer circle. The panels shall be alternated for left-handed throwers.

*Note 2: A weight-throw cage is designed to provide limited protection for spectators, officials and competitors. It does not ensure the safety of the aforementioned personnel. **Any flagged area should not be based on the reduced sector area.***

Circle

ARTICLE 2. The circle shall be constructed in accordance with Figure 17 in Rule 1-10-2.

Sector

ARTICLE 3. The throwing sector shall be marked by two radial lines 5.08 centimeters (2 in.) wide that form a 34.92-degree angle, extended from the center of the circle. The inside edges of these lines shall mark the sector. The surface within the landing area shall be on the same level as the throwing surface.

SECTION 9. The Weight

Head

ARTICLE 1. The head shall be a solid sphere made of metal not softer than brass, or with a shell made of plastic or other suitable material, designed to protect the landing surface. *[Note: Rubber is not an acceptable material.]*

Handle

ARTICLE 2. The handle shall be made of a round steel rod bent into a triangular form with straight sides and no sides exceeding an inside measurement of 19 centimeters (7.5 in.) nor less than 10 centimeters (4 in.) (see Figure 26-A). A handle with no permanent connection point must have all sides of the same length. The handle must be rigid and not show evidence of elasticity or malformation after the implement is being thrown.

Connection

ARTICLE 3. The grip shall be connected to the ball by means of a chain link, links or steel line whose thickness shall be such that it cannot stretch while the implement is being thrown.

The grip shall be connected to the link(s) or steel line by means of a loop. A functional swivel may not be used.

The link(s) or steel line shall be connected to the ball by means of a swivel that may be either plain or ball-bearing.

Note: Where indoor facilities dictate, synthetic-covered implements with internal movement may be used. Homemade or modified implements are not allowed. Hammer handles are not allowed. Repair of broken implements may be made only with the original manufacturer's replacement parts.

Specifications

ARTICLE 4. The weight shall conform to the following specifications (see Figure 26);

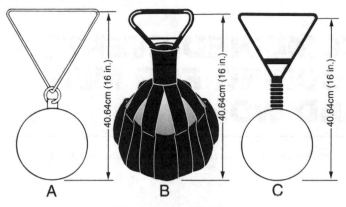

Figure 26—The Weight

	MEN'S	WOMEN'S
Weight (Minimum)	15.880kg (35 lbs.)	9.080kg (20 lbs.)

Length (complete as thrown, measured from inside of the grip)

	MEN'S AND WOMEN'S
(Maximum)	40.64cm (16 in.)

Harness
ARTICLE 5. If the implement includes a harness, it shall be fabricated from a minimum of four straps sewn together to form a sling. Netting shall not be used for this purpose. The harness must not show evidence of elasticity or malformation after the implement has been thrown.

Competition
ARTICLE 6. The rules for the weight throw shall be the same as for the hammer throw (see Rules 6-1-12 through 6-1-17).

Part II:

COMBINED-EVENTS SCORING FOR MEN AND WOMEN

Reprinted by permission of the International Association of Athletics Federations.

Seconds	Points	Seconds	Points	Seconds	Points	Seconds	Points	Seconds	Points
				This table to be used exclusively for fully automatic times.					
9.50	1223	10.00	1096	10.50	975	11.00	861	11.50	753
9.51	1221	10.01	1094	10.51	973	11.01	858	11.51	750
9.52	1218	10.02	1091	10.52	970	11.02	856	11.52	748
9.53	1215	10.03	1089	10.53	968	11.03	854	11.53	746
9.54	1213	10.04	1086	10.54	966	11.04	852	11.54	744
9.55	1210	10.05	1084	10.55	963	11.05	850	11.55	742
9.56	1208	10.06	1081	10.56	961	11.06	847	11.56	740
9.57	1205	10.07	1079	10.57	959	11.07	845	11.57	738
9.58	1202	10.08	1076	10.58	956	11.08	843	11.58	736
9.59	1200	10.09	1074	10.59	954	11.09	841	11.59	734
9.60	1197	10.10	1071	10.60	952	11.10	838	11.60	732
9.61	1195	10.11	1069	10.61	949	11.11	836	11.61	730
9.62	1192	10.12	1066	10.62	947	11.12	834	11.62	728
9.63	1190	10.13	1064	10.63	945	11.13	832	11.63	725
9.64	1187	10.14	1062	10.64	942	11.14	830	11.64	723
9.65	1184	10.15	1059	10.65	940	11.15	827	11.65	721
9.66	1182	10.16	1057	10.66	938	11.16	825	11.66	719
9.67	1179	10.17	1054	10.67	935	11.17	823	11.67	717
9.68	1177	10.18	1052	10.68	933	11.18	821	11.68	715
9.69	1174	10.19	1049	10.69	931	11.19	819	11.69	713
9.70	1172	10.20	1047	10.70	929	11.20	817	11.70	711
9.71	1169	10.21	1044	10.71	926	11.21	814	11.71	709
9.72	1166	10.22	1042	10.72	924	11.22	812	11.72	707
9.73	1164	10.23	1040	10.73	922	11.23	810	11.73	705
9.74	1161	10.24	1037	10.74	919	11.24	808	11.74	703
9.75	1159	10.25	1035	10.75	917	11.25	806	11.75	701
9.76	1156	10.26	1032	10.76	915	11.26	804	11.76	699
9.77	1154	10.27	1030	10.77	912	11.27	801	11.77	697
9.78	1151	10.28	1028	10.78	910	11.28	799	11.78	695
9.79	1149	10.29	1025	10.79	908	11.29	797	11.79	693
9.80	1146	10.30	1023	10.80	906	11.30	795	11.80	691
9.81	1144	10.31	1020	10.81	903	11.31	793	11.81	689
9.82	1141	10.32	1018	10.82	901	11.32	791	11.82	687
9.83	1139	10.33	1016	10.83	899	11.33	789	11.83	685
9.84	1136	10.34	1013	10.84	897	11.34	786	11.84	683
9.85	1134	10.35	1011	10.85	894	11.35	784	11.85	681
9.86	1131	10.36	1008	10.86	892	11.36	782	11.86	679
9.87	1128	10.37	1006	10.87	890	11.37	780	11.87	677
9.88	1126	10.38	1004	10.88	888	11.38	778	11.88	675
9.89	1123	10.39	1001	10.89	885	11.39	776	11.89	673
9.90	1121	10.40	999	10.90	883	11.40	774	11.90	671
9.91	1118	10.41	996	10.91	881	11.41	771	11.91	669
9.92	1116	10.42	994	10.92	878	11.42	769	11.92	667
9.93	1113	10.43	992	10.93	876	11.43	767	11.93	665
9.94	1111	10.44	989	10.94	874	11.44	765	11.94	663
9.95	1108	10.45	987	10.95	872	11.45	763	11.95	661
9.96	1106	10.46	985	10.96	870	11.46	761	11.96	659
9.97	1103	10.47	982	10.97	867	11.47	759	11.97	657
9.98	1101	10.48	980	10.98	865	11.48	757	11.98	655
9.99	1099	10.49	977	10.99	863	11.49	755	11.99	653

This table to be used exclusively for fully automatic times.

Seconds	Points	Seconds	Points	Seconds	Points	Seconds	Points	Seconds	Points
12.00	651	12.50	556	13.00	468	13.50	387	14.00	312
12.01	649	12.51	554	13.01	466	13.51	385	14.01	311
12.02	647	12.52	552	13.02	464	13.52	383	14.02	309
12.03	645	12.53	551	13.03	463	13.53	382	14.03	308
12.04	643	12.54	549	13.04	461	13.54	380	14.04	307
12.05	641	12.55	547	13.05	459	13.55	379	14.05	305
12.06	639	12.56	545	13.06	458	13.56	377	14.06	304
12.07	637	12.57	543	13.07	456	13.57	376	14.07	302
12.08	635	12.58	541	13.08	454	13.58	374	14.08	301
12.09	633	12.59	540	13.09	453	13.59	373	14.09	300
12.10	631	12.60	538	13.10	451	13.60	371	14.10	298
12.11	629	12.61	536	13.11	449	13.61	370	14.11	297
12.12	628	12.62	534	13.12	448	13.62	368	14.12	295
12.13	626	12.63	532	13.13	446	13.63	367	14.13	294
12.14	624	12.64	531	13.14	444	13.64	365	14.14	293
12.15	622	12.65	529	13.15	443	13.65	363	14.15	291
12.16	620	12.66	527	13.16	441	13.66	362	14.16	290
12.17	618	12.67	525	13.17	439	13.67	360	14.17	289
12.18	616	12.68	523	13.18	438	13.68	359	14.18	287
12.19	614	12.69	522	13.19	436	13.69	357	14.19	286
12.20	612	12.70	520	13.20	434	13.70	356	14.20	284
12.21	610	12.71	518	13.21	433	13.71	354	14.21	283
12.22	608	12.72	516	13.22	431	13.72	353	14.22	282
12.23	606	12.73	515	13.23	430	13.73	351	14.23	280
12.24	605	12.74	513	13.24	428	13.74	350	14.24	279
12.25	603	12.75	511	13.25	426	13.75	348	14.25	278
12.26	601	12.76	509	13.26	425	13.76	347	14.26	276
12.27	599	12.77	508	13.27	423	13.77	346	14.27	275
12.28	597	12.78	506	13.28	421	13.78	344	14.28	274
12.29	595	12.79	504	13.29	420	13.79	343	14.29	272
12.30	593	12.80	502	13.30	418	13.80	341	14.30	271
12.31	591	12.81	501	13.31	417	13.81	340	14.31	270
12.32	589	12.82	499	13.32	415	13.82	338	14.32	268
12.33	588	12.83	497	13.33	413	13.83	337	14.33	267
12.34	586	12.84	495	13.34	412	13.84	335	14.34	266
12.35	584	12.85	494	13.35	410	13.85	334	14.35	264
12.36	582	12.86	492	13.36	409	13.86	332	14.36	263
12.37	580	12.87	490	13.37	407	13.87	331	14.37	262
12.38	578	12.88	488	13.38	405	13.88	329	14.38	261
12.39	576	12.89	487	13.39	404	13.89	328	14.39	259
12.40	574	12.90	485	13.40	402	13.90	327	14.40	258
12.41	573	12.91	483	13.41	401	13.91	325	14.41	257
12.42	571	12.92	481	13.42	399	13.92	324	14.42	255
12.43	569	12.93	480	13.43	397	13.93	322	14.43	254
12.44	567	12.94	478	13.44	396	13.94	321	14.44	253
12.45	565	12.95	476	13.45	394	13.95	319	14.45	251
12.46	563	12.96	475	13.46	393	13.96	318	14.46	250
12.47	562	12.97	473	13.47	391	13.97	316	14.47	249
12.48	560	12.98	471	13.48	390	13.98	315	14.48	248
12.49	558	12.99	470	13.49	388	13.99	314	14.49	246

Seconds	Points	Seconds	Points	Seconds	Points	Seconds	Points	Seconds	Points
				This table to be used exclusively for fully automatic times.					
14.50	245	15.00	185	15.50	133	16.07	83	16.84	33
14.51	244	15.01	184	15.51	132	16.09	82	16.86	32
14.52	243	15.02	183	15.52	131	16.10	81	16.88	31
14.53	241	15.03	182	15.53	130	16.11	80	16.90	30
14.54	240	15.04	181	15.54	129	16.12	79	16.92	29
14.55	239	15.05	180	15.55	128	16.14	78	16.94	28
14.56	238	15.06	179	15.56	127	16.15	77	16.96	27
14.57	236	15.07	178	15.57	126	16.16	76	16.98	26
14.58	235	15.08	176	15.58	125	16.18	75	17.00	25
14.59	234	15.09	175	15.60	124	16.19	74	17.03	24
14.60	233	15.10	174	15.61	123	16.20	73	17.05	23
14.61	231	15.11	173	15.62	122	16.22	72	17.07	22
14.62	230	15.12	172	15.63	121	16.23	71	17.10	21
14.63	229	15.13	171	15.64	120	16.25	70	17.12	20
14.64	228	15.14	170	15.65	119	16.26	69	17.14	19
14.65	226	15.15	169	15.66	118	16.27	68	17.17	18
14.66	225	15.16	168	15.67	117	16.29	67	17.19	17
14.67	224	15.17	167	15.68	116	16.30	66	17.22	16
14.68	223	15.18	166	15.69	115	16.32	65	17.25	15
14.69	221	15.19	165	15.70	114	16.33	64	17.28	14
14.70	220	15.20	163	15.72	113	16.34	63	17.30	13
14.71	219	15.21	162	15.73	112	16.36	62	17.33	12
14.72	218	15.22	161	15.74	111	16.37	61	17.37	11
14.73	217	15.23	160	15.75	110	16.39	60	17.40	10
14.74	215	15.24	159	15.76	109	16.40	59	17.43	9
14.75	214	15.25	158	15.77	108	16.42	58	17.47	8
14.76	213	15.26	157	15.78	107	16.43	57	17.50	7
14.77	212	15.27	156	15.79	106	16.45	56	17.54	6
14.78	211	15.28	155	15.81	105	16.46	55	17.59	5
14.79	209	15.29	154	15.82	104	16.48	54	17.64	4
14.80	208	15.30	153	15.83	103	16.49	53	17.69	3
14.81	207	15.31	152	15.84	102	16.51	52	17.75	2
14.82	206	15.32	151	15.85	101	16.53	51	17.83	1
14.83	205	15.33	150	15.86	100	16.54	50		
14.84	204	15.34	149	15.88	99	16.56	49		
14.85	202	15.35	148	15.89	98	16.57	48		
14.86	201	15.36	147	15.90	97	16.59	47		
14.87	200	15.37	146	15.91	96	16.61	46		
14.88	199	15.38	145	15.92	95	16.62	45		
14.89	198	15.39	144	15.94	94	16.64	44		
14.90	197	15.40	143	15.95	93	16.66	43		
14.91	195	15.41	142	15.96	92	16.68	42		
14.92	194	15.42	141	15.97	91	16.69	41		
14.93	193	15.43	140	15.98	90	16.71	40		
14.94	192	15.44	139	16.00	89	16.73	39		
14.95	191	15.45	138	16.01	88	16.75	38		
14.96	190	15.46	137	16.02	87	16.76	37		
14.97	189	15.47	136	16.03	86	16.78	36		
14.98	188	15.48	135	16.05	85	16.80	35		
14.99	186	15.49	134	16.06	84	16.82	34		

Seconds	Points	Seconds	Points	Seconds	Points	Seconds	Points	Seconds	Points

THIS TABLE IS TO BE USED EXCLUSIVELY FOR HAND TIMES

A UTILISER UNIQUEMENT EN CAS DE CHRONOMETRAGE MANUEL

Seconds	Points	Seconds	Points	Seconds	Points	Seconds	Points	Seconds	Points
9.0	1292	11.0	808	13.0	428	15.0	159	17.0	15
9.1	1265	11.1	786	13.1	412	15.1	149	17.1	11
9.2	1239	11.2	765	13.2	396	15.2	139	17.2	8
9.3	1213	11.3	744	13.3	380	15.3	129	17.3	6
9.4	1187	11.4	723	13.4	365	15.4	120	17.4	4
9.5	1161	11.5	703	13.5	350	15.5	111	17.5	2
9.6	1136	11.6	683	13.6	335	15.6	102		
9.7	1111	11.7	663	13.7	321	15.7	94		
9.8	1086	11.8	643	13.8	307	15.8	85		
9.9	1062	11.9	624	13.9	293	15.9	78		
10.0	1037	12.0	605	14.0	279	16.0	70		
10.1	1013	12.1	586	14.1	266	16.1	63		
10.2	989	12.2	567	14.2	253	16.2	56		
10.3	966	12.3	549	14.3	240	16.3	50		
10.4	942	12.4	531	14.4	228	16.4	44		
10.5	919	12.5	513	14.5	215	16.5	38		
10.6	897	12.6	495	14.6	204	16.6	33		
10.7	874	12.7	478	14.7	192	16.7	28		
10.8	852	12.8	461	14.8	181	16.8	23		
10.9	830	12.9	444	14.9	170	16.9	19		

Metres	Points	Metres	Points	Metres	Points	Metres	Points	Metres	Points
8.99	1323	8.49	1188	7.99	1058	7.49	932	6.99	811
8.98	1320	8.48	1186	7.98	1056	7.48	930	6.98	809
8.97	1317	8.47	1183	7.97	1053	7.47	927	6.97	807
8.96	1314	8.46	1180	7.96	1050	7.46	925	6.96	804
8.95	1312	8.45	1178	7.95	1048	7.45	922	6.95	802
8.94	1309	8.44	1175	7.94	1045	7.44	920	6.94	799
8.93	1306	8.43	1172	7.93	1043	7.43	918	6.93	797
8.92	1304	8.42	1170	7.92	1040	7.42	915	6.92	795
8.91	1301	8.41	1167	7.91	1038	7.41	913	6.91	792
8.90	1298	8.40	1164	7.90	1035	7.40	910	6.90	790
8.89	1295	8.39	1162	7.89	1033	7.39	908	6.89	788
8.88	1293	8.38	1159	7.88	1030	7.38	905	6.88	785
8.87	1290	8.37	1157	7.87	1027	7.37	903	6.87	783
8.86	1287	8.36	1154	7.86	1025	7.36	900	6.86	781
8.85	1285	8.35	1151	7.85	1022	7.35	898	6.85	778
8.84	1282	8.34	1149	7.84	1020	7.34	896	6.84	776
8.83	1279	8.33	1146	7.83	1017	7.33	893	6.83	774
8.82	1276	8.32	1143	7.82	1015	7.32	891	6.82	771
8.81	1274	8.31	1141	7.81	1012	7.31	888	6.81	769
8.80	1271	8.30	1138	7.80	1010	7.30	886	6.80	767
8.79	1268	8.29	1136	7.79	1007	7.29	883	6.79	764
8.78	1266	8.28	1133	7.78	1005	7.28	881	6.78	762
8.77	1263	8.27	1130	7.77	1002	7.27	878	6.77	760
8.76	1260	8.26	1128	7.76	1000	7.26	876	6.76	757
8.75	1258	8.25	1125	7.75	997	7.25	874	6.75	755
8.74	1255	8.24	1123	7.74	995	7.24	871	6.74	753
8.73	1252	8.23	1120	7.73	992	7.23	869	6.73	750
8.72	1250	8.22	1117	7.72	990	7.22	866	6.72	748
8.71	1247	8.21	1115	7.71	987	7.21	864	6.71	746
8.70	1244	8.20	1112	7.70	985	7.20	862	6.70	743
8.69	1241	8.19	1110	7.69	982	7.19	859	6.69	741
8.68	1239	8.18	1107	7.68	980	7.18	857	6.68	739
8.67	1236	8.17	1104	7.67	977	7.17	854	6.67	736
8.66	1233	8.16	1102	7.66	975	7.16	852	6.66	734
8.65	1231	8.15	1099	7.65	972	7.15	850	6.65	732
8.64	1228	8.14	1097	7.64	970	7.14	847	6.64	729
8.63	1225	8.13	1094	7.63	967	7.13	845	6.63	727
8.62	1223	8.12	1092	7.62	965	7.12	842	6.62	725
8.61	1220	8.11	1089	7.61	962	7.11	840	6.61	723
8.60	1217	8.10	1086	7.60	960	7.10	838	6.60	720
8.59	1215	8.09	1084	7.59	957	7.09	835	6.59	718
8.58	1212	8.08	1081	7.58	955	7.08	833	6.58	716
8.57	1209	8.07	1079	7.57	952	7.07	830	6.57	713
8.56	1207	8.06	1076	7.56	950	7.06	828	6.56	711
8.55	1204	8.05	1073	7.55	947	7.05	826	6.55	709
8.54	1201	8.04	1071	7.54	945	7.04	823	6.54	707
8.53	1199	8.03	1068	7.53	942	7.03	821	6.53	704
8.52	1196	8.02	1066	7.52	940	7.02	818	6.52	702
8.51	1194	8.01	1063	7.51	937	7.01	816	6.51	700
8.50	1191	8.00	1061	7.50	935	7.00	814	6.50	697

Men   Long Jump — Saut en Longueur   Hommes

Metres	Points	Metres	Points	Metres	Points	Metres	Points	Metres	Points
6.49	695	5.99	584	5.49	479	4.99	380	4.49	288
6.48	693	5.98	582	5.48	477	4.98	378	4.48	287
6.47	691	5.97	580	5.47	475	4.97	377	4.47	285
6.46	688	5.96	578	5.46	473	4.96	375	4.46	283
6.45	686	5.95	576	5.45	471	4.95	373	4.45	281
6.44	684	5.94	574	5.44	469	4.94	371	4.44	280
6.43	682	5.93	571	5.43	467	4.93	369	4.43	278
6.42	679	5.92	569	5.42	465	4.92	367	4.42	276
6.41	677	5.91	567	5.41	463	4.91	365	4.41	274
6.40	675	5.90	565	5.40	461	4.90	363	4.40	273
6.39	673	5.89	563	5.39	459	4.89	361	4.39	271
6.38	670	5.88	561	5.38	457	4.88	360	4.38	269
6.37	668	5.87	559	5.37	455	4.87	358	4.37	267
6.36	666	5.86	556	5.36	453	4.86	356	4.36	266
6.35	664	5.85	554	5.35	451	4.85	354	4.35	264
6.34	661	5.84	552	5.34	449	4.84	352	4.34	262
6.33	659	5.83	550	5.33	447	4.83	350	4.33	261
6.32	657	5.82	548	5.32	445	4.82	348	4.32	259
6.31	655	5.81	546	5.31	443	4.81	346	4.31	257
6.30	652	5.80	544	5.30	441	4.80	345	4.30	255
6.29	650	5.79	542	5.29	439	4.79	343	4.29	254
6.28	648	5.78	540	5.28	437	4.78	341	4.28	252
6.27	646	5.77	537	5.27	435	4.77	339	4.27	250
6.26	644	5.76	535	5.26	433	4.76	337	4.26	249
6.25	641	5.75	533	5.25	431	4.75	335	4.25	247
6.24	639	5.74	531	5.24	429	4.74	333	4.24	245
6.23	637	5.73	529	5.23	427	4.73	332	4.23	244
6.22	635	5.72	527	5.22	425	4.72	330	4.22	242
6.21	632	5.71	525	5.21	423	4.71	328	4.21	240
6.20	630	5.70	523	5.20	421	4.70	326	4.20	239
6.19	628	5.69	521	5.19	419	4.69	324	4.19	237
6.18	626	5.68	519	5.18	417	4.68	323	4.18	235
6.17	624	5.67	516	5.17	415	4.67	321	4.17	234
6.16	621	5.66	514	5.16	413	4.66	319	4.16	232
6.15	619	5.65	512	5.15	411	4.65	317	4.15	230
6.14	617	5.64	510	5.14	409	4.64	315	4.14	229
6.13	615	5.63	508	5.13	407	4.63	313	4.13	227
6.12	613	5.62	506	5.12	405	4.62	312	4.12	225
6.11	610	5.61	504	5.11	404	4.61	310	4.11	224
6.10	608	5.60	502	5.10	402	4.60	308	4.10	222
6.09	606	5.59	500	5.09	400	4.59	306	4.09	220
6.08	604	5.58	498	5.08	398	4.58	304	4.08	219
6.07	602	5.57	496	5.07	396	4.57	303	4.07	217
6.06	600	5.56	494	5.06	394	4.56	301	4.06	215
6.05	597	5.55	492	5.05	392	4.55	299	4.05	214
6.04	595	5.54	490	5.04	390	4.54	297	4.04	212
6.03	593	5.53	487	5.03	388	4.53	295	4.03	211
6.02	591	5.52	485	5.02	386	4.52	294	4.02	209
6.01	589	5.51	483	5.01	384	4.51	292	4.01	207
6.00	587	5.50	481	5.00	382	4.50	290	4.00	206

Men   **Long Jump — Saut en Longueur**   **Hommes**

Metres	Points	Metres	Points	Metres	Points	Metres	Points	Metres	Points
3.99	204	3.59	143	3.19	89	2.79	43	2.29	3
3.98	203	3.58	142	3.18	88	2.78	42	2.27	2
3.97	201	3.57	140	3.17	86	2.77	41	2.25	1
3.96	199	3.56	139	3.16	85	2.76	40		
3.95	198	3.55	137	3.15	84	2.75	39		
3.94	196	3.54	136	3.14	83	2.74	38		
3.93	195	3.53	135	3.13	81	2.73	37		
3.92	193	3.52	133	3.12	80	2.72	36		
3.91	191	3.51	132	3.11	79	2.71	35		
3.90	190	3.50	130	3.10	78	2.70	34		
3.89	188	3.49	129	3.09	76	2.69	33		
3.88	187	3.48	127	3.08	75	2.68	32		
3.87	185	3.47	126	3.07	74	2.67	31		
3.86	184	3.46	125	3.06	73	2.66	30		
3.85	182	3.45	123	3.05	72	2.65	29		
3.84	181	3.44	122	3.04	70	2.64	28		
3.83	179	3.43	121	3.03	69	2.63	27		
3.82	177	3.42	119	3.02	68	2.62	26		
3.81	176	3.41	118	3.01	67	2.60	25		
3.80	174	3.40	116	3.00	66	2.59	24		
3.79	173	3.39	115	2.99	65	2.58	23		
3.78	171	3.38	114	2.98	63	2.57	22		
3.77	170	3.37	112	2.97	62	2.56	21		
3.76	168	3.36	111	2.96	61	2.54	20		
3.75	167	3.35	110	2.95	60	2.53	19		
3.74	165	3.34	108	2.94	59	2.52	18		
3.73	164	3.33	107	2.93	58	2.51	17		
3.72	162	3.32	106	2.92	57	2.49	16		
3.71	161	3.31	104	2.91	56	2.48	15		
3.70	159	3.30	103	2.90	54	2.47	14		
3.69	158	3.29	102	2.89	53	2.45	13		
3.68	156	3.28	100	2.88	52	2.44	12		
3.67	155	3.27	99	2.87	51	2.43	11		
3.66	153	3.26	98	2.86	50	2.41	10		
3.65	152	3.25	96	2.85	49	2.40	9		
3.64	150	3.24	95	2.84	48	2.38	8		
3.63	149	3.23	94	2.83	47	2.37	7		
3.62	147	3.22	93	2.82	46	2.35	6		
3.61	146	3.21	91	2.81	45	2.33	5		
3.60	145	3.20	90	2.80	44	2.31	4		

Men   Putting the Shot — Lancement du Poids   Hommes

Metres	Points	Metres	Points	Metres	Points	Metres	Points	Metres	Points
22.38	1249	21.59	1199	20.79	1149	19.99	1099	19.19	1049
22.37	1248	21.57	1198	20.77	1148	19.97	1098	19.17	1048
22.35	1247	21.55	1197	20.76	1147	19.96	1097	19.15	1047
22.34	1246	21.54	1196	20.74	1146	19.94	1096	19.14	1046
22.32	1245	21.52	1195	20.72	1145	19.92	1095	19.12	1045
22.30	1244	21.51	1194	20.71	1144	19.91	1094	19.11	1044
22.29	1243	21.49	1193	20.69	1143	19.89	1093	19.09	1043
22.27	1242	21.48	1192	20.68	1142	19.88	1092	19.07	1042
22.26	1241	21.46	1191	20.66	1141	19.86	1091	19.06	1041
22.24	1240	21.44	1190	20.64	1140	19.84	1090	19.04	1040
22.22	1239	21.43	1189	20.63	1139	19.83	1089	19.03	1039
22.21	1238	21.41	1188	20.61	1138	19.81	1088	19.01	1038
22.19	1237	21.40	1187	20.60	1137	19.80	1087	18.99	1037
22.18	1236	21.38	1186	20.58	1136	19.78	1086	18.98	1036
22.16	1235	21.36	1185	20.56	1135	19.76	1085	18.96	1035
22.14	1234	21.35	1184	20.55	1134	19.75	1084	18.95	1034
22.13	1233	21.33	1183	20.53	1133	19.73	1083	18.93	1033
22.11	1232	21.32	1182	20.52	1132	19.72	1082	18.91	1032
22.10	1231	21.30	1181	20.50	1131	19.70	1081	18.90	1031
22.08	1230	21.28	1180	20.48	1130	19.68	1080	18.88	1030
22.06	1229	21.27	1179	20.47	1129	19.67	1079	18.87	1029
22.05	1228	21.25	1178	20.45	1128	19.65	1078	18.85	1028
22.03	1227	21.24	1177	20.44	1127	19.64	1077	18.83	1027
22.02	1226	21.22	1176	20.42	1126	19.62	1076	18.82	1026
22.00	1225	21.20	1175	20.40	1125	19.60	1075	18.80	1025
21.99	1224	21.19	1174	20.39	1124	19.59	1074	18.79	1024
21.97	1223	21.17	1173	20.37	1123	19.57	1073	18.77	1023
21.95	1222	21.16	1172	20.36	1122	19.56	1072	18.75	1022
21.94	1221	21.14	1171	20.34	1121	19.54	1071	18.74	1021
21.92	1220	21.12	1170	20.32	1120	19.52	1070	18.72	1020
21.91	1219	21.11	1169	20.31	1119	19.51	1069	18.70	1019
21.89	1218	21.09	1168	20.29	1118	19.49	1068	18.69	1018
21.87	1217	21.08	1167	20.28	1117	19.48	1067	18.67	1017
21.86	1216	21.06	1166	20.26	1116	19.46	1066	18.66	1016
21.84	1215	21.04	1165	20.24	1115	19.44	1065	18.64	1015
21.83	1214	21.03	1164	20.23	1114	19.43	1064	18.62	1014
21.81	1213	21.01	1163	20.21	1113	19.41	1063	18.61	1013
21.79	1212	21.00	1162	20.20	1112	19.40	1062	18.59	1012
21.78	1211	20.98	1161	20.18	1111	19.38	1061	18.58	1011
21.76	1210	20.96	1160	20.16	1110	19.36	1060	18.56	1010
21.75	1209	20.95	1159	20.15	1109	19.35	1059	18.54	1009
21.73	1208	20.93	1158	20.13	1108	19.33	1058	18.53	1008
21.71	1207	20.92	1157	20.12	1107	19.31	1057	18.51	1007
21.70	1206	20.90	1156	20.10	1106	19.30	1056	18.50	1006
21.68	1205	20.88	1155	20.08	1105	19.28	1055	18.48	1005
21.67	1204	20.87	1154	20.07	1104	19.27	1054	18.46	1004
21.65	1203	20.85	1153	20.05	1103	19.25	1053	18.45	1003
21.63	1202	20.84	1152	20.04	1102	19.23	1052	18.43	1002
21.62	1201	20.82	1151	20.02	1101	19.22	1051	18.42	1001
21.60	1200	20.80	1150	20.00	1100	19.20	1050	18.40	1000

Metres	Points	Metres	Points	Metres	Points	Metres	Points	Metres	Points
18.38	999	17.58	949	16.77	899	15.96	849	15.15	799
18.37	998	17.56	948	16.75	898	15.94	848	15.13	798
18.35	997	17.55	947	16.74	897	15.93	847	15.12	797
18.33	996	17.53	946	16.72	896	15.91	846	15.10	796
18.32	995	17.51	945	16.71	895	15.90	845	15.08	795
18.30	994	17.50	944	16.69	894	15.88	844	15.07	794
18.29	993	17.48	943	16.67	893	15.86	843	15.05	793
18.27	992	17.46	942	16.66	892	15.85	842	15.03	792
18.25	991	17.45	941	16.64	891	15.83	841	15.02	791
18.24	990	17.43	940	16.62	890	15.81	840	15.00	790
18.22	989	17.42	939	16.61	889	15.80	839	14.99	789
18.21	988	17.40	938	16.59	888	15.78	838	14.97	788
18.19	987	17.38	937	16.58	887	15.77	837	14.95	787
18.17	986	17.37	936	16.56	886	15.75	836	14.94	786
18.16	985	17.35	935	16.54	885	15.73	835	14.92	785
18.14	984	17.34	934	16.53	884	15.72	834	14.90	784
18.13	983	17.32	933	16.51	883	15.70	833	14.89	783
18.11	982	17.30	932	16.49	882	15.68	832	14.87	782
18.09	981	17.29	931	16.48	881	15.67	831	14.86	781
18.08	980	17.27	930	16.46	880	15.65	830	14.84	780
18.06	979	17.25	929	16.45	879	15.64	829	14.82	779
18.04	978	17.24	928	16.43	878	15.62	828	14.81	778
18.03	977	17.22	927	16.41	877	15.60	827	14.79	777
18.01	976	17.21	926	16.40	876	15.59	826	14.77	776
18.00	975	17.19	925	16.38	875	15.57	825	14.76	775
17.98	974	17.17	924	16.37	874	15.55	824	14.74	774
17.96	973	17.16	923	16.35	873	15.54	823	14.73	773
17.95	972	17.14	922	16.33	872	15.52	822	14.71	772
17.93	971	17.13	921	16.32	871	15.51	821	14.69	771
17.92	970	17.11	920	16.30	870	15.49	820	14.68	770
17.90	969	17.09	919	16.28	869	15.47	819	14.66	769
17.88	968	17.08	918	16.27	868	15.46	818	14.64	768
17.87	967	17.06	917	16.25	867	15.44	817	14.63	767
17.85	966	17.04	916	16.24	866	15.42	816	14.61	766
17.84	965	17.03	915	16.22	865	15.41	815	14.59	765
17.82	964	17.01	914	16.20	864	15.39	814	14.58	764
17.80	963	17.00	913	16.19	863	15.38	813	14.56	763
17.79	962	16.98	912	16.17	862	15.36	812	14.55	762
17.77	961	16.96	911	16.15	861	15.34	811	14.53	761
17.75	960	16.95	910	16.14	860	15.33	810	14.51	760
17.74	959	16.93	909	16.12	859	15.31	809	14.50	759
17.72	958	16.92	908	16.11	858	15.29	808	14.48	758
17.71	957	16.90	907	16.09	857	15.28	807	14.46	757
17.69	956	16.88	906	16.07	856	15.26	806	14.45	756
17.67	955	16.87	905	16.06	855	15.25	805	14.43	755
17.66	954	16.85	904	16.04	854	15.23	804	14.42	754
17.64	953	16.83	903	16.03	853	15.21	803	14.40	753
17.63	952	16.82	902	16.01	852	15.20	802	14.38	752
17.61	951	16.80	901	15.99	851	15.18	801	14.37	751
17.59	950	16.79	900	15.98	850	15.16	800	14.35	750

Metres	Points	Metres	Points	Metres	Points	Metres	Points	Metres	Points
14.33	749	13.52	699	12.70	649	11.87	599	11.05	549
14.32	748	13.50	698	12.68	648	11.86	598	11.03	548
14.30	747	13.48	697	12.66	647	11.84	597	11.02	547
14.29	746	13.47	696	12.65	646	11.83	596	11.00	546
14.27	745	13.45	695	12.63	645	11.81	595	10.98	545
14.25	744	13.44	694	12.62	644	11.79	594	10.97	544
14.24	743	13.42	693	12.60	643	11.78	593	10.95	543
14.22	742	13.40	692	12.58	642	11.76	592	10.93	542
14.20	741	13.39	691	12.57	641	11.74	591	10.92	541
14.19	740	13.37	690	12.55	640	11.73	590	10.90	540
14.17	739	13.35	689	12.53	639	11.71	589	10.88	539
14.15	738	13.34	688	12.52	638	11.69	588	10.87	538
14.14	737	13.32	687	12.50	637	11.68	587	10.85	537
14.12	736	13.30	686	12.48	636	11.66	586	10.83	536
14.11	735	13.29	685	12.47	635	11.64	585	10.82	535
14.09	734	13.27	684	12.45	634	11.63	584	10.80	534
14.07	733	13.26	683	12.43	633	11.61	583	10.78	533
14.06	732	13.24	682	12.42	632	11.59	582	10.77	532
14.04	731	13.22	681	12.40	631	11.58	581	10.75	531
14.02	730	13.21	680	12.39	630	11.56	580	10.73	530
14.01	729	13.19	679	12.37	629	11.54	579	10.72	529
13.99	728	13.17	678	12.35	628	11.53	578	10.70	528
13.97	727	13.16	677	12.34	627	11.51	577	10.68	527
13.96	726	13.14	676	12.32	626	11.50	576	10.67	526
13.94	725	13.12	675	12.30	625	11.48	575	10.65	525
13.93	724	13.11	674	12.29	624	11.46	574	10.63	524
13.91	723	13.09	673	12.27	623	11.45	573	10.62	523
13.89	722	13.07	672	12.25	622	11.43	572	10.60	522
13.88	721	13.06	671	12.24	621	11.41	571	10.58	521
13.86	720	13.04	670	12.22	620	11.40	570	10.57	520
13.84	719	13.03	669	12.20	619	11.38	569	10.55	519
13.83	718	13.01	668	12.19	618	11.36	568	10.53	518
13.81	717	12.99	667	12.17	617	11.35	567	10.52	517
13.80	716	12.98	666	12.15	616	11.33	566	10.50	516
13.78	715	12.96	665	12.14	615	11.31	565	10.48	515
13.76	714	12.94	664	12.12	614	11.30	564	10.47	514
13.75	713	12.93	663	12.11	613	11.28	563	10.45	513
13.73	712	12.91	662	12.09	612	11.26	562	10.43	512
13.71	711	12.89	661	12.07	611	11.25	561	10.42	511
13.70	710	12.88	660	12.06	610	11.23	560	10.40	510
13.68	709	12.86	659	12.04	609	11.21	559	10.39	509
13.66	708	12.85	658	12.02	608	11.20	558	10.37	508
13.65	707	12.83	657	12.01	607	11.18	557	10.35	507
13.63	706	12.81	656	11.99	606	11.16	556	10.34	506
13.62	705	12.80	655	11.97	605	11.15	555	10.32	505
13.60	704	12.78	654	11.96	604	11.13	554	10.30	504
13.58	703	12.76	653	11.94	603	11.11	553	10.29	503
13.57	702	12.75	652	11.92	602	11.10	552	10.27	502
13.55	701	12.73	651	11.91	601	11.08	551	10.25	501
13.53	700	12.71	650	11.89	600	11.07	550	10.24	500

Men   Putting the Shot — Lancement du Poids   Hommes

Metres	Points	Metres	Points	Metres	Points	Metres	Points	Metres	Points
10.22	499	9.39	449	8.55	399	7.70	349	6.86	299
10.20	498	9.37	448	8.53	398	7.69	348	6.84	298
10.19	497	9.35	447	8.51	397	7.67	347	6.82	297
10.17	496	9.34	446	8.50	396	7.65	346	6.80	296
10.15	495	9.32	445	8.48	395	7.64	345	6.79	295
10.14	494	9.30	444	8.46	394	7.62	344	6.77	294
10.12	493	9.28	443	8.45	393	7.60	343	6.75	293
10.10	492	9.27	442	8.43	392	7.59	342	6.74	292
10.09	491	9.25	441	8.41	391	7.57	341	6.72	291
10.07	490	9.23	440	8.40	390	7.55	340	6.70	290
10.05	489	9.22	439	8.38	389	7.53	339	6.68	289
10.04	488	9.20	438	8.36	388	7.52	338	6.67	288
10.02	487	9.18	437	8.35	387	7.50	337	6.65	287
10.00	486	9.17	436	8.33	386	7.48	336	6.63	286
9.99	485	9.15	435	8.31	385	7.47	335	6.62	285
9.97	484	9.13	434	8.29	384	7.45	334	6.60	284
9.95	483	9.12	433	8.28	383	7.43	333	6.58	283
9.94	482	9.10	432	8.26	382	7.42	332	6.57	282
9.92	481	9.08	431	8.24	381	7.40	331	6.55	281
9.90	480	9.07	430	8.23	380	7.38	330	6.53	280
9.89	479	9.05	429	8.21	379	7.37	329	6.51	279
9.87	478	9.03	428	8.19	378	7.35	328	6.50	278
9.85	477	9.02	427	8.18	377	7.33	327	6.48	277
9.84	476	9.00	426	8.16	376	7.31	326	6.46	276
9.82	475	8.98	425	8.14	375	7.30	325	6.45	275
9.80	474	8.97	424	8.13	374	7.28	324	6.43	274
9.79	473	8.95	423	8.11	373	7.26	323	6.41	273
9.77	472	8.93	422	8.09	372	7.25	322	6.39	272
9.75	471	8.92	421	8.08	371	7.23	321	6.38	271
9.74	470	8.90	420	8.06	370	7.21	320	6.36	270
9.72	469	8.88	419	8.04	369	7.20	319	6.34	269
9.70	468	8.87	418	8.03	368	7.18	318	6.33	268
9.69	467	8.85	417	8.01	367	7.16	317	6.31	267
9.67	466	8.83	416	7.99	366	7.14	316	6.29	266
9.65	465	8.82	415	7.97	365	7.13	315	6.27	265
9.64	464	8.80	414	7.96	364	7.11	314	6.26	264
9.62	463	8.78	413	7.94	363	7.09	313	6.24	263
9.60	462	8.77	412	7.92	362	7.08	312	6.22	262
9.59	461	8.75	411	7.91	361	7.06	311	6.21	261
9.57	460	8.73	410	7.89	360	7.04	310	6.19	260
9.55	459	8.72	409	7.87	359	7.03	309	6.17	259
9.54	458	8.70	408	7.86	358	7.01	308	6.15	258
9.52	457	8.68	407	7.84	357	6.99	307	6.14	257
9.50	456	8.66	406	7.82	356	6.97	306	6.12	256
9.49	455	8.65	405	7.81	355	6.96	305	6.10	255
9.47	454	8.63	404	7.79	354	6.94	304	6.09	254
9.45	453	8.61	403	7.77	353	6.92	303	6.07	253
9.44	452	8.60	402	7.75	352	6.91	302	6.05	252
9.42	451	8.58	401	7.74	351	6.89	301	6.03	251
9.40	450	8.56	400	7.72	350	6.87	300	6.02	250

Metres	Points	Metres	Points	Metres	Points	Metres	Points	Metres	Points
6.00	249	5.14	199	4.26	149	3.37	99	2.46	49
5.98	248	5.12	198	4.24	148	3.35	98	2.44	48
5.97	247	5.10	197	4.23	147	3.34	97	2.42	47
5.95	246	5.08	196	4.21	146	3.32	96	2.40	46
5.93	245	5.07	195	4.19	145	3.30	95	2.39	45
5.91	244	5.05	194	4.17	144	3.28	94	2.37	44
5.90	243	5.03	193	4.16	143	3.26	93	2.35	43
5.88	242	5.01	192	4.14	142	3.25	92	2.33	42
5.86	241	5.00	191	4.12	141	3.23	91	2.31	41
5.84	240	4.98	190	4.10	140	3.21	90	2.29	40
5.83	239	4.96	189	4.08	139	3.19	89	2.27	39
5.81	238	4.94	188	4.07	138	3.17	88	2.26	38
5.79	237	4.93	187	4.05	137	3.16	87	2.24	37
5.78	236	4.91	186	4.03	136	3.14	86	2.22	36
5.76	235	4.89	185	4.01	135	3.12	85	2.20	35
5.74	234	4.87	184	4.00	134	3.10	84	2.18	34
5.72	233	4.86	183	3.98	133	3.08	83	2.16	33
5.71	232	4.84	182	3.96	132	3.07	82	2.14	32
5.69	231	4.82	181	3.94	131	3.05	81	2.12	31
5.67	230	4.80	180	3.93	130	3.03	80	2.10	30
5.66	229	4.79	179	3.91	129	3.01	79	2.08	29
5.64	228	4.77	178	3.89	128	2.99	78	2.07	28
5.62	227	4.75	177	3.87	127	2.97	77	2.05	27
5.60	226	4.73	176	3.85	126	2.96	76	2.03	26
5.59	225	4.72	175	3.84	125	2.94	75	2.01	25
5.57	224	4.70	174	3.82	124	2.92	74	1.99	24
5.55	223	4.68	173	3.80	123	2.90	73	1.97	23
5.53	222	4.66	172	3.78	122	2.88	72	1.95	22
5.52	221	4.65	171	3.77	121	2.87	71	1.93	21
5.50	220	4.63	170	3.75	120	2.85	70	1.91	20
5.48	219	4.61	169	3.73	119	2.83	69	1.89	19
5.46	218	4.59	168	3.71	118	2.81	68	1.87	18
5.45	217	4.58	167	3.69	117	2.79	67	1.85	17
5.43	216	4.56	166	3.68	116	2.77	66	1.83	16
5.41	215	4.54	165	3.66	115	2.76	65	1.81	15
5.40	214	4.52	164	3.64	114	2.74	64	1.79	14
5.38	213	4.51	163	3.62	113	2.72	63	1.78	13
5.36	212	4.49	162	3.61	112	2.70	62	1.76	12
5.34	211	4.47	161	3.59	111	2.68	61	1.74	11
5.33	210	4.45	160	3.57	110	2.66	60	1.72	10
5.31	209	4.44	159	3.55	109	2.65	59	1.70	9
5.29	208	4.42	158	3.53	108	2.63	58	1.68	8
5.27	207	4.40	157	3.52	107	2.61	57	1.65	7
5.26	206	4.38	156	3.50	106	2.59	56	1.63	6
5.24	205	4.37	155	3.48	105	2.57	55	1.61	5
5.22	204	4.35	154	3.46	104	2.55	54	1.59	4
5.21	203	4.33	153	3.44	103	2.53	53	1.57	3
5.19	202	4.31	152	3.43	102	2.52	52	1.55	2
5.17	201	4.30	151	3.41	101	2.50	51	1.53	1
5.15	200	4.28	150	3.39	100	2.48	50		

Men · High Jump — Saut en Hauteur · Hommes

Metres	Points	Metres	Points	Metres	Points	Metres	Points	Metres	Points
2.49	1285	2.09	887	1.69	536	1.29	244	0.89	35
2.48	1275	2.08	878	1.68	528	1.28	237	0.88	32
2.47	1264	2.07	868	1.67	520	1.27	231	0.87	28
2.46	1254	2.06	859	1.66	512	1.26	225	0.86	25
2.45	1244	2.05	850	1.65	504	1.25	218	0.85	22
2.44	1233	2.04	840	1.64	496	1.24	212	0.84	19
2.43	1223	2.03	831	1.63	488	1.23	206	0.83	16
2.42	1213	2.02	822	1.62	480	1.22	200	0.82	13
2.41	1202	2.01	813	1.61	472	1.21	194	0.81	10
2.40	1192	2.00	803	1.60	464	1.20	188	0.80	8
2.39	1182	1.99	794	1.59	457	1.19	182	0.79	6
2.38	1172	1.98	785	1.58	449	1.18	176	0.78	4
2.37	1161	1.97	776	1.57	441	1.17	170	0.77	2
2.36	1151	1.96	767	1.56	434	1.16	165		
2.35	1141	1.95	758	1.55	426	1.15	159		
2.34	1131	1.94	749	1.54	419	1.14	153		
2.33	1121	1.93	740	1.53	411	1.13	148		
2.32	1111	1.92	731	1.52	404	1.12	142		
2.31	1101	1.91	723	1.51	396	1.11	137		
2.30	1091	1.90	714	1.50	389	1.10	131		
2.29	1081	1.89	705	1.49	381	1.09	126		
2.28	1071	1.88	696	1.48	374	1.08	121		
2.27	1061	1.87	687	1.47	367	1.07	116		
2.26	1051	1.86	679	1.46	360	1.06	111		
2.25	1041	1.85	670	1.45	352	1.05	105		
2.24	1031	1.84	661	1.44	345	1.04	100		
2.23	1021	1.83	653	1.43	338	1.03	96		
2.22	1012	1.82	644	1.42	331	1.02	91		
2.21	1002	1.81	636	1.41	324	1.01	86		
2.20	992	1.80	627	1.40	317	1.00	81		
2.19	982	1.79	619	1.39	310	0.99	77		
2.18	973	1.78	610	1.38	303	0.98	72		
2.17	963	1.77	602	1.37	297	0.97	68		
2.16	953	1.76	593	1.36	290	0.96	63		
2.15	944	1.75	585	1.35	283	0.95	59		
2.14	934	1.74	577	1.34	276	0.94	55		
2.13	925	1.73	569	1.33	270	0.93	51		
2.12	915	1.72	560	1.32	263	0.92	47		
2.11	906	1.71	552	1.31	257	0.91	43		
2.10	896	1.70	544	1.30	250	0.90	39		

Men   400 metres — 400 mètres   Hommes

Seconds	Points	Seconds	Points	Seconds	Points	Seconds	Points	Seconds	Points
			This table to be used exclusively for fully automatic times.						
41.49	1249	42.39	1199	43.31	1149	44.25	1099	45.21	1049
41.50	1248	42.41	1198	43.33	1148	44.27	1098	45.23	1048
41.52	1247	42.43	1197	43.35	1147	44.29	1097	45.25	1047
41.54	1246	42.44	1196	43.37	1146	44.31	1096	45.27	1046
41.56	1245	42.46	1195	43.39	1145	44.33	1095	45.29	1045
41.58	1244	42.48	1194	43.40	1144	44.35	1094	45.31	1044
41.59	1243	42.50	1193	43.42	1143	44.36	1093	45.33	1043
41.61	1242	42.52	1192	43.44	1142	44.38	1092	45.34	1042
41.63	1241	42.54	1191	43.46	1141	44.40	1091	45.36	1041
41.65	1240	42.55	1190	43.48	1140	44.42	1090	45.38	1040
41.67	1239	42.57	1189	43.50	1139	44.44	1089	45.40	1039
41.68	1238	42.59	1188	43.52	1138	44.46	1088	45.42	1038
41.70	1237	42.61	1187	43.53	1137	44.48	1087	45.44	1037
41.72	1236	42.63	1186	43.55	1136	44.50	1086	45.46	1036
41.74	1235	42.65	1185	43.57	1135	44.52	1085	45.48	1035
41.76	1234	42.66	1184	43.59	1134	44.54	1084	45.50	1034
41.77	1233	42.68	1183	43.61	1133	44.55	1083	45.52	1033
41.79	1232	42.70	1182	43.63	1132	44.57	1082	45.54	1032
41.81	1231	42.72	1181	43.65	1131	44.59	1081	45.56	1031
41.83	1230	42.74	1180	43.67	1130	44.61	1080	45.58	1030
41.85	1229	42.76	1179	43.68	1129	44.63	1079	45.60	1029
41.86	1228	42.77	1178	43.70	1128	44.65	1078	45.62	1028
41.88	1227	42.79	1177	43.72	1127	44.67	1077	45.64	1027
41.90	1226	42.81	1176	43.74	1126	44.69	1076	45.66	1026
41.92	1225	42.83	1175	43.76	1125	44.71	1075	45.68	1025
41.94	1224	42.85	1174	43.78	1124	44.73	1074	45.70	1024
41.95	1223	42.87	1173	43.80	1123	44.75	1073	45.72	1023
41.97	1222	42.88	1172	43.82	1122	44.77	1072	45.73	1022
41.99	1221	42.90	1171	43.83	1121	44.78	1071	45.75	1021
42.01	1220	42.92	1170	43.85	1120	44.80	1070	45.77	1020
42.03	1219	42.94	1169	43.87	1119	44.82	1069	45.79	1019
42.04	1218	42.96	1168	43.89	1118	44.84	1068	45.81	1018
42.06	1217	42.98	1167	43.91	1117	44.86	1067	45.83	1017
42.08	1216	43.00	1166	43.93	1116	44.88	1066	45.85	1016
42.10	1215	43.01	1165	43.95	1115	44.90	1065	45.87	1015
42.12	1214	43.03	1164	43.97	1114	44.92	1064	45.89	1014
42.13	1213	43.05	1163	43.99	1113	44.94	1063	45.91	1013
42.15	1212	43.07	1162	44.00	1112	44.96	1062	45.93	1012
42.17	1211	43.09	1161	44.02	1111	44.98	1061	45.95	1011
42.19	1210	43.11	1160	44.04	1110	45.00	1060	45.97	1010
42.21	1209	43.13	1159	44.06	1109	45.02	1059	45.99	1009
42.23	1208	43.14	1158	44.08	1108	45.03	1058	46.01	1008
42.24	1207	43.16	1157	44.10	1107	45.05	1057	46.03	1007
42.26	1206	43.18	1156	44.12	1106	45.07	1056	46.05	1006
42.28	1205	43.20	1155	44.14	1105	45.09	1055	46.07	1005
42.30	1204	43.22	1154	44.16	1104	45.11	1054	46.09	1004
42.32	1203	43.24	1153	44.17	1103	45.13	1053	46.11	1003
42.33	1202	43.26	1152	44.19	1102	45.15	1052	46.13	1002
42.35	1201	43.27	1151	44.21	1101	45.17	1051	46.15	1001
42.37	1200	43.29	1150	44.23	1100	45.19	1050	46.17	1000

Seconds	Points	Seconds	Points	Seconds	Points	Seconds	Points	Seconds	Points
				This table to be used exclusively for fully automatic times.					
46.19	999	47.19	949	48.22	899	49.27	849	50.35	799
46.21	998	47.21	948	48.24	898	49.29	848	50.37	798
46.23	997	47.23	947	48.26	897	49.31	847	50.39	797
46.25	996	47.25	946	48.28	896	49.33	846	50.41	796
46.27	995	47.27	945	48.30	895	49.35	845	50.43	795
46.29	994	47.29	944	48.32	894	49.37	844	50.46	794
46.31	993	47.31	943	48.34	893	49.39	843	50.48	793
46.33	992	47.33	942	48.36	892	49.42	842	50.50	792
46.35	991	47.35	941	48.38	891	49.44	841	50.52	791
46.37	990	47.37	940	48.40	890	49.46	840	50.54	790
46.39	989	47.39	939	48.42	889	49.48	839	50.57	789
46.41	988	47.41	938	48.44	888	49.50	838	50.59	788
46.43	987	47.43	937	48.46	887	49.52	837	50.61	787
46.45	986	47.45	936	48.49	886	49.54	836	50.63	786
46.47	985	47.47	935	48.51	885	49.57	835	50.65	785
46.49	984	47.49	934	48.53	884	49.59	834	50.68	784
46.51	983	47.52	933	48.55	883	49.61	833	50.70	783
46.53	982	47.54	932	48.57	882	49.63	832	50.72	782
46.55	981	47.56	931	48.59	881	49.65	831	50.74	781
46.57	980	47.58	930	48.61	880	49.67	830	50.76	780
46.59	979	47.60	929	48.63	879	49.69	829	50.79	779
46.61	978	47.62	928	48.65	878	49.72	828	50.81	778
46.63	977	47.64	927	48.67	877	49.74	827	50.83	777
46.65	976	47.66	926	48.70	876	49.76	826	50.85	776
46.67	975	47.68	925	48.72	875	49.78	825	50.87	775
46.69	974	47.70	924	48.74	874	49.80	824	50.90	774
46.71	973	47.72	923	48.76	873	49.82	823	50.92	773
46.73	972	47.74	922	48.78	872	49.85	822	50.94	772
46.75	971	47.76	921	48.80	871	49.87	821	50.96	771
46.77	970	47.78	920	48.82	870	49.89	820	50.99	770
46.79	969	47.80	919	48.84	869	49.91	819	51.01	769
46.81	968	47.82	918	48.86	868	49.93	818	51.03	768
46.83	967	47.84	917	48.88	867	49.95	817	51.05	767
46.85	966	47.86	916	48.91	866	49.98	816	51.07	766
46.87	965	47.88	915	48.93	865	50.00	815	51.10	765
46.89	964	47.90	914	48.95	864	50.02	814	51.12	764
46.91	963	47.93	913	48.97	863	50.04	813	51.14	763
46.93	962	47.95	912	48.99	862	50.06	812	51.16	762
46.95	961	47.97	911	49.01	861	50.08	811	51.19	761
46.97	960	47.99	910	49.03	860	50.11	810	51.21	760
46.99	959	48.01	909	49.05	859	50.13	809	51.23	759
47.01	958	48.03	908	49.08	858	50.15	808	51.25	758
47.03	957	48.05	907	49.10	857	50.17	807	51.28	757
47.05	956	48.07	906	49.12	856	50.19	806	51.30	756
47.07	955	48.09	905	49.14	855	50.21	805	51.32	755
47.09	954	48.11	904	49.16	854	50.24	804	51.34	754
47.11	953	48.13	903	49.18	853	50.26	803	51.37	753
47.13	952	48.15	902	49.20	852	50.28	802	51.39	752
47.15	951	48.17	901	49.22	851	50.30	801	51.41	751
47.17	950	48.19	900	49.24	850	50.32	800	51.43	750

This table to be used exclusively for fully automatic times.

Seconds	Points	Seconds	Points	Seconds	Points	Seconds	Points	Seconds	Points
51.46	749	52.60	699	53.78	649	55.00	599	56.27	549
51.48	748	52.62	698	53.80	648	55.03	598	56.30	548
51.50	747	52.65	697	53.83	647	55.05	597	56.32	547
51.52	746	52.67	696	53.85	646	55.08	596	56.35	546
51.55	745	52.69	695	53.88	645	55.10	595	56.38	545
51.57	744	52.72	694	53.90	644	55.13	594	56.40	544
51.59	743	52.74	693	53.92	643	55.15	593	56.43	543
51.61	742	52.76	692	53.95	642	55.18	592	56.45	542
51.64	741	52.79	691	53.97	641	55.20	591	56.48	541
51.66	740	52.81	690	54.00	640	55.23	590	56.51	540
51.68	739	52.83	689	54.02	639	55.25	589	56.53	539
51.70	738	52.86	688	54.05	638	55.28	588	56.56	538
51.73	737	52.88	687	54.07	637	55.30	587	56.58	537
51.75	736	52.90	686	54.09	636	55.33	586	56.61	536
51.77	735	52.93	685	54.12	635	55.35	585	56.64	535
51.80	734	52.95	684	54.14	634	55.38	584	56.66	534
51.82	733	52.97	683	54.17	633	55.40	583	56.69	533
51.84	732	53.00	682	54.19	632	55.43	582	56.72	532
51.86	731	53.02	681	54.22	631	55.45	581	56.74	531
51.89	730	53.04	680	54.24	630	55.48	580	56.77	530
51.91	729	53.07	679	54.26	629	55.50	579	56.79	529
51.93	728	53.09	678	54.29	628	55.53	578	56.82	528
51.95	727	53.11	677	54.31	627	55.56	577	56.85	527
51.98	726	53.14	676	54.34	626	55.58	576	56.87	526
52.00	725	53.16	675	54.36	625	55.61	575	56.90	525
52.02	724	53.18	674	54.39	624	55.63	574	56.93	524
52.05	723	53.21	673	54.41	623	55.66	573	56.95	523
52.07	722	53.23	672	54.44	622	55.68	572	56.98	522
52.09	721	53.26	671	54.46	621	55.71	571	57.01	521
52.11	720	53.28	670	54.48	620	55.73	570	57.03	520
52.14	719	53.30	669	54.51	619	55.76	569	57.06	519
52.16	718	53.33	668	54.53	618	55.78	568	57.08	518
52.18	717	53.35	667	54.56	617	55.81	567	57.11	517
52.21	716	53.37	666	54.58	616	55.83	566	57.14	516
52.23	715	53.40	665	54.61	615	55.86	565	57.16	515
52.25	714	53.42	664	54.63	614	55.89	564	57.19	514
52.28	713	53.45	663	54.66	613	55.91	563	57.22	513
52.30	712	53.47	662	54.68	612	55.94	562	57.24	512
52.32	711	53.49	661	54.71	611	55.96	561	57.27	511
52.34	710	53.52	660	54.73	610	55.99	560	57.30	510
52.37	709	53.54	659	54.75	609	56.01	559	57.32	509
52.39	708	53.56	658	54.78	608	56.04	558	57.35	508
52.41	707	53.59	657	54.80	607	56.07	557	57.38	507
52.44	706	53.61	656	54.83	606	56.09	556	57.41	506
52.46	705	53.64	655	54.85	605	56.12	555	57.43	505
52.48	704	53.66	654	54.88	604	56.14	554	57.46	504
52.51	703	53.68	653	54.90	603	56.17	553	57.49	503
52.53	702	53.71	652	54.93	602	56.19	552	57.51	502
52.55	701	53.73	651	54.95	601	56.22	551	57.54	501
52.58	700	53.76	650	54.98	600	56.25	550	57.57	500

Seconds	Points	Seconds	Points	Seconds	Points	Seconds	Points	Seconds	Points
		This table to be used exclusively for fully automatic times.							
57.59	499	58.98	449	60.43	399	61.97	349	63.61	299
57.62	498	59.00	448	60.46	398	62.00	348	63.64	298
57.65	497	59.03	447	60.49	397	62.03	347	63.68	297
57.67	496	59.06	446	60.52	396	62.06	346	63.71	296
57.70	495	59.09	445	60.55	395	62.09	345	63.74	295
57.73	494	59.12	444	60.58	394	62.13	344	63.78	294
57.76	493	59.15	443	60.61	393	62.16	343	63.81	293
57.78	492	59.18	442	60.64	392	62.19	342	63.85	292
57.81	491	59.20	441	60.67	391	62.22	341	63.88	291
57.84	490	59.23	440	60.70	390	62.25	340	63.92	290
57.87	489	59.26	439	60.73	389	62.29	339	63.95	289
57.89	488	59.29	438	60.76	388	62.32	338	63.98	288
57.92	487	59.32	437	60.79	387	62.35	337	64.02	287
57.95	486	59.35	436	60.82	386	62.38	336	64.05	286
57.97	485	59.38	435	60.85	385	62.42	335	64.09	285
58.00	484	59.40	434	60.88	384	62.45	334	64.12	284
58.03	483	59.43	433	60.91	383	62.48	333	64.16	283
58.06	482	59.46	432	60.94	382	62.51	332	64.19	282
58.08	481	59.49	431	60.97	381	62.55	331	64.23	281
58.11	480	59.52	430	61.00	380	62.58	330	64.26	280
58.14	479	59.55	429	61.03	379	62.61	329	64.30	279
58.17	478	59.58	428	61.06	378	62.64	328	64.33	278
58.19	477	59.61	427	61.10	377	62.68	327	64.37	277
58.22	476	59.64	426	61.13	376	62.71	326	64.40	276
58.25	475	59.66	425	61.16	375	62.74	325	64.44	275
58.28	474	59.69	424	61.19	374	62.77	324	64.47	274
58.30	473	59.72	423	61.22	373	62.81	323	64.51	273
58.33	472	59.75	422	61.25	372	62.84	322	64.54	272
58.36	471	59.78	421	61.28	371	62.87	321	64.58	271
58.39	470	59.81	420	61.31	370	62.90	320	64.62	270
58.42	469	59.84	419	61.34	369	62.94	319	64.65	269
58.44	468	59.87	418	61.37	368	62.97	318	64.69	268
58.47	467	59.90	417	61.40	367	63.00	317	64.72	267
58.50	466	59.93	416	61.43	366	63.04	316	64.76	266
58.53	465	59.96	415	61.47	365	63.07	315	64.79	265
58.55	464	59.99	414	61.50	364	63.10	314	64.83	264
58.58	463	60.02	413	61.53	363	63.14	313	64.87	263
58.61	462	60.04	412	61.56	362	63.17	312	64.90	262
58.64	461	60.07	411	61.59	361	63.20	311	64.94	261
58.67	460	60.10	410	61.62	360	63.24	310	64.97	260
58.69	459	60.13	409	61.65	359	63.27	309	65.01	259
58.72	458	60.16	408	61.68	358	63.30	308	65.05	258
58.75	457	60.19	407	61.72	357	63.34	307	65.08	257
58.78	456	60.22	406	61.75	356	63.37	306	65.12	256
58.81	455	60.25	405	61.78	355	63.40	305	65.16	255
58.84	454	60.28	404	61.81	354	63.44	304	65.19	254
58.86	453	60.31	403	61.84	353	63.47	303	65.23	253
58.89	452	60.34	402	61.87	352	63.51	302	65.27	252
58.92	451	60.37	401	61.90	351	63.54	301	65.30	251
58.95	450	60.40	400	61.94	350	63.57	300	65.34	250

149

Men 400 metres — 400 mètres Hommes

Seconds	Points	Seconds	Points	Seconds	Points	Seconds	Points	Seconds	Points
				This table to be used exclusively for fully automatic times.					
65.38	249	67.31	199	69.48	149	72.01	99	75.23	49
65.41	248	67.35	198	69.53	148	72.07	98	75.30	48
65.45	247	67.39	197	69.57	147	72.12	97	75.38	47
65.49	246	67.43	196	69.62	146	72.18	96	75.46	46
65.52	245	67.48	195	69.67	145	72.24	95	75.54	45
65.56	244	67.52	194	69.71	144	72.29	94	75.62	44
65.60	243	67.56	193	69.76	143	72.35	93	75.70	43
65.64	242	67.60	192	69.81	142	72.41	92	75.78	42
65.67	241	67.64	191	69.86	141	72.47	91	75.86	41
65.71	240	67.68	190	69.90	140	72.52	90	75.94	40
65.75	239	67.72	189	69.95	139	72.58	89	76.03	39
65.79	238	67.77	188	70.00	138	72.64	88	76.11	38
65.82	237	67.81	187	70.05	137	72.70	87	76.20	37
65.86	236	67.85	186	70.10	136	72.76	86	76.29	36
65.90	235	67.89	185	70.14	135	72.82	85	76.37	35
65.94	234	67.93	184	70.19	134	72.88	84	76.46	34
65.97	233	67.98	183	70.24	133	72.94	83	76.55	33
66.01	232	68.02	182	70.29	132	73.00	82	76.65	32
66.05	231	68.06	181	70.34	131	73.06	81	76.74	31
66.09	230	68.10	180	70.39	130	73.12	80	76.83	30
66.13	229	68.15	179	70.44	129	73.18	79	76.93	29
66.17	228	68.19	178	70.49	128	73.24	78	77.03	28
66.20	227	68.23	177	70.54	127	73.31	77	77.12	27
66.24	226	68.27	176	70.59	126	73.37	76	77.23	26
66.28	225	68.32	175	70.64	125	73.43	75	77.33	25
66.32	224	68.36	174	70.69	124	73.49	74	77.43	24
66.36	223	68.40	173	70.74	123	73.56	73	77.54	23
66.40	222	68.45	172	70.79	122	73.62	72	77.65	22
66.44	221	68.49	171	70.84	121	73.69	71	77.76	21
66.47	220	68.54	170	70.89	120	73.75	70	77.87	20
66.51	219	68.58	169	70.94	119	73.82	69	77.98	19
66.55	218	68.62	168	70.99	118	73.88	68	78.10	18
66.59	217	68.67	167	71.05	117	73.95	67	78.22	17
66.63	216	68.71	166	71.10	116	74.01	66	78.35	16
66.67	215	68.76	165	71.15	115	74.08	65	78.48	15
66.71	214	68.80	164	71.20	114	74.15	64	78.61	14
66.75	213	68.84	163	71.25	113	74.22	63	78.74	13
66.79	212	68.89	162	71.31	112	74.29	62	78.88	12
66.83	211	68.93	161	71.36	111	74.35	61	79.03	11
66.87	210	68.98	160	71.41	110	74.42	60	79.18	10
66.91	209	69.02	159	71.47	109	74.49	59	79.34	9
66.95	208	69.07	158	71.52	108	74.56	58	79.51	8
66.99	207	69.11	157	71.57	107	74.64	57	79.68	7
67.03	206	69.16	156	71.63	106	74.71	56	79.87	6
67.07	205	69.20	155	71.68	105	74.78	55	80.08	5
67.11	204	69.25	154	71.74	104	74.85	54	80.30	4
67.15	203	69.30	153	71.79	103	74.93	53	80.55	3
67.19	202	69.34	152	71.84	102	75.00	52	80.84	2
67.23	201	69.39	151	71.90	101	75.07	51	81.21	1
67.27	200	69.43	150	71.96	100	75.15	50		

THIS TABLE IS TO BE USED EXCLUSIVELY FOR HAND TIMES

A UTILISER UNIQUEMENT EN CAS DE CHRONOMETRAGE MANUEL

Seconds	Points	Seconds	Points	Seconds	Points	Seconds	Points	Seconds	Points
41.0	1268	45.0	1052	49.0	855	53.0	676	57.0	516
41.1	1263	45.1	1047	49.1	850	53.1	671	57.1	512
41.2	1257	45.2	1042	49.2	845	53.2	667	57.2	508
41.3	1251	45.3	1037	49.3	841	53.3	663	57.3	504
41.4	1246	45.4	1032	49.4	836	53.4	659	57.4	501
41.5	1240	45.5	1027	49.5	831	53.5	655	57.5	497
41.6	1235	45.6	1021	49.6	827	53.6	650	57.6	493
41.7	1229	45.7	1016	49.7	822	53.7	646	57.7	490
41.8	1224	45.8	1011	49.8	817	53.8	642	57.8	486
41.9	1218	45.9	1006	49.9	813	53.9	638	57.9	482
42.0	1212	46.0	1001	50.0	808	54.0	634	58.0	479
42.1	1207	46.1	996	50.1	804	54.1	630	58.1	475
42.2	1201	46.2	991	50.2	799	54.2	626	58.2	471
42.3	1196	46.3	986	50.3	794	54.3	622	58.3	468
42.4	1191	46.4	981	50.4	790	54.4	617	58.4	464
42.5	1185	46.5	976	50.5	785	54.5	613	58.5	461
42.6	1180	46.6	971	50.6	781	54.6	609	58.6	457
42.7	1174	46.7	966	50.7	776	54.7	605	58.7	454
42.8	1169	46.8	961	50.8	772	54.8	601	58.8	450
42.9	1163	46.9	956	50.9	767	54.9	597	58.9	446
43.0	1158	47.0	951	51.0	763	55.0	593	59.0	443
43.1	1153	47.1	946	51.1	758	55.1	589	59.1	439
43.2	1147	47.2	941	51.2	754	55.2	585	59.2	436
43.3	1142	47.3	936	51.3	749	55.3	581	59.3	432
43.4	1136	47.4	932	51.4	745	55.4	577	59.4	429
43.5	1131	47.5	927	51.5	741	55.5	573	59.5	426
43.6	1126	47.6	922	51.6	736	55.6	569	59.6	422
43.7	1120	47.7	917	51.7	732	55.7	565	59.7	419
43.8	1115	47.8	912	51.8	727	55.8	562	59.8	415
43.9	1110	47.9	907	51.9	723	55.9	558	59.9	412
44.0	1105	48.0	902	52.0	719	56.0	554	60.0	408
44.1	1099	48.1	898	52.1	714	56.1	550	60.1	405
44.2	1094	48.2	893	52.2	710	56.2	546	60.2	402
44.3	1089	48.3	888	52.3	706	56.3	542	60.3	398
44.4	1084	48.4	883	52.4	701	56.4	538	60.4	395
44.5	1078	48.5	878	52.5	697	56.5	535	60.5	392
44.6	1073	48.6	874	52.6	693	56.6	531	60.6	388
44.7	1068	48.7	869	52.7	688	56.7	527	60.7	385
44.8	1063	48.8	864	52.8	684	56.8	523	60.8	382
44.9	1057	48.9	859	52.9	680	56.9	519	60.9	378

Men   400 metres — 1/10 sec — 400 mètres   Hommes

THIS TABLE IS TO BE USED EXCLUSIVELY FOR HAND TIMES

A UTILISER UNIQUEMENT EN CAS DE CHRONOMETRAGE MANUEL

Seconds	Points	Seconds	Points	Seconds	Points	Seconds	Points	Seconds	Points
61.0	375	65.0	255	69.0	156	73.0	79	77.0	26
61.1	372	65.1	252	69.1	154	73.1	78	77.1	25
61.2	369	65.2	250	69.2	152	73.2	76	77.2	24
61.3	365	65.3	247	69.3	149	73.3	74	77.4	23
61.4	362	65.4	244	69.4	147	73.4	73	77.5	22
61.5	359	65.5	242	69.5	145	73.5	71	77.6	21
61.6	356	65.6	239	69.6	143	73.6	70	77.7	20
61.7	353	65.7	236	69.7	141	73.7	68	77.8	19
61.8	350	65.8	234	69.8	139	73.8	67	77.9	18
61.9	346	65.9	231	69.9	137	73.9	65	78.0	17
62.0	343	66.0	228	70.0	135	74.0	64	78.2	16
62.1	340	66.1	226	70.1	133	74.1	62	78.3	15
62.2	337	66.2	223	70.2	131	74.2	61	78.4	14
62.3	334	66.3	221	70.3	129	74.3	59	78.6	13
62.4	331	66.4	218	70.4	127	74.4	58	78.7	12
62.5	328	66.5	215	70.5	125	74.5	57	78.8	11
62.6	325	66.6	213	70.6	123	74.6	55	79.0	10
62.7	322	66.7	210	70.7	121	74.7	54	79.2	9
62.8	319	66.8	208	70.8	119	74.8	52	79.3	8
62.9	316	66.9	205	70.9	117	74.9	51	79.5	7
63.0	313	67.0	203	71.0	115	75.0	50	79.7	6
63.1	310	67.1	200	71.1	113	75.1	48	79.9	5
63.2	307	67.2	198	71.2	111	75.2	47	80.1	4
63.3	304	67.3	195	71.3	109	75.3	46	80.4	3
63.4	301	67.4	193	71.4	107	75.4	45	80.7	2
63.5	298	67.5	191	71.5	105	75.5	43	81.0	1
63.6	295	67.6	188	71.6	104	75.6	42		
63.7	292	67.7	186	71.7	102	75.7	41		
63.8	289	67.8	183	71.8	100	75.8	40		
63.9	286	67.9	181	71.9	98	75.9	38		
64.0	283	68.0	179	72.0	96	76.0	37		
64.1	280	68.1	176	72.1	95	76.1	36		
64.2	277	68.2	174	72.2	93	76.2	35		
64.3	275	68.3	172	72.3	91	76.3	34		
64.4	272	68.4	170	72.4	89	76.4	33		
64.5	269	68.5	167	72.5	88	76.5	32		
64.6	266	68.6	165	72.6	86	76.6	31		
64.7	263	68.7	163	72.7	84	76.7	29		
64.8	261	68.8	160	72.8	83	76.8	28		
64.9	258	68.9	158	72.9	81	76.9	27		

Seconds	Points	Seconds	Points	Seconds	Points	Seconds	Points	Seconds	Points
				This table to be used exclusively for fully automatic times.					
12.00	1249	12.50	1177	13.00	1108	13.50	1040	14.00	975
12.01	1248	12.51	1176	13.01	1106	13.51	1039	14.01	973
12.02	1246	12.52	1175	13.02	1105	13.52	1037	14.02	972
12.03	1245	12.53	1173	13.03	1104	13.53	1036	14.03	971
12.04	1243	12.54	1172	13.04	1102	13.54	1035	14.04	969
12.05	1242	12.55	1170	13.05	1101	13.55	1033	14.05	968
12.06	1240	12.56	1169	13.06	1099	13.56	1032	14.06	967
12.07	1239	12.57	1167	13.07	1098	13.57	1031	14.07	965
12.08	1237	12.58	1166	13.08	1097	13.58	1029	14.08	964
12.09	1236	12.59	1165	13.09	1095	13.59	1028	14.09	963
12.10	1235	12.60	1163	13.10	1094	13.60	1027	14.10	962
12.11	1233	12.61	1162	13.11	1093	13.61	1025	14.11	960
12.12	1232	12.62	1160	13.12	1091	13.62	1024	14.12	959
12.13	1230	12.63	1159	13.13	1090	13.63	1023	14.13	958
12.14	1229	12.64	1158	13.14	1089	13.64	1022	14.14	957
12.15	1227	12.65	1156	13.15	1087	13.65	1020	14.15	955
12.16	1226	12.66	1155	13.16	1086	13.66	1019	14.16	954
12.17	1224	12.67	1153	13.17	1084	13.67	1018	14.17	953
12.18	1223	12.68	1152	13.18	1083	13.68	1016	14.18	951
12.19	1222	12.69	1151	13.19	1082	13.69	1015	14.19	950
12.20	1220	12.70	1149	13.20	1080	13.70	1014	14.20	949
12.21	1219	12.71	1148	13.21	1079	13.71	1012	14.21	948
12.22	1217	12.72	1146	13.22	1078	13.72	1011	14.22	946
12.23	1216	12.73	1145	13.23	1076	13.73	1010	14.23	945
12.24	1214	12.74	1144	13.24	1075	13.74	1008	14.24	944
12.25	1213	12.75	1142	13.25	1074	13.75	1007	14.25	942
12.26	1212	12.76	1141	13.26	1072	13.76	1006	14.26	941
12.27	1210	12.77	1139	13.27	1071	13.77	1004	14.27	940
12.28	1209	12.78	1138	13.28	1070	13.78	1003	14.28	939
12.29	1207	12.79	1137	13.29	1068	13.79	1002	14.29	937
12.30	1206	12.80	1135	13.30	1067	13.80	1000	14.30	936
12.31	1204	12.81	1134	13.31	1066	13.81	999	14.31	935
12.32	1203	12.82	1133	13.32	1064	13.82	998	14.32	934
12.33	1201	12.83	1131	13.33	1063	13.83	997	14.33	932
12.34	1200	12.84	1130	13.34	1061	13.84	995	14.34	931
12.35	1199	12.85	1128	13.35	1060	13.85	994	14.35	930
12.36	1197	12.86	1127	13.36	1059	13.86	993	14.36	929
12.37	1196	12.87	1126	13.37	1057	13.87	991	14.37	927
12.38	1194	12.88	1124	13.38	1056	13.88	990	14.38	926
12.39	1193	12.89	1123	13.39	1055	13.89	989	14.39	925
12.40	1192	12.90	1121	13.40	1053	13.90	987	14.40	924
12.41	1190	12.91	1120	13.41	1052	13.91	986	14.41	922
12.42	1189	12.92	1119	13.42	1051	13.92	985	14.42	921
12.43	1187	12.93	1117	13.43	1049	13.93	984	14.43	920
12.44	1186	12.94	1116	13.44	1048	13.94	982	14.44	918
12.45	1184	12.95	1115	13.45	1047	13.95	981	14.45	917
12.46	1183	12.96	1113	13.46	1045	13.96	980	14.46	916
12.47	1182	12.97	1112	13.47	1044	13.97	978	14.47	915
12.48	1180	12.98	1110	13.48	1043	13.98	977	14.48	913
12.49	1179	12.99	1109	13.49	1041	13.99	976	14.49	912

Seconds	Points	Seconds	Points	Seconds	Points	Seconds	Points	Seconds	Points
				This table to be used exclusively for fully automatic times.					
14.50	911	15.00	850	15.50	790	16.00	733	16.50	677
14.51	910	15.01	848	15.51	789	16.01	732	16.51	676
14.52	908	15.02	847	15.52	788	16.02	730	16.52	675
14.53	907	15.03	846	15.53	787	16.03	729	16.53	674
14.54	906	15.04	845	15.54	785	16.04	728	16.54	673
14.55	905	15.05	843	15.55	784	16.05	727	16.55	672
14.56	903	15.06	842	15.56	783	16.06	726	16.56	671
14.57	902	15.07	841	15.57	782	16.07	725	16.57	670
14.58	901	15.08	840	15.58	781	16.08	724	16.58	669
14.59	900	15.09	839	15.59	780	16.09	723	16.59	668
14.60	899	15.10	837	15.60	778	16.10	722	16.60	667
14.61	897	15.11	836	15.61	777	16.11	720	16.61	666
14.62	896	15.12	835	15.62	776	16.12	719	16.62	665
14.63	895	15.13	834	15.63	775	16.13	718	16.63	663
14.64	894	15.14	833	15.64	774	16.14	717	16.64	662
14.65	892	15.15	831	15.65	773	16.15	716	16.65	661
14.66	891	15.16	830	15.66	772	16.16	715	16.66	660
14.67	890	15.17	829	15.67	770	16.17	714	16.67	659
14.68	889	15.18	828	15.68	769	16.18	713	16.68	658
14.69	887	15.19	827	15.69	768	16.19	711	16.69	657
14.70	886	15.20	825	15.70	767	16.20	710	16.70	656
14.71	885	15.21	824	15.71	766	16.21	709	16.71	655
14.72	884	15.22	823	15.72	765	16.22	708	16.72	654
14.73	882	15.23	822	15.73	763	16.23	707	16.73	653
14.74	881	15.24	821	15.74	762	16.24	706	16.74	652
14.75	880	15.25	820	15.75	761	16.25	705	16.75	651
14.76	879	15.26	818	15.76	760	16.26	704	16.76	650
14.77	878	15.27	817	15.77	759	16.27	703	16.77	648
14.78	876	15.28	816	15.78	758	16.28	702	16.78	647
14.79	875	15.29	815	15.79	757	16.29	700	16.79	646
14.80	874	15.30	814	15.80	755	16.30	699	16.80	645
14.81	873	15.31	812	15.81	754	16.31	698	16.81	644
14.82	871	15.32	811	15.82	753	16.32	697	16.82	643
14.83	870	15.33	810	15.83	752	16.33	696	16.83	642
14.84	869	15.34	809	15.84	751	16.34	695	16.84	641
14.85	868	15.35	808	15.85	750	16.35	694	16.85	640
14.86	867	15.36	807	15.86	749	16.36	693	16.86	639
14.87	865	15.37	805	15.87	747	16.37	692	16.87	638
14.88	864	15.38	804	15.88	746	16.38	691	16.88	637
14.89	863	15.39	803	15.89	745	16.39	689	16.89	636
14.90	862	15.40	802	15.90	744	16.40	688	16.90	635
14.91	860	15.41	801	15.91	743	16.41	687	16.91	634
14.92	859	15.42	799	15.92	742	16.42	686	16.92	633
14.93	858	15.43	798	15.93	741	16.43	685	16.93	632
14.94	857	15.44	797	15.94	740	16.44	684	16.94	631
14.95	856	15.45	796	15.95	738	16.45	683	16.95	629
14.96	854	15.46	795	15.96	737	16.46	682	16.96	628
14.97	853	15.47	794	15.97	736	16.47	681	16.97	627
14.98	852	15.48	792	15.98	735	16.48	680	16.98	626
14.99	851	15.49	791	15.99	734	16.49	679	16.99	625

This table to be used exclusively for fully automatic times.

Seconds	Points	Seconds	Points	Seconds	Points	Seconds	Points	Seconds	Points
17.00	624	17.50	573	18.01	523	18.55	473	19.11	423
17.01	623	17.51	572	18.02	522	18.56	472	19.12	422
17.02	622	17.52	571	18.03	521	18.57	471	19.13	421
17.03	621	17.53	570	18.04	520	18.58	470	19.14	420
17.04	620	17.54	569	18.05	519	18.59	469	19.16	419
17.05	619	17.55	568	18.06	518	18.60	468	19.17	418
17.06	618	17.56	567	18.07	517	18.61	467	19.18	417
17.07	617	17.57	566	18.09	516	18.62	466	19.19	416
17.08	616	17.58	565	18.10	515	18.63	465	19.20	415
17.09	615	17.59	564	18.11	514	18.65	464	19.21	414
17.10	614	17.60	563	18.12	513	18.66	463	19.23	413
17.11	613	17.61	562	18.13	512	18.67	462	19.24	412
17.12	612	17.62	561	18.14	511	18.68	461	19.25	411
17.13	611	17.63	560	18.15	510	18.69	460	19.26	410
17.14	610	17.64	559	18.16	509	18.70	459	19.27	409
17.15	609	17.65	558	18.17	508	18.71	458	19.28	408
17.16	608	17.66	557	18.18	507	18.72	457	19.30	407
17.17	607	17.67	556	18.19	506	18.73	456	19.31	406
17.18	606	17.68	555	18.20	505	18.75	455	19.32	405
17.19	605	17.69	554	18.21	504	18.76	454	19.33	404
17.20	604	17.70	553	18.22	503	18.77	453	19.34	403
17.21	603	17.71	552	18.23	502	18.78	452	19.35	402
17.22	602	17.72	551	18.24	501	18.79	451	19.37	401
17.23	600	17.73	550	18.25	500	18.80	450	19.38	400
17.24	599	17.74	549	18.27	499	18.81	449	19.39	399
17.25	598	17.75	548	18.28	498	18.82	448	19.40	398
17.26	597	17.76	547	18.29	497	18.84	447	19.41	397
17.27	596	17.77	546	18.30	496	18.85	446	19.43	396
17.28	595	17.78	545	18.31	495	18.86	445	19.44	395
17.29	594	17.79	544	18.32	494	18.87	444	19.45	394
17.30	593	17.81	543	18.33	493	18.88	443	19.46	393
17.31	592	17.82	542	18.34	492	18.89	442	19.47	392
17.32	591	17.83	541	18.35	491	18.90	441	19.49	391
17.33	590	17.84	540	18.36	490	18.91	440	19.50	390
17.34	589	17.85	539	18.37	489	18.93	439	19.51	389
17.35	588	17.86	538	18.38	488	18.94	438	19.52	388
17.36	587	17.87	537	18.39	487	18.95	437	19.53	387
17.37	586	17.88	536	18.41	486	18.96	436	19.55	386
17.38	585	17.89	535	18.42	485	18.97	435	19.56	385
17.39	584	17.90	534	18.43	484	18.98	434	19.57	384
17.40	583	17.91	533	18.44	483	18.99	433	19.58	383
17.41	582	17.92	532	18.45	482	19.01	432	19.59	382
17.42	581	17.93	531	18.46	481	19.02	431	19.61	381
17.43	580	17.94	530	18.47	480	19.03	430	19.62	380
17.44	579	17.95	529	18.48	479	19.04	429	19.63	379
17.45	578	17.96	528	18.49	478	19.05	428	19.64	378
17.46	577	17.97	527	18.50	477	19.06	427	19.66	377
17.47	576	17.98	526	18.51	476	19.07	426	19.67	376
17.48	575	17.99	525	18.52	475	19.09	425	19.68	375
17.49	574	18.00	524	18.54	474	19.10	424	19.69	374

Seconds	Points	Seconds	Points	Seconds	Points	Seconds	Points	Seconds	Points
				This table to be used exclusively for fully automatic times.					
19.70	373	20.34	323	21.02	273	21.77	223	22.60	173
19.72	372	20.35	322	21.04	272	21.79	222	22.62	172
19.73	371	20.37	321	21.05	271	21.80	221	22.64	171
19.74	370	20.38	320	21.07	270	21.82	220	22.66	170
19.75	369	20.39	319	21.08	269	21.83	219	22.67	169
19.77	368	20.41	318	21.09	268	21.85	218	22.69	168
19.78	367	20.42	317	21.11	267	21.87	217	22.71	167
19.79	366	20.43	316	21.12	266	21.88	216	22.73	166
19.80	365	20.44	315	21.14	265	21.90	215	22.75	165
19.82	364	20.46	314	21.15	264	21.91	214	22.76	164
19.83	363	20.47	313	21.17	263	21.93	213	22.78	163
19.84	362	20.48	312	21.18	262	21.95	212	22.80	162
19.85	361	20.50	311	21.20	261	21.96	211	22.82	161
19.87	360	20.51	310	21.21	260	21.98	210	22.84	160
19.88	359	20.53	309	21.23	259	21.99	209	22.86	159
19.89	358	20.54	308	21.24	258	22.01	208	22.88	158
19.90	357	20.55	307	21.25	257	22.03	207	22.89	157
19.92	356	20.57	306	21.27	256	22.04	206	22.91	156
19.93	355	20.58	305	21.28	255	22.06	205	22.93	155
19.94	354	20.59	304	21.30	254	22.08	204	22.95	154
19.95	353	20.61	303	21.31	253	22.09	203	22.97	153
19.97	352	20.62	302	21.33	252	22.11	202	22.99	152
19.98	351	20.63	301	21.34	251	22.12	201	23.01	151
19.99	350	20.65	300	21.36	250	22.14	200	23.03	150
20.00	349	20.66	299	21.37	249	22.16	199	23.04	149
20.02	348	20.67	298	21.39	248	22.17	198	23.06	148
20.03	347	20.69	297	21.40	247	22.19	197	23.08	147
20.04	346	20.70	296	21.42	246	22.21	196	23.10	146
20.05	345	20.72	295	21.43	245	22.22	195	23.12	145
20.07	344	20.73	294	21.45	244	22.24	194	23.14	144
20.08	343	20.74	293	21.46	243	22.26	193	23.16	143
20.09	342	20.76	292	21.48	242	22.27	192	23.18	142
20.11	341	20.77	291	21.49	241	22.29	191	23.20	141
20.12	340	20.78	290	21.51	240	22.31	190	23.22	140
20.13	339	20.80	289	21.52	239	22.33	189	23.24	139
20.14	338	20.81	288	21.54	238	22.34	188	23.26	138
20.16	337	20.83	287	21.55	237	22.36	187	23.28	137
20.17	336	20.84	286	21.57	236	22.38	186	23.30	136
20.18	335	20.85	285	21.58	235	22.39	185	23.32	135
20.20	334	20.87	284	21.60	234	22.41	184	23.34	134
20.21	333	20.88	283	21.61	233	22.43	183	23.36	133
20.22	332	20.90	282	21.63	232	22.45	182	23.38	132
20.23	331	20.91	281	21.65	231	22.46	181	23.40	131
20.25	330	20.92	280	21.66	230	22.48	180	23.42	130
20.26	329	20.94	279	21.68	229	22.50	179	23.44	129
20.27	328	20.95	278	21.69	228	22.52	178	23.46	128
20.29	327	20.97	277	21.71	227	22.53	177	23.48	127
20.30	326	20.98	276	21.72	226	22.55	176	23.50	126
20.31	325	20.99	275	21.74	225	22.57	175	23.52	125
20.33	324	21.01	274	21.75	224	22.59	174	23.54	124

Seconds	Points	Seconds	Points	Seconds	Points	Seconds	Points	Seconds	Points
				This table to be used exclusively for fully automatic times.					
23.56	123	24.23	93	25.01	63	26.01	33	27.78	3
23.58	122	24.25	92	25.04	62	26.05	32	27.92	2
23.60	121	24.28	91	25.07	61	26.09	31	28.09	1
23.63	120	24.30	90	25.10	60	26.13	30		
23.65	119	24.33	89	25.13	59	26.17	29		
23.67	118	24.35	88	25.16	58	26.21	28		
23.69	117	24.38	87	25.19	57	26.26	27		
23.71	116	24.40	86	25.22	56	26.30	26		
23.73	115	24.43	85	25.25	55	26.34	25		
23.75	114	24.45	84	25.28	54	26.39	24		
23.78	113	24.48	83	25.31	53	26.44	23		
23.80	112	24.50	82	25.34	52	26.48	22		
23.82	111	24.53	81	25.38	51	26.53	21		
23.84	110	24.55	80	25.41	50	26.58	20		
23.86	109	24.58	79	25.44	49	26.63	19		
23.89	108	24.60	78	25.47	48	26.68	18		
23.91	107	24.63	77	25.51	47	26.74	17		
23.93	106	24.66	76	25.54	46	26.79	16		
23.95	105	24.68	75	25.57	45	26.85	15		
23.98	104	24.71	74	25.61	44	26.90	14		
24.00	103	24.74	73	25.64	43	26.96	13		
24.02	102	24.76	72	25.68	42	27.03	12		
24.04	101	24.79	71	25.71	41	27.09	11		
24.07	100	24.82	70	25.75	40	27.16	10		
24.09	99	24.84	69	25.78	39	27.23	9		
24.11	98	24.87	68	25.82	38	27.31	8		
24.14	97	24.90	67	25.86	37	27.39	7		
24.16	96	24.93	66	25.89	36	27.47	6		
24.18	95	24.96	65	25.93	35	27.56	5		
24.21	94	24.98	64	25.97	34	27.67	4		

Seconds	Points	Seconds	Points	Seconds	Points	Seconds	Points	Seconds	Points

THIS TABLE IS TO BE USED EXCLUSIVELY FOR HAND TIMES

A UTILISER UNIQUEMENT EN CAS DE CHRONOMETRAGE MANUEL

Seconds	Points	Seconds	Points	Seconds	Points	Seconds	Points
12.0	1214	16.0	706	20.0	330	24.0	92
12.1	1200	16.1	695	20.1	323	24.1	88
12.2	1186	16.2	684	20.2	315	24.2	84
12.3	1172	16.3	673	20.3	308	24.3	80
12.4	1158	16.4	662	20.4	300	24.4	76
12.5	1144	16.5	652	20.5	293	24.5	73
12.6	1130	16.6	641	20.6	286	24.6	69
12.7	1116	16.7	631	20.7	279	24.7	65
12.8	1102	16.8	620	20.8	272	24.8	62
12.9	1089	16.9	610	20.9	265	24.9	58
13.0	1075	17.0	599	21.0	258	25.0	55
13.1	1061	17.1	589	21.1	251	25.1	52
13.2	1048	17.2	579	21.2	244	25.2	49
13.3	1035	17.3	569	21.3	238	25.3	46
13.4	1022	17.4	559	21.4	231	25.4	43
13.5	1008	17.5	549	21.5	225	25.5	40
13.6	995	17.6	540	21.6	218	25.6	37
13.7	982	17.7	530	21.7	212	25.7	34
13.8	969	17.8	520	21.8	206	25.8	32
13.9	957	17.9	511	21.9	200	25.9	29
14.0	944	18.0	501	22.0	194	26.0	27
14.1	931	18.1	492	22.1	188	26.1	25
14.2	918	18.2	483	22.2	182	26.2	23
14.3	906	18.3	474	22.3	176	26.3	20
14.4	894	18.4	464	22.4	171	26.4	18
14.5	881	18.5	455	22.5	165	26.5	17
14.6	869	18.6	447	22.6	160	26.6	15
14.7	857	18.7	438	22.7	154	26.7	13
14.8	845	18.8	429	22.8	149	26.8	11
14.9	833	18.9	420	22.9	144	26.9	10
15.0	821	19.0	412	23.0	139	27.0	8
15.1	809	19.1	403	23.1	134	27.1	7
15.2	797	19.2	395	23.2	129	27.2	6
15.3	785	19.3	386	23.3	124	27.3	5
15.4	774	19.4	378	23.4	119	27.4	4
15.5	762	19.5	370	23.5	114	27.5	3
15.6	751	19.6	362	23.6	110	27.6	2
15.7	740	19.7	354	23.7	105	27.8	1
15.8	728	19.8	346	23.8	101		
15.9	717	19.9	338	23.9	97		

Perf.	Points	Perf.	Points	Perf.	Points	Perf.	Points	Perf.	Points
79.41	1500	77.13	1450	74.83	1400	72.53	1350	70.22	1300
79.37	1499	77.08	1449	74.78	1399	72.48	1349	70.17	1299
79.32	1498	77.03	1448	74.74	1398	72.43	1348	70.12	1298
79.28	1497	76.99	1447	74.69	1397	72.39	1347	70.08	1297
79.23	1496	76.94	1446	74.65	1396	72.34	1346	70.03	1296
79.19	1495	76.90	1445	74.60	1395	72.30	1345	69.98	1295
79.14	1494	76.85	1444	74.55	1394	72.25	1344	69.94	1294
79.09	1493	76.80	1443	74.51	1393	72.20	1343	69.89	1293
79.05	1492	76.76	1442	74.46	1392	72.16	1342	69.84	1292
79.00	1491	76.71	1441	74.42	1391	72.11	1341	69.80	1291
78.96	1490	76.67	1440	74.37	1390	72.06	1340	69.75	1290
78.91	1489	76.62	1439	74.32	1389	72.02	1339	69.71	1289
78.87	1488	76.57	1438	74.28	1388	71.97	1338	69.66	1288
78.82	1487	76.53	1437	74.23	1387	71.93	1337	69.61	1287
78.77	1486	76.48	1436	74.19	1386	71.88	1336	69.57	1286
78.73	1485	76.44	1435	74.14	1385	71.83	1335	69.52	1285
78.68	1484	76.39	1434	74.09	1384	71.79	1334	69.47	1284
78.64	1483	76.35	1433	74.05	1383	71.74	1333	69.43	1283
78.59	1482	76.30	1432	74.00	1382	71.70	1332	69.38	1282
78.55	1481	76.25	1431	73.96	1381	71.65	1331	69.33	1281
78.50	1480	76.21	1430	73.91	1380	71.60	1330	69.29	1280
78.45	1479	76.16	1429	73.86	1379	71.56	1329	69.24	1279
78.41	1478	76.12	1428	73.82	1378	71.51	1328	69.20	1278
78.36	1477	76.07	1427	73.77	1377	71.46	1327	69.15	1277
78.32	1476	76.02	1426	73.72	1376	71.42	1326	69.10	1276
78.27	1475	75.98	1425	73.68	1375	71.37	1325	69.06	1275
78.22	1474	75.93	1424	73.63	1374	71.33	1324	69.01	1274
78.18	1473	75.89	1423	73.59	1373	71.28	1323	68.96	1273
78.13	1472	75.84	1422	73.54	1372	71.23	1322	68.92	1272
78.09	1471	75.79	1421	73.49	1371	71.19	1321	68.87	1271
78.04	1470	75.75	1420	73.45	1370	71.14	1320	68.82	1270
78.00	1469	75.70	1419	73.40	1369	71.09	1319	68.78	1269
77.95	1468	75.66	1418	73.36	1368	71.05	1318	68.73	1268
77.90	1467	75.61	1417	73.31	1367	71.00	1317	68.69	1267
77.86	1466	75.56	1416	73.26	1366	70.96	1316	68.64	1266
77.81	1465	75.52	1415	73.22	1365	70.91	1315	68.59	1265
77.77	1464	75.47	1414	73.17	1364	70.86	1314	68.55	1264
77.72	1463	75.43	1413	73.13	1363	70.82	1313	68.50	1263
77.68	1462	75.38	1412	73.08	1362	70.77	1312	68.45	1262
77.63	1461	75.34	1411	73.03	1361	70.72	1311	68.41	1261
77.58	1460	75.29	1410	72.99	1360	70.68	1310	68.36	1260
77.54	1459	75.24	1409	72.94	1359	70.63	1309	68.31	1259
77.49	1458	75.20	1408	72.90	1358	70.59	1308	68.27	1258
77.45	1457	75.15	1407	72.85	1357	70.54	1307	68.22	1257
77.40	1456	75.11	1406	72.80	1356	70.49	1306	68.17	1256
77.35	1455	75.06	1405	72.76	1355	70.45	1305	68.13	1255
77.31	1454	75.01	1404	72.71	1354	70.40	1304	68.08	1254
77.26	1453	74.97	1403	72.66	1353	70.35	1303	68.04	1253
77.22	1452	74.92	1402	72.62	1352	70.31	1302	67.99	1252
77.17	1451	74.88	1401	72.57	1351	70.26	1301	67.94	1251

159

Perf.	Points	Perf.	Points	Perf.	Points	Perf.	Points	Perf.	Points
67.90	1250	65.57	1200	63.23	1150	60.89	1100	58.53	1050
67.85	1249	65.52	1199	63.19	1149	60.84	1099	58.48	1049
67.80	1248	65.48	1198	63.14	1148	60.79	1098	58.44	1048
67.76	1247	65.43	1197	63.09	1147	60.75	1097	58.39	1047
67.71	1246	65.38	1196	63.04	1146	60.70	1096	58.34	1046
67.66	1245	65.34	1195	63.00	1145	60.65	1095	58.29	1045
67.62	1244	65.29	1194	62.95	1144	60.60	1094	58.25	1044
67.57	1243	65.24	1193	62.90	1143	60.56	1093	58.20	1043
67.52	1242	65.20	1192	62.86	1142	60.51	1092	58.15	1042
67.48	1241	65.15	1191	62.81	1141	60.46	1091	58.11	1041
67.43	1240	65.10	1190	62.76	1140	60.42	1090	58.06	1040
67.38	1239	65.06	1189	62.72	1139	60.37	1089	58.01	1039
67.34	1238	65.01	1188	62.67	1138	60.32	1088	57.96	1038
67.29	1237	64.96	1187	62.62	1137	60.27	1087	57.92	1037
67.25	1236	64.92	1186	62.58	1136	60.23	1086	57.87	1036
67.20	1235	64.87	1185	62.53	1135	60.18	1085	57.82	1035
67.15	1234	64.82	1184	62.48	1134	60.13	1084	57.78	1034
67.11	1233	64.78	1183	62.44	1133	60.09	1083	57.73	1033
67.06	1232	64.73	1182	62.39	1132	60.04	1082	57.68	1032
67.01	1231	64.68	1181	62.34	1131	59.99	1081	57.63	1031
66.97	1230	64.63	1180	62.29	1130	59.95	1080	57.59	1030
66.92	1229	64.59	1179	62.25	1129	59.90	1079	57.54	1029
66.87	1228	64.54	1178	62.20	1128	59.85	1078	57.49	1028
66.83	1227	64.49	1177	62.15	1127	59.80	1077	57.44	1027
66.78	1226	64.45	1176	62.11	1126	59.76	1076	57.40	1026
66.73	1225	64.40	1175	62.06	1125	59.71	1075	57.35	1025
66.69	1224	64.35	1174	62.01	1124	59.66	1074	57.30	1024
66.64	1223	64.31	1173	61.97	1123	59.62	1073	57.25	1023
66.59	1222	64.26	1172	61.92	1122	59.57	1072	57.21	1022
66.55	1221	64.21	1171	61.87	1121	59.52	1071	57.16	1021
66.50	1220	64.17	1170	61.83	1120	59.47	1070	57.11	1020
66.45	1219	64.12	1169	61.78	1119	59.43	1069	57.07	1019
66.41	1218	64.07	1168	61.73	1118	59.38	1068	57.02	1018
66.36	1217	64.03	1167	61.68	1117	59.33	1067	56.97	1017
66.31	1216	63.98	1166	61.64	1116	59.29	1066	56.92	1016
66.27	1215	63.93	1165	61.59	1115	59.24	1065	56.88	1015
66.22	1214	63.89	1164	61.54	1114	59.19	1064	56.83	1014
66.17	1213	63.84	1163	61.50	1113	59.14	1063	56.78	1013
66.13	1212	63.79	1162	61.45	1112	59.10	1062	56.73	1012
66.08	1211	63.75	1161	61.40	1111	59.05	1061	56.69	1011
66.03	1210	63.70	1160	61.36	1110	59.00	1060	56.64	1010
65.99	1209	63.65	1159	61.31	1109	58.96	1059	56.59	1009
65.94	1208	63.61	1158	61.26	1108	58.91	1058	56.54	1008
65.89	1207	63.56	1157	61.22	1107	58.86	1057	56.50	1007
65.85	1206	63.51	1156	61.17	1106	58.81	1056	56.45	1006
65.80	1205	63.47	1155	61.12	1105	58.77	1055	56.40	1005
65.75	1204	63.42	1154	61.07	1104	58.72	1054	56.35	1004
65.71	1203	63.37	1153	61.03	1103	58.67	1053	56.31	1003
65.66	1202	63.33	1152	60.98	1102	58.63	1052	56.26	1002
65.62	1201	63.28	1151	60.93	1101	58.58	1051	56.21	1001

160

Perf.	Points	Perf.	Points	Perf.	Points	Perf.	Points	Perf.	Points
56.17	1000	53.79	950	51.40	900	49.00	850	46.59	800
56.12	999	53.74	949	51.35	899	48.95	849	46.54	799
56.07	998	53.69	948	51.31	898	48.90	848	46.49	798
56.02	997	53.65	947	51.26	897	48.86	847	46.44	797
55.98	996	53.60	946	51.21	896	48.81	846	46.39	796
55.93	995	53.55	945	51.16	895	48.76	845	46.35	795
55.88	994	53.50	944	51.11	894	48.71	844	46.30	794
55.83	993	53.46	943	51.07	893	48.66	843	46.25	793
55.79	992	53.41	942	51.02	892	48.62	842	46.20	792
55.74	991	53.36	941	50.97	891	48.57	841	46.15	791
55.69	990	53.31	940	50.92	890	48.52	840	46.10	790
55.64	989	53.26	939	50.87	889	48.47	839	46.06	789
55.60	988	53.22	938	50.83	888	48.42	838	46.01	788
55.55	987	53.17	937	50.78	887	48.38	837	45.96	787
55.50	986	53.12	936	50.73	886	48.33	836	45.91	786
55.45	985	53.07	935	50.68	885	48.28	835	45.86	785
55.41	984	53.03	934	50.63	884	48.23	834	45.81	784
55.36	983	52.98	933	50.59	883	48.18	833	45.76	783
55.31	982	52.93	932	50.54	882	48.13	832	45.72	782
55.26	981	52.88	931	50.49	881	48.09	831	45.67	781
55.22	980	52.84	930	50.44	880	48.04	830	45.62	780
55.17	979	52.79	929	50.39	879	47.99	829	45.57	779
55.12	978	52.74	928	50.35	878	47.94	828	45.52	778
55.07	977	52.69	927	50.30	877	47.89	827	45.47	777
55.03	976	52.64	926	50.25	876	47.84	826	45.43	776
54.98	975	52.60	925	50.20	875	47.80	825	45.38	775
54.93	974	52.55	924	50.15	874	47.75	824	45.33	774
54.88	973	52.50	923	50.11	873	47.70	823	45.28	773
54.84	972	52.45	922	50.06	872	47.65	822	45.23	772
54.79	971	52.41	921	50.01	871	47.60	821	45.18	771
54.74	970	52.36	920	49.96	870	47.56	820	45.13	770
54.69	969	52.31	919	49.91	869	47.51	819	45.09	769
54.65	968	52.26	918	49.87	868	47.46	818	45.04	768
54.60	967	52.21	917	49.82	867	47.41	817	44.99	767
54.55	966	52.17	916	49.77	866	47.36	816	44.94	766
54.50	965	52.12	915	49.72	865	47.31	815	44.89	765
54.46	964	52.07	914	49.67	864	47.27	814	44.84	764
54.41	963	52.02	913	49.63	863	47.22	813	44.79	763
54.36	962	51.98	912	49.58	862	47.17	812	44.75	762
54.31	961	51.93	911	49.53	861	47.12	811	44.70	761
54.27	960	51.88	910	49.48	860	47.07	810	44.65	760
54.22	959	51.83	909	49.43	859	47.02	809	44.60	759
54.17	958	51.78	908	49.39	858	46.98	808	44.55	758
54.12	957	51.74	907	49.34	857	46.93	807	44.50	757
54.07	956	51.69	906	49.29	856	46.88	806	44.45	756
54.03	955	51.64	905	49.24	855	46.83	805	44.41	755
53.98	954	51.59	904	49.19	854	46.78	804	44.36	754
53.93	953	51.54	903	49.15	853	46.73	803	44.31	753
53.88	952	51.50	902	49.10	852	46.69	802	44.26	752
53.84	951	51.45	901	49.05	851	46.64	801	44.21	751

Perf.	Points	Perf.	Points	Perf.	Points	Perf.	Points	Perf.	Points
44.16	750	41.72	700	39.26	650	36.79	600	34.30	550
44.11	749	41.67	699	39.21	649	36.74	599	34.25	549
44.06	748	41.62	698	39.16	648	36.69	598	34.20	548
44.02	747	41.57	697	39.12	647	36.64	597	34.15	547
43.97	746	41.52	696	39.07	646	36.59	596	34.10	546
43.92	745	41.48	695	39.02	645	36.54	595	34.05	545
43.87	744	41.43	694	38.97	644	36.49	594	33.99	544
43.82	743	41.38	693	38.92	643	36.44	593	33.94	543
43.77	742	41.33	692	38.87	642	36.39	592	33.89	542
43.72	741	41.28	691	38.82	641	36.34	591	33.84	541
43.67	740	41.23	690	38.77	640	36.29	590	33.79	540
43.63	739	41.18	689	38.72	639	36.24	589	33.74	539
43.58	738	41.13	688	38.67	638	36.19	588	33.69	538
43.53	737	41.08	687	38.62	637	36.14	587	33.64	537
43.48	736	41.03	686	38.57	636	36.09	586	33.59	536
43.43	735	40.99	685	38.52	635	36.04	585	33.54	535
43.38	734	40.94	684	38.47	634	35.99	584	33.49	534
43.33	733	40.89	683	38.42	633	35.94	583	33.44	533
43.28	732	40.84	682	38.37	632	35.89	582	33.39	532
43.24	731	40.79	681	38.33	631	35.84	581	33.34	531
43.19	730	40.74	680	38.28	630	35.79	580	33.29	530
43.14	729	40.69	679	38.23	629	35.74	579	33.24	529
43.09	728	40.64	678	38.18	628	35.69	578	33.19	528
43.04	727	40.59	677	38.13	627	35.64	577	33.14	527
42.99	726	40.54	676	38.08	626	35.59	576	33.09	526
42.94	725	40.49	675	38.03	625	35.54	575	33.04	525
42.89	724	40.44	674	37.98	624	35.49	574	32.99	524
42.85	723	40.40	673	37.93	623	35.44	573	32.94	523
42.80	722	40.35	672	37.88	622	35.39	572	32.89	522
42.75	721	40.30	671	37.83	621	35.35	571	32.84	521
42.70	720	40.25	670	37.78	620	35.30	570	32.79	520
42.65	719	40.20	669	37.73	619	35.25	569	32.74	519
42.60	718	40.15	668	37.68	618	35.20	568	32.69	518
42.55	717	40.10	667	37.63	617	35.15	567	32.64	517
42.50	716	40.05	666	37.58	616	35.10	566	32.59	516
42.45	715	40.00	665	37.53	615	35.05	565	32.54	515
42.41	714	39.95	664	37.48	614	35.00	564	32.49	514
42.36	713	39.90	663	37.43	613	34.95	563	32.44	513
42.31	712	39.85	662	37.38	612	34.90	562	32.39	512
42.26	711	39.81	661	37.33	611	34.85	561	32.34	511
42.21	710	39.76	660	37.29	610	34.80	560	32.29	510
42.16	709	39.71	659	37.24	609	34.75	559	32.24	509
42.11	708	39.66	658	37.19	608	34.70	558	32.19	508
42.06	707	39.61	657	37.14	607	34.65	557	32.13	507
42.01	706	39.56	656	37.09	606	34.60	556	32.08	506
41.97	705	39.51	655	37.04	605	34.55	555	32.03	505
41.92	704	39.46	654	36.99	604	34.50	554	31.98	504
41.87	703	39.41	653	36.94	603	34.45	553	31.93	503
41.82	702	39.36	652	36.89	602	34.40	552	31.88	502
41.77	701	39.31	651	36.84	601	34.35	551	31.83	501

Perf.	Points	Perf.	Points	Perf.	Points	Perf.	Points	Perf.	Points
31.78	500	29.24	450	26.68	400	24.09	350	21.46	300
31.73	499	29.19	449	26.63	399	24.04	349	21.41	299
31.68	498	29.14	448	26.58	398	23.98	348	21.36	298
31.63	497	29.09	447	26.53	397	23.93	347	21.30	297
31.58	496	29.04	446	26.48	396	23.88	346	21.25	296
31.53	495	28.99	445	26.42	395	23.83	345	21.20	295
31.48	494	28.94	444	26.37	394	23.78	344	21.15	294
31.43	493	28.89	443	26.32	393	23.72	343	21.09	293
31.38	492	28.84	442	26.27	392	23.67	342	21.04	292
31.33	491	28.79	441	26.22	391	23.62	341	20.99	291
31.28	490	28.73	440	26.17	390	23.57	340	20.93	290
31.23	489	28.68	439	26.11	389	23.51	339	20.88	289
31.17	488	28.63	438	26.06	388	23.46	338	20.83	288
31.12	487	28.58	437	26.01	387	23.41	337	20.77	287
31.07	486	28.53	436	25.96	386	23.36	336	20.72	286
31.02	485	28.48	435	25.91	385	23.31	335	20.67	285
30.97	484	28.43	434	25.86	384	23.25	334	20.61	284
30.92	483	28.38	433	25.80	383	23.20	333	20.56	283
30.87	482	28.32	432	25.75	382	23.15	332	20.51	282
30.82	481	28.27	431	25.70	381	23.10	331	20.45	281
30.77	480	28.22	430	25.65	380	23.04	330	20.40	280
30.72	479	28.17	429	25.60	379	22.99	329	20.35	279
30.67	478	28.12	428	25.54	378	22.94	328	20.30	278
30.62	477	28.07	427	25.49	377	22.89	327	20.24	277
30.57	476	28.02	426	25.44	376	22.83	326	20.19	276
30.52	475	27.97	425	25.39	375	22.78	325	20.14	275
30.47	474	27.92	424	25.34	374	22.73	324	20.08	274
30.41	473	27.86	423	25.29	373	22.68	323	20.03	273
30.36	472	27.81	422	25.23	372	22.62	322	19.98	272
30.31	471	27.76	421	25.18	371	22.57	321	19.92	271
30.26	470	27.71	420	25.13	370	22.52	320	19.87	270
30.21	469	27.66	419	25.08	369	22.47	319	19.82	269
30.16	468	27.61	418	25.03	368	22.41	318	19.76	268
30.11	467	27.56	417	24.97	367	22.36	317	19.71	267
30.06	466	27.50	416	24.92	366	22.31	316	19.65	266
30.01	465	27.45	415	24.87	365	22.25	315	19.60	265
29.96	464	27.40	414	24.82	364	22.20	314	19.55	264
29.91	463	27.35	413	24.77	363	22.15	313	19.49	263
29.86	462	27.30	412	24.71	362	22.10	312	19.44	262
29.80	461	27.25	411	24.66	361	22.04	311	19.39	261
29.75	460	27.20	410	24.61	360	21.99	310	19.33	260
29.70	459	27.14	409	24.56	359	21.94	309	19.28	259
29.65	458	27.09	408	24.51	358	21.89	308	19.23	258
29.60	457	27.04	407	24.45	357	21.83	307	19.17	257
29.55	456	26.99	406	24.40	356	21.78	306	19.12	256
29.50	455	26.94	405	24.35	355	21.73	305	19.07	255
29.45	454	26.89	404	24.30	354	21.67	304	19.01	254
29.40	453	26.84	403	24.25	353	21.62	303	18.96	253
29.35	452	26.78	402	24.19	352	21.57	302	18.90	252
29.30	451	26.73	401	24.14	351	21.52	301	18.85	251

Perf.	Points	Perf.	Points	Perf.	Points	Perf.	Points	Perf.	Points
18.80	250	16.08	200	13.30	150	10.44	100	7.43	50
18.74	249	16.03	199	13.25	149	10.38	99	7.37	49
18.69	248	15.97	198	13.19	148	10.32	98	7.30	48
18.64	247	15.92	197	13.13	147	10.26	97	7.24	47
18.58	246	15.86	196	13.08	146	10.20	96	7.18	46
18.53	245	15.81	195	13.02	145	10.14	95	7.12	45
18.47	244	15.75	194	12.96	144	10.08	94	7.05	44
18.42	243	15.70	193	12.91	143	10.03	93	6.99	43
18.37	242	15.64	192	12.85	142	9.97	92	6.93	42
18.31	241	15.59	191	12.79	141	9.91	91	6.86	41
18.26	240	15.53	190	12.74	140	9.85	90	6.80	40
18.20	239	15.48	189	12.68	139	9.79	89	6.74	39
18.15	238	15.42	188	12.62	138	9.73	88	6.67	38
18.10	237	15.36	187	12.57	137	9.67	87	6.61	37
18.04	236	15.31	186	12.51	136	9.61	86	6.55	36
17.99	235	15.25	185	12.45	135	9.55	85	6.48	35
17.93	234	15.20	184	12.40	134	9.49	84	6.42	34
17.88	233	15.14	183	12.34	133	9.43	83	6.35	33
17.83	232	15.09	182	12.28	132	9.37	82	6.29	32
17.77	231	15.03	181	12.22	131	9.31	81	6.22	31
17.72	230	14.98	180	12.17	130	9.25	80	6.16	30
17.66	229	14.92	179	12.11	129	9.20	79	6.09	29
17.61	228	14.87	178	12.05	128	9.14	78	6.03	28
17.55	227	14.81	177	12.00	127	9.08	77	5.96	27
17.50	226	14.76	176	11.94	126	9.02	76	5.89	26
17.45	225	14.70	175	11.88	125	8.96	75	5.83	25
17.39	224	14.64	174	11.82	124	8.90	74	5.76	24
17.34	223	14.59	173	11.77	123	8.84	73	5.70	23
17.28	222	14.53	172	11.71	122	8.78	72	5.63	22
17.23	221	14.48	171	11.65	121	8.72	71	5.56	21
17.17	220	14.42	170	11.59	120	8.65	70	5.49	20
17.12	219	14.37	169	11.54	119	8.59	69	5.43	19
17.06	218	14.31	168	11.48	118	8.53	68	5.36	18
17.01	217	14.25	167	11.42	117	8.47	67	5.29	17
16.96	216	14.20	166	11.36	116	8.41	66	5.22	16
16.90	215	14.14	165	11.31	115	8.35	65	5.15	15
16.85	214	14.09	164	11.25	114	8.29	64	5.08	14
16.79	213	14.03	163	11.19	113	8.23	63	5.01	13
16.74	212	13.98	162	11.13	112	8.17	62	4.94	12
16.68	211	13.92	161	11.08	111	8.11	61	4.87	11
16.63	210	13.86	160	11.02	110	8.05	60	4.80	10
16.57	209	13.81	159	10.96	109	7.99	59	4.73	9
16.52	208	13.75	158	10.90	108	7.92	58	4.65	8
16.46	207	13.70	157	10.84	107	7.86	57	4.58	7
16.41	206	13.64	156	10.79	106	7.80	56	4.50	6
16.35	205	13.58	155	10.73	105	7.74	55	4.43	5
16.30	204	13.53	154	10.67	104	7.68	54	4.35	4
16.25	203	13.47	153	10.61	103	7.62	53	4.27	3
16.19	202	13.41	152	10.55	102	7.55	52	4.19	2
16.14	201	13.36	151	10.49	101	7.49	51	4.10	1

Metres	Points	Metres	Points	Metres	Points	Metres	Points	Metres	Points
5.99	1227	5.49	1064	4.99	907	4.49	757	3.99	614
5.98	1224	5.48	1061	4.98	904	4.48	754	3.98	612
5.97	1221	5.47	1058	4.97	901	4.47	751	3.97	609
5.96	1217	5.46	1055	4.96	898	4.46	748	3.96	606
5.95	1214	5.45	1051	4.95	895	4.45	746	3.95	603
5.94	1211	5.44	1048	4.94	892	4.44	743	3.94	601
5.93	1207	5.43	1045	4.93	889	4.43	740	3.93	598
5.92	1204	5.42	1042	4.92	886	4.42	737	3.92	595
5.91	1201	5.41	1039	4.91	883	4.41	734	3.91	592
5.90	1198	5.40	1035	4.90	880	4.40	731	3.90	590
5.89	1194	5.39	1032	4.89	877	4.39	728	3.89	587
5.88	1191	5.38	1029	4.88	874	4.38	725	3.88	584
5.87	1188	5.37	1026	4.87	871	4.37	722	3.87	581
5.86	1184	5.36	1023	4.86	868	4.36	719	3.86	579
5.85	1181	5.35	1020	4.85	865	4.35	716	3.85	576
5.84	1178	5.34	1016	4.84	862	4.34	714	3.84	573
5.83	1174	5.33	1013	4.83	859	4.33	711	3.83	570
5.82	1171	5.32	1010	4.82	856	4.32	708	3.82	568
5.81	1168	5.31	1007	4.81	852	4.31	705	3.81	565
5.80	1165	5.30	1004	4.80	849	4.30	702	3.80	562
5.79	1161	5.29	1001	4.79	846	4.29	699	3.79	560
5.78	1158	5.28	998	4.78	843	4.28	696	3.78	557
5.77	1155	5.27	994	4.77	840	4.27	693	3.77	554
5.76	1152	5.26	991	4.76	837	4.26	691	3.76	551
5.75	1148	5.25	988	4.75	834	4.25	688	3.75	549
5.74	1145	5.24	985	4.74	831	4.24	685	3.74	546
5.73	1142	5.23	982	4.73	828	4.23	682	3.73	543
5.72	1138	5.22	979	4.72	825	4.22	679	3.72	541
5.71	1135	5.21	976	4.71	822	4.21	676	3.71	538
5.70	1132	5.20	972	4.70	819	4.20	673	3.70	535
5.69	1129	5.19	969	4.69	816	4.19	671	3.69	533
5.68	1125	5.18	966	4.68	813	4.18	668	3.68	530
5.67	1122	5.17	963	4.67	810	4.17	665	3.67	527
5.66	1119	5.16	960	4.66	807	4.16	662	3.66	525
5.65	1116	5.15	957	4.65	804	4.15	659	3.65	522
5.64	1112	5.14	954	4.64	802	4.14	656	3.64	519
5.63	1109	5.13	951	4.63	799	4.13	654	3.63	517
5.62	1106	5.12	947	4.62	796	4.12	651	3.62	514
5.61	1103	5.11	944	4.61	793	4.11	648	3.61	511
5.60	1100	5.10	941	4.60	790	4.10	645	3.60	509
5.59	1096	5.09	938	4.59	787	4.09	642	3.59	506
5.58	1093	5.08	935	4.58	784	4.08	640	3.58	503
5.57	1090	5.07	932	4.57	781	4.07	637	3.57	501
5.56	1087	5.06	929	4.56	778	4.06	634	3.56	498
5.55	1083	5.05	926	4.55	775	4.05	631	3.55	496
5.54	1080	5.04	923	4.54	772	4.04	628	3.54	493
5.53	1077	5.03	920	4.53	769	4.03	626	3.53	490
5.52	1074	5.02	917	4.52	766	4.02	623	3.52	488
5.51	1071	5.01	913	4.51	763	4.01	620	3.51	485
5.50	1067	5.00	910	4.50	760	4.00	617	3.50	482

Metres	Points	Metres	Points	Metres	Points	Metres	Points	Metres	Points
3.49	480	2.99	354	2.49	240	1.99	138	1.49	53
3.48	477	2.98	352	2.48	237	1.98	136	1.48	52
3.47	475	2.97	350	2.47	235	1.97	134	1.47	50
3.46	472	2.96	347	2.46	233	1.96	132	1.46	49
3.45	469	2.95	345	2.45	231	1.95	130	1.45	47
3.44	467	2.94	342	2.44	229	1.94	128	1.44	46
3.43	464	2.93	340	2.43	227	1.93	127	1.43	44
3.42	462	2.92	338	2.42	225	1.92	125	1.42	43
3.41	459	2.91	335	2.41	222	1.91	123	1.41	42
3.40	457	2.90	333	2.40	220	1.90	121	1.40	40
3.39	454	2.89	331	2.39	218	1.89	119	1.39	39
3.38	451	2.88	328	2.38	216	1.88	117	1.38	37
3.37	449	2.87	326	2.37	214	1.87	116	1.37	36
3.36	446	2.86	323	2.36	212	1.86	114	1.36	35
3.35	444	2.85	321	2.35	210	1.85	112	1.35	33
3.34	441	2.84	319	2.34	208	1.84	110	1.34	32
3.33	439	2.83	316	2.33	206	1.83	109	1.33	31
3.32	436	2.82	314	2.32	203	1.82	107	1.32	30
3.31	434	2.81	312	2.31	201	1.81	105	1.31	28
3.30	431	2.80	309	2.30	199	1.80	103	1.30	27
3.29	429	2.79	307	2.29	197	1.79	101	1.29	26
3.28	426	2.78	305	2.28	195	1.78	100	1.28	25
3.27	423	2.77	303	2.27	193	1.77	98	1.27	23
3.26	421	2.76	300	2.26	191	1.76	96	1.26	22
3.25	418	2.75	298	2.25	189	1.75	95	1.25	21
3.24	416	2.74	296	2.24	187	1.74	93	1.24	20
3.23	413	2.73	293	2.23	185	1.73	91	1.23	19
3.22	411	2.72	291	2.22	183	1.72	89	1.22	18
3.21	408	2.71	289	2.21	181	1.71	88	1.21	17
3.20	406	2.70	286	2.20	179	1.70	86	1.20	15
3.19	403	2.69	284	2.19	177	1.69	84	1.19	14
3.18	401	2.68	282	2.18	175	1.68	83	1.18	13
3.17	398	2.67	280	2.17	173	1.67	81	1.17	12
3.16	396	2.66	277	2.16	171	1.66	79	1.16	11
3.15	393	2.65	275	2.15	169	1.65	78	1.15	10
3.14	391	2.64	273	2.14	167	1.64	76	1.14	9
3.13	389	2.63	271	2.13	165	1.63	75	1.12	8
3.12	386	2.62	268	2.12	163	1.62	73	1.11	7
3.11	384	2.61	266	2.11	161	1.61	71	1.10	6
3.10	381	2.60	264	2.10	159	1.60	70	1.09	5
3.09	379	2.59	262	2.09	157	1.59	68	1.08	4
3.08	376	2.58	259	2.08	155	1.58	67	1.06	3
3.07	374	2.57	257	2.07	153	1.57	65	1.05	2
3.06	371	2.56	255	2.06	151	1.56	64	1.03	1
3.05	369	2.55	253	2.05	149	1.55	62		
3.04	367	2.54	251	2.04	147	1.54	61		
3.03	364	2.53	248	2.03	145	1.53	59		
3.02	362	2.52	246	2.02	143	1.52	57		
3.01	359	2.51	244	2.01	142	1.51	56		
3.00	357	2.50	242	2.00	140	1.50	54		

Perf.	Points	Perf.	Points	Perf.	Points	Perf.	Points	Perf.	Points
102.85	1400	99.68	1350	96.49	1300	93.30	1250	90.10	1200
102.79	1399	99.61	1349	96.43	1299	93.24	1249	90.04	1199
102.72	1398	99.55	1348	96.37	1298	93.17	1248	89.97	1198
102.66	1397	99.48	1347	96.30	1297	93.11	1247	89.91	1197
102.60	1396	99.42	1346	96.24	1296	93.05	1246	89.84	1196
102.53	1395	99.36	1345	96.17	1295	92.98	1245	89.78	1195
102.47	1394	99.29	1344	96.11	1294	92.92	1244	89.72	1194
102.41	1393	99.23	1343	96.05	1293	92.85	1243	89.65	1193
102.34	1392	99.17	1342	95.98	1292	92.79	1242	89.59	1192
102.28	1391	99.10	1341	95.92	1291	92.73	1241	89.52	1191
102.21	1390	99.04	1340	95.86	1290	92.66	1240	89.46	1190
102.15	1389	98.98	1339	95.79	1289	92.60	1239	89.39	1189
102.09	1388	98.91	1338	95.73	1288	92.53	1238	89.33	1188
102.02	1387	98.85	1337	95.66	1287	92.47	1237	89.27	1187
101.96	1386	98.79	1336	95.60	1286	92.41	1236	89.20	1186
101.90	1385	98.72	1335	95.54	1285	92.34	1235	89.14	1185
101.83	1384	98.66	1334	95.47	1284	92.28	1234	89.07	1184
101.77	1383	98.59	1333	95.41	1283	92.21	1233	89.01	1183
101.71	1382	98.53	1332	95.35	1282	92.15	1232	88.95	1182
101.64	1381	98.47	1331	95.28	1281	92.09	1231	88.88	1181
101.58	1380	98.40	1330	95.22	1280	92.02	1230	88.82	1180
101.52	1379	98.34	1329	95.15	1279	91.96	1229	88.75	1179
101.45	1378	98.28	1328	95.09	1278	91.89	1228	88.69	1178
101.39	1377	98.21	1327	95.03	1277	91.83	1227	88.62	1177
101.33	1376	98.15	1326	94.96	1276	91.77	1226	88.56	1176
101.26	1375	98.09	1325	94.90	1275	91.70	1225	88.50	1175
101.20	1374	98.02	1324	94.83	1274	91.64	1224	88.43	1174
101.14	1373	97.96	1323	94.77	1273	91.57	1223	88.37	1173
101.07	1372	97.89	1322	94.71	1272	91.51	1222	88.30	1172
101.01	1371	97.83	1321	94.64	1271	91.45	1221	88.24	1171
100.95	1370	97.77	1320	94.58	1270	91.38	1220	88.18	1170
100.88	1369	97.70	1319	94.52	1269	91.32	1219	88.11	1169
100.82	1368	97.64	1318	94.45	1268	91.25	1218	88.05	1168
100.76	1367	97.58	1317	94.39	1267	91.19	1217	87.98	1167
100.69	1366	97.51	1316	94.32	1266	91.13	1216	87.92	1166
100.63	1365	97.45	1315	94.26	1265	91.06	1215	87.85	1165
100.56	1364	97.38	1314	94.20	1264	91.00	1214	87.79	1164
100.50	1363	97.32	1313	94.13	1263	90.93	1213	87.73	1163
100.44	1362	97.26	1312	94.07	1262	90.87	1212	87.66	1162
100.37	1361	97.19	1311	94.00	1261	90.81	1211	87.60	1161
100.31	1360	97.13	1310	93.94	1260	90.74	1210	87.53	1160
100.25	1359	97.07	1309	93.88	1259	90.68	1209	87.47	1159
100.18	1358	97.00	1308	93.81	1258	90.61	1208	87.40	1158
100.12	1357	96.94	1307	93.75	1257	90.55	1207	87.34	1157
100.06	1356	96.88	1306	93.68	1256	90.49	1206	87.28	1156
99.99	1355	96.81	1305	93.62	1255	90.42	1205	87.21	1155
99.93	1354	96.75	1304	93.56	1254	90.36	1204	87.15	1154
99.87	1353	96.68	1303	93.49	1253	90.29	1203	87.08	1153
99.80	1352	96.62	1302	93.43	1252	90.23	1202	87.02	1152
99.74	1351	96.56	1301	93.37	1251	90.16	1201	86.95	1151

Perf.	Points	Perf.	Points	Perf.	Points	Perf.	Points	Perf.	Points
86.89	1150	83.67	1100	80.44	1050	77.19	1000	73.94	950
86.83	1149	83.60	1099	80.37	1049	77.13	999	73.87	949
86.76	1148	83.54	1098	80.31	1048	77.06	998	73.81	948
86.70	1147	83.47	1097	80.24	1047	77.00	997	73.74	947
86.63	1146	83.41	1096	80.18	1046	76.93	996	73.68	946
86.57	1145	83.35	1095	80.11	1045	76.87	995	73.61	945
86.50	1144	83.28	1094	80.05	1044	76.80	994	73.55	944
86.44	1143	83.22	1093	79.98	1043	76.74	993	73.48	943
86.37	1142	83.15	1092	79.92	1042	76.67	992	73.42	942
86.31	1141	83.09	1091	79.85	1041	76.61	991	73.35	941
86.25	1140	83.02	1090	79.79	1040	76.54	990	73.28	940
86.18	1139	82.96	1089	79.72	1039	76.48	989	73.22	939
86.12	1138	82.89	1088	79.66	1038	76.41	988	73.15	938
86.05	1137	82.83	1087	79.59	1037	76.35	987	73.09	937
85.99	1136	82.76	1086	79.53	1036	76.28	986	73.02	936
85.92	1135	82.70	1085	79.46	1035	76.22	985	72.96	935
85.86	1134	82.64	1084	79.40	1034	76.15	984	72.89	934
85.80	1133	82.57	1083	79.33	1033	76.09	983	72.83	933
85.73	1132	82.51	1082	79.27	1032	76.02	982	72.76	932
85.67	1131	82.44	1081	79.21	1031	75.96	981	72.70	931
85.60	1130	82.38	1080	79.14	1030	75.89	980	72.63	930
85.54	1129	82.31	1079	79.08	1029	75.83	979	72.57	929
85.47	1128	82.25	1078	79.01	1028	75.76	978	72.50	928
85.41	1127	82.18	1077	78.95	1027	75.70	977	72.44	927
85.34	1126	82.12	1076	78.88	1026	75.63	976	72.37	926
85.28	1125	82.05	1075	78.82	1025	75.57	975	72.30	925
85.22	1124	81.99	1074	78.75	1024	75.50	974	72.24	924
85.15	1123	81.92	1073	78.69	1023	75.44	973	72.17	923
85.09	1122	81.86	1072	78.62	1022	75.37	972	72.11	922
85.02	1121	81.80	1071	78.56	1021	75.31	971	72.04	921
84.96	1120	81.73	1070	78.49	1020	75.24	970	71.98	920
84.89	1119	81.67	1069	78.43	1019	75.18	969	71.91	919
84.83	1118	81.60	1068	78.36	1018	75.11	968	71.85	918
84.76	1117	81.54	1067	78.30	1017	75.05	967	71.78	917
84.70	1116	81.47	1066	78.23	1016	74.98	966	71.72	916
84.64	1115	81.41	1065	78.17	1015	74.92	965	71.65	915
84.57	1114	81.34	1064	78.10	1014	74.85	964	71.59	914
84.51	1113	81.28	1063	78.04	1013	74.78	963	71.52	913
84.44	1112	81.21	1062	77.97	1012	74.72	962	71.45	912
84.38	1111	81.15	1061	77.91	1011	74.65	961	71.39	911
84.31	1110	81.08	1060	77.84	1010	74.59	960	71.32	910
84.25	1109	81.02	1059	77.78	1009	74.52	959	71.26	909
84.18	1108	80.95	1058	77.71	1008	74.46	958	71.19	908
84.12	1107	80.89	1057	77.65	1007	74.39	957	71.13	907
84.06	1106	80.82	1056	77.58	1006	74.33	956	71.06	906
83.99	1105	80.76	1055	77.52	1005	74.26	955	71.00	905
83.93	1104	80.70	1054	77.45	1004	74.20	954	70.93	904
83.86	1103	80.63	1053	77.39	1003	74.13	953	70.87	903
83.80	1102	80.57	1052	77.32	1002	74.07	952	70.80	902
83.73	1101	80.50	1051	77.26	1001	74.00	951	70.73	901

Perf.	Points	Perf.	Points	Perf.	Points	Perf.	Points	Perf.	Points
70.67	900	67.39	850	64.09	800	60.78	750	57.45	700
70.60	899	67.32	849	64.02	799	60.71	749	57.39	699
70.54	898	67.26	848	63.96	798	60.65	748	57.32	698
70.47	897	67.19	847	63.89	797	60.58	747	57.25	697
70.41	896	67.12	846	63.83	796	60.51	746	57.18	696
70.34	895	67.06	845	63.76	795	60.45	745	57.12	695
70.28	894	66.99	844	63.69	794	60.38	744	57.05	694
70.21	893	66.93	843	63.63	793	60.31	743	56.98	693
70.14	892	66.86	842	63.56	792	60.25	742	56.92	692
70.08	891	66.79	841	63.50	791	60.18	741	56.85	691
70.01	890	66.73	840	63.43	790	60.12	740	56.78	690
69.95	889	66.66	839	63.36	789	60.05	739	56.72	689
69.88	888	66.60	838	63.30	788	59.98	738	56.65	688
69.82	887	66.53	837	63.23	787	59.92	737	56.58	687
69.75	886	66.47	836	63.17	786	59.85	736	56.52	686
69.69	885	66.40	835	63.10	785	59.78	735	56.45	685
69.62	884	66.33	834	63.03	784	59.72	734	56.38	684
69.55	883	66.27	833	62.97	783	59.65	733	56.32	683
69.49	882	66.20	832	62.90	782	59.58	732	56.25	682
69.42	881	66.14	831	62.83	781	59.52	731	56.18	681
69.36	880	66.07	830	62.77	780	59.45	730	56.12	680
69.29	879	66.00	829	62.70	779	59.38	729	56.05	679
69.23	878	65.94	828	62.64	778	59.32	728	55.98	678
69.16	877	65.87	827	62.57	777	59.25	727	55.92	677
69.10	876	65.81	826	62.50	776	59.18	726	55.85	676
69.03	875	65.74	825	62.44	775	59.12	725	55.78	675
68.96	874	65.67	824	62.37	774	59.05	724	55.71	674
68.90	873	65.61	823	62.30	773	58.98	723	55.65	673
68.83	872	65.54	822	62.24	772	58.92	722	55.58	672
68.77	871	65.48	821	62.17	771	58.85	721	55.51	671
68.70	870	65.41	820	62.11	770	58.78	720	55.45	670
68.64	869	65.35	819	62.04	769	58.72	719	55.38	669
68.57	868	65.28	818	61.97	768	58.65	718	55.31	668
68.50	867	65.21	817	61.91	767	58.59	717	55.25	667
68.44	866	65.15	816	61.84	766	58.52	716	55.18	666
68.37	865	65.08	815	61.77	765	58.45	715	55.11	665
68.31	864	65.02	814	61.71	764	58.39	714	55.04	664
68.24	863	64.95	813	61.64	763	58.32	713	54.98	663
68.18	862	64.88	812	61.58	762	58.25	712	54.91	662
68.11	861	64.82	811	61.51	761	58.19	711	54.84	661
68.04	860	64.75	810	61.44	760	58.12	710	54.78	660
67.98	859	64.69	809	61.38	759	58.05	709	54.71	659
67.91	858	64.62	808	61.31	758	57.99	708	54.64	658
67.85	857	64.55	807	61.24	757	57.92	707	54.58	657
67.78	856	64.49	806	61.18	756	57.85	706	54.51	656
67.72	855	64.42	805	61.11	755	57.79	705	54.44	655
67.65	854	64.36	804	61.05	754	57.72	704	54.37	654
67.58	853	64.29	803	60.98	753	57.65	703	54.31	653
67.52	852	64.22	802	60.91	752	57.59	702	54.24	652
67.45	851	64.16	801	60.85	751	57.52	701	54.17	651

Perf.	Points	Perf.	Points	Perf.	Points	Perf.	Points	Perf.	Points
54.11	650	50.74	600	47.36	550	43.95	500	40.51	450
54.04	649	50.67	599	47.29	549	43.88	499	40.45	449
53.97	648	50.61	598	47.22	548	43.81	498	40.38	448
53.90	647	50.54	597	47.15	547	43.74	497	40.31	447
53.84	646	50.47	596	47.08	546	43.67	496	40.24	446
53.77	645	50.40	595	47.02	545	43.61	495	40.17	445
53.70	644	50.34	594	46.95	544	43.54	494	40.10	444
53.64	643	50.27	593	46.88	543	43.47	493	40.03	443
53.57	642	50.20	592	46.81	542	43.40	492	39.96	442
53.50	641	50.13	591	46.74	541	43.33	491	39.89	441
53.43	640	50.07	590	46.68	540	43.26	490	39.82	440
53.37	639	50.00	589	46.61	539	43.19	489	39.75	439
53.30	638	49.93	588	46.54	538	43.13	488	39.69	438
53.23	637	49.86	587	46.47	537	43.06	487	39.62	437
53.17	636	49.80	586	46.40	536	42.99	486	39.55	436
53.10	635	49.73	585	46.34	535	42.92	485	39.48	435
53.03	634	49.66	584	46.27	534	42.85	484	39.41	434
52.96	633	49.59	583	46.20	533	42.78	483	39.34	433
52.90	632	49.53	582	46.13	532	42.71	482	39.27	432
52.83	631	49.46	581	46.06	531	42.65	481	39.20	431
52.76	630	49.39	580	46.00	530	42.58	480	39.13	430
52.70	629	49.32	579	45.93	529	42.51	479	39.06	429
52.63	628	49.25	578	45.86	528	42.44	478	38.99	428
52.56	627	49.19	577	45.79	527	42.37	477	38.93	427
52.49	626	49.12	576	45.72	526	42.30	476	38.86	426
52.43	625	49.05	575	45.65	525	42.23	475	38.79	425
52.36	624	48.98	574	45.59	524	42.17	474	38.72	424
52.29	623	48.92	573	45.52	523	42.10	473	38.65	423
52.22	622	48.85	572	45.45	522	42.03	472	38.58	422
52.16	621	48.78	571	45.38	521	41.96	471	38.51	421
52.09	620	48.71	570	45.31	520	41.89	470	38.44	420
52.02	619	48.65	569	45.25	519	41.82	469	38.37	419
51.96	618	48.58	568	45.18	518	41.75	468	38.30	418
51.89	617	48.51	567	45.11	517	41.68	467	38.23	417
51.82	616	48.44	566	45.04	516	41.62	466	38.16	416
51.75	615	48.37	565	44.97	515	41.55	465	38.09	415
51.69	614	48.31	564	44.90	514	41.48	464	38.02	414
51.62	613	48.24	563	44.84	513	41.41	463	37.95	413
51.55	612	48.17	562	44.77	512	41.34	462	37.89	412
51.48	611	48.10	561	44.70	511	41.27	461	37.82	411
51.42	610	48.04	560	44.63	510	41.20	460	37.75	410
51.35	609	47.97	559	44.56	509	41.13	459	37.68	409
51.28	608	47.90	558	44.49	508	41.07	458	37.61	408
51.21	607	47.83	557	44.43	507	41.00	457	37.54	407
51.15	606	47.76	556	44.36	506	40.93	456	37.47	406
51.08	605	47.70	555	44.29	505	40.86	455	37.40	405
51.01	604	47.63	554	44.22	504	40.79	454	37.33	404
50.94	603	47.56	553	44.15	503	40.72	453	37.26	403
50.88	602	47.49	552	44.08	502	40.65	452	37.19	402
50.81	601	47.42	551	44.02	501	40.58	451	37.12	401

Men Javelin Throw - Lancer du Javelot Hommes

Perf.	Points	Perf.	Points	Perf.	Points	Perf.	Points	Perf.	Points
37.05	400	33.56	350	30.03	300	26.45	250	22.82	200
36.98	399	33.49	349	29.95	299	26.38	249	22.75	199
36.91	398	33.42	348	29.88	298	26.31	248	22.67	198
36.84	397	33.35	347	29.81	297	26.23	247	22.60	197
36.77	396	33.28	346	29.74	296	26.16	246	22.53	196
36.70	395	33.21	345	29.67	295	26.09	245	22.45	195
36.63	394	33.14	344	29.60	294	26.02	244	22.38	194
36.56	393	33.07	343	29.53	293	25.94	243	22.31	193
36.49	392	32.99	342	29.46	292	25.87	242	22.23	192
36.43	391	32.92	341	29.39	291	25.80	241	22.16	191
36.36	390	32.85	340	29.31	290	25.73	240	22.09	190
36.29	389	32.78	339	29.24	289	25.66	239	22.01	189
36.22	388	32.71	338	29.17	288	25.58	238	21.94	188
36.15	387	32.64	337	29.10	287	25.51	237	21.87	187
36.08	386	32.57	336	29.03	286	25.44	236	21.79	186
36.01	385	32.50	335	28.96	285	25.37	235	21.72	185
35.94	384	32.43	334	28.89	284	25.29	234	21.64	184
35.87	383	32.36	333	28.82	283	25.22	233	21.57	183
35.80	382	32.29	332	28.74	282	25.15	232	21.50	182
35.73	381	32.22	331	28.67	281	25.08	231	21.42	181
35.66	380	32.15	330	28.60	280	25.00	230	21.35	180
35.59	379	32.08	329	28.53	279	24.93	229	21.28	179
35.52	378	32.01	328	28.46	278	24.86	228	21.20	178
35.45	377	31.94	327	28.39	277	24.79	227	21.13	177
35.38	376	31.87	326	28.32	276	24.71	226	21.05	176
35.31	375	31.80	325	28.24	275	24.64	225	20.98	175
35.24	374	31.73	324	28.17	274	24.57	224	20.91	174
35.17	373	31.66	323	28.10	273	24.50	223	20.83	173
35.10	372	31.58	322	28.03	272	24.42	222	20.76	172
35.03	371	31.51	321	27.96	271	24.35	221	20.68	171
34.96	370	31.44	320	27.89	270	24.28	220	20.61	170
34.89	369	31.37	319	27.81	269	24.21	219	20.54	169
34.82	368	31.30	318	27.74	268	24.13	218	20.46	168
34.75	367	31.23	317	27.67	267	24.06	217	20.39	167
34.68	366	31.16	316	27.60	266	23.99	216	20.31	166
34.61	365	31.09	315	27.53	265	23.92	215	20.24	165
34.54	364	31.02	314	27.46	264	23.84	214	20.17	164
34.47	363	30.95	313	27.38	263	23.77	213	20.09	163
34.40	362	30.88	312	27.31	262	23.70	212	20.02	162
34.33	361	30.81	311	27.24	261	23.62	211	19.94	161
34.26	360	30.74	310	27.17	260	23.55	210	19.87	160
34.19	359	30.66	309	27.10	259	23.48	209	19.79	159
34.12	358	30.59	308	27.03	258	23.40	208	19.72	158
34.05	357	30.52	307	26.95	257	23.33	207	19.64	157
33.98	356	30.45	306	26.88	256	23.26	206	19.57	156
33.91	355	30.38	305	26.81	255	23.19	205	19.50	155
33.84	354	30.31	304	26.74	254	23.11	204	19.42	154
33.77	353	30.24	303	26.67	253	23.04	203	19.35	153
33.70	352	30.17	302	26.59	252	22.97	202	19.27	152
33.63	351	30.10	301	26.52	251	22.89	201	19.20	151

Men   **Javelin Throw - Lancer du Javelot**

Perf.	Points	Perf.	Points	Perf.	Points	Perf.	Points	Perf.	Points
19.12	150	16.86	120	14.56	90	12.19	60	9.74	30
19.05	149	16.78	119	14.48	89	12.11	59	9.65	29
18.97	148	16.71	118	14.40	88	12.03	58	9.57	28
18.90	147	16.63	117	14.32	87	11.95	57	9.48	27
18.82	146	16.56	116	14.24	86	11.87	56	9.40	26
18.75	145	16.48	115	14.17	85	11.79	55	9.31	25
18.67	144	16.40	114	14.09	84	11.71	54	9.23	24
18.60	143	16.33	113	14.01	83	11.63	53	9.14	23
18.52	142	16.25	112	13.93	82	11.55	52	9.05	22
18.45	141	16.17	111	13.85	81	11.47	51	8.97	21
18.37	140	16.10	110	13.78	80	11.39	50	8.88	20
18.30	139	16.02	109	13.70	79	11.31	49	8.79	19
18.22	138	15.94	108	13.62	78	11.22	48	8.71	18
18.15	137	15.87	107	13.54	77	11.14	47	8.62	17
18.07	136	15.79	106	13.46	76	11.06	46	8.53	16
18.00	135	15.71	105	13.38	75	10.98	45	8.44	15
17.92	134	15.64	104	13.30	74	10.90	44	8.35	14
17.84	133	15.56	103	13.22	73	10.82	43	8.26	13
17.77	132	15.48	102	13.15	72	10.73	42	8.17	12
17.69	131	15.41	101	13.07	71	10.65	41	8.08	11
17.62	130	15.33	100	12.99	70	10.57	40	7.99	10
17.54	129	15.25	99	12.91	69	10.49	39	7.90	9
17.47	128	15.17	98	12.83	68	10.40	38	7.81	8
17.39	127	15.10	97	12.75	67	10.32	37	7.71	7
17.32	126	15.02	96	12.67	66	10.24	36	7.62	6
17.24	125	14.94	95	12.59	65	10.15	35	7.52	5
17.16	124	14.87	94	12.51	64	10.07	34	7.43	4
17.09	123	14.79	93	12.43	63	9.99	33	7.33	3
17.01	122	14.71	92	12.35	62	9.90	32	7.23	2
16.94	121	14.63	91	12.27	61	9.82	31	7.12	1

Men   1500 metres - 1500 mètres   Hommes

Seconds	Points	Seconds	Points	Seconds	Points	Seconds	Points	Seconds	Points
3:22.35	1249	3:28.42	1199	3:34.60	1149	3:40.90	1099	3:47.34	1049
3:22.47	1248	3:28.54	1198	3:34.72	1148	3:41.03	1098	3:47.47	1048
3:22.59	1247	3:28.66	1197	3:34.85	1147	3:41.16	1097	3:47.60	1047
3:22.71	1246	3:28.78	1196	3:34.97	1146	3:41.29	1096	3:47.73	1046
3:22.83	1245	3:28.91	1195	3:35.10	1145	3:41.41	1095	3:47.86	1045
3:22.95	1244	3:29.03	1194	3:35.22	1144	3:41.54	1094	3:48.00	1044
3:23.07	1243	3:29.15	1193	3:35.35	1143	3:41.67	1093	3:48.13	1043
3:23.19	1242	3:29.27	1192	3:35.47	1142	3:41.80	1092	3:48.26	1042
3:23.31	1241	3:29.40	1191	3:35.60	1141	3:41.93	1091	3:48.39	1041
3:23.43	1240	3:29.52	1190	3:35.72	1140	3:42.05	1090	3:48.52	1040
3:23.56	1239	3:29.64	1189	3:35.85	1139	3:42.18	1089	3:48.65	1039
3:23.68	1238	3:29.77	1188	3:35.97	1138	3:42.31	1088	3:48.78	1038
3:23.80	1237	3:29.89	1187	3:36.10	1137	3:42.44	1087	3:48.91	1037
3:23.92	1236	3:30.01	1186	3:36.22	1136	3:42.57	1086	3:49.04	1036
3:24.04	1235	3:30.13	1185	3:36.35	1135	3:42.69	1085	3:49.17	1035
3:24.16	1234	3:30.26	1184	3:36.48	1134	3:42.82	1084	3:49.30	1034
3:24.28	1233	3:30.38	1183	3:36.60	1133	3:42.95	1083	3:49.43	1033
3:24.40	1232	3:30.50	1182	3:36.73	1132	3:43.08	1082	3:49.57	1032
3:24.52	1231	3:30.63	1181	3:36.85	1131	3:43.21	1081	3:49.70	1031
3:24.64	1230	3:30.75	1180	3:36.98	1130	3:43.33	1080	3:49.83	1030
3:24.76	1229	3:30.87	1179	3:37.10	1129	3:43.46	1079	3:49.96	1029
3:24.88	1228	3:31.00	1178	3:37.23	1128	3:43.59	1078	3:50.09	1028
3:25.01	1227	3:31.12	1177	3:37.36	1127	3:43.72	1077	3:50.22	1027
3:25.13	1226	3:31.24	1176	3:37.48	1126	3:43.85	1076	3:50.35	1026
3:25.25	1225	3:31.37	1175	3:37.61	1125	3:43.98	1075	3:50.48	1025
3:25.37	1224	3:31.49	1174	3:37.73	1124	3:44.11	1074	3:50.62	1024
3:25.49	1223	3:31.62	1173	3:37.86	1123	3:44.24	1073	3:50.75	1023
3:25.61	1222	3:31.74	1172	3:37.99	1122	3:44.36	1072	3:50.88	1022
3:25.73	1221	3:31.86	1171	3:38.11	1121	3:44.49	1071	3:51.01	1021
3:25.86	1220	3:31.99	1170	3:38.24	1120	3:44.62	1070	3:51.14	1020
3:25.98	1219	3:32.11	1169	3:38.37	1119	3:44.75	1069	3:51.28	1019
3:26.10	1218	3:32.23	1168	3:38.49	1118	3:44.88	1068	3:51.41	1018
3:26.22	1217	3:32.36	1167	3:38.62	1117	3:45.01	1067	3:51.54	1017
3:26.34	1216	3:32.48	1166	3:38.75	1116	3:45.14	1066	3:51.67	1016
3:26.46	1215	3:32.61	1165	3:38.87	1115	3:45.27	1065	3:51.80	1015
3:26.58	1214	3:32.73	1164	3:39.00	1114	3:45.40	1064	3:51.94	1014
3:26.71	1213	3:32.85	1163	3:39.13	1113	3:45.53	1063	3:52.07	1013
3:26.83	1212	3:32.98	1162	3:39.25	1112	3:45.66	1062	3:52.20	1012
3:26.95	1211	3:33.10	1161	3:39.38	1111	3:45.79	1061	3:52.33	1011
3:27.07	1210	3:33.23	1160	3:39.51	1110	3:45.92	1060	3:52.47	1010
3:27.19	1209	3:33.35	1159	3:39.63	1109	3:46.04	1059	3:52.60	1009
3:27.32	1208	3:33.48	1158	3:39.76	1108	3:46.17	1058	3:52.73	1008
3:27.44	1207	3:33.60	1157	3:39.89	1107	3:46.30	1057	3:52.86	1007
3:27.56	1206	3:33.72	1156	3:40.01	1106	3:46.43	1056	3:53.00	1006
3:27.68	1205	3:33.85	1155	3:40.14	1105	3:46.56	1055	3:53.13	1005
3:27.80	1204	3:33.97	1154	3:40.27	1104	3:46.69	1054	3:53.26	1004
3:27.93	1203	3:34.10	1153	3:40.39	1103	3:46.82	1053	3:53.39	1003
3:28.05	1202	3:34.22	1152	3:40.52	1102	3:46.95	1052	3:53.53	1002
3:28.17	1201	3:34.35	1151	3:40.65	1101	3:47.08	1051	3:53.66	1001
3:28.29	1200	3:34.47	1150	3:40.78	1100	3:47.21	1050	3:53.79	1000

Seconds	Points	Seconds	Points	Seconds	Points	Seconds	Points	Seconds	Points
3:53.93	999	4:00.66	949	4:07.56	899	4:14.64	849	4:21.92	799
3:54.06	998	4:00.80	948	4:07.70	898	4:14.79	848	4:22.06	798
3:54.19	997	4:00.93	947	4:07.84	897	4:14.93	847	4:22.21	797
3:54.33	996	4:01.07	946	4:07.98	896	4:15.07	846	4:22.36	796
3:54.46	995	4:01.21	945	4:08.12	895	4:15.22	845	4:22.51	795
3:54.59	994	4:01.34	944	4:08.26	894	4:15.36	844	4:22.65	794
3:54.73	993	4:01.48	943	4:08.40	893	4:15.50	843	4:22.80	793
3:54.86	992	4:01.62	942	4:08.54	892	4:15.65	842	4:22.95	792
3:54.99	991	4:01.75	941	4:08.68	891	4:15.79	841	4:23.10	791
3:55.13	990	4:01.89	940	4:08.82	890	4:15.94	840	4:23.25	790
3:55.26	989	4:02.03	939	4:08.96	889	4:16.08	839	4:23.40	789
3:55.39	988	4:02.17	938	4:09.10	888	4:16.23	838	4:23.54	788
3:55.53	987	4:02.30	937	4:09.24	887	4:16.37	837	4:23.69	787
3:55.66	986	4:02.44	936	4:09.39	886	4:16.51	836	4:23.84	786
3:55.80	985	4:02.58	935	4:09.53	885	4:16.66	835	4:23.99	785
3:55.93	984	4:02.71	934	4:09.67	884	4:16.80	834	4:24.14	784
3:56.06	983	4:02.85	933	4:09.81	883	4:16.95	833	4:24.29	783
3:56.20	982	4:02.99	932	4:09.95	882	4:17.09	832	4:24.44	782
3:56.33	981	4:03.13	931	4:10.09	881	4:17.24	831	4:24.59	781
3:56.47	980	4:03.26	930	4:10.23	880	4:17.38	830	4:24.73	780
3:56.60	979	4:03.40	929	4:10.37	879	4:17.53	829	4:24.88	779
3:56.74	978	4:03.54	928	4:10.51	878	4:17.67	828	4:25.03	778
3:56.87	977	4:03.68	927	4:10.65	877	4:17.82	827	4:25.18	777
3:57.00	976	4:03.81	926	4:10.80	876	4:17.96	826	4:25.33	776
3:57.14	975	4:03.95	925	4:10.94	875	4:18.11	825	4:25.48	775
3:57.27	974	4:04.09	924	4:11.08	874	4:18.25	824	4:25.63	774
3:57.41	973	4:04.23	923	4:11.22	873	4:18.40	823	4:25.78	773
3:57.54	972	4:04.37	922	4:11.36	872	4:18.54	822	4:25.93	772
3:57.68	971	4:04.51	921	4:11.50	871	4:18.69	821	4:26.08	771
3:57.81	970	4:04.64	920	4:11.65	870	4:18.84	820	4:26.23	770
3:57.95	969	4:04.78	919	4:11.79	869	4:18.98	819	4:26.38	769
3:58.08	968	4:04.92	918	4:11.93	868	4:19.13	818	4:26.53	768
3:58.22	967	4:05.06	917	4:12.07	867	4:19.27	817	4:26.68	767
3:58.35	966	4:05.20	916	4:12.21	866	4:19.42	816	4:26.83	766
3:58.49	965	4:05.34	915	4:12.36	865	4:19.57	815	4:26.98	765
3:58.62	964	4:05.47	914	4:12.50	864	4:19.71	814	4:27.13	764
3:58.76	963	4:05.61	913	4:12.64	863	4:19.86	813	4:27.28	763
3:58.90	962	4:05.75	912	4:12.78	862	4:20.01	812	4:27.43	762
3:59.03	961	4:05.89	911	4:12.93	861	4:20.15	811	4:27.58	761
3:59.17	960	4:06.03	910	4:13.07	860	4:20.30	810	4:27.74	760
3:59.30	959	4:06.17	909	4:13.21	859	4:20.44	809	4:27.89	759
3:59.44	958	4:06.31	908	4:13.35	858	4:20.59	808	4:28.04	758
3:59.57	957	4:06.45	907	4:13.50	857	4:20.74	807	4:28.19	757
3:59.71	956	4:06.59	906	4:13.64	856	4:20.89	806	4:28.34	756
3:59.85	955	4:06.73	905	4:13.78	855	4:21.03	805	4:28.49	755
3:59.98	954	4:06.86	904	4:13.93	854	4:21.18	804	4:28.64	754
4:00.12	953	4:07.00	903	4:14.07	853	4:21.33	803	4:28.79	753
4:00.25	952	4:07.14	902	4:14.21	852	4:21.47	802	4:28.95	752
4:00.39	951	4:07.28	901	4:14.36	851	4:21.62	801	4:29.10	751
4:00.53	950	4:07.42	900	4:14.50	850	4:21.77	800	4:29.25	750

Seconds	Points	Seconds	Points	Seconds	Points	Seconds	Points	Seconds	Points
4:29.40	749	4:37.12	699	4:45.10	649	4:53.36	599	5:01.95	549
4:29.55	748	4:37.28	698	4:45.26	648	4:53.53	598	5:02.13	548
4:29.71	747	4:37.44	697	4:45.42	647	4:53.70	597	5:02.31	547
4:29.86	746	4:37.59	696	4:45.59	646	4:53.87	596	5:02.48	546
4:30.01	745	4:37.75	695	4:45.75	645	4:54.04	595	5:02.66	545
4:30.16	744	4:37.91	694	4:45.91	644	4:54.21	594	5:02.83	544
4:30.32	743	4:38.06	693	4:46.08	643	4:54.38	593	5:03.01	543
4:30.47	742	4:38.22	692	4:46.24	642	4:54.55	592	5:03.18	542
4:30.62	741	4:38.38	691	4:46.40	641	4:54.72	591	5:03.36	541
4:30.77	740	4:38.54	690	4:46.57	640	4:54.89	590	5:03.54	540
4:30.93	739	4:38.70	689	4:46.73	639	4:55.06	589	5:03.71	539
4:31.08	738	4:38.85	688	4:46.89	638	4:55.23	588	5:03.89	538
4:31.23	737	4:39.01	687	4:47.06	637	4:55.40	587	5:04.07	537
4:31.39	736	4:39.17	686	4:47.22	636	4:55.57	586	5:04.25	536
4:31.54	735	4:39.33	685	4:47.38	635	4:55.74	585	5:04.42	535
4:31.69	734	4:39.49	684	4:47.55	634	4:55.91	584	5:04.60	534
4:31.85	733	4:39.65	683	4:47.71	633	4:56.08	583	5:04.78	533
4:32.00	732	4:39.80	682	4:47.88	632	4:56.25	582	5:04.96	532
4:32.15	731	4:39.96	681	4:48.04	631	4:56.42	581	5:05.13	531
4:32.31	730	4:40.12	680	4:48.20	630	4:56.59	580	5:05.31	530
4:32.46	729	4:40.28	679	4:48.37	629	4:56.76	579	5:05.49	529
4:32.61	728	4:40.44	678	4:48.53	628	4:56.93	578	5:05.67	528
4:32.77	727	4:40.60	677	4:48.70	627	4:57.10	577	5:05.85	527
4:32.92	726	4:40.76	676	4:48.86	626	4:57.27	576	5:06.03	526
4:33.08	725	4:40.92	675	4:49.03	625	4:57.44	575	5:06.20	525
4:33.23	724	4:41.08	674	4:49.19	624	4:57.62	574	5:06.38	524
4:33.39	723	4:41.24	673	4:49.36	623	4:57.79	573	5:06.56	523
4:33.54	722	4:41.40	672	4:49.52	622	4:57.96	572	5:06.74	522
4:33.69	721	4:41.56	671	4:49.69	621	4:58.13	571	5:06.92	521
4:33.85	720	4:41.72	670	4:49.86	620	4:58.30	570	5:07.10	520
4:34.00	719	4:41.88	669	4:50.02	619	4:58.48	569	5:07.28	519
4:34.16	718	4:42.04	668	4:50.19	618	4:58.65	568	5:07.46	518
4:34.31	717	4:42.20	667	4:50.35	617	4:58.82	567	5:07.64	517
4:34.47	716	4:42.36	666	4:50.52	616	4:58.99	566	5:07.82	516
4:34.62	715	4:42.52	665	4:50.69	615	4:59.17	565	5:08.00	515
4:34.78	714	4:42.68	664	4:50.85	614	4:59.34	564	5:08.18	514
4:34.94	713	4:42.84	663	4:51.02	613	4:59.51	563	5:08.36	513
4:35.09	712	4:43.00	662	4:51.19	612	4:59.69	562	5:08.54	512
4:35.25	711	4:43.16	661	4:51.35	611	4:59.86	561	5:08.73	511
4:35.40	710	4:43.32	660	4:51.52	610	5:00.03	560	5:08.91	510
4:35.56	709	4:43.48	659	4:51.69	609	5:00.21	559	5:09.09	509
4:35.71	708	4:43.64	658	4:51.85	608	5:00.38	558	5:09.27	508
4:35.87	707	4:43.80	657	4:52.02	607	5:00.56	557	5:09.45	507
4:36.03	706	4:43.97	656	4:52.19	606	5:00.73	556	5:09.63	506
4:36.18	705	4:44.13	655	4:52.36	605	5:00.90	555	5:09.82	505
4:36.34	704	4:44.29	654	4:52.52	604	5:01.08	554	5:10.00	504
4:36.49	703	4:44.45	653	4:52.69	603	5:01.25	553	5:10.18	503
4:36.65	702	4:44.61	652	4:52.86	602	5:01.43	552	5:10.36	502
4:36.81	701	4:44.77	651	4:53.03	601	5:01.60	551	5:10.55	501
4:36.96	700	4:44.94	650	4:53.20	600	5:01.78	550	5:10.73	500

Seconds	Points	Seconds	Points	Seconds	Points	Seconds	Points	Seconds	Points
5:10.91	499	5:20.29	449	5:30.16	399	5:40.62	349	5:51.80	299
5:11.09	498	5:20.48	448	5:30.37	398	5:40.84	348	5:52.03	298
5:11.28	497	5:20.68	447	5:30.57	397	5:41.06	347	5:52.26	297
5:11.46	496	5:20.87	446	5:30.77	396	5:41.27	346	5:52.50	296
5:11.64	495	5:21.06	445	5:30.98	395	5:41.49	345	5:52.73	295
5:11.83	494	5:21.25	444	5:31.18	394	5:41.71	344	5:52.96	294
5:12.01	493	5:21.45	443	5:31.39	393	5:41.93	343	5:53.20	293
5:12.20	492	5:21.64	442	5:31.59	392	5:42.14	342	5:53.43	292
5:12.38	491	5:21.84	441	5:31.80	391	5:42.36	341	5:53.67	291
5:12.57	490	5:22.03	440	5:32.00	390	5:42.58	340	5:53.90	290
5:12.75	489	5:22.22	439	5:32.21	389	5:42.80	339	5:54.14	289
5:12.94	488	5:22.42	438	5:32.41	388	5:43.02	338	5:54.37	288
5:13.12	487	5:22.61	437	5:32.62	387	5:43.24	337	5:54.61	287
5:13.31	486	5:22.81	436	5:32.82	386	5:43.46	336	5:54.84	286
5:13.49	485	5:23.00	435	5:33.03	385	5:43.68	335	5:55.08	285
5:13.68	484	5:23.20	434	5:33.24	384	5:43.90	334	5:55.32	284
5:13.86	483	5:23.39	433	5:33.44	383	5:44.12	333	5:55.56	283
5:14.05	482	5:23.59	432	5:33.65	382	5:44.34	332	5:55.79	282
5:14.24	481	5:23.78	431	5:33.86	381	5:44.56	331	5:56.03	281
5:14.42	480	5:23.98	430	5:34.06	380	5:44.78	330	5:56.27	280
5:14.61	479	5:24.18	429	5:34.27	379	5:45.00	329	5:56.51	279
5:14.80	478	5:24.37	428	5:34.48	378	5:45.22	328	5:56.75	278
5:14.98	477	5:24.57	427	5:34.69	377	5:45.44	327	5:56.99	277
5:15.17	476	5:24.77	426	5:34.90	376	5:45.67	326	5:57.23	276
5:15.36	475	5:24.96	425	5:35.11	375	5:45.89	325	5:57.47	275
5:15.54	474	5:25.16	424	5:35.31	374	5:46.11	324	5:57.71	274
5:15.73	473	5:25.36	423	5:35.52	373	5:46.34	323	5:57.95	273
5:15.92	472	5:25.56	422	5:35.73	372	5:46.56	322	5:58.19	272
5:16.11	471	5:25.75	421	5:35.94	371	5:46.78	321	5:58.44	271
5:16.30	470	5:25.95	420	5:36.15	370	5:47.01	320	5:58.68	270
5:16.48	469	5:26.15	419	5:36.36	369	5:47.23	319	5:58.92	269
5:16.67	468	5:26.35	418	5:36.57	368	5:47.46	318	5:59.16	268
5:16.86	467	5:26.55	417	5:36.78	367	5:47.68	317	5:59.41	267
5:17.05	466	5:26.75	416	5:37.00	366	5:47.91	316	5:59.65	266
5:17.24	465	5:26.95	415	5:37.21	365	5:48.14	315	5:59.90	265
5:17.43	464	5:27.15	414	5:37.42	364	5:48.36	314	6:00.14	264
5:17.62	463	5:27.34	413	5:37.63	363	5:48.59	313	6:00.39	263
5:17.81	462	5:27.54	412	5:37.84	362	5:48.82	312	6:00.63	262
5:18.00	461	5:27.75	411	5:38.05	361	5:49.04	311	6:00.88	261
5:18.19	460	5:27.95	410	5:38.27	360	5:49.27	310	6:01.13	260
5:18.38	459	5:28.15	409	5:38.48	359	5:49.50	309	6:01.38	259
5:18.57	458	5:28.35	408	5:38.69	358	5:49.73	308	6:01.62	258
5:18.76	457	5:28.55	407	5:38.91	357	5:49.96	307	6:01.87	257
5:18.95	456	5:28.75	406	5:39.12	356	5:50.19	306	6:02.12	256
5:19.14	455	5:28.95	405	5:39.33	355	5:50.42	305	6:02.37	255
5:19.33	454	5:29.15	404	5:39.55	354	5:50.65	304	6:02.62	254
5:19.52	453	5:29.35	403	5:39.76	353	5:50.88	303	6:02.87	253
5:19.71	452	5:29.56	402	5:39.98	352	5:51.11	302	6:03.12	252
5:19.91	451	5:29.76	401	5:40.19	351	5:51.34	301	6:03.37	251
5:20.10	450	5:29.96	400	5:40.41	350	5:51.57	300	6:03.62	250

Seconds	Points	Seconds	Points	Seconds	Points	Seconds	Points	Seconds	Points
6:03.87	249	6:17.12	199	6:32.02	149	6:49.46	99	7:11.77	49
6:04.13	248	6:17.40	198	6:32.34	148	6:49.85	98	7:12.30	48
6:04.38	247	6:17.68	197	6:32.66	147	6:50.24	97	7:12.84	47
6:04.63	246	6:17.97	196	6:32.98	146	6:50.63	96	7:13.39	46
6:04.89	245	6:18.25	195	6:33.30	145	6:51.02	95	7:13.94	45
6:05.14	244	6:18.53	194	6:33.63	144	6:51.41	94	7:14.49	44
6:05.39	243	6:18.81	193	6:33.95	143	6:51.81	93	7:15.06	43
6:05.65	242	6:19.10	192	6:34.28	142	6:52.20	92	7:15.62	42
6:05.91	241	6:19.38	191	6:34.60	141	6:52.60	91	7:16.20	41
6:06.16	240	6:19.67	190	6:34.93	140	6:53.00	90	7:16.78	40
6:06.42	239	6:19.95	189	6:35.26	139	6:53.41	89	7:17.37	39
6:06.68	238	6:20.24	188	6:35.59	138	6:53.81	88	7:17.96	38
6:06.93	237	6:20.52	187	6:35.92	137	6:54.22	87	7:18.56	37
6:07.19	236	6:20.81	186	6:36.25	136	6:54.63	86	7:19.17	36
6:07.45	235	6:21.10	185	6:36.59	135	6:55.04	85	7:19.79	35
6:07.71	234	6:21.39	184	6:36.92	134	6:55.46	84	7:20.41	34
6:07.97	233	6:21.68	183	6:37.26	133	6:55.87	83	7:21.05	33
6:08.23	232	6:21.97	182	6:37.60	132	6:56.29	82	7:21.69	32
6:08.49	231	6:22.26	181	6:37.93	131	6:56.71	81	7:22.34	31
6:08.75	230	6:22.56	180	6:38.27	130	6:57.14	80	7:23.00	30
6:09.01	229	6:22.85	179	6:38.61	129	6:57.56	79	7:23.67	29
6:09.27	228	6:23.14	178	6:38.95	128	6:57.99	78	7:24.36	28
6:09.54	227	6:23.44	177	6:39.30	127	6:58.42	77	7:25.05	27
6:09.80	226	6:23.73	176	6:39.64	126	6:58.85	76	7:25.76	26
6:10.06	225	6:24.03	175	6:39.99	125	6:59.29	75	7:26.47	25
6:10.33	224	6:24.32	174	6:40.33	124	6:59.73	74	7:27.21	24
6:10.59	223	6:24.62	173	6:40.68	123	7:00.17	73	7:27.95	23
6:10.86	222	6:24.92	172	6:41.03	122	7:00.62	72	7:28.71	22
6:11.12	221	6:25.22	171	6:41.38	121	7:01.06	71	7:29.49	21
6:11.39	220	6:25.52	170	6:41.73	120	7:01.51	70	7:30.28	20
6:11.66	219	6:25.82	169	6:42.09	119	7:01.97	69	7:31.10	19
6:11.93	218	6:26.12	168	6:42.44	118	7:02.42	68	7:31.93	18
6:12.19	217	6:26.42	167	6:42.80	117	7:02.88	67	7:32.78	17
6:12.46	216	6:26.73	166	6:43.15	116	7:03.34	66	7:33.66	16
6:12.73	215	6:27.03	165	6:43.51	115	7:03.81	65	7:34.56	15
6:13.00	214	6:27.34	164	6:43.87	114	7:04.28	64	7:35.49	14
6:13.27	213	6:27.64	163	6:44.23	113	7:04.75	63	7:36.46	13
6:13.54	212	6:27.95	162	6:44.60	112	7:05.23	62	7:37.45	12
6:13.82	211	6:28.26	161	6:44.96	111	7:05.71	61	7:38.49	11
6:14.09	210	6:28.57	160	6:45.33	110	7:06.19	60	7:39.57	10
6:14.36	209	6:28.87	159	6:45.70	109	7:06.68	59	7:40.70	9
6:14.63	208	6:29.19	158	6:46.07	108	7:07.17	58	7:41.89	8
6:14.91	207	6:29.50	157	6:46.44	107	7:07.66	57	7:43.15	7
6:15.18	206	6:29.81	156	6:46.81	106	7:08.16	56	7:44.50	6
6:15.46	205	6:30.12	155	6:47.18	105	7:08.66	55	7:45.95	5
6:15.73	204	6:30.44	154	6:47.56	104	7:09.17	54	7:47.55	4
6:16.01	203	6:30.75	153	6:47.94	103	7:09.68	53	7:49.34	3
6:16.29	202	6:31.07	152	6:48.31	102	7:10.19	52	7:51.44	2
6:16.57	201	6:31.38	151	6:48.70	101	7:10.71	51	7:54.11	1
6:16.84	200	6:31.70	150	6:49.08	100	7:11.24	50		

Women — 100m Hurdles — 100m Haies — Femmes

Seconds	Points	Seconds	Points	Seconds	Points	Seconds	Points	Seconds	Points
				This table to be used exclusively for fully automatic times.					
12.00	1280	12.50	1201	13.00	1124	13.50	1050	14.00	978
12.01	1278	12.51	1199	13.01	1123	13.51	1049	14.01	977
12.02	1276	12.52	1198	13.02	1121	13.52	1047	14.02	976
12.03	1275	12.53	1196	13.03	1120	13.53	1046	14.03	974
12.04	1273	12.54	1195	13.04	1118	13.54	1044	14.04	973
12.05	1272	12.55	1193	13.05	1117	13.55	1043	14.05	971
12.06	1270	12.56	1192	13.06	1115	13.56	1041	14.06	970
12.07	1268	12.57	1190	13.07	1114	13.57	1040	14.07	968
12.08	1267	12.58	1189	13.08	1112	13.58	1039	14.08	967
12.09	1265	12.59	1187	13.09	1111	13.59	1037	14.09	966
12.10	1264	12.60	1185	13.10	1109	13.60	1036	14.10	964
12.11	1262	12.61	1184	13.11	1108	13.61	1034	14.11	963
12.12	1261	12.62	1182	13.12	1106	13.62	1033	14.12	961
12.13	1259	12.63	1181	13.13	1105	13.63	1031	14.13	960
12.14	1257	12.64	1179	13.14	1103	13.64	1030	14.14	959
12.15	1256	12.65	1178	13.15	1102	13.65	1028	14.15	957
12.16	1254	12.66	1176	13.16	1100	13.66	1027	14.16	956
12.17	1253	12.67	1175	13.17	1099	13.67	1026	14.17	954
12.18	1251	12.68	1173	13.18	1097	13.68	1024	14.18	953
12.19	1249	12.69	1172	13.19	1096	13.69	1023	14.19	952
12.20	1248	12.70	1170	13.20	1094	13.70	1021	14.20	950
12.21	1246	12.71	1168	13.21	1093	13.71	1020	14.21	949
12.22	1245	12.72	1167	13.22	1091	13.72	1018	14.22	947
12.23	1243	12.73	1165	13.23	1090	13.73	1017	14.23	946
12.24	1242	12.74	1164	13.24	1089	13.74	1015	14.24	945
12.25	1240	12.75	1162	13.25	1087	13.75	1014	14.25	943
12.26	1238	12.76	1161	13.26	1086	13.76	1013	14.26	942
12.27	1237	12.77	1159	13.27	1084	13.77	1011	14.27	941
12.28	1235	12.78	1158	13.28	1083	13.78	1010	14.28	939
12.29	1234	12.79	1156	13.29	1081	13.79	1008	14.29	938
12.30	1232	12.80	1155	13.30	1080	13.80	1007	14.30	936
12.31	1231	12.81	1153	13.31	1078	13.81	1005	14.31	935
12.32	1229	12.82	1152	13.32	1077	13.82	1004	14.32	934
12.33	1227	12.83	1150	13.33	1075	13.83	1003	14.33	932
12.34	1226	12.84	1149	13.34	1074	13.84	1001	14.34	931
12.35	1224	12.85	1147	13.35	1072	13.85	1000	14.35	929
12.36	1223	12.86	1146	13.36	1071	13.86	998	14.36	928
12.37	1221	12.87	1144	13.37	1069	13.87	997	14.37	927
12.38	1220	12.88	1143	13.38	1068	13.88	995	14.38	925
12.39	1218	12.89	1141	13.39	1066	13.89	994	14.39	924
12.40	1216	12.90	1140	13.40	1065	13.90	993	14.40	923
12.41	1215	12.91	1138	13.41	1063	13.91	991	14.41	921
12.42	1213	12.92	1136	13.42	1062	13.92	990	14.42	920
12.43	1212	12.93	1135	13.43	1060	13.93	988	14.43	918
12.44	1210	12.94	1133	13.44	1059	13.94	987	14.44	917
12.45	1209	12.95	1132	13.45	1058	13.95	985	14.45	916
12.46	1207	12.96	1130	13.46	1056	13.96	984	14.46	914
12.47	1206	12.97	1129	13.47	1055	13.97	983	14.47	913
12.48	1204	12.98	1127	13.48	1053	13.98	981	14.48	912
12.49	1202	12.99	1126	13.49	1052	13.99	980	14.49	910

178

Seconds	Points	Seconds	Points	Seconds	Points	Seconds	Points	Seconds	Points
				This table to be used exclusively for fully automatic times.					
14.50	909	15.00	842	15.50	777	16.00	714	16.50	654
14.51	907	15.01	840	15.51	775	16.01	713	16.51	653
14.52	906	15.02	839	15.52	774	16.02	712	16.52	652
14.53	905	15.03	838	15.53	773	16.03	711	16.53	651
14.54	903	15.04	836	15.54	772	16.04	709	16.54	649
14.55	902	15.05	835	15.55	770	16.05	708	16.55	648
14.56	901	15.06	834	15.56	769	16.06	707	16.56	647
14.57	899	15.07	832	15.57	768	16.07	706	16.57	646
14.58	898	15.08	831	15.58	767	16.08	704	16.58	645
14.59	897	15.09	830	15.59	765	16.09	703	16.59	644
14.60	895	15.10	828	15.60	764	16.10	702	16.60	642
14.61	894	15.11	827	15.61	763	16.11	701	16.61	641
14.62	892	15.12	826	15.62	762	16.12	700	16.62	640
14.63	891	15.13	825	15.63	760	16.13	698	16.63	639
14.64	890	15.14	823	15.64	759	16.14	697	16.64	638
14.65	888	15.15	822	15.65	758	16.15	696	16.65	637
14.66	887	15.16	821	15.66	756	16.16	695	16.66	635
14.67	886	15.17	819	15.67	755	16.17	694	16.67	634
14.68	884	15.18	818	15.68	754	16.18	692	16.68	633
14.69	883	15.19	817	15.69	753	16.19	691	16.69	632
14.70	882	15.20	815	15.70	751	16.20	690	16.70	631
14.71	880	15.21	814	15.71	750	16.21	689	16.71	630
14.72	879	15.22	813	15.72	749	16.22	688	16.72	628
14.73	878	15.23	811	15.73	748	16.23	686	16.73	627
14.74	876	15.24	810	15.74	746	16.24	685	16.74	626
14.75	875	15.25	809	15.75	745	16.25	684	16.75	625
14.76	874	15.26	808	15.76	744	16.26	683	16.76	624
14.77	872	15.27	806	15.77	743	16.27	682	16.77	623
14.78	871	15.28	805	15.78	741	16.28	680	16.78	622
14.79	870	15.29	804	15.79	740	16.29	679	16.79	620
14.80	868	15.30	802	15.80	739	16.30	678	16.80	619
14.81	867	15.31	801	15.81	738	16.31	677	16.81	618
14.82	866	15.32	800	15.82	736	16.32	676	16.82	617
14.83	864	15.33	799	15.83	735	16.33	674	16.83	616
14.84	863	15.34	797	15.84	734	16.34	673	16.84	615
14.85	862	15.35	796	15.85	733	16.35	672	16.85	614
14.86	860	15.36	795	15.86	732	16.36	671	16.86	612
14.87	859	15.37	793	15.87	730	16.37	670	16.87	611
14.88	858	15.38	792	15.88	729	16.38	668	16.88	610
14.89	856	15.39	791	15.89	728	16.39	667	16.89	609
14.90	855	15.40	790	15.90	727	16.40	666	16.90	608
14.91	854	15.41	788	15.91	725	16.41	665	16.91	607
14.92	852	15.42	787	15.92	724	16.42	664	16.92	606
14.93	851	15.43	786	15.93	723	16.43	662	16.93	604
14.94	850	15.44	784	15.94	722	16.44	661	16.94	603
14.95	848	15.45	783	15.95	720	16.45	660	16.95	602
14.96	847	15.46	782	15.96	719	16.46	659	16.96	601
14.97	846	15.47	781	15.97	718	16.47	658	16.97	600
14.98	844	15.48	779	15.98	717	16.48	657	16.98	599
14.99	843	15.49	778	15.99	715	16.49	655	16.99	598

Women   100m Hurdles — 100m Haies   Femmes

This table to be used exclusively for fully automatic times.

Seconds	Points	Seconds	Points	Seconds	Points	Seconds	Points	Seconds	Points
17.00	596	17.50	541	18.00	488	18.50	438	19.03	388
17.01	595	17.51	540	18.01	487	18.51	437	19.04	387
17.02	594	17.52	539	18.02	486	18.52	436	19.05	386
17.03	593	17.53	538	18.03	485	18.53	435	19.06	385
17.04	592	17.54	537	18.04	484	18.54	434	19.07	384
17.05	591	17.55	536	18.05	483	18.55	433	19.08	383
17.06	590	17.56	535	18.06	482	18.56	432	19.09	382
17.07	589	17.57	534	18.07	481	18.57	431	19.10	381
17.08	587	17.58	533	18.08	480	18.58	430	19.11	380
17.09	586	17.59	532	18.09	479	18.59	429	19.12	379
17.10	585	17.60	530	18.10	478	18.60	428	19.13	378
17.11	584	17.61	529	18.11	477	18.61	427	19.14	377
17.12	583	17.62	528	18.12	476	18.62	426	19.16	376
17.13	582	17.63	527	18.13	475	18.63	425	19.17	375
17.14	581	17.64	526	18.14	474	18.65	424	19.18	374
17.15	580	17.65	525	18.15	473	18.66	423	19.19	373
17.16	579	17.66	524	18.16	472	18.67	422	19.20	372
17.17	577	17.67	523	18.17	471	18.68	421	19.21	371
17.18	576	17.68	522	18.18	470	18.69	420	19.22	370
17.19	575	17.69	521	18.19	469	18.70	419	19.23	369
17.20	574	17.70	520	18.20	468	18.71	418	19.24	368
17.21	573	17.71	519	18.21	467	18.72	417	19.25	367
17.22	572	17.72	518	18.22	466	18.73	416	19.27	366
17.23	571	17.73	517	18.23	465	18.74	415	19.28	365
17.24	570	17.74	516	18.24	464	18.75	414	19.29	364
17.25	569	17.75	515	18.25	463	18.76	413	19.30	363
17.26	567	17.76	513	18.26	462	18.77	412	19.31	362
17.27	566	17.77	512	18.27	461	18.78	411	19.32	361
17.28	565	17.78	511	18.28	460	18.79	410	19.33	360
17.29	564	17.79	510	18.29	459	18.80	409	19.34	359
17.30	563	17.80	509	18.30	458	18.81	408	19.35	358
17.31	562	17.81	508	18.31	457	18.82	407	19.37	357
17.32	561	17.82	507	18.32	456	18.83	406	19.38	356
17.33	560	17.83	506	18.33	455	18.84	405	19.39	355
17.34	559	17.84	505	18.34	454	18.85	404	19.40	354
17.35	558	17.85	504	18.35	453	18.86	403	19.41	353
17.36	556	17.86	503	18.36	452	18.88	402	19.42	352
17.37	555	17.87	502	18.37	451	18.89	401	19.43	351
17.38	554	17.88	501	18.38	450	18.90	400	19.44	350
17.39	553	17.89	500	18.39	449	18.91	399	19.46	349
17.40	552	17.90	499	18.40	448	18.92	398	19.47	348
17.41	551	17.91	498	18.41	447	18.93	397	19.48	347
17.42	550	17.92	497	18.42	446	18.94	396	19.49	346
17.43	549	17.93	496	18.43	445	18.95	395	19.50	345
17.44	548	17.94	495	18.44	444	18.96	394	19.51	344
17.45	547	17.95	494	18.45	443	18.97	393	19.52	343
17.46	546	17.96	493	18.46	442	18.98	392	19.53	342
17.47	544	17.97	492	18.47	441	18.99	391	19.55	341
17.48	543	17.98	491	18.48	440	19.00	390	19.56	340
17.49	542	17.99	489	18.49	439	19.01	389	19.57	339

Women 100m Hurdles — 100m Haies Femmes

Seconds	Points	Seconds	Points	Seconds	Points	Seconds	Points	Seconds	Points
				This table to be used exclusively for fully automatic times.					
19.58	338	20.17	288	20.82	238	21.53	188	22.33	138
19.59	337	20.19	287	20.83	237	21.54	187	22.35	137
19.60	336	20.20	286	20.85	236	21.56	186	22.36	136
19.62	335	20.21	285	20.86	235	21.57	185	22.38	135
19.63	334	20.22	284	20.87	234	21.59	184	22.40	134
19.64	333	20.24	283	20.89	233	21.60	183	22.42	133
19.65	332	20.25	282	20.90	232	21.62	182	22.43	132
19.66	331	20.26	281	20.91	231	21.63	181	22.45	131
19.67	330	20.27	280	20.93	230	21.65	180	22.47	130
19.68	329	20.29	279	20.94	229	21.66	179	22.49	129
19.70	328	20.30	278	20.95	228	21.68	178	22.50	128
19.71	327	20.31	277	20.97	227	21.69	177	22.52	127
19.72	326	20.32	276	20.98	226	21.71	176	22.54	126
19.73	325	20.34	275	21.00	225	21.73	175	22.56	125
19.74	324	20.35	274	21.01	224	21.74	174	22.58	124
19.75	323	20.36	273	21.02	223	21.76	173	22.59	123
19.77	322	20.37	272	21.04	222	21.77	172	22.61	122
19.78	321	20.39	271	21.05	221	21.79	171	22.63	121
19.79	320	20.40	270	21.06	220	21.80	170	22.65	120
19.80	319	20.41	269	21.08	219	21.82	169	22.67	119
19.81	318	20.43	268	21.09	218	21.83	168	22.69	118
19.82	317	20.44	267	21.11	217	21.85	167	22.70	117
19.84	316	20.45	266	21.12	216	21.87	166	22.72	116
19.85	315	20.46	265	21.14	215	21.88	165	22.74	115
19.86	314	20.48	264	21.15	214	21.90	164	22.76	114
19.87	313	20.49	263	21.16	213	21.91	163	22.78	113
19.88	312	20.50	262	21.18	212	21.93	162	22.80	112
19.90	311	20.52	261	21.19	211	21.95	161	22.82	111
19.91	310	20.53	260	21.21	210	21.96	160	22.84	110
19.92	309	20.54	259	21.22	209	21.98	159	22.86	109
19.93	308	20.55	258	21.23	208	21.99	158	22.87	108
19.94	307	20.57	257	21.25	207	22.01	157	22.89	107
19.96	306	20.58	256	21.26	206	22.03	156	22.91	106
19.97	305	20.59	255	21.28	205	22.04	155	22.93	105
19.98	304	20.61	254	21.29	204	22.06	154	22.95	104
19.99	303	20.62	253	21.31	203	22.08	153	22.97	103
20.00	302	20.63	252	21.32	202	22.09	152	22.99	102
20.02	301	20.65	251	21.34	201	22.11	151	23.01	101
20.03	300	20.66	250	21.35	200	22.13	150	23.03	100
20.04	299	20.67	249	21.36	199	22.14	149	23.05	99
20.05	298	20.69	248	21.38	198	22.16	148	23.07	98
20.06	297	20.70	247	21.39	197	22.18	147	23.09	97
20.08	296	20.71	246	21.41	196	22.19	146	23.11	96
20.09	295	20.72	245	21.42	195	22.21	145	23.13	95
20.10	294	20.75	244	21.44	194	22.23	144	23.15	94
20.11	293	20.75	243	21.45	193	22.24	143	23.17	93
20.13	292	20.76	242	21.47	192	22.26	142	23.19	92
20.14	291	20.78	241	21.48	191	22.28	141	23.21	91
20.15	290	20.79	240	21.50	190	22.29	140	23.24	90
20.16	289	20.81	239	21.51	189	22.31	139	23.26	89

Women   100m Hurdles — 100m Haies   Femmes

Seconds	Points	Seconds	Points	Seconds	Points	Seconds	Points	Seconds	Points
				This table to be used exclusively for fully automatic times.					
23.28	88	23.73	68	24.24	48	24.86	28	25.77	8
23.30	87	23.75	67	24.27	47	24.90	27	25.83	7
23.32	86	23.77	66	24.30	46	24.94	26	25.90	6
23.34	85	23.80	65	24.32	45	24.97	25	25.98	5
23.36	84	23.82	64	24.35	44	25.01	24	26.06	4
23.39	83	23.85	63	24.38	43	25.05	23	26.15	3
23.41	82	23.87	62	24.41	42	25.09	22	26.26	2
23.43	81	23.90	61	24.44	41	25.13	21	26.40	1
23.45	80	23.92	60	24.47	40	25.17	20		
23.47	79	23.95	59	24.50	39	25.21	19		
23.50	78	23.97	58	24.53	38	25.26	18		
23.52	77	24.00	57	24.56	37	25.30	17		
23.54	76	24.02	56	24.60	36	25.35	16		
23.56	75	24.05	55	24.63	35	25.39	15		
23.59	74	24.08	54	24.66	34	25.44	14		
23.61	73	24.10	53	24.69	33	25.49	13		
23.63	72	24.13	52	24.73	32	25.54	12		
23.66	71	24.16	51	24.76	31	25.59	11		
23.68	70	24.18	50	24.79	30	25.65	10		
23.70	69	24.21	49	24.83	29	25.71	9		

Women   100m Hurdles — 1/10 sec — 100m Haies   Femmes

THIS TABLE IS TO BE USED EXCLUSIVELY FOR HAND TIMES
A UTILISER UNIQUEMENT EN CAS DE CHRONOMETRAGE MANUEL

Seconds	Points	Seconds	Points	Seconds	Points	Seconds	Points	Seconds	Points
12.0	1242	15.0	810	18.0	464	21.0	207	24.0	48
12.1	1226	15.1	797	18.1	454	21.1	201	24.1	44
12.2	1210	15.2	784	18.2	444	21.2	194	24.2	41
12.3	1195	15.3	772	18.3	434	21.3	187	24.3	37
12.4	1179	15.4	759	18.4	424	21.4	180	24.4	34
12.5	1164	15.5	746	18.5	415	21.5	174	24.5	31
12.6	1149	15.6	734	18.6	405	21.6	167	24.6	28
12.7	1133	15.7	722	18.7	396	21.7	161	24.7	26
12.8	1118	15.8	709	18.8	387	21.8	155	24.8	23
12.9	1103	15.9	697	18.9	377	21.9	149	24.9	20
13.0	1089	16.0	685	19.0	368	22.0	143	25.0	18
13.1	1074	16.1	673	19.1	359	22.1	137	25.1	16
13.2	1059	16.2	661	19.2	350	22.2	131	25.2	14
13.3	1044	16.3	649	19.3	341	22.3	126	25.3	12
13.4	1030	16.4	638	19.4	333	22.4	120	25.4	10
13.5	1015	16.5	626	19.5	324	22.5	115	25.5	8
13.6	1001	16.6	615	19.6	316	22.6	110	25.6	6
13.7	987	16.7	603	19.7	307	22.7	104	25.7	5
13.8	973	16.8	592	19.8	299	22.8	99	25.8	4
13.9	959	16.9	581	19.9	291	22.9	94	25.9	3
14.0	945	17.0	570	20.0	283	23.0	90	26.0	2
14.1	931	17.1	559	20.1	275	23.1	85	26.1	1
14.2	917	17.2	548	20.2	267	23.2	80		
14.3	903	17.3	537	20.3	259	23.3	76		
14.4	890	17.4	526	20.4	251	23.4	71		
14.5	876	17.5	516	20.5	244	23.5	67		
14.6	863	17.6	505	20.6	236	23.6	63		
14.7	850	17.7	495	20.7	229	23.7	59		
14.8	836	17.8	484	20.8	222	23.8	55		
14.9	823	17.9	474	20.9	215	23.9	51		

Metres	Points	Metres	Points	Metres	Points	Metres	Points	Metres	Points
2.09	1359	1.79	966	1.49	610	1.19	302	0.89	64
2.08	1345	1.78	953	1.48	599	1.18	293	0.88	58
2.07	1332	1.77	941	1.47	588	1.17	284	0.87	52
2.06	1318	1.76	928	1.46	577	1.16	275	0.86	46
2.05	1305	1.75	916	1.45	566	1.15	266	0.85	41
2.04	1291	1.74	903	1.44	555	1.14	257	0.84	35
2.03	1278	1.73	891	1.43	544	1.13	248	0.83	30
2.02	1264	1.72	879	1.42	534	1.12	239	0.82	25
2.01	1251	1.71	867	1.41	523	1.11	231	0.81	20
2.00	1237	1.70	855	1.40	512	1.10	222	0.80	16
1.99	1224	1.69	842	1.39	502	1.09	214	0.79	11
1.98	1211	1.68	830	1.38	491	1.08	205	0.78	8
1.97	1198	1.67	818	1.37	481	1.07	197	0.77	4
1.96	1184	1.66	806	1.36	470	1.06	188	0.76	1
1.95	1171	1.65	795	1.35	460	1.05	180		
1.94	1158	1.64	783	1.34	449	1.04	172		
1.93	1145	1.63	771	1.33	439	1.03	164		
1.92	1132	1.62	759	1.32	429	1.02	156		
1.91	1119	1.61	747	1.31	419	1.01	149		
1.90	1106	1.60	736	1.30	409	1.00	141		
1.89	1093	1.59	724	1.29	399	0.99	133		
1.88	1080	1.58	712	1.28	389	0.98	126		
1.87	1067	1.57	701	1.27	379	0.97	119		
1.86	1054	1.56	689	1.26	369	0.96	111		
1.85	1041	1.55	678	1.25	359	0.95	104		
1.84	1029	1.54	666	1.24	350	0.94	97		
1.83	1016	1.53	655	1.23	340	0.93	90		
1.82	1003	1.52	644	1.22	331	0.92	84		
1.81	991	1.51	632	1.21	321	0.91	77		
1.80	978	1.50	621	1.20	312	0.90	71		

Metres	Points	Metres	Points	Metres	Points	Metres	Points	Metres	Points
22.93	1399	22.20	1349	21.47	1299	20.74	1249	20.00	1199
22.92	1398	22.19	1348	21.45	1298	20.72	1248	19.99	1198
22.90	1397	22.17	1347	21.44	1297	20.71	1247	19.97	1197
22.89	1396	22.16	1346	21.42	1296	20.69	1246	19.96	1196
22.87	1395	22.14	1345	21.41	1295	20.68	1245	19.94	1195
22.86	1394	22.13	1344	21.40	1294	20.66	1244	19.93	1194
22.84	1393	22.11	1343	21.38	1293	20.65	1243	19.91	1193
22.83	1392	22.10	1342	21.37	1292	20.63	1242	19.90	1192
22.81	1391	22.08	1341	21.35	1291	20.62	1241	19.88	1191
22.80	1390	22.07	1340	21.34	1290	20.60	1240	19.87	1190
22.78	1389	22.05	1339	21.32	1289	20.59	1239	19.86	1189
22.77	1388	22.04	1338	21.31	1288	20.58	1238	19.84	1188
22.75	1387	22.02	1337	21.29	1287	20.56	1237	19.83	1187
22.74	1386	22.01	1336	21.28	1286	20.55	1236	19.81	1186
22.73	1385	22.00	1335	21.26	1285	20.53	1235	19.80	1185
22.71	1384	21.98	1334	21.25	1284	20.52	1234	19.78	1184
22.70	1383	21.97	1333	21.23	1283	20.50	1233	19.77	1183
22.68	1382	21.95	1332	21.22	1282	20.49	1232	19.75	1182
22.67	1381	21.94	1331	21.21	1281	20.47	1231	19.74	1181
22.65	1380	21.92	1330	21.19	1280	20.46	1230	19.72	1180
22.64	1379	21.91	1329	21.18	1279	20.44	1229	19.71	1179
22.62	1378	21.89	1328	21.16	1278	20.43	1228	19.69	1178
22.61	1377	21.88	1327	21.15	1277	20.41	1227	19.68	1177
22.59	1376	21.86	1326	21.13	1276	20.40	1226	19.66	1176
22.58	1375	21.85	1325	21.12	1275	20.38	1225	19.65	1175
22.57	1374	21.83	1324	21.10	1274	20.37	1224	19.63	1174
22.55	1373	21.82	1323	21.09	1273	20.35	1223	19.62	1173
22.54	1372	21.81	1322	21.07	1272	20.34	1222	19.61	1172
22.52	1371	21.79	1321	21.06	1271	20.33	1221	19.59	1171
22.51	1370	21.78	1320	21.04	1270	20.31	1220	19.58	1170
22.49	1369	21.76	1319	21.03	1269	20.30	1219	19.56	1169
22.48	1368	21.75	1318	21.01	1268	20.28	1218	19.55	1168
22.46	1367	21.73	1317	21.00	1267	20.27	1217	19.53	1167
22.45	1366	21.72	1316	20.99	1266	20.25	1216	19.52	1166
22.43	1365	21.70	1315	20.97	1265	20.24	1215	19.50	1165
22.42	1364	21.69	1314	20.96	1264	20.22	1214	19.49	1164
22.40	1363	21.67	1313	20.94	1263	20.21	1213	19.47	1163
22.39	1362	21.66	1312	20.93	1262	20.19	1212	19.46	1162
22.38	1361	21.64	1311	20.91	1261	20.18	1211	19.44	1161
22.36	1360	21.63	1310	20.90	1260	20.16	1210	19.43	1160
22.35	1359	21.62	1309	20.88	1259	20.15	1209	19.41	1159
22.33	1358	21.60	1308	20.87	1258	20.13	1208	19.40	1158
22.32	1357	21.59	1307	20.85	1257	20.12	1207	19.38	1157
22.30	1356	21.57	1306	20.84	1256	20.11	1206	19.37	1156
22.29	1355	21.56	1305	20.82	1255	20.09	1205	19.36	1155
22.27	1354	21.54	1304	20.81	1254	20.08	1204	19.34	1154
22.26	1353	21.53	1303	20.80	1253	20.06	1203	19.33	1153
22.24	1352	21.51	1302	20.78	1252	20.05	1202	19.31	1152
22.23	1351	21.50	1301	20.77	1251	20.03	1201	19.30	1151
22.21	1350	21.48	1300	20.75	1250	20.02	1200	19.28	1150

Women   Putting the Shot — Lancement du Poids   Femmes

Metres	Points	Metres	Points	Metres	Points	Metres	Points	Metres	Points
19.27	1149	18.53	1099	17.79	1049	17.05	999	16.31	949
19.25	1148	18.52	1098	17.78	1048	17.04	998	16.29	948
19.24	1147	18.50	1097	17.76	1047	17.02	997	16.28	947
19.22	1146	18.49	1096	17.75	1046	17.01	996	16.26	946
19.21	1145	18.47	1095	17.73	1045	16.99	995	16.25	945
19.19	1144	18.46	1094	17.72	1044	16.98	994	16.24	944
19.18	1143	18.44	1093	17.70	1043	16.96	993	16.22	943
19.16	1142	18.43	1092	17.69	1042	16.95	992	16.21	942
19.15	1141	18.41	1091	17.67	1041	16.93	991	16.19	941
19.13	1140	18.40	1090	17.66	1040	16.92	990	16.18	940
19.12	1139	18.38	1089	17.64	1039	16.90	989	16.16	939
19.11	1138	18.37	1088	17.63	1038	16.89	988	16.15	938
19.09	1137	18.35	1087	17.61	1037	16.87	987	16.13	937
19.08	1136	18.34	1086	17.60	1036	16.86	986	16.12	936
19.06	1135	18.32	1085	17.58	1035	16.84	985	16.10	935
19.05	1134	18.31	1084	17.57	1034	16.83	984	16.09	934
19.03	1133	18.29	1083	17.55	1033	16.81	983	16.07	933
19.02	1132	18.28	1082	17.54	1032	16.80	982	16.06	932
19.00	1131	18.26	1081	17.53	1031	16.78	981	16.04	931
18.99	1130	18.25	1080	17.51	1030	16.77	980	16.03	930
18.97	1129	18.23	1079	17.50	1029	16.75	979	16.01	929
18.96	1128	18.22	1078	17.48	1028	16.74	978	16.00	928
18.94	1127	18.21	1077	17.47	1027	16.73	977	15.98	927
18.93	1126	18.19	1076	17.45	1026	16.71	976	15.97	926
18.91	1125	18.18	1075	17.44	1025	16.70	975	15.95	925
18.90	1124	18.16	1074	17.42	1024	16.68	974	15.94	924
18.88	1123	18.15	1073	17.41	1023	16.67	973	15.92	923
18.87	1122	18.13	1072	17.39	1022	16.65	972	15.91	922
18.85	1121	18.12	1071	17.38	1021	16.64	971	15.89	921
18.84	1120	18.10	1070	17.36	1020	16.62	970	15.88	920
18.83	1119	18.09	1069	17.35	1019	16.61	969	15.86	919
18.81	1118	18.07	1068	17.33	1018	16.59	968	15.85	918
18.80	1117	18.06	1067	17.32	1017	16.58	967	15.83	917
18.78	1116	18.04	1066	17.30	1016	16.56	966	15.82	916
18.77	1115	18.03	1065	17.29	1015	16.55	965	15.80	915
18.75	1114	18.01	1064	17.27	1014	16.53	964	15.79	914
18.74	1113	18.00	1063	17.26	1013	16.52	963	15.77	913
18.72	1112	17.98	1062	17.24	1012	16.50	962	15.76	912
18.71	1111	17.97	1061	17.23	1011	16.49	961	15.74	911
18.69	1110	17.95	1060	17.21	1010	16.47	960	15.73	910
18.68	1109	17.94	1059	17.20	1009	16.46	959	15.71	909
18.66	1108	17.92	1058	17.18	1008	16.44	958	15.70	908
18.65	1107	17.91	1057	17.17	1007	16.43	957	15.68	907
18.63	1106	17.90	1056	17.16	1006	16.41	956	15.67	906
18.62	1105	17.88	1055	17.14	1005	16.40	955	15.66	905
18.60	1104	17.87	1054	17.13	1004	16.38	954	15.64	904
18.59	1103	17.85	1053	17.11	1003	16.37	953	15.63	903
18.57	1102	17.84	1052	17.10	1002	16.35	952	15.61	902
18.56	1101	17.82	1051	17.08	1001	16.34	951	15.60	901
18.54	1100	17.81	1050	17.07	1000	16.32	950	15.58	900

186

Women — Putting the Shot — Lancement du Poids — Femmes

Metres	Points	Metres	Points	Metres	Points	Metres	Points	Metres	Points
15.57	899	14.82	845	14.07	799	13.32	749	12.57	699
15.55	898	14.80	848	14.06	798	13.31	748	12.55	698
15.54	897	14.79	847	14.04	797	13.29	747	12.54	697
15.52	896	14.78	846	14.03	796	13.28	746	12.52	696
15.51	895	14.76	845	14.01	795	13.26	745	12.51	695
15.49	894	14.75	844	14.00	794	13.25	744	12.49	694
15.48	893	14.73	843	13.98	793	13.23	743	12.48	693
15.46	892	14.72	842	13.97	792	13.22	742	12.46	692
15.45	891	14.70	841	13.95	791	13.20	741	12.45	691
15.43	890	14.69	840	13.94	790	13.19	740	12.43	690
15.42	889	14.67	839	13.92	789	13.17	739	12.42	689
15.40	888	14.66	838	13.91	788	13.16	738	12.40	688
15.39	887	14.64	837	13.89	787	13.14	737	12.39	687
15.37	886	14.63	836	13.88	786	13.13	736	12.37	686
15.36	885	14.61	835	13.86	785	13.11	735	12.36	685
15.34	884	14.60	834	13.85	784	13.10	734	12.34	684
15.33	883	14.58	833	13.83	783	13.08	733	12.33	683
15.31	882	14.57	832	13.82	782	13.07	732	12.31	682
15.30	881	14.55	831	13.80	781	13.05	731	12.30	681
15.28	880	14.54	830	13.79	780	13.04	730	12.28	680
15.27	879	14.52	829	13.77	779	13.02	729	12.27	679
15.25	878	14.51	828	13.76	778	13.01	728	12.25	678
15.24	877	14.49	827	13.74	777	12.99	727	12.24	677
15.22	876	14.48	826	13.73	776	12.98	726	12.22	676
15.21	875	14.46	825	13.71	775	12.96	725	12.21	675
15.19	874	14.45	824	13.70	774	12.95	724	12.19	674
15.18	873	14.43	823	13.68	773	12.93	723	12.18	673
15.16	872	14.42	822	13.67	772	12.92	722	12.16	672
15.15	871	14.40	821	13.65	771	12.90	721	12.15	671
15.13	870	14.39	820	13.64	770	12.89	720	12.13	670
15.12	869	14.37	819	13.62	769	12.87	719	12.12	669
15.10	868	14.36	818	13.61	768	12.86	718	12.10	668
15.09	867	14.34	817	13.59	767	12.84	717	12.09	667
15.07	866	14.33	816	13.58	766	12.83	716	12.07	666
15.06	865	14.31	815	13.56	765	12.81	715	12.06	665
15.04	864	14.30	814	13.55	764	12.80	714	12.04	664
15.03	863	14.28	813	13.53	763	12.78	713	12.03	663
15.01	862	14.27	812	13.52	762	12.77	712	12.01	662
15.00	861	14.25	811	13.50	761	12.75	711	12.00	661
14.98	860	14.24	810	13.49	760	12.74	710	11.98	660
14.97	859	14.22	809	13.47	759	12.72	709	11.97	659
14.95	858	14.21	808	13.46	758	12.71	708	11.95	658
14.94	857	14.19	807	13.44	757	12.69	707	11.94	657
14.92	856	14.18	806	13.43	756	12.67	706	11.92	656
14.91	855	14.16	805	13.41	755	12.66	705	11.91	655
14.89	854	14.15	804	13.40	754	12.64	704	11.89	654
14.88	853	14.13	803	13.38	753	12.63	703	11.87	653
14.86	852	14.12	802	13.37	752	12.61	702	11.86	652
14.85	851	14.10	801	13.35	751	12.60	701	11.84	651
14.83	850	14.09	800	13.34	750	12.58	700	11.83	650

Metres	Points	Metres	Points	Metres	Points	Metres	Points	Metres	Points
15.57	899	14.82	849	14.07	799	13.32	749	12.57	699
15.55	898	14.80	848	14.06	798	13.31	748	12.55	698
15.54	897	14.79	847	14.04	797	13.29	747	12.54	697
15.52	896	14.78	846	14.03	796	13.28	746	12.52	696
15.51	895	14.76	845	14.01	795	13.26	745	12.51	695
15.49	894	14.75	844	14.00	794	13.25	744	12.49	694
15.48	893	14.73	843	13.98	793	13.23	743	12.48	693
15.46	892	14.72	842	13.97	792	13.22	742	12.46	692
15.45	891	14.70	841	13.95	791	13.20	741	12.45	691
15.43	890	14.69	840	13.94	790	13.19	740	12.43	690
15.42	889	14.67	839	13.92	789	13.17	739	12.42	689
15.40	888	14.66	838	13.91	788	13.16	738	12.40	688
15.39	887	14.64	837	13.89	787	13.14	737	12.39	687
15.37	886	14.63	836	13.88	786	13.13	736	12.37	686
15.36	885	14.61	835	13.86	785	13.11	735	12.36	685
15.34	884	14.60	834	13.85	784	13.10	734	12.34	684
15.33	883	14.58	833	13.83	783	13.08	733	12.33	683
15.31	882	14.57	832	13.82	782	13.07	732	12.31	682
15.30	881	14.55	831	13.80	781	13.05	731	12.30	681
15.28	880	14.54	830	13.79	780	13.04	730	12.28	680
15.27	879	14.52	829	13.77	779	13.02	729	12.27	679
15.25	878	14.51	828	13.76	778	13.01	728	12.25	678
15.24	877	14.49	827	13.74	777	12.99	727	12.24	677
15.22	876	14.48	826	13.73	776	12.98	726	12.22	676
15.21	875	14.46	825	13.71	775	12.96	725	12.21	675
15.19	874	14.45	824	13.70	774	12.95	724	12.19	674
15.18	873	14.43	823	13.68	773	12.93	723	12.18	673
15.16	872	14.42	822	13.67	772	12.92	722	12.16	672
15.15	871	14.40	821	13.65	771	12.90	721	12.15	671
15.13	870	14.39	820	13.64	770	12.89	720	12.13	670
15.12	869	14.37	819	13.62	769	12.87	719	12.12	669
15.10	868	14.36	818	13.61	768	12.86	718	12.10	668
15.09	867	14.34	817	13.59	767	12.84	717	12.09	667
15.07	866	14.33	816	13.58	766	12.83	716	12.07	666
15.06	865	14.31	815	13.56	765	12.81	715	12.06	665
15.04	864	14.30	814	13.55	764	12.80	714	12.04	664
15.03	863	14.28	813	13.53	763	12.78	713	12.03	663
15.01	862	14.27	812	13.52	762	12.77	712	12.01	662
15.00	861	14.25	811	13.50	761	12.75	711	12.00	661
14.98	860	14.24	810	13.49	760	12.74	710	11.98	660
14.97	859	14.22	809	13.47	759	12.72	709	11.97	659
14.95	858	14.21	808	13.46	758	12.71	708	11.95	658
14.94	857	14.19	807	13.44	757	12.69	707	11.94	657
14.92	856	14.18	806	13.43	756	12.67	706	11.92	656
14.91	855	14.16	805	13.41	755	12.66	705	11.91	655
14.89	854	14.15	804	13.40	754	12.64	704	11.89	654
14.88	853	14.13	803	13.38	753	12.63	703	11.87	653
14.86	852	14.12	802	13.37	752	12.61	702	11.86	652
14.85	851	14.10	801	13.35	751	12.60	701	11.84	651
14.83	850	14.09	800	13.34	750	12.58	700	11.83	650

Women   Putting the Shot — Lancement du Poids   Femmes

Metres	Points	Metres	Points	Metres	Points	Metres	Points	Metres	Points
7.99	399	7.22	349	6.43	299	5.64	249	4.85	199
7.98	398	7.20	348	6.42	298	5.63	248	4.83	198
7.96	397	7.18	347	6.40	297	5.61	247	4.82	197
7.95	396	7.17	346	6.39	296	5.60	246	4.80	196
7.93	395	7.15	345	6.37	295	5.58	245	4.79	195
7.91	394	7.14	344	6.35	294	5.57	244	4.77	194
7.90	393	7.12	343	6.34	293	5.55	243	4.75	193
7.88	392	7.11	342	6.32	292	5.53	242	4.74	192
7.87	391	7.09	341	6.31	291	5.52	241	4.72	191
7.85	390	7.07	340	6.29	290	5.50	240	4.70	190
7.84	389	7.06	339	6.28	289	5.49	239	4.69	189
7.82	388	7.04	338	6.26	288	5.47	238	4.67	188
7.81	387	7.03	337	6.24	287	5.45	237	4.66	187
7.79	386	7.01	336	6.23	286	5.44	236	4.64	186
7.77	385	7.00	335	6.21	285	5.42	235	4.62	185
7.76	384	6.98	334	6.20	284	5.41	234	4.61	184
7.74	383	6.97	333	6.18	283	5.39	233	4.59	183
7.73	382	6.95	332	6.17	282	5.38	232	4.58	182
7.71	381	6.93	331	6.15	281	5.36	231	4.56	181
7.70	380	6.92	330	6.13	280	5.34	230	4.54	180
7.68	379	6.90	329	6.12	279	5.33	229	4.53	179
7.67	378	6.89	328	6.10	278	5.31	228	4.51	178
7.65	377	6.87	327	6.09	277	5.30	227	4.50	177
7.64	376	6.86	326	6.07	276	5.28	226	4.48	176
7.62	375	6.84	325	6.06	275	5.26	225	4.46	175
7.60	374	6.82	324	6.04	274	5.25	224	4.45	174
7.59	373	6.81	323	6.02	273	5.23	223	4.43	173
7.57	372	6.79	322	6.01	272	5.22	222	4.42	172
7.56	371	6.78	321	5.99	271	5.20	221	4.40	171
7.54	370	6.76	320	5.98	270	5.18	220	4.38	170
7.53	369	6.75	319	5.96	269	5.17	219	4.37	169
7.51	368	6.73	318	5.95	268	5.15	218	4.35	168
7.50	367	6.72	317	5.93	267	5.14	217	4.33	167
7.48	366	6.70	316	5.91	266	5.12	216	4.32	166
7.46	365	6.68	315	5.90	265	5.10	215	4.30	165
7.45	364	6.67	314	5.88	264	5.09	214	4.29	164
7.43	363	6.65	313	5.87	263	5.07	213	4.27	163
7.42	362	6.64	312	5.85	262	5.06	212	4.25	162
7.40	361	6.62	311	5.83	261	5.04	211	4.24	161
7.39	360	6.61	310	5.82	260	5.02	210	4.22	160
7.37	359	6.59	309	5.80	259	5.01	209	4.21	159
7.36	358	6.57	308	5.79	258	4.99	208	4.19	158
7.34	357	6.56	307	5.77	257	4.98	207	4.17	157
7.32	356	6.54	306	5.76	256	4.96	206	4.16	156
7.31	355	6.53	305	5.74	255	4.95	205	4.14	155
7.29	354	6.51	304	5.72	254	4.93	204	4.12	154
7.28	353	6.50	303	5.71	253	4.91	203	4.11	153
7.26	352	6.48	302	5.69	252	4.90	202	4.09	152
7.25	351	6.46	301	5.68	251	4.88	201	4.08	151
7.23	350	6.45	300	5.66	250	4.87	200	4.06	150

Women   Putting the Shot — Lancement du Poids   Femmes

Metres	Points	Metres	Points	Metres	Points	Metres	Points	Metres	Points
4.04	149	3.55	119	3.06	89	2.56	59	2.04	29
4.03	148	3.54	118	3.04	88	2.54	58	2.02	28
4.01	147	3.52	117	3.03	87	2.52	57	2.00	27
3.99	146	3.51	116	3.01	86	2.50	56	1.99	26
3.98	145	3.49	115	2.99	85	2.49	55	1.97	25
3.96	144	3.47	114	2.98	84	2.47	54	1.95	24
3.95	143	3.46	113	2.96	83	2.45	53	1.93	23
3.93	142	3.44	112	2.94	82	2.44	52	1.92	22
3.91	141	3.42	111	2.93	81	2.42	51	1.90	21
3.90	140	3.41	110	2.91	80	2.40	50	1.88	20
3.88	139	3.39	109	2.89	79	2.39	49	1.86	19
3.86	138	3.37	108	2.88	78	2.37	48	1.84	18
3.85	137	3.36	107	2.86	77	2.35	47	1.83	17
3.83	136	3.34	106	2.84	76	2.33	46	1.81	16
3.82	135	3.32	105	2.83	75	2.32	45	1.79	15
3.80	134	3.31	104	2.81	74	2.30	44	1.77	14
3.78	133	3.29	103	2.79	73	2.28	43	1.75	13
3.77	132	3.27	102	2.77	72	2.27	42	1.74	12
3.75	131	3.26	101	2.76	71	2.25	41	1.72	11
3.73	130	3.24	100	2.74	70	2.23	40	1.70	10
3.72	129	3.22	99	2.72	69	2.21	39	1.68	9
3.70	128	3.21	98	2.71	68	2.20	38	1.66	8
3.69	127	3.19	97	2.69	67	2.18	37	1.64	7
3.67	126	3.18	96	2.67	66	2.16	36	1.62	6
3.65	125	3.16	95	2.66	65	2.14	35	1.61	5
3.64	124	3.14	94	2.64	64	2.13	34	1.59	4
3.62	123	3.13	93	2.62	63	2.11	33	1.57	3
3.60	122	3.11	92	2.61	62	2.09	32	1.55	2
3.59	121	3.09	91	2.59	61	2.07	31	1.53	1
3.57	120	3.08	90	2.57	60	2.06	30		

Seconds	Points	Seconds	Points	Seconds	Points	Seconds	Points	Seconds	Points
				This table to be used exclusively for fully automatic times.					
21.50	1234	22.00	1181	22.50	1129	23.00	1079	23.50	1029
21.51	1233	22.01	1180	22.51	1128	23.01	1078	23.51	1028
21.52	1232	22.02	1179	22.52	1127	23.02	1077	23.52	1027
21.53	1231	22.03	1178	22.53	1126	23.03	1076	23.53	1026
21.54	1229	22.04	1177	22.54	1125	23.04	1075	23.54	1025
21.55	1228	22.05	1176	22.55	1124	23.05	1074	23.55	1024
21.56	1227	22.06	1175	22.56	1123	23.06	1073	23.56	1023
21.57	1226	22.07	1174	22.57	1122	23.07	1072	23.57	1022
21.58	1225	22.08	1173	22.58	1121	23.08	1071	23.58	1021
21.59	1224	22.09	1172	22.59	1120	23.09	1070	23.59	1020
21.60	1223	22.10	1171	22.60	1119	23.10	1069	23.60	1019
21.61	1222	22.11	1170	22.61	1118	23.11	1068	23.61	1018
21.62	1221	22.12	1169	22.62	1117	23.12	1067	23.63	1017
21.63	1220	22.13	1168	22.63	1116	23.13	1066	23.64	1016
21.64	1219	22.14	1166	22.64	1115	23.14	1065	23.65	1015
21.65	1218	22.15	1165	22.65	1114	23.15	1064	23.66	1014
21.66	1217	22.16	1164	22.66	1113	23.16	1063	23.67	1013
21.67	1216	22.17	1163	22.67	1112	23.17	1062	23.68	1012
21.68	1215	22.18	1162	22.68	1111	23.18	1061	23.69	1011
21.69	1214	22.19	1161	22.69	1110	23.19	1060	23.70	1010
21.70	1213	22.20	1160	22.70	1109	23.20	1059	23.71	1009
21.71	1211	22.21	1159	22.71	1108	23.21	1058	23.72	1008
21.72	1210	22.22	1158	22.72	1107	23.22	1057	23.73	1007
21.73	1209	22.23	1157	22.73	1106	23.23	1056	23.74	1006
21.74	1208	22.24	1156	22.74	1105	23.24	1055	23.75	1005
21.75	1207	22.25	1155	22.75	1104	23.25	1054	23.76	1004
21.76	1206	22.26	1154	22.76	1103	23.26	1053	23.77	1003
21.77	1205	22.27	1153	22.77	1102	23.27	1052	23.78	1002
21.78	1204	22.28	1152	22.78	1101	23.28	1051	23.79	1001
21.79	1203	22.29	1151	22.79	1100	23.29	1050	23.80	1000
21.80	1202	22.30	1150	22.80	1099	23.30	1049	23.81	999
21.81	1201	22.31	1149	22.81	1098	23.31	1048	23.82	998
21.82	1200	22.32	1148	22.82	1097	23.32	1047	23.83	997
21.83	1199	22.33	1147	22.83	1096	23.33	1046	23.84	996
21.84	1198	22.34	1146	22.84	1095	23.34	1045	23.85	995
21.85	1197	22.35	1145	22.85	1094	23.35	1044	23.86	994
21.86	1196	22.36	1144	22.86	1093	23.36	1043	23.87	993
21.87	1195	22.37	1143	22.87	1092	23.37	1042	23.88	992
21.88	1194	22.38	1142	22.88	1091	23.38	1041	23.89	991
21.89	1193	22.39	1141	22.89	1090	23.39	1040	23.90	990
21.90	1191	22.40	1140	22.90	1089	23.40	1039	23.91	989
21.91	1190	22.41	1139	22.91	1088	23.41	1038	23.92	988
21.92	1189	22.42	1138	22.92	1087	23.42	1037	23.93	987
21.93	1188	22.43	1137	22.93	1086	23.43	1036	23.95	986
21.94	1187	22.44	1136	22.94	1085	23.44	1035	23.96	985
21.95	1186	22.45	1135	22.95	1084	23.45	1034	23.97	984
21.96	1185	22.46	1133	22.96	1083	23.46	1033	23.98	983
21.97	1184	22.47	1132	22.97	1082	23.47	1032	23.99	982
21.98	1183	22.48	1131	22.98	1081	23.48	1031	24.00	981
21.99	1182	22.49	1130	22.99	1080	23.49	1030	24.01	980

Seconds	Points	Seconds	Points	Seconds	Points	Seconds	Points	Seconds	Points
				This table to be used exclusively for fully automatic times.					
24.02	979	24.55	929	25.09	879	25.64	829	26.21	779
24.03	978	24.56	928	25.10	878	25.65	828	26.22	778
24.04	977	24.57	927	25.11	877	25.66	827	26.23	777
24.05	976	24.58	926	25.12	876	25.67	826	26.24	776
24.06	975	24.59	925	25.13	875	25.68	825	26.26	775
24.07	974	24.60	924	25.14	874	25.70	824	26.27	774
24.08	973	24.61	923	25.15	873	25.71	823	26.28	773
24.09	972	24.62	922	25.16	872	25.72	822	26.29	772
24.10	971	24.63	921	25.17	871	25.73	821	26.30	771
24.11	970	24.64	920	25.18	870	25.74	820	26.31	770
24.12	969	24.65	919	25.20	869	25.75	819	26.33	769
24.13	968	24.66	918	25.21	868	25.76	818	26.34	768
24.14	967	24.67	917	25.22	867	25.78	817	26.35	767
24.15	966	24.68	916	25.23	866	25.79	816	26.36	766
24.16	965	24.70	915	25.24	865	25.80	815	26.37	765
24.17	964	24.71	914	25.25	864	25.81	814	26.38	764
24.19	963	24.72	913	25.26	863	25.82	813	26.40	763
24.20	962	24.73	912	25.27	862	25.83	812	26.41	762
24.21	961	24.74	911	25.28	861	25.84	811	26.42	761
24.22	960	24.75	910	25.29	860	25.85	810	26.43	760
24.23	959	24.76	909	25.31	859	25.87	809	26.44	759
24.24	958	24.77	908	25.32	858	25.88	808	26.45	758
24.25	957	24.78	907	25.33	857	25.89	807	26.47	757
24.26	956	24.79	906	25.34	856	25.90	806	26.48	756
24.27	955	24.80	905	25.35	855	25.91	805	26.49	755
24.28	954	24.81	904	25.36	854	25.92	804	26.50	754
24.29	953	24.82	903	25.37	853	25.93	803	26.51	753
24.30	952	24.84	902	25.38	852	25.95	802	26.52	752
24.31	951	24.85	901	25.39	851	25.96	801	26.54	751
24.32	950	24.86	900	25.41	850	25.97	800	26.55	750
24.33	949	24.87	899	25.42	849	25.98	799	26.56	749
24.34	948	24.88	898	25.43	848	25.99	798	26.57	748
24.35	947	24.89	897	25.44	847	26.00	797	26.58	747
24.36	946	24.90	896	25.45	846	26.01	796	26.59	746
24.38	945	24.91	895	25.46	845	26.03	795	26.61	745
24.39	944	24.92	894	25.47	844	26.04	794	26.62	744
24.40	943	24.93	893	25.48	843	26.05	793	26.63	743
24.41	942	24.94	892	25.49	842	26.06	792	26.64	742
24.42	941	24.95	891	25.51	841	26.07	791	26.65	741
24.43	940	24.97	890	25.52	840	26.08	790	26.67	740
24.44	939	24.98	889	25.53	839	26.09	789	26.68	739
24.45	938	24.99	888	25.54	838	26.11	788	26.69	738
24.46	937	25.00	887	25.55	837	26.12	787	26.70	737
24.47	936	25.01	886	25.56	836	26.13	786	26.71	736
24.48	935	25.02	885	25.57	835	26.14	785	26.72	735
24.49	934	25.03	884	25.58	834	26.15	784	26.74	734
24.50	933	25.04	883	25.60	833	26.16	783	26.75	733
24.51	932	25.05	882	25.61	832	26.17	782	26.76	732
24.52	931	25.06	881	25.62	831	26.19	781	26.77	731
24.53	930	25.07	880	25.63	830	26.20	780	26.78	730

Perf.	Points	Perf.	Points	Perf.	Points	Perf.	Points	Perf.	Points
2:30.19	986	2:34.49	936	2:38.91	886	2:43.44	836	2:48.10	786
2:30.27	985	2:34.58	935	2:39.00	885	2:43.53	835	2:48.19	785
2:30.36	984	2:34.67	934	2:39.09	884	2:43.62	834	2:48.29	784
2:30.44	983	2:34.76	933	2:39.18	883	2:43.72	833	2:48.38	783
2:30.53	982	2:34.84	932	2:39.27	882	2:43.81	832	2:48.48	782
2:30.61	981	2:34.93	931	2:39.36	881	2:43.90	831	2:48.57	781
2:30.70	980	2:35.02	930	2:39.45	880	2:43.99	830	2:48.67	780
2:30.78	979	2:35.11	929	2:39.54	879	2:44.09	829	2:48.76	779
2:30.87	978	2:35.19	928	2:39.63	878	2:44.18	828	2:48.86	778
2:30.95	977	2:35.28	927	2:39.72	877	2:44.27	827	2:48.95	777
2:31.04	976	2:35.37	926	2:39.81	876	2:44.36	826	2:49.05	776
2:31.13	975	2:35.46	925	2:39.90	875	2:44.45	825	2:49.14	775
2:31.21	974	2:35.54	924	2:39.99	874	2:44.55	824	2:49.24	774
2:31.30	973	2:35.63	923	2:40.08	873	2:44.64	823	2:49.33	773
2:31.38	972	2:35.72	922	2:40.17	872	2:44.73	822	2:49.43	772
2:31.47	971	2:35.81	921	2:40.26	871	2:44.82	821	2:49.52	771
2:31.55	970	2:35.90	920	2:40.35	870	2:44.92	820	2:49.62	770
2:31.64	969	2:35.98	919	2:40.44	869	2:45.01	819	2:49.71	769
2:31.73	968	2:36.07	918	2:40.53	868	2:45.10	818	2:49.81	768
2:31.81	967	2:36.16	917	2:40.62	867	2:45.20	817	2:49.90	767
2:31.90	966	2:36.25	916	2:40.71	866	2:45.29	816	2:50.00	766
2:31.98	965	2:36.34	915	2:40.80	865	2:45.38	815	2:50.10	765
2:32.07	964	2:36.42	914	2:40.89	864	2:45.47	814	2:50.19	764
2:32.16	963	2:36.51	913	2:40.98	863	2:45.57	813	2:50.29	763
2:32.24	962	2:36.60	912	2:41.07	862	2:45.66	812	2:50.38	762
2:32.33	961	2:36.69	911	2:41.16	861	2:45.75	811	2:50.48	761
2:32.41	960	2:36.78	910	2:41.25	860	2:45.85	810	2:50.57	760
2:32.50	959	2:36.87	909	2:41.34	859	2:45.94	809	2:50.67	759
2:32.59	958	2:36.95	908	2:41.43	858	2:46.03	808	2:50.77	758
2:32.67	957	2:37.04	907	2:41.52	857	2:46.13	807	2:50.86	757
2:32.76	956	2:37.13	906	2:41.61	856	2:46.22	806	2:50.96	756
2:32.85	955	2:37.22	905	2:41.70	855	2:46.31	805	2:51.05	765
2:32.93	954	2:37.31	904	2:41.80	854	2:46.41	804	2:51.15	754
2:33.02	953	2:37.40	903	2:41.89	853	2:46.50	803	2:51.25	753
2:33.11	952	2:37.48	902	2:41.98	852	2:46.59	802	2:51.34	752
2:33.19	951	2:37.57	901	2:42.07	851	2:46.69	801	2:51.44	751
2:33.28	950	2:37.66	900	2:42.16	850	2:46.78	800	2:51.54	750
2:33.36	949	2:37.75	899	2:42.25	849	2:46.87	799	2:51.63	749
2:33.45	948	2:37.84	898	2:42.34	848	2:46.97	798	2:51.73	748
2:33.54	947	2:37.93	897	2:42.43	847	2:47.06	797	2:51.83	747
2:33.62	946	2:38.02	896	2:42.53	846	2:47.16	796	2:51.92	746
2:33.71	945	2:38.11	895	2:42.62	845	2:47.25	795	2:52.02	745
2:33.80	944	2:38.20	894	2:42.71	844	2:47.34	794	2:52.12	744
2:33.89	943	2:38.29	893	2:42.80	843	2:47.44	793	2:52.21	743
2:33.97	942	2:38.37	892	2:42.89	842	2:47.53	792	2:52.31	742
2:34.06	941	2:38.46	891	2:42.98	841	2:47.63	791	2:52.41	741
2:34.15	940	2:38.55	890	2:43.07	840	2:47.72	790	2:52.51	740
2:34.23	939	2:38.64	889	2:43.17	839	2:47.82	789	2:52.60	739
2:34.32	938	2:38.73	888	2:43.26	838	2:47.91	788	2:52.70	738
2:34.41	937	2:38.82	887	2:43.35	837	2:48.00	787	2:52.80	737

IAAF Scoring Tables for Combined Events / Tables de Cotation pour les Epreuves Combinées

Perf.	Points	Perf.	Points	Perf.	Points	Perf.	Points	Perf.	Points
2:52.89	736	2:57.84	686	3:02.96	636	3:08.26	586	3:13.78	536
2:52.99	735	2:57.94	685	3:03.06	635	3:08.37	585	3:13.89	535
2:53.09	734	2:58.04	684	3:03.17	634	3:08.48	584	3:14.01	534
2:53.19	733	2:58.14	683	3:03.27	633	3:08.59	583	3:14.12	533
2:53.28	732	2:58.25	682	3:03.38	632	3:08.70	582	3:14.23	532
2:53.38	731	2:58.35	681	3:03.48	631	3:08.81	581	3:14.35	531
2:53.48	730	2:58.45	680	3:03.58	630	3:08.91	580	3:14.46	530
2:53.58	729	2:58.55	679	3:03.69	629	3:09.02	579	3:14.57	529
2:53.68	728	2:58.65	678	3:03.79	628	3:09.13	578	3:14.69	528
2:53.77	727	2:58.75	677	3:03.90	627	3:09.24	577	3:14.80	527
2:53.87	726	2:58.85	676	3:04.00	626	3:09.35	576	3:14.91	526
2:53.97	725	2:58.95	675	3:04.11	625	3:09.46	575	3:15.03	525
2:54.07	724	2:59.05	674	3:04.21	624	3:09.57	574	3:15.14	524
2:54.17	723	2:59.16	673	3:04.32	623	3:09.68	573	3:15.25	523
2:54.26	722	2:59.26	672	3:04.42	622	3:09.79	572	3:15.37	522
2:54.36	721	2:59.36	671	3:04.53	621	3:09.90	571	3:15.48	521
2:54.46	720	2:59.46	670	3:04.63	620	3:10.00	570	3:15.60	520
2:54.56	719	2:59.56	669	3:04.74	619	3:10.11	569	3:15.71	519
2:54.66	718	2:59.66	668	3:04.85	618	3:10.22	568	3:15.83	518
2:54.76	717	2:59.77	667	3:04.95	617	3:10.33	567	3:15.94	517
2:54.85	716	2:59.87	666	3:05.06	616	3:10.44	566	3:16.05	516
2:54.95	715	2:59.97	665	3:05.16	615	3:10.55	565	3:16.17	515
2:55.05	714	3:00.07	664	3:05.27	614	3:10.66	564	3:16.28	514
2:55.15	713	3:00.17	663	3:05.37	613	3:10.77	563	3:16.40	513
2:55.25	712	3:00.28	662	3:05.48	612	3:10.88	562	3:16.51	512
2:55.35	711	3:00.38	661	3:05.59	611	3:10.99	561	3:16.63	511
2:55.45	710	3:00.48	660	3:05.69	610	3:11.10	560	3:16.74	510
2:55.55	709	3:00.58	659	3:05.80	609	3:11.22	559	3:16.86	509
2:55.65	708	3:00.69	658	3:05.90	608	3:11.33	558	3:16.97	508
2:55.74	707	3:00.79	657	3:06.01	607	3:11.44	557	3:17.09	507
2:55.84	706	3:00.89	656	3:06.12	606	3:11.55	556	3:17.21	506
2:55.94	705	3:00.99	655	3:06.22	605	3:11.66	555	3:17.32	505
2:56.04	704	3:01.10	654	3:06.33	604	3:11.77	554	3:17.44	504
2:56.14	703	3:01.20	653	3:06.44	603	3:11.88	553	3:17.55	503
2:56.24	702	3:01.30	652	3:06.54	602	3:11.99	552	3:17.67	502
2:56.34	701	3:01.40	651	3:06.65	601	3:12.10	551	3:17.79	501
2:56.44	700	3:01.51	650	3:06.76	600	3:12.21	550	3:17.90	500
2:56.54	699	3:01.61	649	3:06.87	599	3:12.32	549	3:18.02	499
2:56.64	698	3:01.71	648	3:06.97	598	3:12.44	548	3:18.13	498
2:56.74	697	3:01.82	647	3:07.08	597	3:12.55	547	3:18.25	497
2:56.84	696	3:01.92	646	3:07.19	596	3:12.66	546	3:18.37	496
2:56.94	695	3:02.02	645	3:07.29	595	3:12.77	545	3:18.48	495
2:57.04	694	3:02.13	644	3:07.40	594	3:12.88	544	3:18.60	494
2:57.14	693	3:02.23	643	3:07.51	593	3:13.00	543	3:18.72	493
2:57.24	692	3:02.34	642	3:07.62	592	3:13.11	542	3:18.84	492
2:57.34	691	3:02.44	641	3:07.72	591	3:13.22	541	3:18.95	491
2:57.44	690	3:02.54	640	3:07.83	590	3:13.33	540	3:19.07	490
2:57.54	689	3:02.65	639	3:07.94	589	3:13.44	539	3:19.19	489
2:57.64	688	3:02.75	638	3:08.05	588	3:13.56	538	3:19.31	488
2:57.74	687	3:02.85	637	3:08.16	587	3:13.67	537	3:19.42	487

IAAF Scoring Tables for Combined Events / Tables de Cotation pour les Epreuves Combinées

1000 Metres - 1000 Mètres

Hommes

Perf.	Points	Perf.	Points	Perf.	Points	Perf.	Points	Perf.	Points
3:19.54	486	3:25.58	436	3:31.95	386	3:38.70	336	3:45.94	286
3:19.66	485	3:25.70	435	3:32.08	385	3:38.84	335	3:46.09	285
3:19.78	484	3:25.83	434	3:32.21	384	3:38.98	334	3:46.24	284
3:19.89	483	3:25.95	433	3:32.34	383	3:39.12	333	3:46.40	283
3:20.01	482	3:26.08	432	3:32.47	382	3:39.26	332	3:46.55	282
3:20.13	481	3:26.20	431	3:32.60	381	3:39.41	331	3:46.70	281
3:20.25	480	3:26.33	430	3:32.74	380	3:39.55	330	3:46.85	280
3:20.37	479	3:26.45	429	3:32.87	379	3:39.69	329	3:47.00	279
3:20.49	478	3:26.57	428	3:33.00	378	3:39.83	328	3:47.15	278
3:20.61	477	3:26.70	427	3:33.13	377	3:39.97	327	3:47.31	277
3:20.72	476	3:26.83	426	3:33.26	376	3:40.11	326	3:47.46	276
3:20.84	475	3:26.95	425	3:33.40	375	3:40.25	325	3:47.61	275
3:20.96	474	3:27.08	424	3:33.53	374	3:40.39	324	3:47.77	274
3:21.08	473	3:27.20	423	3:33.66	373	3:40.54	323	3:47.92	273
3:21.20	472	3:27.33	422	3:33.80	372	3:40.68	322	3:48.07	272
3:21.32	471	3:27.45	421	3:33.93	371	3:40.82	321	3:48.23	271
3:21.44	470	3:27.58	420	3:34.06	370	3:40.96	320	3:48.38	270
3:21.56	469	3:27.70	419	3:34.20	369	3:41.11	319	3:48.54	269
3:21.68	468	3:27.83	418	3:34.33	368	3:41.25	318	3:48.69	268
3:21.80	467	3:27.96	417	3:34.46	367	3:41.39	317	3:48.85	267
3:21.92	466	3:28.08	416	3:34.60	366	3:41.54	316	3:49.00	266
3:22.04	465	3:28.21	415	3:34.73	365	3:41.68	315	3:49.16	265
3:22.16	464	3:28.34	414	3:34.87	364	3:41.82	314	3:49.31	264
3:22.28	463	3:28.46	413	3:35.00	363	3:41.97	313	3:49.47	263
3:22.40	462	3:28.59	412	3:35.14	362	3:42.11	312	3:49.62	262
3:22.52	461	3:28.72	411	3:35.27	361	3:42.26	311	3:49.78	261
3:22.64	460	3:28.85	410	3:35.41	360	3:42.40	310	3:49.94	260
3:22.76	459	3:28.97	409	3:35.54	359	3:42.55	309	3:50.10	259
3:22.89	458	3:29.10	408	3:35.68	358	3:42.69	308	3:50.25	258
3:23.01	457	3:29.23	407	3:35.81	357	3:42.84	307	3:50.41	257
3:23.13	456	3:29.36	406	3:35.95	356	3:42.98	306	3:50.57	256
3:23.25	455	3:29.48	405	3:36.09	355	3:43.13	305	3:50.73	255
3:23.37	454	3:29.61	404	3:36.22	354	3:43.28	304	3:50.89	254
3:23.49	453	3:29.74	403	3:36.36	353	3:43.42	303	3:51.04	253
3:23.61	452	3:29.87	402	3:36.49	352	3:43.57	302	3:51.20	252
3:23.74	451	3:30.00	401	3:36.63	351	3:43.71	301	3:51.36	251
3:23.86	450	3:30.13	400	3:36.77	350	3:43.86	300	3:51.52	250
3:23.98	449	3:30.26	399	3:36.91	349	3:44.01	299	3:51.68	249
3:24.10	448	3:30.39	398	3:37.04	348	3:44.16	298	3:51.84	248
3:24.22	447	3:30.51	397	3:37.18	347	3:44.30	297	3:52.00	247
3:24.35	446	3:30.64	396	3:37.32	346	3:44.45	296	3:52.17	246
3:24.47	445	3:30.77	395	3:37.46	345	3:44.60	295	3:52.33	245
3:24.59	444	3:30.90	394	3:37.59	344	3:44.75	294	3:52.49	244
3:24.72	443	3:31.03	393	3:37.73	343	3:44.90	293	3:52.65	243
3:24.84	442	3:31.16	392	3:37.87	342	3:45.05	292	3:52.81	242
3:24.96	441	3:31.29	391	3:38.01	341	3:45.19	291	3:52.97	241
3:25.09	440	3:31.42	390	3:38.15	340	3:45.34	290	3:53.14	240
3:25.21	439	3:31.55	389	3:38.29	339	3:45.49	289	3:53.30	239
3:25.33	438	3:31.68	388	3:38.43	338	3:45.64	288	3:53.46	238
3:25.46	437	3:31.82	387	3:38.57	337	3:45.79	287	3:53.63	237

IAAF Scoring Tables for Combined Events / Tables de Cotation pour les Epreuves Combinées

Perf.	Points	Perf.	Points	Perf.	Points	Perf.	Points	Perf.	Points
3:53.79	236	4:02.45	186	4:12.27	136	4:23.95	86	4:39.55	36
3:53.96	235	4:02.63	185	4:12.48	135	4:24.21	85	4:39.94	35
3:54.12	234	4:02.82	184	4:12.69	134	4:24.47	84	4:40.34	34
3:54.29	233	4:03.00	183	4:12.90	133	4:24.74	83	4:40.74	33
3:54.45	232	4:03.19	182	4:13.12	132	4:25.00	82	4:41.15	32
3:54.62	231	4:03.37	181	4:13.33	131	4:25.27	81	4:41.56	31
3:54.78	230	4:03.56	180	4:13.55	130	4:25.54	80	4:41.98	30
3:54.95	229	4:03.74	179	4:13.77	129	4:25.81	79	4:42.41	29
3:55.12	228	4:03.93	178	4:13.98	128	4:26.08	78	4:42.84	28
3:55.28	227	4:04.12	177	4:14.20	127	4:26.36	77	4:43.28	27
3:55.45	226	4:04.31	176	4:14.42	126	4:26.63	76	4:43.73	26
3:55.62	225	4:04.49	175	4:14.64	125	4:26.91	75	4:44.19	25
3:55.79	224	4:04.68	174	4:14.86	124	4:27.19	74	4:44.65	24
3:55.95	223	4:04.87	173	4:15.08	123	4:27.47	73	4:45.13	23
3:56.12	222	4:05.06	172	4:15.30	122	4:27.75	72	4:45.61	22
3:56.29	221	4:05.25	171	4:15.52	121	4:28.04	71	4:46.10	21
3:56.46	220	4:05.44	170	4:15.75	120	4:28.32	70	4:46.61	20
3:56.63	219	4:05.63	169	4:15.97	119	4:28.61	69	4:47.13	19
3:56.80	218	4:05.83	168	4:16.20	118	4:28.90	68	4:47.65	18
3:56.97	217	4:06.02	167	4:16.42	117	4:29.19	67	4:48.20	17
3:57.14	216	4:06.21	166	4:16.65	116	4:29.49	66	4:48.75	16
3:57.31	215	4:06.40	165	4:16.88	115	4:29.78	65	4:49.33	15
3:57.49	214	4:06.60	164	4:17.11	114	4:30.08	64	4:49.92	14
3:57.66	213	4:06.79	163	4:17.34	113	4:30.38	63	4:50.53	13
3:57.83	212	4:06.99	162	4:17.57	112	4:30.68	62	4:51.17	12
3:58.00	211	4:07.18	161	4:17.80	111	4:30.99	61	4:51.82	11
3:58.18	210	4:07.38	160	4:18.03	110	4:31.29	60	4:52.51	10
3:58.35	209	4:07.58	159	4:18.27	109	4:31.60	59	4:53.23	9
3:58.52	208	4:07.77	158	4:18.50	108	4:31.91	58	4:53.99	8
3:58.70	207	4:07.97	157	4:18.74	107	4:32.23	57	4:54.79	7
3:58.87	206	4:08.17	156	4:18.97	106	4:32.55	56	4:55.64	6
3:59.05	205	4:08.37	155	4:19.21	105	4:32.86	55	4:56.57	5
3:59.22	204	4:08.57	154	4:19.45	104	4:33.19	54	4:57.58	4
3:59.40	203	4:08.77	153	4:19.69	103	4:33.51	53	4:58.72	3
3:59.57	202	4:08.97	152	4:19.93	102	4:33.84	52	5:00.05	2
3:59.75	201	4:09.17	151	4:20.17	101	4:34.17	51	5:01.75	1
3:59.93	200	4:09.37	150	4:20.42	100	4:34.50	50		
4:00.11	199	4:09.57	149	4:20.66	99	4:34.84	49		
4:00.28	198	4:09.78	148	4:20.91	98	4:35.18	48		
4:00.46	197	4:09.98	147	4:21.15	97	4:35.52	47		
4:00.64	196	4:10.19	146	4:21.40	96	4:35.87	46		
4:00.82	195	4:10.39	145	4:21.65	95	4:36.22	45		
4:01.00	194	4:10.60	144	4:21.90	94	4:36.57	44		
4:01.18	193	4:10.80	143	4:22.15	93	4:36.93	43		
4:01.36	192	4:11.01	142	4:22.40	92	4:37.29	42		
4:01.54	191	4:11.22	141	4:22.66	91	4:37.66	41		
4:01.72	190	4:11.43	140	4:22.91	90	4:38.02	40		
4:01.90	189	4:11.63	139	4:23.17	89	4:38.40	39		
4:02.09	188	4:11.84	138	4:23.43	88	4:38.78	38		
4:02.27	187	4:12.06	137	4:23.69	87	4:39.16	37		

IAAF Scoring Tables for Combined Events / Tables de Cotation pour les Epreuves Combinées

Perf.	Points	Perf.	Points	Perf.	Points	Perf.	Points	Perf.	Points
7.00	1371	7.50	1247	8.00	1130	8.50	1017	9.00	910
7.01	1368	7.51	1245	8.01	1127	8.51	1015	9.01	908
7.02	1366	7.52	1243	8.02	1125	8.52	1013	9.02	906
7.03	1363	7.53	1240	8.03	1123	8.53	1010	9.03	904
7.04	1361	7.54	1238	8.04	1120	8.54	1008	9.04	902
7.05	1358	7.55	1235	8.05	1118	8.55	1006	9.05	900
7.06	1356	7.56	1233	8.06	1116	8.56	1004	9.06	897
7.07	1353	7.57	1231	8.07	1113	8.57	1002	9.07	895
7.08	1351	7.58	1228	8.08	1111	8.58	1000	9.08	893
7.09	1348	7.59	1226	8.09	1109	8.59	997	9.09	891
7.10	1346	7.60	1223	8.10	1107	8.60	995	9.10	889
7.11	1343	7.61	1221	8.11	1104	8.61	993	9.11	887
7.12	1341	7.62	1219	8.12	1102	8.62	991	9.12	885
7.13	1338	7.63	1216	8.13	1100	8.63	989	9.13	883
7.14	1336	7.64	1214	8.14	1098	8.64	987	9.14	881
7.15	1333	7.65	1212	8.15	1095	8.65	984	9.15	879
7.16	1331	7.66	1209	8.16	1093	8.66	982	9.16	877
7.17	1328	7.67	1207	8.17	1091	8.67	980	9.17	875
7.18	1326	7.68	1204	8.18	1088	8.68	978	9.18	873
7.19	1323	7.69	1202	8.19	1086	8.69	976	9.19	871
7.20	1321	7.70	1200	8.20	1084	8.70	974	9.20	869
7.21	1318	7.71	1197	8.21	1082	8.71	971	9.21	867
7.22	1316	7.72	1195	8.22	1079	8.72	969	9.22	865
7.23	1313	7.73	1193	8.23	1077	8.73	967	9.23	862
7.24	1311	7.74	1190	8.24	1075	8.74	965	9.24	860
7.25	1308	7.75	1188	8.25	1073	8.75	963	9.25	858
7.26	1306	7.76	1185	8.26	1070	8.76	961	9.26	856
7.27	1303	7.77	1183	8.27	1068	8.77	959	9.27	854
7.28	1301	7.78	1181	8.28	1066	8.78	956	9.28	852
7.29	1299	7.79	1178	8.29	1064	8.79	954	9.29	850
7.30	1296	7.80	1176	8.30	1061	8.80	952	9.30	848
7.31	1294	7.81	1174	8.31	1059	8.81	950	9.31	846
7.32	1291	7.82	1171	8.32	1057	8.82	948	9.32	844
7.33	1289	7.83	1169	8.33	1055	8.83	946	9.33	842
7.34	1286	7.84	1167	8.34	1052	8.84	944	9.34	840
7.35	1284	7.85	1164	8.35	1050	8.85	941	9.35	838
7.36	1281	7.86	1162	8.36	1048	8.86	939	9.36	836
7.37	1279	7.87	1160	8.37	1046	8.87	937	9.37	834
7.38	1277	7.88	1157	8.38	1044	8.88	935	9.38	832
7.39	1274	7.89	1155	8.39	1041	8.89	933	9.39	830
7.40	1272	7.90	1153	8.40	1039	8.90	931	9.40	828
7.41	1269	7.91	1150	8.41	1037	8.91	929	9.41	826
7.42	1267	7.92	1148	8.42	1035	8.92	927	9.42	824
7.43	1264	7.93	1146	8.43	1032	8.93	925	9.43	822
7.44	1262	7.94	1143	8.44	1030	8.94	922	9.44	820
7.45	1260	7.95	1141	8.45	1028	8.95	920	9.45	818
7.46	1257	7.96	1139	8.46	1026	8.96	918	9.46	816
7.47	1255	7.97	1136	8.47	1024	8.97	916	9.47	814
7.48	1252	7.98	1134	8.48	1021	8.98	914	9.48	812
7.49	1250	7.99	1132	8.49	1019	8.99	912	9.49	810

IAAF Scoring Tables for Combined Events / Tables de Cotation pour les Epreuves Combinées

Perf.	Points	Perf.	Points	Perf.	Points	Perf.	Points	Perf.	Points
9.50	808	10.00	712	10.50	621	11.00	537	11.50	457
9.51	806	10.01	710	10.51	620	11.01	535	11.51	456
9.52	804	10.02	708	10.52	618	11.02	533	11.52	454
9.53	802	10.03	706	10.53	616	11.03	532	11.53	453
9.54	800	10.04	705	10.54	614	11.04	530	11.54	451
9.55	798	10.05	703	10.55	613	11.05	528	11.55	450
9.56	796	10.06	701	10.56	611	11.06	527	11.56	448
9.57	794	10.07	699	10.57	609	11.07	525	11.57	447
9.58	792	10.08	697	10.58	607	11.08	523	11.58	445
9.59	791	10.09	695	10.59	606	11.09	522	11.59	444
9.60	789	10.10	693	10.60	604	11.10	520	11.60	442
9.61	787	10.11	692	10.61	602	11.11	519	11.61	441
9.62	785	10.12	690	10.62	601	11.12	517	11.62	439
9.63	783	10.13	688	10.63	599	11.13	515	11.63	438
9.64	781	10.14	686	10.64	597	11.14	514	11.64	436
9.65	779	10.15	684	10.65	595	11.15	512	11.65	435
9.66	777	10.16	682	10.66	594	11.16	511	11.66	433
9.67	775	10.17	681	10.67	592	11.17	509	11.67	432
9.68	773	10.18	679	10.68	590	11.18	507	11.68	430
9.69	771	10.19	677	10.69	589	11.19	506	11.69	429
9.70	769	10.20	675	10.70	587	11.20	504	11.70	427
9.71	767	10.21	673	10.71	585	11.21	503	11.71	426
9.72	765	10.22	672	10.72	583	11.22	501	11.72	424
9.73	763	10.23	670	10.73	582	11.23	499	11.73	423
9.74	761	10.24	668	10.74	580	11.24	498	11.74	421
9.75	759	10.25	666	10.75	578	11.25	496	11.75	420
9.76	758	10.26	664	10.76	577	11.26	495	11.76	418
9.77	756	10.27	662	10.77	575	11.27	493	11.77	417
9.78	754	10.28	661	10.78	573	11.28	491	11.78	415
9.79	752	10.29	659	10.79	571	11.29	490	11.79	414
9.80	750	10.30	657	10.80	570	11.30	488	11.80	412
9.81	748	10.31	655	10.81	568	11.31	487	11.81	411
9.82	746	10.32	653	10.82	566	11.32	485	11.82	410
9.83	744	10.33	652	10.83	565	11.33	484	11.83	408
9.84	742	10.34	650	10.84	563	11.34	482	11.84	407
9.85	740	10.35	648	10.85	561	11.35	480	11.85	405
9.86	738	10.36	646	10.86	560	11.36	479	11.86	404
9.87	737	10.37	644	10.87	558	11.37	477	11.87	402
9.88	735	10.38	643	10.88	556	11.38	476	11.88	401
9.89	733	10.39	641	10.89	555	11.39	474	11.89	399
9.90	731	10.40	639	10.90	553	11.40	473	11.90	398
9.91	729	10.41	637	10.91	551	11.41	471	11.91	397
9.92	727	10.42	636	10.92	550	11.42	470	11.92	395
9.93	725	10.43	634	10.93	548	11.43	468	11.93	394
9.94	723	10.44	632	10.94	546	11.44	466	11.94	392
9.95	721	10.45	630	10.95	545	11.45	465	11.95	391
9.96	720	10.46	629	10.96	543	11.46	463	11.96	389
9.97	718	10.47	627	10.97	541	11.47	462	11.97	388
9.98	716	10.48	625	10.98	540	11.48	460	11.98	387
9.99	714	10.49	623	10.99	538	11.49	459	11.99	385

IAAF Scoring Tables for Combined Events / Tables de Cotation pour les Epreuves Combinées

Perf.	Points	Perf.	Points	Perf.	Points	Perf.	Points	Perf.	Points
12.00	384	12.50	316	13.00	255	13.50	199	14.01	149
12.01	382	12.51	315	13.01	254	13.51	198	14.02	148
12.02	381	12.52	314	13.02	252	13.52	197	14.03	147
12.03	380	12.53	312	13.03	251	13.53	196	14.04	146
12.04	378	12.54	311	13.04	250	13.54	195	14.06	145
12.05	377	12.55	310	13.05	249	13.55	194	14.07	144
12.06	375	12.56	309	13.06	248	13.56	193	14.08	143
12.07	374	12.57	307	13.07	247	13.57	192	14.09	142
12.08	373	12.58	306	13.08	245	13.58	191	14.10	141
12.09	371	12.59	305	13.09	244	13.59	190	14.11	140
12.10	370	12.60	303	13.10	243	13.60	189	14.12	139
12.11	368	12.61	302	13.11	242	13.61	188	14.13	138
12.12	367	12.62	301	13.12	241	13.62	187	14.14	137
12.13	366	12.63	300	13.13	240	13.63	186	14.16	136
12.14	364	12.64	298	13.14	239	13.64	185	14.17	135
12.15	363	12.65	297	13.15	237	13.65	184	14.18	134
12.16	362	12.66	296	13.16	236	13.66	183	14.19	133
12.17	360	12.67	295	13.17	235	13.67	182	14.20	132
12.18	359	12.68	293	13.18	234	13.68	181	14.21	131
12.19	357	12.69	292	13.19	233	13.69	180	14.23	130
12.20	356	12.70	291	13.20	232	13.70	179	14.24	129
12.21	355	12.71	290	13.21	231	13.71	178	14.25	128
12.22	353	12.72	288	13.22	230	13.72	177	14.26	127
12.23	352	12.73	287	13.23	228	13.73	176	14.27	126
12.24	351	12.74	286	13.24	227	13.74	175	14.28	125
12.25	349	12.75	285	13.25	226	13.75	174	14.30	124
12.26	348	12.76	283	13.26	225	13.76	173	14.31	123
12.27	347	12.77	282	13.27	224	13.77	172	14.32	122
12.28	345	12.78	281	13.28	223	13.78	171	14.33	121
12.29	344	12.79	280	13.29	222	13.79	170	14.34	120
12.30	343	12.80	279	13.30	221	13.80	169	14.36	119
12.31	341	12.81	277	13.31	220	13.81	168	14.37	118
12.32	340	12.82	276	13.32	218	13.82	167	14.38	117
12.33	339	12.83	275	13.33	217	13.83	166	14.39	116
12.34	337	12.84	274	13.34	216	13.84	165	14.40	115
12.35	336	12.85	273	13.35	215	13.85	164	14.42	114
12.36	335	12.86	271	13.36	214	13.86	163	14.43	113
12.37	333	12.87	270	13.37	213	13.87	162	14.44	112
12.38	332	12.88	269	13.38	212	13.88	161	14.45	111
12.39	331	12.89	268	13.39	211	13.89	160	14.47	110
12.40	329	12.90	267	13.40	210	13.90	159	14.48	109
12.41	328	12.91	265	13.41	209	13.91	158	14.49	108
12.42	327	12.92	264	13.42	208	13.93	157	14.50	107
12.43	325	12.93	263	13.43	207	13.94	156	14.52	106
12.44	324	12.94	262	13.44	206	13.95	155	14.53	105
12.45	323	12.95	261	13.45	204	13.96	154	14.54	104
12.46	321	12.96	259	13.46	203	13.97	153	14.56	103
12.47	320	12.97	258	13.47	202	13.98	152	14.57	102
12.48	319	12.98	257	13.48	201	13.99	151	14.58	101
12.49	318	12.99	256	13.49	200	14.00	150	14.59	100

IAAF Scoring Tables for Combined Events / Tables de Cotation pour les Epreuves Combinées

Perf.	Points	Perf.	Points	Perf.	Points	Perf.	Points	Perf.	Points
14.61	99	14.88	79	15.19	59	15.56	39	16.02	19
14.62	98	14.90	78	15.21	58	15.58	38	16.05	18
14.63	97	14.91	77	15.23	57	15.60	37	16.08	17
14.65	96	14.93	76	15.24	56	15.62	36	16.11	16
14.66	95	14.94	75	15.26	55	15.64	35	16.14	15
14.67	94	14.96	74	15.28	54	15.66	34	16.17	14
14.69	93	14.97	73	15.30	53	15.68	33	16.21	13
14.70	92	14.99	72	15.31	52	15.70	32	16.24	12
14.71	91	15.00	71	15.33	51	15.73	31	16.27	11
14.73	90	15.02	70	15.35	50	15.75	30	16.31	10
14.74	89	15.03	69	15.37	49	15.77	29	16.35	9
14.76	88	15.05	68	15.39	48	15.80	28	16.39	8
14.77	87	15.06	67	15.40	47	15.82	27	16.43	7
14.78	86	15.08	66	15.42	46	15.84	26	16.48	6
14.80	85	15.10	65	15.44	45	15.87	25	16.53	5
14.81	84	15.11	64	15.46	44	15.89	24	16.58	4
14.83	83	15.13	63	15.48	43	15.92	23	16.64	3
14.84	82	15.14	62	15.50	42	15.94	22	16.71	2
14.85	81	15.16	61	15.52	41	15.97	21	16.80	1
14.87	80	15.18	60	15.54	40	16.00	20		

IAAF Scoring Tables for Combined Events / Tables de Cotation pour les Epreuves Combinées

Perf.	Points	Perf.	Points	Perf.	Points	Perf.	Points	Perf.	Points

THIS TABLE IS TO BE USED EXCLUSIVELY FOR HAND TIMES

A UTILISER UNIQUEMENT EN CAS DE CHRONOMETRAGE MANUEL

Perf.	Points	Perf.	Points	Perf.	Points	Perf.	Points	Perf.	Points
7.0	1311	9.0	860	11.0	498	13.0	227	15.0	56
7.1	1286	9.1	840	11.1	482	13.1	216	15.2	45
7.2	1262	9.2	820	11.2	466	13.2	206	15.3	40
7.3	1238	9.3	800	11.3	451	13.3	195	15.4	35
7.4	1214	9.4	781	11.4	436	13.4	185	15.5	30
7.5	1190	9.5	761	11.5	421	13.5	175	15.6	26
7.6	1167	9.6	742	11.6	407	13.6	165	15.7	22
7.7	1143	9.7	723	11.7	392	13.7	156	15.8	18
7.8	1120	9.8	705	11.8	378	13.8	146	15.9	15
7.9	1098	9.9	686	11.9	364	13.9	137	16.0	12
8.0	1075	10.0	668	12.0	351	14.0	129	16.1	9
8.1	1052	10.1	650	12.1	337	14.1	120	16.2	6
8.2	1030	10.2	632	12.2	324	14.2	112	16.3	4
8.3	1008	10.3	614	12.3	311	14.3	104	16.4	3
8.4	987	10.4	597	12.4	298	14.4	96	16.5	1
8.5	965	10.5	580	12.5	286	14.5	89		
8.6	944	10.6	563	12.6	274	14.6	82		
8.7	922	10.7	546	12.7	262	14.7	75		
8.8	902	10.8	530	12.8	250	14.8	68		
8.9	881	10.9	514	12.9	239	14.9	62		

IAAF Scoring Tables for Combined Events / Tables de Cotation pour les Epreuves Combinées

This table to be used exclusively for fully automatic times.

Perf.	Points	Perf.	Points	Perf.	Points	Perf.	Points	Perf.	Points
6.60	1413	7.10	1271	7.60	1135	8.10	1007	8.60	886
6.61	1410	7.11	1268	7.61	1133	8.11	1004	8.61	883
6.62	1407	7.12	1265	7.62	1130	8.12	1002	8.62	881
6.63	1404	7.13	1262	7.63	1127	8.13	999	8.63	879
6.64	1401	7.14	1260	7.64	1125	8.14	997	8.64	876
6.65	1399	7.15	1257	7.65	1122	8.15	994	8.65	874
6.66	1396	7.16	1254	7.66	1120	8.16	992	8.66	871
6.67	1393	7.17	1251	7.67	1117	8.17	990	8.67	869
6.68	1390	7.18	1249	7.68	1114	8.18	987	8.68	867
6.69	1387	7.19	1246	7.69	1112	8.19	985	8.69	864
6.70	1384	7.20	1243	7.70	1109	8.20	982	8.70	862
6.71	1381	7.21	1240	7.71	1107	8.21	980	8.71	860
6.72	1378	7.22	1238	7.72	1104	8.22	977	8.72	857
6.73	1375	7.23	1235	7.73	1101	8.23	975	8.73	855
6.74	1373	7.24	1232	7.74	1099	8.24	972	8.74	853
6.75	1370	7.25	1229	7.75	1096	8.25	970	8.75	851
6.76	1367	7.26	1227	7.76	1094	8.26	967	8.76	848
6.77	1364	7.27	1224	7.77	1091	8.27	965	8.77	846
6.78	1361	7.28	1221	7.78	1088	8.28	962	8.78	844
6.79	1358	7.29	1218	7.79	1086	8.29	960	8.79	841
6.80	1355	7.30	1216	7.80	1083	8.30	958	8.80	839
6.81	1352	7.31	1213	7.81	1081	8.31	955	8.81	837
6.82	1350	7.32	1210	7.82	1078	8.32	953	8.82	834
6.83	1347	7.33	1208	7.83	1075	8.33	950	8.83	832
6.84	1344	7.34	1205	7.84	1073	8.34	948	8.84	830
6.85	1341	7.35	1202	7.85	1070	8.35	945	8.85	828
6.86	1338	7.36	1199	7.86	1068	8.36	943	8.86	825
6.87	1335	7.37	1197	7.87	1065	8.37	941	8.87	823
6.88	1333	7.38	1194	7.88	1063	8.38	938	8.88	821
6.89	1330	7.39	1191	7.89	1060	8.39	936	8.89	818
6.90	1327	7.40	1189	7.90	1057	8.40	933	8.90	816
6.91	1324	7.41	1186	7.91	1055	8.41	931	8.91	814
6.92	1321	7.42	1183	7.92	1052	8.42	928	8.92	812
6.93	1318	7.43	1181	7.93	1050	8.43	926	8.93	809
6.94	1316	7.44	1178	7.94	1047	8.44	924	8.94	807
6.95	1313	7.45	1175	7.95	1045	8.45	921	8.95	805
6.96	1310	7.46	1173	7.96	1042	8.46	919	8.96	803
6.97	1307	7.47	1170	7.97	1040	8.47	916	8.97	800
6.98	1304	7.48	1167	7.98	1037	8.48	914	8.98	798
6.99	1301	7.49	1165	7.99	1035	8.49	912	8.99	796
7.00	1299	7.50	1162	8.00	1032	8.50	909	9.00	794
7.01	1296	7.51	1159	8.01	1030	8.51	907	9.01	791
7.02	1293	7.52	1157	8.02	1027	8.52	905	9.02	789
7.03	1290	7.53	1154	8.03	1024	8.53	902	9.03	787
7.04	1287	7.54	1151	8.04	1022	8.54	900	9.04	785
7.05	1285	7.55	1149	8.05	1019	8.55	897	9.05	782
7.06	1282	7.56	1146	8.06	1017	8.56	895	9.06	780
7.07	1279	7.57	1143	8.07	1014	8.57	893	9.07	778
7.08	1276	7.58	1141	8.08	1012	8.58	890	9.08	776
7.09	1274	7.59	1138	8.09	1009	8.59	888	9.09	774

Women   55-Meter Hurdles

This table to be used exclusively for fully automatic times.

Perf.	Points	Perf.	Points	Perf.	Points	Perf.	Points	Perf.	Points
9.10	771	9.60	664	10.10	565	10.60	472	11.10	388
9.11	769	9.61	662	10.11	563	10.61	471	11.11	386
9.12	767	9.62	660	10.12	561	10.62	469	11.12	384
9.13	765	9.63	658	10.13	559	10.63	467	11.13	383
9.14	762	9.64	656	10.14	557	10.64	465	11.14	381
9.15	760	9.65	654	10.15	555	10.65	463	11.15	380
9.16	758	9.66	652	10.16	553	10.66	462	11.16	378
9.17	756	9.67	650	10.17	551	10.67	460	11.17	376
9.18	754	9.68	648	10.18	549	10.68	458	11.18	375
9.19	752	9.69	646	10.19	547	10.69	456	11.19	373
9.20	749	9.70	644	10.20	546	10.70	455	11.20	372
9.21	747	9.71	642	10.21	544	10.71	453	11.21	370
9.22	745	9.72	640	10.22	542	10.72	451	11.22	368
9.23	743	9.73	638	10.23	540	10.73	450	11.23	367
9.24	741	9.74	636	10.24	538	10.74	448	11.24	365
9.25	738	9.75	634	10.25	536	10.75	446	11.25	364
9.26	736	9.76	632	10.26	534	10.76	444	11.26	362
9.27	734	9.77	630	10.27	532	10.77	443	11.27	360
9.28	732	9.78	628	10.28	531	10.78	441	11.28	359
9.29	730	9.79	626	10.29	529	10.79	439	11.29	357
9.30	728	9.80	624	10.30	527	10.80	437	11.30	356
9.31	725	9.81	622	10.31	525	10.81	436	11.31	354
9.32	723	9.82	620	10.32	523	10.82	434	11.32	353
9.33	721	9.83	618	10.33	521	10.83	432	11.33	351
9.34	719	9.84	616	10.34	519	10.84	431	11.34	350
9.35	717	9.85	614	10.35	518	10.85	429	11.35	348
9.36	715	9.86	612	10.36	516	10.86	427	11.36	347
9.37	713	9.87	610	10.37	514	10.87	426	11.37	345
9.38	710	9.88	608	10.38	512	10.88	424	11.38	343
9.39	708	9.89	606	10.39	510	10.89	422	11.39	342
9.40	706	9.90	604	10.40	508	10.90	421	11.40	340
9.41	704	9.91	602	10.41	506	10.91	419	11.41	339
9.42	702	9.92	600	10.42	505	10.92	417	11.42	337
9.43	700	9.93	598	10.43	503	10.93	416	11.43	336
9.44	698	9.94	596	10.44	501	10.94	414	11.44	334
9.45	696	9.95	594	10.45	499	10.95	412	11.45	333
9.46	694	9.96	592	10.46	497	10.96	411	11.46	331
9.47	691	9.97	590	10.47	496	10.97	409	11.47	330
9.48	689	9.98	588	10.48	494	10.98	407	11.48	328
9.49	687	9.99	586	10.49	492	10.99	406	11.49	327
9.50	685	10.00	584	10.50	490	11.00	404	11.50	325
9.51	683	10.01	582	10.51	488	11.01	402	11.51	324
9.52	681	10.02	580	10.52	487	11.02	401	11.52	322
9.53	679	10.03	578	10.53	485	11.03	399	11.53	321
9.54	677	10.04	576	10.54	483	11.04	397	11.54	319
9.55	675	10.05	574	10.55	481	11.05	396	11.55	318
9.56	673	10.06	572	10.56	479	11.06	394	11.56	316
9.57	671	10.07	570	10.57	478	11.07	392	11.57	315
9.58	668	10.08	568	10.58	476	11.08	391	11.58	313
9.59	666	10.09	567	10.59	474	11.09	389	11.59	312

This table to be used exclusively for fully automatic times.

Perf.	Points	Perf.	Points	Perf.	Points	Perf.	Points	Perf.	Points
11.60	311	11.90	268	12.20	228	12.50	192	12.80	158
11.61	309	11.91	267	12.21	227	12.51	190	12.81	157
11.62	308	11.92	265	12.22	226	12.52	189	12.82	156
11.63	306	11.93	264	12.23	225	12.53	188	12.83	155
11.64	305	11.94	263	12.24	223	12.54	187	12.84	154
11.65	303	11.95	261	12.25	222	12.55	186	12.85	153
11.66	302	11.96	260	12.26	221	12.56	185	12.86	151
11.67	300	11.97	259	12.27	220	12.57	184	12.87	150
11.68	299	11.98	257	12.28	218	12.58	182	12.88	149
11.69	297	11.99	256	12.29	217	12.59	181	12.89	148
11.70	296	12.00	254	12.30	216	12.60	180		
11.71	295	12.01	253	12.31	215	12.61	179		
11.72	293	12.02	252	12.32	213	12.62	178		
11.73	292	12.03	250	12.33	212	12.63	177		
11.74	290	12.04	249	12.34	211	12.64	176		
11.75	289	12.05	248	12.35	210	12.65	174		
11.76	287	12.06	247	12.36	208	12.66	173		
11.77	286	12.07	245	12.37	207	12.67	172		
11.78	285	12.08	244	12.38	206	12.68	171		
11.79	283	12.09	243	12.39	205	12.69	170		
11.80	282	12.10	241	12.40	204	12.70	169		
11.81	280	12.11	240	12.41	202	12.71	168		
11.82	279	12.12	239	12.42	201	12.72	167		
11.83	278	12.13	237	12.43	200	12.73	165		
11.84	276	12.14	236	12.44	199	12.74	164		
11.85	275	12.15	235	12.45	198	12.75	163		
11.86	274	12.16	234	12.46	196	12.76	162		
11.87	272	12.17	232	12.47	195	12.77	161		
11.88	271	12.18	231	12.48	194	12.78	160		
11.89	269	12.19	230	12.49	193	12.79	159		

*This table to be used exclusively for **hand times**.*

Perf.	Points	Perf.	Points	Perf.	Points	Perf.	Points	Perf.	Points
6.6	1344	8.1	948	9.6	616	11.1	350	12.1	211
6.7	1316	8.2	924	9.7	596	11.2	334	12.2	199
6.8	1287	8.3	900	9.8	576	11.3	319	12.3	187
6.9	1260	8.4	876	9.9	557	11.4	305	12.4	176
7.0	1232	8.5	853	10.0	538	11.5	290	12.5	164
		8.6	830			11.6	276		
7.1	1205	8.7	807	10.1	519	11.7	263		
7.2	1178	8.8	785	10.2	501	11.8	249		
7.3	1151	8.9	763	10.3	483	11.9	236		
7.4	1125	9.0	741	10.4	465	12.0	223		
7.5	1099			10.5	448				
7.6	1073	9.1	719	10.6	431				
7.7	1047	9.2	698	10.7	414				
7.8	1022	9.3	677	10.8	397				
7.9	997	9.4	656	10.9	381				
8.0	972	9.5	636	11.0	365				

Part III:

2005 NCAA Qualifying

Administrative procedures for NCAA track and field championships are contained in the men's and women's indoor and outdoor track championships handbooks. Copies may be obtained via the NCAA Web site (www.ncaa.org).

Men's and Women's National Championships Qualifying Procedures

1. The NCAA Men's and Women's Track and Field Committee recognizes the differences in event conversions from fully automatic timing (FAT) to manual timing (MT). The standards encourage the use of FAT qualifying for NCAA championships based on the accuracy inherent in FAT.

2. The entry blank for national championships should include all eligible competitors.

3. A qualifying mark for entry into national championships (regional meets for Division I outdoor, except in the 10,000-meter run and the combined events) must be made between the following dates:

Indoor

Division I—December 1, 2004 - March 5, 2005 (**Exception:** Conference championships conducted March 6 have until 3 p.m. [Central time].)

Division II—December 3, 2004 - February 27, 2005

Division III—November 29, 2004 - March 5, 2005 (**Exception:** Conference championships conducted March 6.)

Outdoor

Division I—March 1 - May 15, 2005

Division II—February 24 - May 15, 2005

Division III—February 28 - May 21, 2005

The qualifying marks must be made in a scheduled collegiate or open track and field meet.

4. Marks will not be acceptable if they are set in meets or events:

a. Where fewer than two four-year institutions with a minimum of 14 athletes per gender per institution compete, or fewer than five four-year institutions participate (Divisions I and II); where fewer than two four-year institutions with a minimum of 10 athletes per gender per institution compete, or fewer than five four-year institutions participate (Division III);

b. Where fewer than 10 collegiate or open events per gender are contested;

c. Where men and women compete together in a running event (except the 10,000 meters);

d. Where contestants or spectators are asked to officiate;

e. Held on other than certified (i.e., at the time of construction) and regularly used facilities;

f. Where official results are not kept and available for inspection (i.e., retain photos, hand times and field-event results through July 1, 2005);

g. Involving only combined-events competition in which fewer than six contestants start or all participants are from the same team;

h. Where a combined-events contestant who obtains a qualifying mark abandons the combined-events competition, unless the competitor is medically excused from further competition by a medical doctor/certified trainer assigned by meet management (see Rule 9-2-8);

i. Where all implements are not measured and weighed before competition;

j. Where intermediate times are taken from a longer race (e.g., 800 meters during 1,000 meters);

k. Where wind readings are not recorded in the 100 meters, 200 meters, 100- and 110-meter hurdles, and long jump and triple jump (Divisions I and II only). In Division II, the wind readings must appear in the official meet results;

l. Where wind readings exceed 4.0 meters per second in the 100 meters, 200 meters, 100- and 110-meter hurdles, and long jump and triple jump (Divisions I and II only);

m. Where contestants are given a second opportunity to compete in the same event(s) on the same calendar day at the same site, unless it is in accordance with the normal established advancement procedure;

    n.   Where trials and finals of the dash and hurdles are not contested at the same distance;

    o.   Where competitors run any turn on indoor tracks that are 400 meters or longer; or

    p.   Held on outdoor tracks that are longer than 400 meters.

5. Photos, hand times and field-event results may be requested by the games committee for the verification of performance.

6. To meet the qualifying standards for relays, only athletes eligible for national championships (NCAA Bylaw 14) may be used.

    Relay times shall not be accepted for individual events.

    In relay races, the names of four athletes who ran a qualifying time shall be entered. In the final declaration, four athletes must be designated as the team.

    Qualification for the distance medley relay for Division I must be contested in the following order: 1,200, 400, 800 and 1,600 meters; or 1,320, 440, 880 and 1,760 yards.

7. All collegiate meets shall be run in accordance with NCAA false-start rules. However, athletes may qualify for NCAA championships in meets conducted under IAAF or USATF rules.

8. Field-event measurements:

    a.   Field-event marks for the Division I championships must be measured, recorded and entered metrically.

    b.   Field-event marks for the Divisions II and III championships may be measured, recorded and entered metrically or imperially. Metrics is the preferred system of measurement.

9. Indoor procedures:

    a.   Qualifying marks must be made using an indoor facility, with the exception of the weight throws, which may be conducted outdoors.

    b.   Qualifying standards in oval events may not be met on banked tracks of more than 220 yards.

    c.   Qualifying standards in the 400 meters and opening leg of the 1,600-meter (mile) relay may not be met using more than a two-turn stagger on a track of 220 yards or less. On a track of more than 220 yards, no more than a one-turn stagger may be used.

   d. The minimum diameter of the head of the weight: Men–145 mm;
       and women–120 mm.

   e. Division I institutions wanting to host an indoor meet, other than a
       conference meet, February 28-March 5, 2005, must petition the
       NCAA for sanctioning before January 12, 2005. Requests should be
       submitted to Donna Thomas, senior associate athletics director,
       University of Tennessee, Knoxville, 117 Stokley Athletics Center,
       Knoxville, Tennessee 37996. Individual institutions may apply to
       host only one meet during this period. The gender of the meet must
       be specified. Additional information regarding the application
       process can be found on the NCAA Web site at www1.ncaa.org/
       membership/champadmin/track/2005/d1_indoor_qual_criteria.

   f. Division III institutions wanting to host an indoor meet, other than
       a conference meet, February 28-March 5, 2005, must petition the
       NCAA for sanctioning before January 31, 2005. Institutions must
       complete the final qualifying meet criteria form that can be found
       on the NCAA Web site at www1.ncaa.org/membership/champad-
       min/track/FORMLastChanceMeets.doc, and should submit the
       request to Kristin Steckmesser, assistant director of championships,
       NCAA, P.O. Box 6222, Indianapolis, Indiana 46206-6222. Individual
       institutions may apply to host only one meet during this period. The
       gender of the meet must be specified.

10. Outdoor procedures:

   a. Qualifying standards must be competed in meters, except for the
       400- and 1,600-meter relays (all divisions), and the 1,500-meter run
       (Divisions I and III only), which may be competed in yards.

   b. Qualifying marks for Division I must be made using an outdoor
       facility.

   c. Qualifying marks for Division II must be made using an outdoor
       facility, unless the high jump or pole vault are moved indoors for
       safety reasons by a decision of a competition's games committee.

   d. Qualifying marks for Division III must be made using an outdoor
       facility, unless field events are moved indoors for safety reasons by
       a decision of a competition's games committee.

   e. Division III institutions wanting to host an outdoor meet, other than
       a conference meet, May 16-21, 2005, must petition the NCAA for
       sanctioning before January 31, 2005. Institutions must complete the

final qualifying meet criteria form that can be found on the NCAA Web site at www1.ncaa.org/membership/champadmin/track/FORMLastChanceMeets.doc, and should submit the request to Kristin Steckmesser, assistant director of championships, NCAA, P.O. Box 6222, Indianapolis, Indiana 46206-6222. Individual institutions may apply to host only one meet during this period. The gender of the meet must be specified.

Men's and Women's Indoor Qualifying Standards
DIVISION I INDOOR—MEN
(SEA LEVEL)

Event	AUTOMATIC		PROVISIONAL	
	FAT	MT	FAT	MT
55 Meters	6.14@	—	6.24@	—
60 Meters	6.62@	—	6.72@	—
55-Meter Hurdles	7.17@	—	7.38@	—
60-Meter Hurdles	7.70@	—	7.91@	—
200 Meters				
(Under 200m/220 yds)*	21.33	—	21.73	—
(200m/220 yds)*	21.08	—	21.48	—
(Banked or Over 200m/220 yds)*	20.83	—	21.23	—
400 Meters				
(Under 200m/220 yds)*	46.85	46.6	48.05	47.8
(200m/220 yds)*	46.45	46.2	47.65	47.4
(Banked or Over 200m/220 yds)*	46.05	45.8	47.25	47.0
800 Meters#				
(200m/220 yds or less)*	1:48.60	1:48.3	1:50.10	1:49.8
(Banked or Over 200m/220 yds)*	1:48.00	1:47.7	1:49.50	1:49.2
Mile#				
(200m/220 yds or less)*	4:00.10	3:59.8	4:05.70	4:05.4
(Banked or Over 200m/220 yds)*	3:59.30	3:59.0	4:04.90	4:04.6
3,000 Meters#				
(200m/220 yds or less)*	7:57.30	7:57.0	8:06.30	8:06.0
(Banked or Over 200m/220 yds)*	7:56.00	7:55.7	8:05.00	8:04.7
5,000 Meters#				
(200m/220 yds or less)*	13:55.00	13:54.7	14:16.90	14:16.6
(Banked or Over 200m/220 yds)*	13:53.10	13:52.8	14:15.00	14:14.7

Event	AUTOMATIC		PROVISIONAL	
	FAT	MT	FAT	MT
1,600-Meter Relay				
(Under 200m/220 yds)*	3:09.30	3:09.0	3:13.60	3:13.3
(200m/220 yds)*	3:07.70	3:07.4	3:12.00	3:11.7
(Banked or Over 200m/220 yds)*	3:06.10	3:05.8	3:10.40	3:10.1
Mile Relay				
(Under 200m/220 yds)*	3:10.50	3:10.2	3:14.80	3:14.5
(200m/220 yds)*	3:08.90	3:08.6	3:13.20	3:12.9
(Banked or Over 200m/220 yds)*	3:07.30	3:07.0	3:11.60	3:11.3
Distance Medley Relay—Meters#				
(200m/220 yds or less)*	9:35.25	9:34.9	9:45.95	9:45.5
(Banked or Over 200m/220 yds)*	9:33.00	9:32.7	9:43.70	9:43.4
Distance Medley Relay—Yards#				
(200 m/220 yds or less)*	9:38.75	9:38.4	9:49.45	9:48.9
(Banked or Over 200 m/220 yds)*	9:36.50	9:36.2	9:47.20	9:46.9

@ Qualifying times attained at altitude of 6,000 feet and above, add .04 seconds.
Times attained at altitude of 3,000-5,999 feet, add .02 seconds.

	METRIC	METRIC
High Jump	2.23	2.17
Pole Vault	5.50	5.20
Long Jump	7.85	7.45
Triple Jump	16.20	15.50
Shot Put	19.30	17.75
35-Pound Weight	21.20	19.00
Heptathlon	5,650 points	5,200 points

*—Size of track.
#—Altitude adjustment available.

DIVISION I INDOOR—WOMEN
(SEA LEVEL)

Event	AUTOMATIC		PROVISIONAL	
	FAT	MT	FAT	MT
55 Meters	6.75@	—	6.92@	—
60 Meters	7.27@	—	7.44@	—
55-Meter Hurdles	7.58@	—	7.86@	—
60-Meter Hurdles	8.15@	—	8.43@	—

Event	AUTOMATIC		PROVISIONAL	
	FAT	MT	FAT	MT
200 Meters				
(Under 200m/220 yds)*	23.70	—	24.30	—
(200m/220 yds)*	23.50	—	24.10	—
(Banked or Over 200m/220 yds)*	23.30	—	23.90	—
400 Meters				
(Under 200m/220 yds)*	53.00	52.7	55.00	54.7
(200m/220 yds)*	52.70	52.4	54.70	54.4
(Banked or Over 200m/220 yds)*	52.40	52.1	54.40	54.1
800 Meters#				
(200m/220 yds or less)*	2:06.05	2:05.8	2:09.40	2:09.1
(Banked or Over 200m/220 yds)*	2:05.65	2:05.4	2:09.00	2:08.7
Mile#				
(200m/220 yds or less)*	4:39.10	4:38.8	4:47.60	4:47.3
(Banked or Over 200m/220 yds)*	4:38.50	4:38.2	4:47.00	4:46.7
3,000 Meters#				
(200m/220 yds or less)*	9:16.80	9:16.5	9:35.80	9:35.5
(Banked or Over 200m/220 yds)*	9:16.00	9:15.7	9:35.00	9:34.7
5,000 Meters#				
(200m/220 yds or less)*	16:11.60	16:11.3	16:46.60	16:46.3
(Banked or Over 200m/220 yds)*	16:10.00	16:09.7	16:45.00	16:44.7
1,600-Meter Relay				
(Under 200m/220 yds)*	3:35.90	3:35.6	3:42.40	3:42.1
(200m/220 yds)*	3:34.70	3:34.4	3:41.20	3:40.9
(Banked or Over 200m/220 yds)*	3:33.50	3:33.2	3:40.00	3:39.7
Mile Relay				
(Under 200m/220 yds)*	3:37.10	3:36.8	3:43.65	3:43.4
(200m/220 yds)*	3:35.90	3:35.6	3:42.45	3:42.2
(Banked or Over 200m/220 yds)*	3:34.70	3:34.4	3:41.25	3:41.0
Distance Medley Relay—Meters#				
(200m/220 yds or less)*	11:11.00	11:10.7	11:30.00	11:29.7
(Banked or Over 200m/220 yds)*	11:09.00	11:08.7	11:28.00	11:27.7
Distance Medley Relay—Yards#				
(200m/220 yds or less)*	11:14.50	11:14.2	11:34.20	11:33.9
(Banked or Over 200m/220 yds)*	11:12.50	11:12.2	11:32.20	11:31.9

@ Qualifying times attained at altitude of 6,000 feet and above, add .04 seconds.
Times attained at altitude of 3,000-5,999 feet, add .02 seconds.

	METRIC	METRIC
High Jump	1.84	1.78
Pole Vault	4.20	3.95
Long Jump	6.40	6.10
Triple Jump	13.30	12.65
Shot Put	16.90	15.40
20-Pound Weight	20.50	18.50
Pentathlon	4,050 points	3,700 points

*—Size of track.
#—Altitude adjustment available.

DIVISION II INDOOR—MEN
(SEA LEVEL)

Event	AUTOMATIC FAT	MT	PROVISIONAL FAT	MT
55 Meters	6.22	—	6.38	—
60 Meters	6.70	—	6.86	—
55-Meter Hurdles	7.40	—	7.71	—
60-Meter Hurdles	7.93	—	8.24	—
200 Meters				
(Under 200m/220 yds)*	—	—	22.80	—
(200m/220 yds-Flat)*	—	—	22.60	—
(200m/220 yds-Banked)*	—	—	22.30	—
(Over 200m/220 yds)*	—	—	22.00	—
400 Meters				
(Under 200m/220 yds)*	48.30	47.9	49.60	49.2
(200m/220 yds-Flat)*	48.00	47.6	49.30	48.9
(200m/220 yds-Banked)*	47.60	47.2	48.90	48.5
(Over 200m/220 yds)*	47.50	47.1	48.80	48.4
800 Meters#				
(Under 200m/220 yds)*	1:51.70	1:51.4	1:54.70	1:54.4
(200m/220 yds-Flat)*	1:51.30	1:51.0	1:54.30	1:54.0
(200m/220 yds-Banked)*	1:50.80	1:50.5	1:53.80	1:53.5
(Over 200m/220 yds)*	1:50.70	1:50.4	1:53.70	1:53.4
Mile#				
(Under 200m/220 yds)*	4:08.80	4:08.5	4:16.80	4:16.5
(200m/220 yds-Flat)*	4:08.30	4:08.0	4:16.30	4:16.0
(200m/220 yds-Banked)*	4:07.50	4:07.2	4:15.50	4:15.2
(Over 200m/220 yds)*	4:07.10	4:06.8	4:15.10	4:14.8

Event	AUTOMATIC		PROVISIONAL	
	FAT	MT	FAT	MT
5,000 Meters#				
(Under 200m/220 yds)*	14:19.70	14:19.4	14:57.70	14:57.4
(200m/220 yds-Flat)*	14:17.20	14:16.9	14:55.20	14:54.9
(200m/220 yds-Banked)*	14:15.00	14:14.7	14:53.00	14:52.7
(Over 200m/220 yds)*	14:14.00	14:13.7	14:52.00	14:51.7
1,600-Meter Relay				
(Under 200m/220 yds)*	3:15.10	3:14.8	3:20.60	3:20.3
(200m/220 yds-Flat)*	3:13.60	3:13.3	3:19.10	3:18.8
(200m/220 yds-Banked)*	3:12.00	3:11.7	3:17.50	3:17.2
(Over 200m/220 yds)*	3:11.60	3:11.3	3:17.10	3:16.8
Mile Relay				
(Under 200m/220 yds)*	3:16.30	3:16.0	3:21.80	3:21.5
(200m/220 yds-Flat)*	3:14.80	3:14.5	3:20.30	3:20.0
(200m/220 yds-Banked)*	3:13.20	3:12.9	3:18.70	3:18.4
(Over 200m/220 yds)*	3:12.80	3:12.5	3:18.30	3:18.0
Distance Medley Relay—Meters#				
(Under 200m/220 yds)*	—	—	10:34.00	10:33.7
(200m/220 yds-Flat)*	—	—	10:32.40	10:32.1
(200m/220 yds-Banked)*	—	—	10:30.00	10:29.7
(Over 200m/220 yds)*	—	—	10:29.10	10:28.8
Distance Medley Relay—Yards#				
(Under 200m/220 yds)*	—	—	10:37.50	10:37.2
(200m/220 yds-Flat)*	—	—	10:35.90	10:35.6
(200m/220 yds-Banked)*	—	—	10:33.50	10:33.2
(Over 200m/220 yds)*	—	—	10:32.60	10:32.3

	METRIC	IMPERIAL	METRIC	IMPERIAL
High Jump	2.16	7'1"	2.04	6'8-1/4"
Pole Vault	5.10	16'8-3/4"	4.71	15'5-1/2"
Long Jump	7.62	25'	7.10	23'3-1/2"
Triple Jump	15.70	51'6-1/4"	14.33	47'1/4"
Shot Put	17.68	58'1/4"	16.00	52'6"
35-Pound Weight	19.50	63'11-3/4"	16.90	55'5-1/2"

*—Size of track.

#—Altitude adjustment available.

DIVISION II INDOOR—WOMEN
(SEA LEVEL)

Event	AUTOMATIC		PROVISIONAL	
	FAT	MT	FAT	MT
55 Meters	6.95	—	7.23	—
60 Meters	7.48	—	7.76	—
55-Meter Hurdles	8.08	—	8.42	—
60-Meter Hurdles	8.65	—	8.99	—
200 Meters				
(Under 200m/220 yds)*	—	—	26.20	—
(200m/220 yds-Flat)*	—	—	26.00	—
(200m/220 yds-Banked)*	—	—	25.70	—
(Over 200m/220 yds)*	—	—	25.40	—
400 Meters				
(Under 200m/220 yds)*	55.90	55.5	58.00	57.6
(200m/220 yds-Flat)*	55.60	55.2	57.70	57.3
(200m/220 yds-Banked)*	55.30	54.9	57.40	57.0
(Over 200m/220 yds)*	55.20	54.8	57.30	56.9
800 Meters#				
(Under 200m/220 yds)*	2:10.60	2:10.3	2:17.40	2:17.1
(200m/220 yds-Flat)*	2:10.30	2:10.0	2:17.10	2:16.8
(200m/220 yds-Banked)*	2:10.00	2:09.7	2:16.80	2:16.5
(Over 200m/220 yds)*	2:09.90	2:09.6	2:16.70	2:16.4
Mile#				
(Under 200m/220 yds)*	4:53.10	4:52.8	5:03.10	5:02.8
(200m/220 yds-Flat)*	4:52.60	4:52.3	5:02.60	5:02.3
(200m/220 yds-Banked)*	4:52.00	4:51.7	5:02.00	5:01.7
(Over 200m/220 yds)*	4:51.60	4:51.3	5:01.60	5:01.3
5,000 Meters#				
(Under 200m/220 yds)*	16:59.30	16:59.0	18:03.30	18:03.0
(200m/220 yds-Flat)*	16:56.80	16:56.5	18:00.80	18:00.5
(200m/220 yds-Banked)*	16:55.00	16:54.7	17:59.00	17:58.7
(Over 200m/220 yds)*	16:54.30	16:54.0	17:58.30	17:58.0
1,600-Meter Relay				
(Under 200m/220 yds)*	3:48.30	3:48.0	3:58.30	3:58.0
(200m/220 yds-Flat)*	3:46.80	3:46.5	3:56.80	3:56.5
(200m/220 yds-Banked)*	3:45.60	3:45.3	3:55.60	3:55.3
(Over 200m/220 yds)*	3:45.20	3:44.9	3:55.20	3:54.9

Event	AUTOMATIC		PROVISIONAL	
	FAT	MT	FAT	MT
Mile Relay				
(Under 200m/220 yds)*	3:49.50	3:49.2	3:59.50	3:59.2
(200m/220 yds-Flat)*	3:48.00	3:47.7	3:58.00	3:57.7
(200m/220 yds-Banked)*	3:46.80	3:46.5	3:56.80	3:56.5
(Over 200m/220 yds)*	3:46.40	3:46.1	3:56.40	3:56.1
Distance Medley Relay—Meters#				
(Under 200m/220 yds)*	—	—	12:43.20	12:42.9
(200m/220 yds-Flat)*	—	—	12:41.70	12:41.4
(200m/220 yds-Banked)*	—	—	12:40.00	12:39.7
(Over 200m/220 yds)*	—	—	12:39.10	12:38.8
Distance Medley Relay—Yards#				
(Under 200m/220 yds)*	—	—	12:46.70	12:46.4
(200m/220 yds-Flat)*	—	—	12:45.20	12:44.9
(200m/220 yds-Banked)*	—	—	12:43.50	12:43.2
(Over 200m/220 yds)*	—	—	12:42.60	12:42.3

	METRIC	IMPERIAL	METRIC	IMPERIAL
High Jump	1.76	5'9-1/4"	1.66	5'5-1/4"
Pole Vault	3.89	12'9"	3.50	11'5-3/4"
Long Jump	6.15	20'2"	5.60	18'4-1/2"
Triple Jump	12.40	40'8-3/4"	11.50	37'8-3/4"
Shot Put	14.95	49'3/4"	13.11	43'1/4"
20-Pound Weight	18.29	60'1/4"	15.85	52'

*—Size of track.

#—Altitude adjustment available.

DIVISION III INDOOR—MEN
(SEA LEVEL)

Event	AUTOMATIC		PROVISIONAL	
	FAT	MT	FAT	MT
55 Meters	6.36	—	6.50	—
60 Meters	6.84	—	6.98	—
55-Meter Hurdles	7.55	—	7.75	—
60-Meter Hurdles	8.08	—	8.28	—
400 Meters				
(Under 200m/220 yds)*	49.10	—	50.00	—
(200m/220 yds-Flat)*	48.80	—	49.70	—
(200m/220 yds-Banked)*	48.50	—	49.40	—
(Over 200m/220 yds)*	48.30	—	49.20	—

Event	AUTOMATIC		PROVISIONAL	
	FAT	MT	FAT	MT
800 Meters#				
(Under 200m/220 yds)*	1:53.40	1:53.1	1:55.40	1:55.1
(200m/220 yds-Flat)*	1:53.00	1:52.7	1:55.00	1:54.7
(200m/220 yds-Banked)*	1:52.60	1:52.3	1:54.60	1:54.3
(Over 200m/220 yds)*	1:52.00	1:51.7	1:54.00	1:53.7
1,500 Meters#				
(Under 200m/220 yds)*	3:52.80	3:52.5	3:58.20	3:57.9
(200m/220 yds-Flat)*	3:52.30	3:52.0	3:57.70	3:57.4
(200m/220 yds-Banked)*	3:51.80	3:51.5	3:57.20	3:56.9
(Over 200m/220 yds)*	3:50.30	3:50.0	3:55.70	3:55.4
Mile#				
(Under 200m/220 yds)*	4:11.30	4:11.0	4:17.20	4:16.9
(200m/220 yds-Flat)*	4:10.80	4:10.5	4:16.70	4:16.4
(200m/220 yds-Banked)*	4:10.30	4:10.0	4:16.20	4:15.9
(Over 200m/220 yds)*	4:08.80	4:08.5	4:14.70	4:14.4
5,000 Meters#				
(Under 200m/220 yds)*	14:35.50	14:35.2	14:57.50	14:57.2
(200m/220 yds-Flat)*	14:33.00	14:32.7	14:55.00	14:54.7
(200m/220 yds-Banked)*	14:30.50	14:30.2	14:52.50	14:52.2
(Over 200m/220 yds)*	14:29.00	14:28.7	14:51.00	14:50.7
1,600 Meter Relay				
(Under 200m/220 yds)*	3:17.80	3:17.5	3:22.40	3:22.1
(200m/220 yds-Flat)*	3:16.60	3:16.3	3:21.20	3:20.9
(200m/220 yds-Banked)*	3:15.40	3:15.1	3:20.00	3:19.7
(Over 200m/220 yds)*	3:14.60	3:14.3	3:19.20	3:18.9
Mile Relay				
(Under 200m/220 yds)*	3:19.00	3:18.7	3:23.60	3:23.3
(200m/220 yds-Flat)*	3:17.80	3:17.5	3:22.40	3:22.1
(200m/220 yds-Banked)*	3:16.60	3:16.3	3:21.20	3:20.9
(Over 200m/220 yds)*	3:15.80	3:15.5	3:20.40	3:20.1
Distance Medley Relay—Meters#				
(Under 200m/220 yds)*	10:04.20	10:03.9	10:16.50	10:16.2
(200m/220 yds-Flat)*	10:02.60	10:02.3	10:14.90	10:14.6
(200m/220 yds-Banked)*	10:01.00	10:00.7	10:13.30	10:13.0
(Over 200m/220 yds)*	9:58.10	9:57.8	10:10.40	10:10.1
Distance Medley Relay—Yards#				
(Under 200m/220 yds)*	10:07.70	10:07.4	10:20.00	10:19.7
(200m/220 yds-Flat)*	10:06.10	10:05.8	10:18.40	10:18.1
(200m/220 yds-Banked)*	10:04.50	10:04.2	10:16.80	10:16.5
(Over 200m/220 yds)*	10:01.60	10:01.3	10:13.90	10:13.6

	METRIC	METRIC
High Jump	2.10	2.02
Pole Vault	5.03	4.64
Long Jump	7.26	6.95
Triple Jump	14.82	14.00
Shot Put	17.11	15.54
35-Pound Weight	—	16.20

*—Size of track.
#—Altitude adjustment available.

DIVISION III INDOOR—WOMEN
(SEA LEVEL)

Event	AUTOMATIC		PROVISIONAL	
	FAT	MT	FAT	MT
55 Meters	7.14	—	7.32	—
60 Meters	7.67	—	7.85	—
55-Meter Hurdles	8.25	—	8.60	—
60-Meter Hurdles	8.82	—	9.17	—
400 Meters				
(Under 200m/220 yds)*	57.00	—	59.00	—
(200m/220 yds-Flat)*	56.80	—	58.80	—
(200m/220 yds-Banked)*	56.60	—	58.60	—
(Over 200m/220 yds)*	56.40	—	58.40	—
800 Meters#				
(Under 200m/220 yds)*	2:14.80	2:14.5	2:18.30	2:18.0
(200m/220 yds-Flat)*	2:14.50	2:14.2	2:18.00	2:17.7
(200m/220 yds-Banked)*	2:14.20	2:13.9	2:17.70	2:17.4
(Over 200m/220 yds)*	2:13.70	2:13.4	2:17.20	2:16.9
1,500 Meters#				
(Under 200m/220 yds)*	4:34.40	4:34.1	4:43.60	4:43.3
(200m/220 yds-Flat)*	4:34.00	4:33.7	4:43.20	4:42.9
(200m/220 yds-Banked)*	4:33.60	4:33.3	4:42.80	4:42.5
(Over 200m/220 yds)*	4:32.40	4:32.1	4:41.60	4:41.3
Mile#				
(Under 200m/220 yds)*	4:56.30	4:56.0	5:06.20	5:05.9
(200m/220 yds-Flat)*	4:55.90	4:55.6	5:05.80	5:05.5
(200m/220 yds-Banked)*	4:55.50	4:55.2	5:05.40	5:05.1
(Over 200m/220 yds)*	4:54.30	4:54.0	5:04.20	5:03.9

Event	AUTOMATIC		PROVISIONAL	
	FAT	MT	FAT	MT
5,000 Meters#				
(Under 200m/220 yds)*	17:12.50	17:12.2	17:57.50	17:57.2
(200m/220 yds-Flat)*	17:10.00	17:09.7	17:55.00	17:54.7
(200m/220 yds-Banked)*	17:07.50	17:07.2	17:52.50	17:52.2
(Over 200m/220 yds)*	17:06.00	17:05.7	17:51.00	17:50.7
1,600 Meter Relay				
(Under 200m/220 yds)*	3:55.80	3:55.5	4:01.80	4:01.5
(200m/220 yds-Flat)*	3:55.00	3:54.7	4:01.00	4:00.7
(200m/220 yds-Banked)*	3:54.20	3:53.9	4:00.20	3:59.9
(Over 200m/220 yds)*	3:53.40	3:53.1	3:59.40	3:59.1
Mile Relay				
(Under 200m/220 yds)*	3:57.20	3:56.9	4:03.20	4:02.9
(200m/220 yds-Flat)*	3:56.40	3:56.1	4:02.40	4:02.1
(200m/220 yds-Banked)*	3:55.60	3:55.3	4:01.60	4:01.3
(Over 200m/220 yds)*	3:54.80	3:54.5	4:00.80	4:00.5
Distance Medley Relay—Meters#				
(Under 200m/220 yds)*	11:52.50	11:52.2	12:21.20	12:20.9
(200m/220 yds-Flat)*	11:51.30	11:51.0	12:20.00	12:19.7
(200m/220 yds-Banked)*	11:50.10	11:49.8	12:18.80	12:18.5
(Over 200m/220 yds)*	11:47.70	11:47.4	12:16.40	12:16.1
Distance Medley Relay—Yards#				
(Under 200m/220 yds)*	11:56.70	11:56.4	12:25.40	12:25.1
(200m/220 yds-Flat)*	11:55.50	11:55.2	12:24.20	12:23.9
(200m/220 yds-Banked)*	11:54.30	11:54.0	12:23.00	12:22.7
(Over 200m/220 yds)*	11:51.90	11:51.6	12:20.60	12:20.3

	METRIC	METRIC
High Jump	1.71	1.63
Pole Vault	3.71	3.30
Long Jump	5.73	5.40
Triple Jump	11.90	11.18
Shot Put	14.00	12.84
20-Pound Weight	—	14.85

*—Size of track.

#—Altitude adjustment available.

Men's and Women's
Indoor Automatic Qualifying Standards
Altitude Adjustments
Time allowance for altitude (seconds) in parentheses

Note 1: To determine altitude adjustments for provisional standards add the allowance indicated in parentheses for the automatic standard to the sea-level provisional standard listed on pages 241-250.

Note 2: The automatic and provisional qualifying marks for altitude are determined by adding the allowance indicated in parentheses to the following sea-level qualifying standards: Division I—tracks that are banked or over 200 meters/220 yards; Division II—200-meter/220-yard tracks that are banked; and Division III—200-meter/220-yard tracks that are flat.

AIR FORCE ACADEMY, COLORADO   ALTITUDE: 7,048

	WOMEN			MEN		
EVENT	I	II	III	I	II	III
5,000 M	16:57.17	17:44.33	17:59.89	14:33.61	14:56.53	15:15.26
	(47.17)	(49.33)	(49.89)	(40.51)	(41.53)	(42.26)
3,000 M	9:41.12			8:17.51		
	(25.12)			(21.51)		
1,500 M			4:44.70			4:01.34
			(10.70)			(9.04)
1 MILE	4:49.44	5:03.45	5:07.46	4:08.70	4:17.20	4:20.57
	(10.94)	(11.45)	(11.56)	(9.40)	(9.70)	(9.77)
800 M	2:07.13	2:11.53	2:16.07	1:49.27	1:52.10	1:54.32
	(1.48)	(1.53)	(1.57)	(1.27)	(1.30)	(1.32)
DMR	11:27.05	12:59.57	12:10.37	9:48.51	10:46.56	10:18.72
	(18.05)	(19.57)	(19.07)	(15.51)	(16.56)	(16.12)

ALAMOSA, COLORADO   ALTITUDE: 7,544

	WOMEN			MEN		
EVENT	I	II	III	I	II	III
5,000 M	17:02.87	17:50.28	18:05.92	14:38.51	15:01.55	15:20.36
	(52.87)	(55.28)	(55.92)	(45.41)	(46.55)	(47.36)
3,000 M	9:44.14			8:20.09		
	(28.14)			(24.09)		
1,500 M			4:45.99			4:02.44
			(11.99)			(10.14)
1 MILE	4:50.76	5:04.83	5:08.85	4:09.83	4:18.37	4:21.75
	(12.26)	(12.83)	(12.95)	(10.53)	(10.87)	(10.95)

EVENT	WOMEN I	WOMEN II	WOMEN III	MEN I	MEN II	MEN III
800 M	2:07.37 (1.72)	2:11.78 (1.78)	2:16.33 (1.83)	1:49.48 (1.48)	1:52.32 (1.52)	1:54.53 (1.53)
DMR	11:29.22 (20.22)	13:01.93 (21.93)	12:12.67 (21.37)	9:50.38 (17.38)	10:48.55 (18.55)	10:20.67 (18.07)

ALBUQUERQUE, NEW MEXICO   ALTITUDE: 4,958

EVENT	WOMEN I	WOMEN II	WOMEN III	MEN I	MEN II	MEN III
5,000 M	16:36.35 (26.35)	17:22.56 (27.56)	17:37.87 (27.87)	14:15.73 (22.63)	14:38.20 (23.20)	14:56.61 (23.61)
3,000 M	9:30.04 (14.04)			8:08.02 (12.02)		
1,500 M			4:40.07 (6.07)			3:57.43 (5.13)
1 MILE	4:44.70 (6.20)	4:58.49 (6.49)	5:02.45 (6.55)	4:04.63 (5.33)	4:13.00 (5.50)	4:16.34 (5.54)
800 M	2:06.36 (0.71)	2:10.73 (0.73)	2:15.25 (0.75)	1:48.61 (0.61)	1:51.42 (0.62)	1:53.63 (0.63)
DMR	11:19.23 (10.23)	12:51.10 (11.10)	12:02.11 (10.81)	9:41.79 (8.79)	10:39.39 (9.39)	10:11.74 (9.14)

AMARILLO, TEXAS   ALTITUDE: 3,676

EVENT	WOMEN I	WOMEN II	WOMEN III	MEN I	MEN II	MEN III
5,000 M	16:26.13 (16.13)	17:11.86 (16.86)	17:25.06 (17.06)	14:06.95 (13.85)	14:29.20 (14.20)	14:47.45 (14.45)
3,000 M	9:24.52 (8.52)			8:03.30 (7.30)		
1,500 M			4:37.87 (3.87)			3:55.57 (3.27)
1 MILE	4:42.46 (3.96)	4:56.14 (4.14)	5:00.08 (4.18)	4:02.70 (3.40)	4:11.01 (3.51)	4:14.34 (3.54)
800 M	2:06.08 (0.43)	2:10.44 (0.44)	2:14.95 (0.45)	1:48.37 (0.37)	1:51.18 (0.38)	1:53.38 (0.38)
DMR	11:15.53 (6.53)	12:47.08 (7.08)	11:58.20 (6.90)	9:38.61 (5.61)	10:35.99 (5.99)	10:08.43 (5.83)

BILLINGS, MONTANA   ALTITUDE: 3,124

EVENT	WOMEN I	WOMEN II	WOMEN III	MEN I	MEN II	MEN III
5,000 M	16:22.32 (12.32)	17:07.88 (12.88)	17:23.03 (13.03)	14:03.68 (10.58)	14:25.85 (10.85)	14:44.04 (11.04)

	WOMEN			MEN		
EVENT	**I**	**II**	**III**	**I**	**II**	**III**
3,000 M	9:22.45			8:01.52		
	(6.45)			(5.52)		
1,500 M			4:37.08			3:54.90
			(3.08)			(2.60)
1 MILE	4:41.65	4:55.30	4:59.23	4:02.00	4:10.29	4:13.61
	(3.15)	(3.30)	(3.33)	(2.70)	(2.79)	(2.81)
800 M	2:06.00	2:10.36	2:14.87	1:48.30	1:51.11	1:53.31
	(0.35)	(0.36)	(0.37)	(0.30)	(0.31)	(0.31)
DMR	11:14.19	12:45.63	11:56.79	9:37.46	10:34.76	10:07.24
	(5.19)	(5.63)	(5.49)	(4.46)	(4.76)	(4.64)

BOONE, NORTH CAROLINA — ALTITUDE: 3,333

	WOMEN			MEN		
EVENT	**I**	**II**	**III**	**I**	**II**	**III**
5,000 M	16:23.72	17:09.34	17:24.51	14:04.88	14:27.08	14:45.29
	(13.72)	(14.34)	(14.51)	(11.78)	(12.08)	(12.29)
3,000 M	9:23.21			8:02.18		
	(7.21)			(6.18)		
1,500 M			4:37.37			3:55.15
			(3.37)			(2.85)
1 MILE	4:41.94	4:55.61	4:59.54	4:02.26	4:10.66	4:13.88
	(3.44)	(3.61)	(3.64)	(2.96)	(3.06)	(3.08)
800 M	2:06.03	2:10.39	2:14.90	1:48.32	1:51.13	1:53.34
	(0.38)	(0.39)	(0.40)	(0.32)	(0.33)	(0.34)
DMR	11:14.68	12:46.16	11:57.30	9:37.88	10:35.21	10:07.68
	(5.68)	(6.16)	(6.00)	(4.88)	(5.21)	(5.08)

BOULDER, COLORADO — ALTITUDE: 5,378

	WOMEN			MEN		
EVENT	**I**	**II**	**III**	**I**	**II**	**III**
5,000 M	16:40.12	17:26.50	17:41.86	14:18.97	14:41.52	14:59.99
	(30.12)	(31.50)	(31.86)	(25.87)	(26.52)	(26.99)
3,000 M	9:32.06			8:09.75		
	(16.06)			(13.75)		
1,500 M			4:40.89			3:58.13
			(6.89)			(5.83)
1 MILE	4:45.55	4:59.38	5:03.35	4:05.35	4:13.75	4:17.09
	(7.05)	(7.38)	(7.45)	(6.05)	(6.25)	(6.29)
800 M	2:06.48	2:10.86	2:15.38	1:48.71	1:51.53	1:53.74
	(0.83)	(0.86)	(0.88)	(0.71)	(0.73)	(0.74)
DMR	11:20.63	12:52.61	12:03.59	9:42.99	10:40.67	10:12.99
	(11.63)	(12.61)	(12.29)	(9.99)	(10.67)	(10.39)

BOZEMAN, MONTANA   ALTITUDE: 4,926

		WOMEN			MEN	
EVENT	**I**	**II**	**III**	**I**	**II**	**III**
5,000 M	16:36.07 (26.07)	17:22.26 (27.26)	17:37.58 (27.58)	14:15.49 (22.39)	14:37.96 (22.96)	14:56.36 (23.36)
3,000 M	9:29.89 (13.89)			8:07.89 (11.89)		
1,500 M			4:40.01 (6.01)			3:57.38 (5.08)
1 MILE	4:44.64 (6.14)	4:58.43 (6.43)	5:02.39 (6.49)	4:04.58 (5.28)	4:12.95 (5.45)	4:16.28 (5.48)
800 M	2:06.35 (0.70)	2:10.72 (0.72)	2:15.24 (0.74)	1:48.60 (0.60)	1:51.41 (0.61)	1:53.62 (0.62)
DMR	11:19.13 (10.13)	12:50.99 (10.99)	12:02.01 (10.71)	9:41.70 (8.70)	10:39.29 (9.29)	10:11.65 (9.05)

CALGARY, ALBERTA, CANADA   ALTITUDE: 3,438

		WOMEN			MEN	
EVENT	**I**	**II**	**III**	**I**	**II**	**III**
5,000 M	16:24.44 (14.44)	17:10.10 (15.10)	17:25.27 (15.27)	14:05.50 (12.40)	14:27.71 (12.71)	14:45.94 (12.94)
3,000 M	9:23.61 (7.61)			8:02.51 (6.51)		
1,500 M			4:37.52 (3.52)			3:55.27 (2.97)
1 MILE	4:42.10 (3.60)	4:55.77 (3.77)	4:59.70 (3.80)	4:02.39 (3.09)	4:10.69 (3.19)	4:14.01 (3.21)
800 M	2:06.04 (0.39)	2:10.40 (0.40)	2:14.92 (0.42)	1:48.34 (0.34)	1:51.14 (0.34)	1:53.35 (0.35)
DMR	11:14.94 (5.94)	12:46.44 (6.44)	11:57.57 (6.27)	9:38.10 (5.10)	10:35.45 (5.45)	10:07.90 (5.30)

CEDAR CITY, UTAH   ALTITUDE: 5,782

		WOMEN			MEN	
EVENT	**I**	**II**	**III**	**I**	**II**	**III**
5,000 M	16:43.95 (33.95)	17:30.50 (35.50)	17:45.91 (35.91)	14:22.26 (29.16)	14:44.89 (29.89)	15:03.41 (30.41)
3,000 M	9:34.10 (18.10)			8:11.50 (15.50)		
1,500 M			4:41.74 (7.74)			3:58.84 (6.54)
1 MILE	4:46.41 (7.91)	5:00.28 (8.28)	5:04.26 (8.36)	4:06.10 (6.80)	4:14.52 (7.02)	4:17.87 (7.07)

	WOMEN			MEN		
EVENT	I	II	III	I	II	III
800 M	2:06.61	2:11.00	2:15.53	1:48.83	1:51.65	1:53.86
	(0.96)	(1.00)	(1.03)	(0.83)	(0.85)	(0.86)
DMR	11:22.05	12:54.15	12:05.09	9:44.21	10:41.97	10:14.26
	(13.05)	(14.15)	(13.79)	(11.21)	(11.97)	(11.66)

CHADRON, NEBRASKA　　　　　ALTITUDE: 3,281

	WOMEN			MEN		
EVENT	I	II	III	I	II	III
5,000 M	16:23.37	17:08.98	17:24.14	14:04.58	14:26.77	14:44.97
	(13.37)	(13.98)	(14.14)	(11.48)	(11.77)	(11.97)
3,000 M	9:23.02			8:02.01		
	(7.02)			(6.01)		
1,500 M			4:37.29			3:55.09
			(3.29)			(2.79)
1 MILE	4:41.87	4:55.53	4:59.46	4:02.19	4:10.49	4:13.81
	(3.37)	(3.53)	(3.56)	(2.89)	(2.99)	(3.01)
800 M	2:06.02	2:10.38	2:14.89	1:48.32	1:51.13	1:53.33
	(0.37)	(0.38)	(0.39)	(0.32)	(0.33)	(0.33)
DMR	11:14.56	12:46.03	11:57.17	9:37.78	10:35.10	10:07.57
	(5.56)	(6.03)	(5.87)	(4.78)	(5.10)	(4.97)

COLORADO SPRINGS, COLORADO　　　ALTITUDE: 6,007

	WOMEN			MEN		
EVENT	I	II	III	I	II	III
5,000 M	16:46.16	17:32.81	17:48.25	14:24.16	14:46.83	15:05.39
	(36.16)	(37.81)	(38.25)	(31.06)	(31.83)	(32.39)
3,000 M	9:35.28			8:12.51		
	(19.28)			(16.51)		
1,500 M			4:42.03			3:59.26
			(8.23)			(6.96)
1 MILE	4:46.91	5:00.81	5:04.79	4:06.53	4:14.96	4:18.31
	(8.41)	(8.81)	(8.89)	(7.23)	(7.46)	(7.51)
800 M	2:06.69	2:11.08	2:15.61	1:48.90	1:51.72	1:53.93
	(1.04)	(1.08)	(1.11)	(0.90)	(0.92)	(0.93)
DMR	11:22.88	12:55.05	12:05.97	9:44.93	10:42.73	10:15.00
	(13.88)	(15.05)	(14.67)	(11.93)	(12.73)	(12.40)

DENVER, COLORADO   ALTITUDE: 5,279

	WOMEN			MEN		
EVENT	I	II	III	I	II	III
5,000 M	16:39.22 (29.22)	17:25.55 (30.55)	17:40.90 (30.90)	14:18.19 (25.09)	14:40.72 (25.72)	14:59.17 (26.17)
3,000 M	9:31.58 (15.58)			8:09.33 (13.33)		
1,500 M			4:40.69 (6.69)			3:57.96 (5.66)
1 MILE	4:45.34 (6.84)	4:59.16 (7.16)	5:03.13 (7.23)	4:05.18 (5.88)	4:13.57 (6.07)	4:16.91 (6.11)
800 M	2:06.45 (0.80)	2:10.83 (0.83)	2:15.35 (0.85)	1:48.69 (0.69)	1:51.50 (0.70)	1:53.71 (0.71)
DMR	11:20.29 (11.29)	12:52.24 (12.24)	12:03.23 (11.93)	9:42.70 (9.70)	10:40.36 (10.36)	10:12.69 (10.09)

EL PASO, TEXAS   ALTITUDE: 3,894

	WOMEN			MEN		
EVENT	I	II	III	I	II	III
5,000 M	16:27.73 (17.73)	17:13.54 (18.54)	17:28.75 (18.75)	14:08.33 (15.23)	14:30.61 (15.61)	14:48.88 (15.88)
3,000 M	9:25.39 (9.39)			8:04.04 (8.04)		
1,500 M			4:38.21 (4.21)			3:55.86 (3.56)
1 MILE	4:42.80 (4.30)	4:56.51 (4.51)	5:00.45 (4.55)	4:03.00 (3.70)	4:11.32 (3.82)	4:14.65 (3.85)
800 M	2:06.11 (0.46)	2:10.48 (0.48)	2:14.99 (0.49)	1:48.40 (0.40)	1:51.21 (0.41)	1:53.41 (0.41)
DMR	11:16.10 (7.10)	12:47.70 (7.70)	11:58.81 (7.51)	9:39.10 (6.10)	10:36.52 (6.52)	10:08.94 (6.34)

FLAGSTAFF, ARIZONA   ALTITUDE: 6,877

	WOMEN			MEN		
EVENT	I	II	III	I	II	III
5,000 M	16:55.27 (45.27)	17:42.34 (47.34)	17:57.89 (47.89)	14:31.99 (38.89)	14:54.86 (39.86)	15:13.56 (40.56)
3,000 M	9:40.12 (24.12)			8:16.65 (20.65)		
1,500 M			4:44.27 (10.27)			4:00.98 (8.68)
1 MILE	4:49.00 (10.50)	5:02.99 (10.99)	5:07.00 (11.10)	4:08.32 (9.02)	4:16.82 (9.32)	4:20.18 (9.38)

	WOMEN			**MEN**		
EVENT	**I**	**II**	**III**	**I**	**II**	**III**
800 M	2:07.05	2:11.45	2:15.99	1:49.20	1:52.03	1:54.25
	(1.40)	(1.45)	(1.49)	(1.20)	(1.23)	(1.25)
DMR	11:26.32	12:58.79	12:09.61	9:47.89	10:45.89	10:18.08
	(17.32)	(18.79)	(18.31)	(14.89)	(15.89)	(15.48)

FORT COLLINS, COLORADO   ALTITUDE: 5,081

	WOMEN			**MEN**		
EVENT	**I**	**II**	**III**	**I**	**II**	**III**
5,000 M	16:37.43	17:23.69	17:39.02	14:16.66	14:39.15	14:57.58
	(27.43)	(28.69)	(29.02)	(23.56)	(24.15)	(24.58)
3,000 M	9:30.62			8:08.52		
	(14.62)			(12.52)		
1,500 M			4:40.30			3:57.63
			(6.30)			(5.33)
1 MILE	4:44.94	4:58.75	5:02.71	4:04.84	4:13.22	4:16.56
	(6.44)	(6.75)	(6.81)	(5.54)	(5.72)	(5.76)
800 M	2:06.39	2:10.77	2:15.29	1:48.64	1:51.45	1:53.66
	(0.74)	(0.77)	(0.79)	(0.64)	(0.65)	(0.66)
DMR	11:19.63	12:51.53	12:02.54	9:42.14	10:39.75	10:12.10
	(10.63)	(11.53)	(11.24)	(9.14)	(9.75)	(9.50)

GOLDEN, COLORADO   ALTITUDE: 5,675

	WOMEN			**MEN**		
EVENT	**I**	**II**	**III**	**I**	**II**	**III**
5,000 M	16:42.92	17:29.42	17:44.82	14:21.37	14:43.98	15:02.49
	(32.92)	(34.42)	(34.82)	(28.27)	(28.98)	(29.49)
3,000 M	9:33.55			8:11.03		
	(17.55)			(15.03)		
1,500 M			4:41.51			3:58.65
			(7.51)			(6.35)
1 MILE	4:46.18	5:00.04	5:04.01	4:05.90	4:14.31	4:17.66
	(7.68)	(8.04)	(8.11)	(6.60)	(6.81)	(6.86)
800 M	2:06.58	2:10.96	2:15.49	1:48.80	1:51.62	1:53.83
	(0.93)	(0.96)	(0.99)	(0.80)	(0.82)	(0.83)
DMR	11:21.67	12:53.73	12:04.68	9:43.88	10:41.62	10:13.91
	(12.67)	(13.73)	(13.38)	(10.88)	(11.62)	(11.31)

GREELEY, COLORADO   ALTITUDE: 4,760

	WOMEN			**MEN**		
EVENT	**I**	**II**	**III**	**I**	**II**	**III**
5,000 M	16:34.65	17:20.77	17:36.07	14:14.27	14:36.70	14:55.08
	(24.65)	(25.77)	(26.07)	(21.17)	(21.70)	(22.08)

EVENT	WOMEN			MEN		
	I	II	III	I	II	III
3,000 M	9:29.13			8:07.24		
	(13.13)			(11.24)		
1,500 M			4:39.70			3:57.11
			(5.70)			(4.81)
1 MILE	4:44.32	4:58.10	5:02.05	4:04.30	4:12.67	4:16.00
	(5.82)	(6.10)	(6.15)	(5.00)	(5.17)	(5.20)
800 M	2:06.30	2:10.68	2:15.19	1:48.56	1:51.38	1:53.58
	(0.65)	(0.68)	(0.69)	(0.56)	(0.58)	(0.58)
DMR	11:18.61	12:50.42	12:01.45	9:41.25	10:38.81	10:11.18
	(9.61)	(10.42)	(10.15)	(8.25)	(8.81)	(8.58)

GUNNISON, COLORADO   ALTITUDE: 7,703

EVENT	WOMEN			MEN		
	I	II	III	I	II	III
5,000 M	17:04.75	17:52.26	18:07.92	14:40.13	15:03.21	15:22.05
	(54.75)	(57.26)	(57.92)	(47.03)	(48.21)	(49.05)
3,000 M	9:45.13			8:20.94		
	(29.13)			(24.94)		
1,500 M			4:46.42			4:02.80
			(12.42)			(10.50)
1 MILE	4:51.20	5:05.29	5:09.32	4:10.21	4:18.76	4:22.14
	(12.70)	(13.29)	(13.42)	(10.91)	(11.26)	(11.34)
800 M	2:07.45	2:11.86	2:16.42	1:49.55	1:52.39	1:54.61
	(1.80)	(1.86)	(1.92)	(1.55)	(1.59)	(1.61)
DMR	11:29.95	13:02.72	12:13.44	9:51.00	10:49.22	10:21.31
	(20.95)	(22.72)	(22.14)	(18.00)	(19.22)	(18.71)

LAS CRUCES, NEW MEXICO   ALTITUDE: 3,896

EVENT	WOMEN			MEN		
	I	II	III	I	II	III
5,000 M	16:27.74	17:13.55	17:28.77	14:08.34	14:30.62	14:48.90
	(17.74)	(18.55)	(18.77)	(15.24)	(15.62)	(15.90)
3,000 M	9:25.40			8:04.05		
	(9.40)			(8.05)		
1,500 M			4:38.21			3:55.86
			(4.21)			(3.56)
1 MILE	4:42.81	4:56.51	5:00.45	4:03.00	4:11.32	4:14.65
	(4.31)	(4.51)	(4.55)	(3.70)	(3.82)	(3.85)
800 M	2:06.11	2:10.48	2:14.99	1:48.40	1:51.21	1:53.41
	(0.46)	(0.48)	(0.49)	(0.40)	(0.41)	(0.41)
DMR	11:16.11	12:47.71	11:57.81	9:39.11	10:36.52	10:08.95
	(7.11)	(7.71)	(7.51)	(6.11)	(6.52)	(6.35)

LARAMIE, WYOMING   ALTITUDE: 7,212

	WOMEN			MEN		
EVENT	I	II	III	I	II	III
5,000 M	16:59.02	17:46.26	18:01.85	14:35.20	14:58.16	15:16.92
	(49.02)	(51.26)	(51.85)	(42.10)	(43.16)	(43.92)
3,000 M	9:42.10			8:18.35		
	(26.10)			(22.35)		
1,500 M			4:45.12			4:01.70
			(11.12)			(9.40)
1 MILE	4:49.87	5:03.90	5:07.91	4:09.07	4:17.58	4:20.95
	(11.37)	(11.90)	(12.01)	(9.77)	(10.08)	(10.15)
800 M	2:07.21	2:11.61	2:16.16	1:49.34	1:52.17	1:54.39
	(1.56)	(1.61)	(1.66)	(1.34)	(1.37)	(1.39)
DMR	11:27.75	13:00.33	12:11.12	9:49.11	10:47.20	10:19.35
	(18.75)	(20.33)	(19.82)	(16.11)	(17.20)	(16.75)

LOGAN, UTAH   ALTITUDE: 4,770

	WOMEN			MEN		
EVENT	I	II	III	I	II	III
5,000 M	16:34.73	17:20.86	17:36.16	14:14.34	14:36.77	14:55.16
	(24.73)	(25.86)	(26.16)	(21.24)	(21.77)	(22.16)
3,000 M	9:29.17			8:07.28		
	(13.17)			(11.28)		
1,500 M			4:39.71			3:57.13
			(5.71)			(4.83)
1 MILE	4:44.34	4:58.12	5:02.07	4:04.32	4:12.68	4:16.02
	(5.84)	(6.12)	(6.17)	(5.02)	(5.18)	(5.22)
800 M	2:06.31	2:10.68	2:15.20	1:48.56	1:51.38	1:53.58
	(0.66)	(0.68)	(0.70)	(0.56)	(0.58)	(0.58)
DMR	11:18.64	12:50.45	12:01.49	9:41.28	10:38.84	10:11.21
	(9.64)	(10.45)	(10.19)	(8.28)	(8.84)	(8.61)

LUBBOCK, TEXAS   ALTITUDE: 3,195

	WOMEN			MEN		
EVENT	I	II	III	I	II	III
5,000 M	16:22.79	17:08.37	17:23.53	14:04.08	14:26.26	14:44.46
	(12.79)	(13.37)	(13.53)	(10.98)	(11.26)	(11.46)
3,000 M	9:22.71			8:01.74		
	(6.71)			(5.74)		
1,500 M			4:37.18			3:54.98
			(3.18)			(2.68)
1 MILE	4:41.75	4:55.40	4:59.33	4:02.09	4:10.38	4:13.70
	(3.25)	(3.40)	(3.43)	(2.79)	(2.88)	(2.90)

EVENT	WOMEN			MEN		
	I	II	III	I	II	III
800 M	2:06.01	2:10.37	2:14.88	1:48.31	1:51.12	1:53.32
	(0.36)	(0.37)	(0.38)	(0.31)	(0.32)	(0.32)
DMR	11:14.36	12:45.81	11:56.96	9:37.60	10:34.91	10:07.38
	(5.36)	(5.81)	(5.66)	(4.60)	(4.91)	(4.78)

MISSOULA, MONTANA   ALTITUDE: 3,199

EVENT	WOMEN			MEN		
	I	II	III	I	II	III
5,000 M	16:22.82	17:08.40	17:23.56	14:04.11	14:26.28	14:44.48
	(12.82)	(13.40)	(13.56)	(11.01)	(11.28)	(11.48)
3,000 M	9:22.72			8:01.75		
	(6.72)			(5.75)		
1,500 M			4:37.18			3:54.99
			(3.18)			(2.69)
1 MILE	4:41.75	4:55.40	4:59.34	4:02.09	4:10.39	4:13.71
	(3.25)	(3.40)	(3.44)	(2.79)	(2.89)	(2.91)
800 M	2:06.01	2:10.37	2:14.88	1:48.31	1:51.12	1:53.32
	(0.36)	(0.37)	(0.38)	(0.31)	(0.32)	(0.32)
DMR	11:14.37	12:45.82	11:56.97	9:37.61	10:34.92	10:07.39
	(5.37)	(5.82)	(5.67)	(4.61)	(4.92)	(4.79)

OGDEN, UTAH   ALTITUDE: 4,300

EVENT	WOMEN			MEN		
	I	II	III	I	II	III
5,000 M	16:34.14	17:20.24	17:35.53	14:13.83	14:36.25	14:54.63
	(24.14)	(25.24)	(25.53)	(20.73)	(21.25)	(21.63)
3,000 M	9:28.85			8:07.00		
	(12.85)			(11.00)		
1,500 M			4:39.58			3:57.02
			(5.58)			(4.72)
1 MILE	4:44.21	4:57.98	5:01.93	4:04.21	4:12.57	4:15.90
	(5.71)	(5.98)	(6.03)	(4.91)	(5.07)	(5.10)
800 M	2:06.29	2:10.66	2:15.18	1:48.55	1:51.36	1:53.57
	(0.64)	(0.66)	(0.68)	(0.55)	(0.56)	(0.57)
DMR	11:18.42	12:50.22	12:01.26	9:41.10	10:38.64	10:11.02
	(9.42)	(10.22)	(9.96)	(8.10)	(8.64)	(8.42)

POCATELLO, IDAHO   ALTITUDE: 4,539

	WOMEN			MEN		
EVENT	I	II	III	I	II	III
5,000 M	16:32.80	17:18.84	17:34.11	14:12.68	14:35.07	14:53.42
	(22.80)	(23.84)	(24.11)	(19.58)	(20.07)	(20.42)
3,000 M	9:28.13			8:06.39		
	(12.13)			(10.39)		
1,500 M			4:39.29			3:56.78
			(5.29)			(4.48)
1 MILE	4:43.91	4:57.67	5:01.62	4:03.95	4:12.30	4:15.64
	(5.41)	(5.67)	(5.72)	(4.65)	(4.80)	(4.84)
800 M	2:06.25	2:10.62	2:15.14	1:48.51	1:51.33	1:53.53
	(0.60)	(0.62)	(0.64)	(0.51)	(0.53)	(0.53)
DMR	11:17.93	12:49.69	12:00.74	9:40.67	10:36.19	10:10.58
	(8.93)	(9.69)	(9.44)	(7.67)	(8.19)	(7.98)

PORTALES, NEW MEXICO   ALTITUDE: 4,009

	WOMEN			MEN		
EVENT	I	II	III	I	II	III
5,000 M	16:28.60	17:14.45	17:29.67	14:09.07	14:31.37	14:49.66
	(18.60)	(19.45)	(19.67)	(15.97)	(16.37)	(16.66)
3,000 M	9:25.86			8:04.44		
	(9.86)			(8.44)		
1,500 M			4:38.39			3:56.02
			(4.39)			(3.72)
1 MILE	4:42.99	4:56.70	5:00.65	4:03.16	4:11.49	4:14.81
	(4.49)	(4.70)	(4.75)	(3.86)	(3.99)	(4.01)
800 M	2:06.13	2:10.50	2:15.02	1:48.42	1:51.23	1:53.43
	(0.48)	(0.50)	(0.52)	(0.42)	(0.43)	(0.43)
DMR	11:16.41	12:48.04	11:59.13	9:39.37	10:36.80	10:09.22
	(7.41)	(8.04)	(7.83)	(6.37)	(6.80)	(6.62)

PROVO, UTAH   ALTITUDE: 4,627

	WOMEN			MEN		
EVENT	I	II	III	I	II	III
5,000 M	16:33.53	17:19.60	17:34.88	14:13.31	14:35.71	14:54.08
	(23.53)	(24.60)	(24.88)	(20.21)	(20.71)	(21.08)
3,000 M	9:28.52			8:06.72		
	(12.52)			(10.72)		
1,500 M			4:39.45			3:56.91
			(5.45)			(4.61)
1 MILE	4:44.07	4:57.84	5:01.79	4:04.09	4:12.45	4:15.78
	(5.57)	(5.84)	(5.89)	(4.79)	(4.95)	(4.98)

	WOMEN			MEN		
EVENT	I	II	III	I	II	III
800 M	2:06.27	2:10.64	2:15.16	1:48.53	1:51.35	1:53.55
	(0.62)	(0.64)	(0.66)	(0.53)	(0.55)	(0.55)
DMR	11:18.20	12:49.97	12:01.02	9:40.90	10:38.44	10:10.82
	(9.20)	(9.97)	(9.72)	(7.90)	(8.44)	(8.22)

PUEBLO, COLORADO   ALTITUDE: 4,700

	WOMEN			MEN		
EVENT	I	II	III	I	II	III
5,000 M	16:34.14	17:20.24	17:35.53	14:13.83	14:36.25	14:54.63
	(24.14)	(25.24)	(25.53)	(20.73)	(21.25)	(21.63)
3,000 M	9:28.85			8:07.00		
	(12.85)			(11.00)		
1,500 M			4:39.58			3:57.02
			(5.58)			(4.72)
1 MILE	4:44.21	4:57.98	5:01.93	4:04.21	4:12.57	4:15.90
	(5.71)	(5.98)	(6.03)	(4.91)	(5.07)	(5.10)
800 M	2:06.29	2:10.66	2:15.18	1:48.55	1:51.36	1:53.57
	(0.64)	(0.66)	(0.68)	(0.55)	(0.56)	(0.57)
DMR	11:18.42	12:50.22	12:01.26	9:41.10	10:38.64	10:22.02
	(9.42)	(10.22)	(9.96)	(8.10)	(8.64)	(8.42)

RAPID CITY, SOUTH DAKOTA   ALTITUDE: 3,247

	WOMEN			MEN		
EVENT	I	II	III	I	II	III
5,000 M	16:23.14	17:08.74	17:23.89	14:04.38	14:26.57	14:44.77
	(13.14)	(13.74)	(13.89)	(11.28)	(11.57)	(11.77)
3,000 M	9:22.90			8:01.90		
	(6.90)			(5.90)		
1,500 M			4:37.25			3:55.05
			(3.25)			(2.75)
1 MILE	4:41.82	4:55.48	4:59.41	4:02.15	4:10.45	4:13.77
	(3.32)	(3.48)	(3.51)	(2.85)	(2.95)	(2.97)
800 M	2:06.02	2:10.38	2:14.89	1:48.31	1:51.12	1:53.33
	(0.37)	(0.38)	(0.39)	(0.31)	(0.32)	(0.33)
DMR	11:14.48	12:45.94	11:57.09	9:37.71	10:35.03	10:07.49
	(5.48)	(5.94)	(5.79)	(4.71)	(5.03)	(4.89)

RENO, NEVADA — ALTITUDE: 4,620

EVENT	WOMEN I	WOMEN II	WOMEN III	MEN I	MEN II	MEN III
5,000 M	16:33.47 (23.47)	17:19.54 (24.54)	17:34.82 (24.82)	14:13.26 (20.16)	14:35.66 (20.66)	14:54.02 (21.02)
3,000 M	9:28.49 (12.49)			8:06.69 (10.69)		
1,500 M			4:39.44 (5.44)			3:56.90 (4.60)
1 MILE	4:44.06 (5.56)	4:57.82 (5.82)	5:01.78 (5.88)	4:04.08 (4.78)	4:12.43 (4.93)	4:15.77 (4.97)
800 M	2:06.27 (0.62)	2:10.64 (0.64)	2:15.16 (0.66)	1:48.53 (0.53)	1:51.34 (0.54)	1:53.55 (0.55)
DMR	11:18.18 (9.18)	12:49.95 (9.95)	12:01.00 (9.70)	9:40.88 (7.88)	10:38.42 (8.42)	10:10.80 (8.20)

SALT LAKE CITY, UTAH — ALTITUDE: 4,659

EVENT	WOMEN I	WOMEN II	WOMEN III	MEN I	MEN II	MEN III
5,000 M	16:33.79 (23.79)	17:19.88 (24.88)	17:35.17 (25.17)	14:13.54 (20.44)	14:35.95 (20.95)	14:54.32 (21.32)
3,000 M	9:28.67 (12.67)			8:06.84 (10.84)		
1,500 M			4:39.51 (5.51)			3:56.96 (4.66)
1 MILE	4:44.13 (5.63)	4:57.90 (5.90)	5:01.85 (5.95)	4:04.14 (4.84)	4:12.50 (5.00)	4:15.83 (5.03)
800 M	2:06.28 (0.63)	2:10.65 (0.65)	2:15.17 (0.67)	1:48.54 (0.54)	1:51.35 (0.55)	1:53.56 (0.56)
DMR	11:18.30 (9.30)	12:50.08 (10.08)	12:01.12 (9.82)	9:40.99 (7.99)	10:38.53 (8.53)	10:20.90 (8.30)

SOUTH LAKE TAHOE, NEVADA — ALTITUDE: 6,224

EVENT	WOMEN I	WOMEN II	WOMEN III	MEN I	MEN II	MEN III
5,000 M	16:48.35 (38.35)	17:35.10 (40.10)	17:50.56 (40.56)	14:26.04 (32.94)	14:48.76 (33.76)	15:07.36 (34.36)
3,000 M	9:36.45 (20.45)			8:13.50 (17.50)		
1,500 M			4:42.72 (8.72)			3:59.67 (7.37)
1 MILE	4:47.41 (8.91)	5:01.33 (9.33)	5:05.32 (9.42)	4:06.96 (7.66)	4:15.41 (7.91)	4:18.76 (7.96)

EVENT	WOMEN			MEN		
	I	II	III	I	II	III
800 M	2:06.78	2:11.17	2:15.70	1:48.97	1:51.79	1:54.00
	(1.13)	(1.17)	(1.20)	(0.97)	(0.99)	(1.00)
DMR	11:23.70	12:55.94	12:06.84	9:45.63	10:43.49	10:15.73
	(14.70)	(15.94)	(15.54)	(12.63)	(13.49)	(13.13)

SPEARFISH, SOUTH DAKOTA   ALTITUDE: 3,593

EVENT	WOMEN			MEN		
	I	II	III	I	II	III
5,000 M	16:25.53	17:11.24	17:26.43	14:06.44	14:28.67	14:46.91
	(15.53)	(16.24)	(16.43)	(13.34)	(13.67)	(13.91)
3,000 M	9:24.20			8:03.02		
	(8.20)			(7.02)		
1,500 M			4:37.75			3:55.47
			(3.75)			(3.17)
1 MILE	4:42.33	4:56.01	4:59.95	4:02.59	4:40.50	4:14.22
	(3.83)	(4.01)	(4.05)	(3.29)	(3.40)	(3.42)
800 M	2:06.06	2:10.43	2:14.94	1:48.36	1:51.16	1:53.37
	(0.41)	(0.43)	(0.44)	(0.36)	(0.36)	(0.37)
DMR	11:15.32	12:46.85	11:57.98	9:38.43	10:35.80	10:08.25
	(6.32)	(6.85)	(6.68)	(5.43)	(5.80)	(5.65)

Men's and Women's
Outdoor Qualifying Standards

DIVISION I—MEN
REGIONAL QUALIFYING STANDARDS
(SEA LEVEL)

Event	FAT	MT	ALTITUDE ADJUSTMENT 3k-5,999/6k+
100 Meters	10.50	—	+.03/+.06
200 Meters	21.19	—	+.07/+.12
400 Meters	47.26	47.0	+.11/+.21
800 Meters#	1:50.40	1:51.1	
1,500 Meters#	3:48.21	3:47.9	
Mile#	4:06.61	4:06.3	
3,000-Meter Steeplechase#	9:08.15	9:07.9	
5,000 Meters#	14:15.75	14:15.5	
110-Meter Hurdles	14.33	—	+.04/+.08
400-Meter Hurdles	52.51	52.2	+.11/+.21
400-Meter Relay	40.66	40.4	+.12/+.24
440-Yard Relay	40.86	40.6	+.12/+.24
1,600-Meter Relay	3:10.00	3:09.7	+.44/+.84
Mile Relay	3:11.20	3:10.9	+.44/+.84

	METRIC
High Jump	2.10
Pole Vault	5.05
Long Jump	7.34
Triple Jump	15.08
Shot Put	16.61
Discus	50.37
Javelin	61.62
Hammer	55.63

#—Altitude adjustment available.

DIVISION I—MEN
NATIONAL QUALIFYING STANDARDS
(SEA LEVEL)

	AUTOMATIC		**PROVISIONAL**	
Event	FAT	MT	FAT	MT
10,000 Meters#	29:00.00	28:59.7	29:45.00	29:44.7
Decathlon	7,500 points		7,000 points	

#—Altitude adjustment available.

DIVISION I—WOMEN
REGIONAL QUALIFYING STANDARDS
(SEA LEVEL)

Event	FAT	MT	ALTITUDE ADJUSTMENT 3k-5,999/6k+
100 Meters	11.75	—	+.03/+.07
200 Meters	23.96	—	+.07/+.14
400 Meters	54.61	54.3	+.11/+.21
800 Meters#	2:09.80	2:09.5	
1,500 Meters#	4:27.80	4:27.5	
Mile#	4:49.60	4:49.3	
3,000-Meter Steeplechase#	10:52.10	10:51.8	
5,000 Meters#	16:52.00	16:51.7	
100-Meter Hurdles	13.95	—	+.04/+.08
400-Meter Hurdles	1:00.82	1:00.5	+.11/+.21
400-Meter Relay	45.80	45.5	+.12/+.28
440-Yard Relay	46.00	45.7	+.12/+.28
1,600-Meter Relay	3:42.00	3:41.7	+.44/+.84
Mile Relay	3.43.20	3:42.9	+.44/+.84

	METRIC
High Jump	1.75
Pole Vault	3.80
Long Jump	5.95
Triple Jump	12.26
Shot Put	14.30
Discus	47.30
Javelin	43.15
Hammer	54.15

#—Altitude adjustment available.

DIVISION I—WOMEN
NATIONAL QUALIFYING STANDARDS
(SEA LEVEL)

	AUTOMATIC		PROVISIONAL	
Event	FAT	MT	FAT	MT
10,000 Meters#	34:10.00	34:09.7	35:15.00	35:14.7
Heptathlon 5,500 points			5,000 points	

#—Altitude adjustment available.

DIVISION II OUTDOOR—MEN
(SEA LEVEL)

	AUTOMATIC		PROVISIONAL	
Event	FAT	MT	FAT	MT
100 Meters	10.30	—	10.65	—
200 Meters	20.65	—	21.50	—
400 Meters	46.50	46.1	48.00	47.6
800 Meters#	1:49.40	1:49.1	1:53.00	1:52.7
1,500 Meters#	3:47.00	3:46.7	3:54.00	3:53.7
Mile#	4:05.16	4:04.9	$	@
3,000-Meter Steeplechase#	9:00.00	8:59.7	9:24.00	9:23.7
5,000 Meters#	14:00.00	13:59.7	14:50.00	14:49.7
10,000 Meters#	29:20.00	29:19.7	31:20.00	31:19.7
110-Meter Hurdles	13.90	—	14.75	—
400-Meter Hurdles	51.70	51.3	53.30	53.0
400-Meter Relay	40.00	39.6	41.15	40.8
440-Yard Relay	40.20	39.8	41.35	41.0
1,600-Meter Relay	3:09.00	3:08.7	3:13.30	3:13.0
Mile Relay	3:10.20	3:09.9	3:14.50	3:14.2

	METRIC	IMPERIAL	METRIC	IMPERIAL
High Jump	2.16	7'1"	2.08	6'9-3/4"
Pole Vault	5.18	17'	4.80	15'9"
Long Jump	7.72	25'4"	7.21	23'8"
Triple Jump	15.54	51'	14.55	47'9"
Shot Put	18.29	60'1/4"	16.00	52'6"
Discus	54.86	180'	49.08	161'
Javelin	66.44	218'	58.84	193'
Hammer	60.96	200'	52.42	172'
Decathlon	7,000 points		6,350 points	

#—Altitude adjustment available.

$—Time must be converted to 1,500 Meters by dividing by 1.08. Example: Athlete timed in 4:11.70 (251.70 seconds) in the mile. 251.70÷1.08=233.01 seconds (3:53.01) for 1,500 Meters. Athlete becomes a provisional qualifier. (Note: When the mile is contested at a site where an altitude adjustment is available, subtract the adjustment for the mile from the actual time and then convert the adjusted time to 1,500 meters.)

@—Time must be converted to 1,500 Meters by dividing by 1.08. Example: Athlete timed in 4:13.0 (253.0 seconds) in the mile. 253.0÷1.08=234.3 seconds (3:54.3) for 1,500 Meters. Athlete is not a provisional qualifier. (Note: When the mile is contested at a site where an altitude adjustment is available, subtract the adjustment for the mile from the actual time and then convert the adjusted time to 1,500 meters.)

DIVISION II OUTDOOR—WOMEN
(SEA LEVEL)

Event	AUTOMATIC		PROVISIONAL	
	FAT	MT	FAT	MT
100 Meters	11.50	—	12.10	—
200 Meters	23.80	—	24.80	—
400 Meters	54.00	53.6	56.60	56.2
800 Meters#	2:08.00	2:07.7	2:15.00	2:14.7
1,500 Meters#	4:27.00	4:26.7	4:41.00	4:40.7
Mile#	4:48.36	4:48.1	$	@
3,000 Meters#	9:40.00	9:39.7	10:18.00	10:17.7
3,000-Meter Steeplechase#	10:20.00	10:19.7	11:27.00	11:26.7
5,000 Meters#	16:40.00	16:39.7	17:50.00	17:49.7
10,000 Meters#	35:00.00	34:59.7	37:50.00	37:49.7
100-Meter Hurdles	13.80	—	14.65	—
400-Meter Hurdles	59.00	58.6	1:03.30	1:02.9
400-Meter Relay	45.50	45.1	47.50	47.1
440-Yard Relay	45.70	45.3	48.10	47.7
1,600-Meter Relay	3:42.00	3:41.7	3:52.00	3:51.7
Mile Relay	3:43.20	3:42.9	3:53.20	3:52.9

	METRIC	IMPERIAL	METRIC	IMPERIAL
High Jump	1.79	5'10-1/2"	1.69	5'6-1/2"
Pole Vault	4.00	13'1-1/2"	3.55	11'5-3/4"
Long Jump	6.25	20'6-1/4"	5.69	18'8"
Triple Jump	12.50	41'1/4"	11.60	38'3/4"
Shot Put	15.24	50'	13.26	43'6"
Discus	50.60	166'	44.00	144'4"
Javelin	47.24	155'	40.84	134'

	METRIC	IMPERIAL	METRIC	IMPERIAL
Hammer	56.38	185'	48.75	159'11"
Heptathlon	5,250 points		4,475 points	

#—Altitude adjustment available.

$—Time must be converted to 1,500 Meters by dividing by 1.08. Example: Athlete timed in 5:03.85 (303.85 seconds) in the mile. 303.85÷1.08=281.34 seconds (4:41.34) for 1,500 Meters. Athlete is not a provisional qualifier. (Note: When the mile is contested at a site where an altitude adjustment is available, subtract the adjustment for the mile from the actual time and then convert the adjusted time to 1,500 meters.)

@—Time must be converted to 1,500 Meters by dividing by 1.08. Example: Athlete timed in 4:59.4 (299.4 seconds) in the mile. 299.4÷1.08=277.2 seconds (4:37.2) for 1,500 Meters. Athlete becomes a provisional qualifier. (Note: When the mile is contested at a site where an altitude adjustment is available, subtract the adjustment for the mile from the actual time and then convert the adjusted time to 1,500 meters.)

DIVISION III OUTDOOR—MEN
(SEA LEVEL)

	AUTOMATIC		PROVISIONAL	
Event	FAT	MT	FAT	MT
100 Meters	10.59	—	10.83	—
200 Meters	21.31	—	21.81	—
400 Meters	47.50	—	48.50	—
800 Meters#	1:51.30	1:51.0	1:53.60	1:53.3
1,500 Meters#	3:50.60	3:50.3	3:55.20	3:54.9
Mile#	4:09.00	4:08.7	4:14.00	4:13.7
3,000-Meter Steeplechase#	9:07.00	9:06.7	9:23.00	9:22.7
5,000 Meters#	14:28.00	14:27.7	14:48.00	14:47.7
10,000 Meters#	30:23.00	30:22.7	31:20.00	31:19.7
110-Meter Hurdles	14.44	—	14.90	—
400-Meter Hurdles	52.40	—	54.00	—
400-Meter Relay	41.24	—	42.00	—
1,600-Meter Relay	3:13.50	3:13.2	3:17.50	3:17.2
Mile Relay	3:14.60	3:14.3	3:18.60	3:18.3
	METRIC		METRIC	
High Jump	2.11		2.01	
Pole Vault	5.00		4.63	
Long Jump	7.24		6.95	
Triple Jump	14.90		14.10	
Shot Put	17.17		15.40	

	METRIC	METRIC
Discus	52.50	47.50
Javelin	62.90	57.40
Hammer	57.55	51.00
Decathlon	6,550 points	6,000 points

#—Altitude adjustment available.

DIVISION III OUTDOOR—WOMEN
(SEA LEVEL)

	AUTOMATIC		PROVISIONAL	
Event	FAT	MT	FAT	MT
100 Meters	12.01	—	12.34	—
200 Meters	24.50	—	25.40	—
400 Meters	55.90	—	57.60	—
800 Meters#	2:12.00	2:11.7	2:15.80	2:15.5
1,500 Meters#	4:34.00	4:33.7	4:41.00	4:40.7
Mile#	4:55.90	4:55.6	5:03.40	5:03.1
3,000-Meter Steeplechase#	10:44.00	10:43.7	11:21.00	11:20.7
5,000 Meters#	17:00.00	16:59.7	17:46.00	17:45.7
10,000 Meters#	36:00.00	35:59.7	37:50.00	37:49.7
100-Meter Hurdles	14.43	—	15.10	—
400-Meter Hurdles	1:01.90	—	1:04.30	—
400-Meter Relay	47.50	—	49.00	—
1,600-Meter Relay	3:49.20	3:48.9	3:58.00	3:57.7
Mile Relay	3:50.60	3:50.3	3:59.40	3:59.1

	METRIC	METRIC
High Jump	1.71	1.64
Pole Vault	3.71	3.35
Long Jump	5.80	5.50
Triple Jump	12.00	11.25
Shot Put	14.28	12.90
Discus	46.50	41.50
Javelin	43.40	38.90
Hammer	52.60	46.00
Heptathlon	4,560 points	4,100 points

#—Altitude adjustment available.

Men's and Women's
Outdoor Automatic Qualifying Standards
Altitude Adjustments
Time allowance for altitude (in seconds) is in parentheses.

Note 1: To determine altitude adjustments for provisional standards add the allowance indicated in parentheses for the automatic standard to the sea-level provisional standard listed on pages 265-270.

AIR FORCE ACADEMY, COLORADO   ALTITUDE: 6,981

	WOMEN			**MEN**		
EVENT	**I**	**II**	**III**	**I**	**II**	**III**
10,000 M	36:05.67	36:58.49	38:01.87	30:38.18	30:59.30	32:05.86
	(115.67)	(118.49)	(121.87)	(98.18)	(99.30)	(102.86)
5,000 M	17:40.43	17:27.86	17:48.82	14:56.71	14:40.20	15.09.54
	(48.43)	(47.86)	(48.82)	(40.96)	(40.20)	(41.54)
3,000M SC	11:21.10	10:47.58	11:12.64	9:32.53	9:24.02	9:31.33
	(29.00)	(27.58)	(28.64)	(24.38)	(24.02)	(24.33)
3,000 M		10:05.80				
		(25.80)				
1,500 M	4:38.15	4:37.32	4:44.59	3:57.03	3:55.77	3:59.51
	(10.35)	(10.32)	(10.59)	(8.82)	(8.77)	(8.91)
1 MILE	5:00.79	4:59.51	5:07.34	4:16.14	4:14.64	4:18.62
	(11.19)	(11.15)	(11.44)	(9.53)	(9.48)	(9.62)
800 M	2:11.30	2:09.48	2:13.52	1:51.67	1:50.66	1:52.58
	(1.50)	(1.48)	(1.52)	(1.27)	(1.26)	(1.28)

ALAMOSA, COLORADO   ALTITUDE: 7,544

	WOMEN			**MEN**		
EVENT	**I**	**II**	**III**	**I**	**II**	**III**
10,000 M	36:21.32	37:14.53	38:18.37	30:51.47	31:12.75	32:19.78
	(131.32)	(134.53)	(138.37)	(111.47)	(112.75)	(116.78)
5,000 M	17:47.16	17:34.50	17:55.59	15:02.39	14:45.78	15:15.31
	(55.16)	(54.50)	(55.59)	(46.64)	(45.78)	(47.31)
3,000M SC	11:25.10	10:51.37	11:16.59	9:35.89	9:27.33	9:34.68
	(33.00)	(31.37)	(32.59)	(27.74)	(27.33)	(27.68)
3,000 M		10:09.35				
		(29.35)				
1,500 M	4:39.59	4:38.75	4:46.06	3:58.25	3:56.99	4:00.75
	(11.79)	(11.75)	(12.06)	(10.04)	(9.99)	(10.15)

EVENT	WOMEN			MEN		
	I	II	III	I	II	III
1 MILE	5:02.35	5:01.05	5:08.92	4:17.46	4:15.95	4:19.96
	(12.75)	(12.69)	(13.02)	(10.85)	(10.79)	(10.96)
800 M	2:11.58	2:09.75	2:13.81	1:51.91	1:50.90	1:52.82
	(1.78)	(1.75)	(1.81)	(1.51)	(1.50)	(1.52)

ALBUQUERQUE, NEW MEXICO   ALTITUDE: 5,120

EVENT	WOMEN			MEN		
	I	II	III	I	II	III
1,0000 M	35:19.77	36:11.47	37:13.51	29:59.22	30:19.90	31:25.05
	(69.77)	(71.47)	(73.51)	(59.22)	(59.90)	(62.05)
5,000 M	17:20.98	17:08.64	17:29.21	14:40.26	14:24.06	14:52.86
	(28.98)	(28.64)	(29.21)	(24.51)	(24.06)	(24.86)
3,000M SC	11:09.47	10:36.51	11:01.15	9:22.75	9:14.38	9:21.57
	(17.37)	(16.51)	(17.15)	(14.60)	(14.38)	(14.57)
3,000 M		9:55.45				
		(15.45)				
1,500 M	4:34.07	4:33.25	4:40.42	3:53.55	3:52.32	3:56.00
	(6.27)	(6.25)	(6.42)	(5.34)	(5.32)	(5.40)
1 MILE	4:56.38	4:55.11	5:02.83	4:12.38	4:10.90	4:14.83
	(6.78)	(6.75)	(6.93)	(5.77)	(5.74)	(5.83)
800 M	2:10.58	2:08.77	2:12.79	1:51.06	1:50.05	1:51.97
	(0.78)	(0.77)	(0.79)	(0.66)	(0.65)	(0.67)

AMARILLO, TEXAS   ALTITUDE: 3,676

EVENT	WOMEN			MEN		
	I	II	III	I	II	III
1,0000 M	34:50.36	35:41.34	36:42.52	29:34.25	29:54.65	30:58.89
	(40.36)	(41.34)	(42.52)	(34.25)	(34.65)	(35.89)
5,000 M	17:08.82	16:56.62	17:16.96	14:29.98	14:13.96	14:42.43
	(16.82)	(16.62)	(16.96)	(14.23)	(13.96)	(14.43)
3,000M SC	11:02.10	10:29.51	10:53.87	9:16.55	9:08.28	9:15.39
	(10.00)	(9.51)	(9.87)	(8.40)	(8.28)	(8.39)
3,000 M		9:48.89				
		(8.89)				
1,500 M	4:31.61	4:30.79	4:37.89	3:51.45	3:50.23	3:53.88
	(3.81)	(3.79)	(3.89)	(3.24)	(3.23)	(3.28)

	WOMEN			**MEN**		
EVENT	**I**	**II**	**III**	**I**	**II**	**III**
1 MILE	4:53.72	4:52.46	5:00.11	4:10.12	4:08.64	4:12.54
	(4.12)	(4.10)	(4.21)	(3.51)	(3.48)	(3.54)
800 M	2:10.24	2:08.43	2:12.45	1:50.77	1:49.77	1:51.68
	(0.44)	(0.43)	(0.45)	(0.37)	(0.37)	(0.38)

BANNER ELK, NORTH CAROLINA   ALTITUDE: 3,683

	WOMEN			**MEN**		
EVENT	**I**	**II**	**III**	**I**	**II**	**III**
10,000 M	34:50.49	35:41.47	36:42.66	29:34.36	29:54.76	30:59.00
	(40.49)	(41.47)	(42.66)	(34.36)	(34.76)	(36.00)
5,000 M	17:08.88	16:56.68	17:17.01	14:30.02	14:14.01	14:42.48
	(16.88)	(16.68)	(17.01)	(14.27)	(14.01)	(14.48)
3,000 M SC	11:02.13	10:29.54	10:53.91	9:16.58	9:08.31	9:15.41
	(10.03)	(9.54)	(9.91)	(8.43)	(8.31)	(8.41)
3,000 M		9:48.27				
		(8.27)				
1,500 M	4:31.62	4:30.81	4:37.91	3:51.46	3:50.24	3:53.89
	(3.82)	(3.81)	(3.91)	(3.25)	(3.24)	(3.29)
1 MILE	4:54.05	4:52.80	5:00.45	4:10.40	4:08.93	4:12.83
	(4.45)	(4.44)	(4.55)	(3.79)	(3.77)	(3.83)
800 M	2:10.24	2.08.44	2:12.45	1:50.78	1:49.77	1:51.68
	(0.44)	(0.44)	(0.45)	(0.38)	(0.37)	(0.38)

BILLINGS, MONTANA   ALTITUDE: 3,124

	WOMEN			**MEN**		
EVENT	**I**	**II**	**III**	**I**	**II**	**III**
10,000 M	34:40.54	35:31.29	36:32.18	29:25.93	29:46.22	30:50.16
	(30.54)	(31.29)	(32.18)	(25.93)	(26.22)	(27.16)
5,000 M	17:04.85	16:52.70	17:12.95	14:26.62	14:10.67	14:39.02
	(12.85)	(12.70)	(12.95)	(10.87)	(10.67)	(11.02)
3,000M SC	10:59.66	10:27.19	10:51.47	9:14.51	9:06.26	9:13.34
	(7.56)	(7.19)	(7.47)	(6.36)	(6.26)	(6.34)
3,000 M		9:46.73				
		(6.73)				
1,500 M	4:30.83	4:30.02	4:37.10	3:50.79	3:49.57	3:53.21
	(3.03)	(3.02)	(3.10)	(2.58)	(2.57)	(2.61)
1 MILE	4:52.87	4:51.62	4:59.24	4:09.40	4:07.93	4:11.81
	(3.27)	(3.26)	(3.34)	(2.79)	(2.77)	(2.81)

	WOMEN			MEN		
EVENT	I	II	III	I	II	III
800 M	2:10.16	2:08.36	2:12.37	1:50.71	1:49.71	1:51.61
	(0.36)	(0.36)	(0.37)	(0.31)	(0.31)	(0.31)

BOONE, NORTH CAROLINA   ALTITUDE: 3,333

	WOMEN			MEN		
EVENT	I	II	III	I	II	III
10,000 M	34:44.17	35:35.00	36:36.00	29:29.00	29:49.33	30:53.38
	(34.17)	(35.00)	(36.00)	(29.00)	(29.33)	(30.38)
5,000 M	17:06.31	16:54.14	17:14.43	14:27.85	14:11.88	14:40.28
	(14.31)	(14.14)	(14.43)	(12.10)	(11.88)	(12.28)
3,000M SC	11:00.56	10:28.04	10:52.36	9:15.26	9:07.01	9:14.10
	(8.46)	(8.04)	(8.36)	(7.11)	(7.01)	(7.10)
3,000 M		9:47.53				
		(7.53)				
1,500 M	4:31.11	4:30.30	4:37.39	3:51.03	3:49.81	3:53.45
	(3.31)	(3.30)	(3.39)	(2.82)	(2.81)	(2.85)
1 MILE	4:53.18	4:51.93	4:59.56	4:09.66	4:08.19	4:12.08
	(3.58)	(3.57)	(3.66)	(3.05)	(3.03)	(3.08)
800 M	2:10.19	2:08.38	2:12.40	1:50.73	1:49.73	1:51.63
	(0.39)	(0.38)	(0.40)	(0.33)	(0.33)	(0.33)

BOULDER, COLORADO   ALTITUDE: 5,260

	WOMEN			MEN		
EVENT	I	II	III	I	II	III
10,000 M	35:22.91	36:14.69	37:16.82	30:01.89	30:22.60	31:27.84
	(72.91)	(74.69)	(76.82)	(61.89)	(62.60)	(64.84)
5,000 M	17:22.30	17:09.94	17:30.54	14:41.37	14:25.15	14:53.99
	(30.30)	(29.94)	(30.54)	(25.62)	(25.15)	(25.99)
3,000M SC	11:10.26	10:37.26	11:01.93	9:23.41	9:15.04	9:22.23
	(18.16)	(17.26)	(17.93)	(15.26)	(15.04)	(15.23)
3,000 M		9:56.15				
		(16.15)				
1,500 M	4:34.34	4:33.52	4:40.69	3:53.78	3:52.55	3:56.23
	(6.54)	(6.52)	(6.69)	(5.57)	(5.55)	(5.63)
1 MILE	4:56.67	4:55.40	5:03.13	4:12.63	4:11.15	4:15.08
	(7.07)	(7.04)	(7.23)	(6.02)	(5.99)	(6.08)
800 M	2:10.62	2:08.81	2:12.83	1:51.10	1:50.09	1:52.00
	(0.82)	(0.81)	(0.83)	(0.70)	(0.69)	(0.70)

BOZEMAN, MONTANA   ALTITUDE: 4,926

	WOMEN			MEN		
EVENT	I	II	III	I	II	III
10,000 M	35:15.50	36:07.10	37:09.02	29:55.60	30:16.24	31:21.25
	(65.50)	(67.10)	(69.02)	(55.60)	(56.24)	(58.25)
5,000 M	17:19.20	17:06.88	17:27.42	14:38.75	14:22.58	14:51.33
	(27.20)	(26.88)	(27.42)	(23.00)	(22.58)	(23.33)
3,000M SC	11:08.39	10:35.49	11:00.09	9:21.85	9:13.49	9:20.67
	(16.29)	(15.49)	(16.09)	(13.70)	(13.49)	(13.67)
3,000 M		9:54.49				
		(14.49)				
1,500 M	4:33.70	4:32.89	4:40.04	3:53.24	3:52.00	3:55.68
	(5.90)	(5.89)	(6.04)	(5.03)	(5.00)	(5.08)
1 MILE	4:55.98	4:54.72	5:02.42	4:12.05	4:10.56	4:14.49
	(6.38)	(6.36)	(6.52)	(5.44)	(5.40)	(5.49)
800 M	2:10.52	2:08.71	2:12.73	1:51.01	1:50.01	1:51.92
	(0.72)	(0.71)	(0.73)	(0.61)	(0.61)	(0.62)

CALGARY, ALBERTA, CANADA   ALTITUDE: 3,438

	WOMEN			MEN		
EVENT	I	II	III	I	II	III
10,000 M	34:46.03	35:36.91	36:37.96	29:30.58	29:50.93	30:55.04
	(36.03)	(36.91)	(37.96)	(30.58)	(30.93)	(32.04)
5,000 M	17:07.07	16:54.89	17:15.19	14:28.49	14:12.51	14:40.92
	(15.07)	(14.89)	(15.19)	(12.74)	(12.51)	(12.92)
3,000M SC	11:01.02	10:28.48	10:52.81	9:15.65	9:07.39	9:14.48
	(8.92)	(8.48)	(8.81)	(7.50)	(7.39)	(7.48)
3,000 M		9:47.94				
		(7.94)				
1,500 M	4:31.26	4:30.45	4:37.54	3:51.16	3:49.93	3:53.58
	(3.46)	(3.45)	(3.54)	(2.95)	(2.93)	(2.98)
1 MILE	4:53.34	4:52.08	4:59.72	4:09.80	4:08.33	4:12.22
	(3.74)	(3.72)	(3.82)	(3.19)	(3.17)	(3.22)
800 M	2:10.20	2:08.40	2:12.41	1:50.74	1:49.74	1:51.65
	(0.40)	(0.40)	(0.41)	(0.34)	(0.34)	(0.35)

CEDAR CITY, UTAH   ALTITUDE: 5,782

EVENT	WOMEN			MEN		
	I	II	III	I	II	III
10,000 M	35:35.07	36:27.14	37:29.63	30:12.20	30:33.03	31:38.65
	(85.07)	(87.14)	(89.63)	(72.20)	(73.03)	(75.65)
5,000 M	17:27.42	17:15.00	17:35.70	14:45.70	14:29.40	14:58.38
	(35.42)	(35.00)	(35.70)	(29.95)	(29.40)	(30.38)
3,000M SC	11:13.33	10:40.19	11:04.97	9:26.00	9:17.58	9:24.81
	(21.23)	(20.19)	(20.97)	(17.85)	(17.58)	(17.81)
3,000 M		9:58.88				
		(18.88)				
1,500 M	4:35.41	4:34.58	4:41.78	3:54.69	3:53.45	3:57.15
	(7.61)	(7.58)	(7.78)	(6.48)	(6.45)	(6.55)
1 MILE	4:57.82	4:56.55	5:04.30	4:13.61	4:12.12	4:16.07
	(8.22)	(8.19)	(8.40)	(7.00)	(6.96)	(7.07)
800 M	2:10.80	2:08.98	2:13.01	1:51.25	1:50.24	1:52.15
	(1.00)	(0.98)	(1.01)	(0.85)	(0.84)	(0.85)

COLORADO SPRINGS, COLORADO   ALTITUDE: 6,007

EVENT	WOMEN			MEN		
	I	II	III	I	II	III
10,000 M	35:40.52	36:32.73	37:35.38	30:16.84	30:37.72	31:43.50
	(90.52)	(92.73)	(95.38)	(76.84)	(77.72)	(80.50)
5,000 M	17:29.72	17:17.28	17:38.02	14:47.65	14:31.31	15:00.36
	(37.72)	(37.28)	(38.02)	(31.90)	(31.31)	(32.36)
3,000M SC	11:14.71	10:41.50	11:06.33	9:27.16	9:18.73	9:25.97
	(22.61)	(21.50)	(22.33)	(19.01)	(18.73)	(18.97)
3,000 M		10:00.11				
		(20.11)				
1,500 M	4:35.89	4:35.06	4:42.28	3:55.10	3:53.86	3:57.56
	(8.09)	(8.06)	(8.28)	(6.89)	(6.86)	(6.96)
1 MILE	4:58.35	4:57.07	5:04.84	4:14.06	4:12.56	4:16.52
	(8.75)	(8.71)	(8.94)	(7.45)	(7.40)	(7.52)
800 M	2:10.88	2:09.06	2:13.10	1:51.32	1:50.31	1:52.23
	(1.08)	(1.06)	(1.10)	(0.92)	(0.91)	(0.93)

DENVER, COLORADO
ALTITUDE: 5,279

EVENT	WOMEN			MEN		
	I	II	III	I	II	III
10,000 M	35:23.34	36:15.13	37:17.28	30:02.25	30:22.97	31:28.22
	(73.34)	(75.13)	(77.28)	(62.25)	(62.97)	(65.22)
5,000 M	17:22.48	17:10.12	17:30.72	14:41.52	14:25.30	14:54.14
	(30.48)	(30.12)	(30.72)	(25.77)	(25.30)	(26.14)
3,000M SC	11:10.37	10:37.37	11:02.04	9:23.51	9:15.13	9:22.32
	(18.27)	(17.37)	(18.04)	(15.36)	(15.13)	(15.32)
3,000 M		9:56.25				
		(16.25)				
1,500 M	4:34.38	4:33.56	4:40.73	3:53.82	3:52.58	3:56.27
	(6.58)	(6.56)	(6.73)	(5.61)	(5.58)	(5.67)
1 MILE	4:56.72	4:55.44	5:03.17	4:12.67	4:11.18	4:15.12
	(7.12)	(7.08)	(7.27)	(6.06)	(6.02)	(6.12)
800 M	2:10.63	2:08.81	2:12.84	1:51.10	1:50.10	1:52.01
	(0.83)	(0.81)	(0.84)	(0.70)	(0.70)	(0.71)

EL PASO, TEXAS
ALTITUDE: 3,894

EVENT	WOMEN			MEN		
	I	II	III	I	II	III
10,000 M	34:54.45	35:45.54	36:46.84	29:37.73	29:58.16	31:02.53
	(44.45)	(45.54)	(46.84)	(37.73)	(38.16)	(39.53)
5,000 M	17:10.50	16:58.28	17:18.64	14:31.39	14:15.35	14:43.86
	(18.50)	(18.28)	(18.64)	(15.64)	(15.35)	(15.86)
3,000M SC	11:03.12	10:30.48	10:54.88	9:17.41	9:09.12	9:16.24
	(11.02)	(10.48)	(10.88)	(9.26)	(9.12)	(9.24)
3,000 M		9:49.80				
		(9.80)				
1,500 M	4:31.94	4:31.13	4:38.23	3:51.74	3:50.51	3:54.16
	(4.14)	(4.13)	(4.23)	(3.53)	(3.51)	(3.56)
1 MILE	4:54.08	4:52.82	5:00.47	4:10.42	4:08.95	4:12.85
	(4.48)	(4.46)	(4.57)	(3.81)	(3.79)	(3.85)
800 M	2:10.28	2:08.47	2:12.49	1:50.81	1:49.80	1:51.71
	(0.48)	(0.47)	(0.49)	(0.41)	(0.40)	(0.41)

FLAGSTAFF, ARIZONA   ALTITUDE: 6,888

EVENT	WOMEN			MEN		
	I	II	III	I	II	III
10,000 M	36:03.16	36:55.92	37:59.23	30:36.05	30:57.15	32:03.63
	(113.16)	(115.92)	(119.23)	(96.05)	(97.15)	(100.63)
5,000 M	17:39.36	17:26.80	17:47.74	14:55.80	14:39.31	15:08.62
	(47.36)	(46.80)	(47.74)	(40.05)	(39.31)	(40.62)
3,000M SC	11:20.46	10:46.97	11:12.01	9:31.99	9:23.49	9:30.79
	(28.36)	(26.97)	(28.01)	(23.84)	(23.49)	(23.79)
3,000 M		10:05.23				
		(25.23)				
1,500 M	4:37.92	4:37.09	4:44.36	3:56.84	3:55.58	3:59.32
	(10.12)	(10.09)	(10.36)	(8.63)	(8.58)	(8.72)
1 MILE	5:00.55	4:59.26	5:07.09	4:15.93	4:14.43	4:18.41
	(10.95)	(10.90)	(11.19)	(9.32)	(9.27)	(9.41)
800 M	2:11.25	2:09.43	2:13.48	1:51.64	1:50.62	1:52.55
	(1.45)	(1.43)	(1.48)	(1.24)	(1.22)	(1.25)

FORT COLLINS, COLORADO   ALTITUDE: 5,081

EVENT	WOMEN			MEN		
	I	II	III	I	II	III
10,000 M	35:18.91	36:10.59	37:12.60	29:58.49	30:19.16	31:24.28
	(68.91)	(70.59)	(72.60)	(58.49)	(59.16)	(61.28)
5,000 M	17:20.62	17:08.28	17:28.85	14:39.95	14:23.76	14:52.55
	(28.62)	(28.28)	(28.85)	(24.20)	(23.76)	(24.55)
3,000M SC	11:09.25	10:36.30	11:00.94	9:22.57	9:14.20	9:21.39
	(17.15)	(16.30)	(16.94)	(14.42)	(14.20)	(14.39)
3,000 M		9:55.25				
		(15.25)				
1,500 M	4:34.00	4:33.18	4:40.34	3:53.49	3:52.25	3:55.94
	(6.20)	(6.18)	(6.34)	(5.28)	(5.25)	(5.34)
1 MILE	4:56.30	4:55.03	5:02.75	4:12.32	4:10.83	4:14.76
	(6.70)	(6.67)	(6.85)	(5.71)	(5.67)	(5.76)
800 M	2:10.56	2:08.75	2:12.78	1:51.05	1:50.04	1:51.96
	(0.76)	(0.75)	(0.78)	(0.65)	(0.64)	(0.66)

GOLDEN, COLORADO — ALTITUDE: 5,675

EVENT	WOMEN			MEN		
	I	II	III	I	II	III
10,000 M	35:32.52	36:24.53	37:26.94	30:10.04	30:30.84	31:36.38
	(82.52)	(84.53)	(86.94)	(70.04)	(70.84)	(73.38)
5,000 M	17:26.34	17:13.93	17:34.61	14:44.79	14:28.50	14:57.45
	(34.34)	(33.93)	(34.61)	(29.04)	(28.50)	(29.45)
3,000M SC	11:12.69	10:39.57	11:04.33	9:25.45	9:17.05	9:24.27
	(20.59)	(19.57)	(20.33)	(17.30)	(17.05)	(17.27)
3,000 M		9:58.31				
		(18.31)				
1,500 M	4:35.18	4:34.36	4:41.55	3:54.50	3:53.26	3:56.96
	(7.38)	(7.36)	(7.55)	(6.29)	(6.26)	(6.36)
1 MILE	4:57.58	4:56.31	5:04.06	4:13.41	4:11.92	4:15.86
	(7.98)	(7.95)	(8.16)	(6.80)	(6.76)	(6.86)
800 M	2:10.76	2:08.94	2:12.97	1:51.21	1:50.21	1:52.12
	(0.96)	(0.94)	(0.97)	(0.81)	(0.81)	(0.82)

GREELEY, COLORADO — ALTITUDE: 4,774

EVENT	WOMEN			MEN		
	I	II	III	I	II	III
10,000 M	35:12.23	36:03.75	37:05.57	29:52.82	30:13.43	31:18.34
	(62.23)	(63.75)	(65.57)	(52.82)	(53.43)	(55.34)
5,000 M	17:17.84	17:05.53	17:26.04	14:37.60	14:21.45	14:50.16
	(25.84)	(25.53)	(26.04)	(21.85)	(21.45)	(22.16)
3,000M SC	11:07.57	10:34.71	10:59.28	9:21.15	9:12.81	9:19.98
	(15.47)	(14.71)	(15.28)	(13.00)	(12.81)	(12.98)
3,000 M		9:53.76				
		(13.76)				
1,500 M	4:33.42	4:32.61	4:39.75	3:53.00	3:51.77	3:55.44
	(5.62)	(5.61)	(5.75)	(4.79)	(4.77)	(4.84)
1 MILE	4:55.68	4:54.42	5:02.11	4:11.79	4:10.31	4:14.23
	(6.08)	(6.06)	(6.21)	(5.18)	(5.15)	(5.23)
800 M	2:10.48	2:08.67	2:12.69	1:50.98	1:49.97	1:51.88
	(0.68)	(0.67)	(0.69)	(0.58)	(0.57)	(0.58)

GUNNISON, COLORADO   ALTITUDE: 7,703

EVENT	WOMEN			MEN		
	I	II	III	I	II	III
10,000 M	36:25.90	37:19.21	38:23.19	30:55.35	31:16.67	32:23.85
	(135.90)	(139.21)	(143.19)	(115.35)	(116.67)	(120.85)
5,000 M	17:49.13	17:36.45	17:57.58	15:04.06	14:47.42	15:17.00
	(57.13)	(56.45)	(57.58)	(48.31)	(47.42)	(49.00)
3,000M SC	11:26.27	10:52.48	11:17.74	9:36.87	9:28.29	9:35.66
	(34.17)	(32.48)	(33.74)	(28.72)	(28.29)	(28.66)
3,000 M		10:10.39				
		(30.39)				
1,500 M	4:40.01	4:39.17	4:46.49	3:58.61	3:57.35	4:01.11
	(12.21)	(12.17)	(12.49)	(10.40)	(10.35)	(10.51)
1 MILE	5:02.80	5:01.51	5:09.39	4:17.85	4:16.34	4:20.35
	(13.20)	(13.15)	(13.49)	(11.24)	(11.18)	(11.35)
800 M	2:11.66	2:09.84	2:13.89	1:51.98	1:50.97	1:52.90
	(1.86)	(1.84)	(1.89)	(1.58)	(1.57)	(1.60)

LAS CRUCES, NEW MEXICO   ALTITUDE: 3,896

EVENT	WOMEN			MEN		
	I	II	III	I	II	III
10,000 M	34:54.49	35:45.57	36:46.88	29:37.76	29:58.20	31:02.56
	(44.49)	(45.57)	(46.88)	(37.76)	(38.20)	(39.56)
5,000 M	17:10.51	16:58.29	17:18.66	14:31.40	14:15.37	14:43.88
	(18.51)	(18.29)	(18.66)	(15.65)	(15.37)	(15.88)
3,000M SC	11:03.13	10:30.48	10:54.89	9:17.42	9:09.13	9:16.25
	(11.03)	(10.48)	(10.89)	(9.27)	(9.13)	(9.25)
3,000 M		9:49.81				
		(9.81)				
1,500 M	4:31.94	4:31.13	4:38.24	3:51.74	3:50.51	3:54.17
	(4.14)	(4.13)	(4.24)	(3.53)	(3.51)	(3.57)
1 MILE	4:54.08	4:52.82	5:00.48	4:10.42	4:08.95	4:12.85
	(4.48)	(4.46)	(4.58)	(3.81)	(3.79)	(3.85)
800 M	2:10.28	2:08.47	2:12.49	1:50.81	1:49.80	1:51.71
	(0.48)	(0.47)	(0.49)	(0.41)	(0.40)	(0.41)

LARAMIE, WYOMING   ALTITUDE: 7,163

EVENT	WOMEN I	II	III	MEN I	II	III
10,000 M	36:10.64	37:03.58	38:07.11	30:42.40	31:03.57	32:10.28
	(120.64)	(123.58)	(127.11)	(102.40)	(103.57)	(107.28)
5,000 M	17:42.56	17:29.97	17:50.96	14:58.51	14:41.97	15:11.37
	(50.56)	(49.97)	(50.96)	(42.76)	(41.97)	(43.37)
3,000M SC	11:22.37	10:48.78	11:13.89	9:33.60	9:25.07	9:32.39
	(30.27)	(28.78)	(29.89)	(25.45)	(25.07)	(25.39)
3,000 M		10:06.92				
		(26.92)				
1,500 M	4:38.60	4:37.77	4:45.05	3:57.42	3:56.16	3:59.90
	(10.80)	(10.77)	(11.05)	(9.21)	(9.16)	(9.30)
1 MILE	5:01.28	4:59.99	5:07.84	4:16.56	4:15.05	4:19.05
	(11.68)	(11.63)	(11.94)	(9.95)	(9.89)	(10.05)
800 M	2:11.38	2:09.56	2:13.61	1:51.75	1:50.73	1:52.66
	(1.58)	(1.56)	(1.61)	(1.35)	(1.33)	(1.36)

LOGAN, UTAH   ALTITUDE: 4,680

EVENT	WOMEN I	II	III	MEN I	II	III
10,000 M	35:10.23	36:01.70	37:03.47	29:51.13	30:11.71	31:16.56
	(60.23)	(61.70)	(63.47)	(51.13)	(51.71)	(53.56)
5,000 M	17:17.01	17:04.71	17:25.21	14:36.90	14:20.76	14:49.45
	(25.01)	(24.71)	(25.21)	(21.15)	(20.76)	(21.45)
3,000M SC	11:07.07	10:34.23	10:58.78	9:20.73	9:12.39	9:19.56
	(14.97)	(14.23)	(14.78)	(12.58)	(12.39)	(12.56)
3,000 M		9:53.31				
		(13.31)				
1,500 M	4:33.25	4:32.44	4:39.58	3:52.86	3:51.62	3:55.30
	(5.45)	(5.44)	(5.58)	(4.65)	(4.62)	(4.70)
1 MILE	4:55.50	4:54.23	5:01.93	4:11.63	4:10.15	4:14.07
	(5.90)	(5.87)	(6.03)	(5.02)	(4.99)	(5.07)
800 M	2:10.45	2:08.64	2:12.66	1:50.96	1:49.95	1:51.86
	(0.65)	(0.64)	(0.66)	(0.56)	(0.55)	(0.56)

LUBBOCK, TEXAS   ALTITUDE: 3,281

	WOMEN			MEN		
EVENT	I	II	III	I	II	III
10,000 M	34:43.26	35:34.07	36:35.04	29:28.23	29:48.55	30:52.57
	(33.26)	(34.07)	(35.04)	(28.23)	(28.55)	(29.57)
5,000 M	17:05.94	16:53.78	17:14.05	14:27.54	14:11.57	14:39.96
	(13.94)	(13.78)	(14.05)	(11.79)	(11.57)	(11.96)
3,000M SC	11:00.33	10:27.83	10:52.13	9:15.07	9:06.82	9:13.91
	(8.23)	(7.83)	(8.13)	(6.92)	(6.82)	(6.91)
3,000 M		9:47.32				
		(7.32)				
1,500 M	4:31.04	4:30.23	4:37.31	3:50.97	3:49.75	3:53.39
	(3.24)	(3.23)	(3.31)	(2.76)	(2.75)	(2.79)
1 MILE	4:53.10	4:51.85	4:59.48	4:09.59	4:08.13	4:12.01
	(3.50)	(3.49)	(3.58)	(2.98)	(2.97)	(3.01)
800 M	2:10.18	2:08.38	2:12.39	1:50.73	1:49.72	1:51.63
	(0.38)	(0.38)	(0.39)	(0.33)	(0.32)	(0.33)

MISSOULA, MONTANA   ALTITUDE: 3,199

	WOMEN			MEN		
EVENT	I	II	III	I	II	III
10,000 M	34:41.83	35:32.61	36:33.54	29:27.02	29:47.33	30:51.31
	(31.83)	(32.61)	(33.54)	(27.02)	(27.33)	(28.31)
5,000 M	17:05.37	16:53.21	17:13.48	14:27.06	14:11.10	14:39.47
	(13.37)	(13.21)	(13.48)	(11.31)	(11.10)	(11.47)
3,000M SC	10:59.98	10:27.49	10:51.78	9:14.78	9:06.53	9:13.61
	(7.88)	(7.49)	(7.78)	(6.63)	(6.53)	(6.61)
3,000 M		9:47.01				
		(7.01)				
1,500 M	4:30.93	4:30.12	4:37.20	3:50.87	3:49.65	3:53.29
	(3.13)	(3.12)	(3.20)	(2.66)	(2.65)	(2.69)
1 MILE	4:52.98	4:51.73	4:59.35	4:09.49	4:08.02	4:11.91
	(3.38)	(3.37)	(3.45)	(2.88)	(2.86)	(2.91)
800 M	2:10.17	2:08.37	2:12.38	1:50.72	1:49.71	1:51.62
	(0.37)	(0.37)	(0.38)	(0.32)	(0.31)	(0.32)

OGDEN, UTAH   ALTITUDE: 4,759

EVENT	WOMEN			MEN		
	I	II	III	I	II	III
10,000 M	35:11.91	36:03.42	37:05.23	29:52.55	30:13.15	31:18.05
	(61.91)	(63.42)	(65.23)	(52.55)	(53.15)	(55.05)
5,000 M	17:17.70	17:05.40	17:25.91	14:37.49	14:21.34	14:50.05
	(25.70)	(25.40)	(25.91)	(21.74)	(21.34)	(22.05)
3,000M SC	11:07.49	10:34.63	10:59.20	9:21.09	9:12.74	9:19.91
	(15.39)	(14.63)	(15.20)	(12.94)	(12.74)	(12.91)
3,000 M		9:53.69				
		(13.69)				
1,500 M	4:33.40	4:32.58	4:39.73	3:52.98	3:51.74	3:55.42
	(5.60)	(5.58)	(5.73)	(4.77)	(4.74)	(4.82)
1 MILE	4:55.65	4:54.39	5:02.08	4:11.76	4:10.28	4:14.20
	(6.05)	(6.03)	(6.18)	(5.15)	(5.12)	(5.20)
800 M	2:10.47	2:08.66	2:12.69	1:50.97	1:49.97	1:51.88
	(0.67)	(0.66)	(0.69)	(0.57)	(0.57)	(0.58)

PLAINVIEW, TEXAS   ALTITUDE: 3,230

EVENT	WOMEN			MEN		
	I	II	III	I	II	III
10,000 M	34:42.37	35:33.16	36:34.10	29:27.47	29:47.79	30:51.78
	(32.37)	(33.16)	(34.10)	(27.47)	(27.79)	(28.78)
5,000 M	17:05.59	16:53.42	17:13.69	14:27.24	14:11.28	14:39.65
	(13.59)	(13.42)	(13.69)	(11.49)	(11.28)	(11.65)
3,000M SC	11:00.11	10:27.62	10:51.92	9:14.89	9:06.64	9:13.72
	(8.01)	(7.62)	(7.92)	(6.74)	(6.64)	(6.72)
3,000 M		9:47.13				
		(7.13)				
1,500 M	4:30.97	4:30.16	4:37.24	3:50.91	3:49.69	3:53.33
	(3.17)	(3.16)	(3.24)	(2.70)	(2.69)	(2.73)
1 MILE	4:53.03	4:51.77	4:59.40	4:09.53	4:08.06	4:11.95
	(3.43)	(3.41)	(3.50)	(2.92)	(2.90)	(2.95)
800 M	2:10.18	2:08.37	2:12.38	1:50.72	1:49.72	1:51.62
	(0.38)	(0.37)	(0.38)	(0.32)	(0.32)	(0.32)

POCATELLO, IDAHO   ALTITUDE: 4,465

	WOMEN			MEN		
EVENT	I	II	III	I	II	III
10,000 M	35:05.76	35:57.12	36:58.75	29:47.33	30:07.87	31:12.58
	(55.76)	(57.12)	(58.75)	(47.33)	(47.87)	(49.58)
5,000 M	17:15.15	17:02.88	17:23.33	14:35.33	14:19.22	14:47.86
	(23.15)	(22.88)	(23.33)	(19.58)	(19.22)	(19.86)
3,000M SC	11:05.94	10:33.16	10:57.67	9:19.79	9:11.46	9:18.61
	(13.84)	(13.16)	(13.67)	(11.64)	(11.46)	(11.61)
3,000 M		9:52.31				
		(12.31)				
1,500 M	4:32.88	4:32.06	4:39.19	3:52.54	3:51.30	3:54.97
	(5.08)	(5.06)	(5.19)	(4.33)	(4.30)	(4.37)
1 MILE	4:55.09	4:53.83	5:01.51	4:11.29	4:09.81	4:13.72
	(5.49)	(5.47)	(5.61)	(4.68)	(4.65)	(4.72)
800 M	2:10.40	2:08.59	2:12.61	1:50.91	1:49.91	1:51.81
	(0.60)	(0.59)	(0.61)	(0.51)	(0.51)	(0.51)

PORTALES, NEW MEXICO   ALTITUDE: 4,009

	WOMEN			MEN		
EVENT	I	II	III	I	II	III
10,000 M	34:56.66	35:47.80	36:49.16	29:39.60	30:00.06	31:04.49
	(46.66)	(47.80)	(49.16)	(39.60)	(40.06)	(41.49)
5,000 M	17:11.40	16:59.17	17:19.55	14:32.16	14:16.10	14:44.64
	(19.40)	(19.17)	(19.55)	(16.41)	(16.10)	(16.64)
3,000M SC	11:03.67	10:31.00	10:55.42	9:17.87	9:09.58	9:16.70
	(11.57)	(11.00)	(11.42)	(9.72)	(9.58)	(9.70)
3,000 M		9:50.29				
		(10.29)				
1,500 M	4:32.12	4:31.31	4:38.42	3:51.89	3:50.66	3:54.32
	(4.32)	(4.31)	(4.42)	(3.68)	(3.66)	(3.72)
1 MILE	4:54.27	4:53.01	5:00.67	4:10.59	4:09.11	4:13.02
	(4.67)	(4.65)	(4.77)	(3.98)	(3.95)	(4.02)
800 M	2:10.30	2:08.49	2:12.51	1:50.83	1:49.82	1:51.73
	(0.50)	(0.49)	(0.51)	(0.43)	(0.42)	(0.43)

PROVO, UTAH   ALTITUDE: 4,627

| EVENT | WOMEN | | | MEN | | |
	I	II	III	I	II	III
10,000 M	35:09.12	36:00.56	37:02.29	29:50.18	30:10.76	31:15.57
	(59.12)	(60.56)	(62.29)	(50.18)	(50.76)	(52.57)
5,000 M	17:16.55	17:04.25	17:24.74	14:36.51	14:20.37	14:49.05
	(24.55)	(24.25)	(24.74)	(20.76)	(20.37)	(21.05)
3,000M SC	11:06.79	10:33.97	10:58.51	9:20.50	9:12.16	9:19.32
	(14.69)	(13.97)	(14.51)	(12.35)	(12.16)	(12.32)
3,000 M		9:53.06				
		(13.06)				
1,500 M	4:33.16	4:32.34	4:39.48	3:52.78	3:51.54	3:55.22
	(5.36)	(5.34)	(5.48)	(4.57)	(4.54)	(4.62)
1 MILE	4:55.40	4:54.13	5:01.82	4:11.55	4:10.07	4:13.98
	(5.80)	(5.77)	(5.92)	(4.94)	(4.91)	(4.98)
800 M	2:10.44	2:08.63	2:12.65	1:50.94	1:49.94	1:51.85
	(0.64)	(0.63)	(0.65)	(0.54)	(0.54)	(0.55)

PUEBLO, COLORADO   ALTITUDE: 4,700

| EVENT | WOMEN | | | MEN | | |
	I	II	III	I	II	III
10,000 M	35:10.66	36:02.14	37:03.91	29:51.48	30:12.08	31:16.94
	(60.66)	(62.14)	(63.91)	(51.48)	(52.08)	(53.94)
5,000 M	17:17.18	17:04.89	17:25.38	14:37.05	14:20.90	14:49.60
	(25.18)	(24.89)	(25.38)	(21.30)	(20.90)	(21.60)
3,000M SC	11:07.17	10:34.33	10:58.89	9:20.82	9:12.48	9:19.64
	(15.07)	(14.33)	(14.89)	(12.67)	(12.48)	(12.64)
3,000 M		9:53.41				
		(13.41)				
1,500 M	4:33.29	4:32.47	4:39.62	3:52.89	3:51.65	3:55.33
	(5.49)	(5.47)	(5.62)	(4.68)	(4.65)	(4.73)
1 MILE	4:55.54	4:54.27	5:01.97	4:11.67	4:10.19	4:14.11
	(5.94)	(5.91)	(6.07)	(5.06)	(5.03)	(5.11)
800 M	2:10.46	2:08.65	2:12.67	1:50.96	1:49.96	1:51.86
	(0.66)	(0.65)	(0.67)	(0.56)	(0.56)	(0.56)

RAPID CITY, SOUTH DAKOTA   ALTITUDE: 3,247

	WOMEN			MEN		
EVENT	I	II	III	I	II	III
10,000 M	34:42.66	35:33.46	36:34.42	29:27.72	29:48.04	30:52.05
	(32.66)	(33.46)	(34.42)	(27.72)	(28.04)	(29.05)
5,000 M	17:05.71	16:53.54	17:13.81	14:27.34	14:11.38	14:39.75
	(13.71)	(13.54)	(13.81)	(11.59)	(11.38)	(11.75)
3,000M SC	11:00.19	10:27.69	10:51.99	9:14.95	9:06.70	9:13.78
	(8.09)	(7.69)	(7.99)	(6.80)	(6.70)	(6.78)
3,000 M		9:47.19				
		(7.19)				
1,500 M	4:30.99	4:30.18	4:37.27	3:50.93	3:49.71	3:53.35
	(3.19)	(3.18)	(3.27)	(2.72)	(2.71)	(2.75)
1 MILE	4:53.05	4:51.80	4:59.43	4:09.55	4:08.08	4:11.97
	(3.45)	(3.44)	(3.53)	(2.94)	(2.92)	(2.97)
800 M	2:10.18	2:08.37	2:12.38	1:50.72	1:49.72	1:51.62
	(0.38)	(0.37)	(0.38)	(0.32)	(0.32)	(0.32)

RENO, NEVADA   ALTITUDE: 4,620

	WOMEN			MEN		
EVENT	I	II	III	I	II	III
10,000 M	35:08.97	36:00.41	37:02.14	29:50.06	30:10.63	31:15.44
	(58.97)	(60.41)	(62.14)	(50.06)	(50.63)	(52.44)
5,000 M	17:16.48	17:04.19	17:24.68	14:36.45	14:20.32	14:49.00
	(24.48)	(24.19)	(24.68)	(20.70)	(20.32)	(21.00)
3,000M SC	11:06.75	10:33.93	10:58.47	9:20.47	9:12.13	9:19.29
	(14.65)	(13.93)	(14.47)	(12.32)	(12.13)	(12.29)
3,000 M		9:53.03				
		(13.03)				
1,500 M	4:33.15	4:32.33	4:39.47	3:52.77	3:51.53	3:55.21
	(5.35)	(5.33)	(5.47)	(4.56)	(4.53)	(4.61)
1 MILE	4:55.38	4:54.12	5:01.81	4:11.53	4:10.06	4:13.97
	(5.78)	(5.76)	(5.91)	(4.92)	(4.90)	(4.97)
800 M	2:10.44	2:08.63	2:12.65	1:50.94	1:49.94	1:51.85
	(0.64)	(0.63)	(0.65)	(0.54)	(0.54)	(0.55)

SALT LAKE CITY, UTAH   ALTITUDE: 4,260

EVENT	WOMEN			MEN		
	I	II	III	I	II	III
10,000 M	35:01.60	35:52.86	36:54.37	29:43.80	30:04.30	31:08.89
	(51.60)	(52.86)	(54.37)	(43.80)	(44.30)	(45.89)
5,000 M	17:13.43	17:01.18	17:21.60	14:33.87	14:17.79	14:46.38
	(21.43)	(21.18)	(21.60)	(18.12)	(17.79)	(18.38)
3,000M SC	11:04.90	10:32.17	10:56.64	9:18.91	9:10.60	9:17.74
	(12.80)	(12.17)	(12.64)	(10.76)	(10.60)	(10.74)
3,000 M		9:51.39				
		(11.39)				
1,500 M	4:32.53	4:31.71	4:38.84	3:52.24	3:51.01	3:54.67
	(4.73)	(4.71)	(4.84)	(4.03)	(4.01)	(4.07)
1 MILE	4:54.71	4:53.45	5:01.13	4:10.96	4:09.49	4:13.40
	(5.11)	(5.09)	(5.23)	(4.35)	(4.33)	(4.40)
800 M	2:10.35	2:08.55	2:12.56	1:50.87	1:49.87	1:51.77
	(0.55)	(0.55)	(0.56)	(0.47)	(0.47)	(0.47)

SOUTH LAKE TAHOE, NEVADA   ALTITUDE: 6,224

EVENT	WOMEN			MEN		
	I	II	III	I	II	III
10,000 M	35:45.91	36:38.25	37:41.06	30:21.41	30:42.34	31:48.29
	(95.91)	(98.25)	(101.06)	(81.41)	(82.34)	(85.29)
5,000 M	17:32.01	17:19.54	17:40.33	14:49.58	14:33.21	15:02.32
	(40.01)	(39.54)	(40.33)	(33.83)	(33.21)	(34.32)
3,000M SC	11:16.08	10:42.80	11:07.68	9:28.31	9:19.86	9:27.11
	(23.98)	(22.80)	(23.68)	(20.16)	(19.86)	(20.11)
3,000 M		10:01.33				
		(21.33)				
1,500 M	4:36.37	4:35.54	4:42.77	3:55.51	3:54.26	3:57.98
	(8.57)	(8.54)	(8.77)	(7.30)	(7.26)	(7.38)
1 MILE	4:58.87	4:57.59	5:05.37	4:14.50	4:13.00	4:16.97
	(9.27)	(9.23)	(9.47)	(7.89)	(7.84)	(7.97)
800 M	2:10.96	2:09.15	2:13.18	1:51.39	1:50.38	1:52.30
	(1.16)	(1.15)	(1.18)	(0.99)	(0.98)	(1.00)

SPEARFISH, SOUTH DAKOTA   ALTITUDE: 3,593

EVENT	WOMEN			MEN		
	I	II	III	I	II	III
10,000 M	34:48.83	35:39.78	36:40.92	29:32.96	29:53.34	30:57.53
	(38.83)	(39.78)	(40.92)	(32.96)	(33.34)	(34.53)
5,000 M	17:08.20	16:56.01	17:16.33	14:29.45	14:13.45	14:41.90
	(16.20)	(16.01)	(16.33)	(13.70)	(13.45)	(13.90)
3,000M SC	11:01.72	10:29.14	10:53.50	9:16.24	9:07.96	9:15.07
	(9.62)	(9.14)	(9.50)	(8.09)	(7.96)	(8.07)
3,000 M		9:48.55				
		(8.55)				
1,500 M	4:31.48	4:30.67	4:37.77	3:51.35	3:50.12	3:53.77
	(3.68)	(3.67)	(3.77)	(3.14)	(3.12)	(3.17)
1 MILE	4:53.58	4:52.33	4:59.97	4:10.00	4:08.53	4:12.42
	(3.98)	(3.97)	(4.07)	(3.39)	(3.37)	(3.42)
800 M	2:10.23	2:08.42	2:12.43	1:50.76	1:49.76	1:51.67
	(0.43)	(0.42)	(0.43)	(0.36)	(0.36)	(0.37)

2005 TRACK AND FIELD CASE BOOK

Contents

RULE 2

Equipment

INTERNAL MOVEMENT

Rule 2-8-1 and Rule 10-7-1

SITUATION: While checking in the shot, the implement inspector feels movement inside the shot. The implement inspector impounds the illegal implement. Is this a correct decision?

RULING: No, the shot is a legal implement. Movement within the shot is allowed.

RULE 3

Meet Personnel

DUTIES OF THE MEET REFEREE

Rule 3-5-2b

SITUATION: The meet referee observes a competitor violating the lane running rule. No other officials see the violation. Does the referee have the responsibility to warn or disqualify the athlete?

RULING: In meets in which a games committee has not been established, the referee can only act upon the information provided by the appropriate meet officials. However, if a games committee has been established for this meet, the referee does have the authority to warn or disqualify the competitor.

Rule 3-5-2d and Position Statement (Athletes)

SITUATION: A meet official observes an athlete shortly after competition throwing a baton (or any equipment) in a display of disappointment or anger. The official reports to the referee what was observed. Does the referee have the responsibility to warn or disqualify the athlete?

RULING: Yes. The referee can warn or disqualify due to the fact that the athlete displayed unsporting conduct.

RULE 4

The Meet

HONEST EFFORT

Rule 4-1-2

SITUATION: A competitor starts the 5,000-meter run. After completing five laps, he steps off the track, tells the nearest official that he has severe stomach cramps, then leaves the stadium. The next day, the same competitor reports for the 1,500-meter run, in which he is declared, in the same competition. Should the competitor be allowed to compete in the 1,500?

RULING: No. Competitors must participate honestly in all events in which they are legally declared. This competitor did not follow the proper procedures, which require an injured athlete to be examined by the official meet medical personnel (e.g., medical doctor/athletic trainer), after dropping out of the 5,000-meter run.

SITUATION: A competitor starts the 200-meter dash. Fifty meters into the race, she develops a leg cramp that prevents her from completing the event. She is examined by the official meet medical personnel (e.g., medical doctor/athletic trainer), who determine that she was incapable of completing the 200, but should be able to compete in the 1,600-meter relay several hours later. Should the competitor be allowed to compete in the 1,600 relay?

RULING: Yes. A competitor who has withdrawn from an event shall be allowed to compete in a subsequent event(s) with documentation of an examination by the official meet medical personnel after the withdrawl, and clearance to compete once again from the official meet medical personnel.

STRAPS OF THE UNIFORM

Rule 4-2-1

SITUATION: A competitor reports to the start of the 100-meter dash with the straps of his uniform down and his chest exposed. The referee issues a yellow-card warning. The competitor contends that he is in conformance with the rule since he did not lower his straps in the area of competition. Is the referee's decision correct?

RULING: Yes. Before entering the area of competition, a competitor shall be responsible for wearing a legal uniform. When removing a jacket or shirt that is covering the running top, the uniform straps must already be on the competitor's shoulders.

UNDERGARMENTS

Rule 4-2-1, Rule 4-2-3 and Rule 8-8d

SITUATION: Two competitors from institution A are wearing sport bras underneath their singlets. One is wearing a black sport bra; one is wearing a yellow sport bra. Have they violated the rule that visible undergarments must be of an identical solid color?

RULING: Sport bras are not considered undergarments; therefore, the competitors have not violated the uniform rule. An example of an undergarment would be a T-shirt or turtleneck.

VAULTING HEADGEAR

Rule 4-2-1

SITUATION: A vaulter is denied the opportunity to compete by the event judge because the competitor is wearing a bicycle helmet instead of a vaulting helmet. Is this ruling correct?

RULING: No. NCAA rules do not have specifications for the helmet. Therefore, any type of headgear, or lack thereof, is permissible.

RELAY UNIFORMS

Rule 4-2-3

SITUATION: A relay team comes to the starting line with three members wearing identical tops and pants, shorts or brief(s) of identical color(s). The fourth member is wearing a one-piece body suit. The clerk tells the team that all members must have identical uniforms and cannot compete until all are dressed the same. Is this ruling correct?

RULING: No. It is not necessary for **all** members to be either in one-piece body suits, or in tops and pants, shorts or briefs. However, it is necessary for the primary color of any one-piece body suits worn by members of a relay team to be the same as the primary color of the top of those members not wearing one-piece body suits.

COLOR OF UNIFORM

Rule 4-2-3 and Rule 8-8b

SITUATION: Two runners on the same relay team or cross country team are wearing a different dye-lot color school-issued singlet. Have they violated the rule that any visible garments worn under the shorts or briefs must be of an identical solid color?

RULING: Uniforms of the same color but a different dye lot should be considered to be identical for the purpose of this rule. This ruling applies to visible undergarments also.

RULE 5

Track Events

RUNNING IN ASSIGNED LANE

Rule 5-5-2c

SITUATION: The runner starts the 100 meters in lane one and crosses the finish line in lane three. The runner does not impede another competitor. The referee, after consulting with the appropriate officials, disqualifies the runner. Is this a correct decision?

RULING: Yes. The runner must finish the event in the assigned lane.

WIRELESS COMMUNICATION DEVICES

Rule 5-5-4c and Rule 6-1-7c

SITUATION: During competition, a competitor is observed operating a cellular phone. When questioned, the competitor indicates that he is speaking with a friend who is not in attendance. Is this activity permitted?

RULING: No. The viewing of videotape or photos, or the use of any wireless communication device, by a competitor during event competition is prohibited. This warrants a yellow-card warning, with disqualification to follow if another violation provided by the rules occurs during the meet.

FLUIDS GIVEN DURING RACE

Rule 5-5-4 and Rule 8-6-15

SITUATION: Can fluids be provided to athletes during a distance race on the track or during a cross country race?

RULING: Yes. This is not considered to be a competition aid. Only persons designated by meet management shall make fluids available to all competitors.

ILLEGAL ASSISTANCE

Rule 5-5-4

SITUATION: Team A's coach is standing near the starting line of the 1,500-meter run and is announcing splits to his runners in the race. Meet management has established boundaries as to how close coaches and team personnel may stand to the starting line to announce splits or give encouragement. Team A's coach is outside the boundaries. Is this illegal assistance?

RULING: No. Meet management must establish the boundaries. Announcing splits and giving encouragement from the stands is permissable.

INTERFERENCE AT FINISH OF RELAY

Rule 5-8-6 and Rule 5-9f

SITUATION: In the 1,600-meter relay, Team A wins the event. As the rest of the teams are finishing, a member of Team A steps out on the track to celebrate the win and interferes with Team B's anchor runner five meters from the finish line, knocking the baton from his hand. Team B's anchor finishes the race without the baton. Should Team A be disqualified for interfering with Team B, and should Team B be disqualified for finishing without a baton?

RULING: Team A is disqualified for interfering with Team B. No other disqualification takes place, because Team B was not afforded the opportunity to finish the race with the baton.

RULE 6

Field Events

ALTERNATIVE PROCEDURES

Rule 6-1-2, Rule 6-1-5 and Rule 6-3-1

SITUATION: The games committee for a competition has determined that the alternative procedure will be utilized in the long jump. A competitor is in the first flight and requests to be excused from the jumping order to compete in the 400-meter relay. Is the competitor permitted to jump out of order?

RULING: No. Since the games committee adopted the alternative procedure outlined in Rule 6.3.1, the event is contested as a final with four attempts. The competitor must initiate an attempt in the predetermined order and within one minute after his name is called by the event judge.

ABSENCE FROM COMPETITION

Rule 6-1-5

SITUATION: Competitor A is in the combined event long jump. She leaves to participate in an open event. The combined event official allows the 60-second clock to run down for Competitor A and calls the next competitor to the runway. Competitor A returns to the combined event long jump and requests to take her jump out of order. The official does not allow her to take the jump and charges her with an attempt. Is this the correct ruling?

RULING: Yes. The combined event is treated as a final event. When a competitor in a combined event jump or throw misses an attempt to participate in an open event, the event clock is started. If the competitor fails to report for her attempt within the allotted time, she is charged with an attempt.

CERTIFIED IMPLEMENTS

Rule 6-1-12

SITUATION: All certified implements become the property of meet management. May any competitor use these certified implements?

RULING: A competitor may use another competitor's implement during competition, with the other competitor's permission. If meet management supplies meet implements, then anyone may use the meet implements.

TAPED WEIGHT/HAMMER HANDLE

Rule 6-1-12a
SITUATION: An athlete wants to use a weight or hammer, which has tape on the handle. Is this permissible?

RULING: No. Modifications of implements are not allowed.

EXITING THE THROWING CIRCLES

Rule 6-1-14e
SITUATION: After completing a successful throw, a competitor leaves the throwing circle with one foot on either side of the line dividing the circle from front to back. The first step was taken out the back half of the circle. The event judge calls this a foul because the competitor did not exit through the back half of the circle with both feet. Is this ruling correct?

RULING: No. The competitor had completed a legal throw.

SUBSTANCE ON HANDS

Rule 6-1-14
SITUATION: Is it permissible for competitors in the weight and/or hammer throws to apply a suitable substance to their hands or gloves?

RULING: Yes. Competitors may apply a suitable substance to their hands or gloves.

ADVANCEMENT TO FINALS IN SCORED MEETS

Rule 6-2-2
SITUATION: Four teams are involved in a scored meet in which the top eight places will receive points. Entries are limited to three athletes per event per team. Before the competition, the coaches agree to advance the top eight performers in each event and at least two performers from each institution. This creates the potential of advancing 10 athletes to the finals. Is this method of advancement allowed?

RULING: Yes. In scored meets with four or fewer teams, it is recommended that the top eight performers should advance to the finals, plus a minimum representation of two competitors (if entered) from each institution to conform with Rule 6-2-1.

BREAKING THE PLANE IN VERTICAL JUMPS
Rule 6-5-3 and Rule 6-6-2

SITUATION: A competitor in the high jump or pole vault aborts his approach. During the deceleration process, a body part or the vaulting pole passes through the horizontal plane. The competitor did not make contact with any part of the landing area or ground beyond the plane. Does this constitute a missed attempt?

RULING: No. It is permissable for a competitor to break the horizontal plane above or below the crossbar, provided no contact is made with the ground or landing area beyond the horizontal plane.

MOVING UPRIGHTS

Rule 6-6

SITUATION: A competitor completes an unsuccessful attempt in the pole vault competition. Immediately after the attempt, it is brought to the attention of the head event judge that the uprights were improperly positioned. Should the competitor be credited with a failed attempt?

RULING: No. This is considered a no vault due to the official's error and the competitor should receive another attempt.

SITUATION: A competitor completes a successful attempt in the pole vault competition. Immediately after the attempt, it is brought to the attention of the head event judge that the uprights were improperly positioned. Should the competitor be credited with a successful attempt?

RULING: Yes. This is considered a successful attempt despite the official's error.

WARM-UP TIME

Rule 6-6

SITUATION: Two vaulters have not taken an attempt in one hour. Upon re-entering competition after a height change, Vaulter A uses one of the two allowable warm-up minutes on the runway and landing area without the crossbar. Is Vaulter B allowed to use three minutes (one remaining minute from Vaulter A and the two allowable minutes)?

RULING: No. Each competitor in the pole vault is allowed a maximum of two minutes on the runway and landing area without the crossbar at a height change with the permission of the event official. Subsequent competitors do not have the right to utilize the unused time of previous competitors.

Note: The same ruling applies to the high jump, except that a maximum time of one and one-half minutes is allowed per competitor for warm-up.

DECLARATION OF TAKEOFF BOARD

Rule 6-7-2

SITUATIONS: A. In a dual-meet competition, Competitor A wishes to change the takeoff board in the triple jump for the finals. Is this permissible? B. In a meet in which there is a qualifying round on the first day and the preliminaries and finals on the second day, can the jumper change takeoff boards from the first day to the second day?

RULINGS: A. No. The competitor must declare the board to be used throughout the competition. B. Yes. The competitor may change boards from day one to day two.

EXITING LONG JUMP PIT

Rule 6-7-4

SITUATION: The long jumper completes the jump inside the landing area and then steps out of the landing area nearer the takeoff board. Is this a legal jump?

RULING: No. The jump is declared a foul. The jumper must exit the landing area ahead of the mark made.

REMOVAL OF HEAD GEAR, GLASSES, GLOVES

Rule 6-7-4, Rule 6-8-3c, Rule 6-9-3c, Rule 6-10-4b and Rule 6-11-3b

SITUATION: A competitor in a throwing event or horizontal jump is wearing glasses, gloves, hair ties, etc., that fall off during an attempt and land beyond the foul line, outside the throwing circle, outside or on the runway, or in the landing pit. Is this a foul?

RULING: No. In throwing events, a foul occurs if the competitor touches the outside of the throwing circle, the foul line or run-up lines with any part of the body. In horizontal jumps, a legal jump is measured from the nearest break in the landing area made by any part of the competitor's feet, hands, body or uniform.

TAPING INDIVIDUAL FINGERS

Rule 6-8-2

SITUATION: Is it permissible for a competitor in the shot to tape individual fingers to prevent injury?

RULING: This type of taping is illegal. Tape can only be applied if there is an open wound.

MEASURING OF JAVELIN THROW

Rule 6-10-1

SITUATION: An athlete throws the javelin. Upon landing, the metal head hits the ground first just above the tip. The field judge calls the throw a (flat) foul by raising the red flag. Was the official's call correct?

RULING: No. The javelin did fall metal head (not tip or point) first.

HAMMER- OR WEIGHT-THROW GLOVE

Rule 6-11-1 and Rule 10-9-5

SITUATION: Is it permissible during the hammer or weight throws for an athlete to compete wearing a glove that conceals any or all fingers?

RULING: No. This type of glove is illegal.

RULE 7

Scoring, Records

TIE FIRST PLACE/BAR PLACEMENT/VERTICAL JUMPS

Rule 7-1-5-3a

SITUATION: In the pole vault, Competitors A and B are the final two vaulters in the competition. Both made 4.88 meters (16-0) as their best height. They are tied on the number of jumps and the number of failures. Competitor A attempts to clear 5.03 meters (16-6) three times, but fails at each attempt. Competitor B passes 5.03 meters (16-6) and fails at all three attempts at 5.18 meters (17-0). This forces a jump-off for first place. At what height is the bar placed to begin the jump-off?

RULING: Even though the last height attempted was 5.18 meters (17-0), the jump-off begins with the bar at 5.03 meters (16-6), which is the lowest height attempted by any of the tied competitors above the tying height.

RULE 8

Cross Country

HAY BALES ON CROSS COUNTRY COURSE

Rule 8-2-2b

SITUATION: May hay bales be placed on a cross country course for a collegiate meet?

RULING: No. Obstacles and other hindrances shall be avoided throughout the course.

RULE 9

Combined Events

WITHDRAWING FROM COMBINED EVENT

Rule 9-8

SITUATION: An athlete starts, but does not complete, an event in a combined event competition. Is the athlete permitted to continue to compete in the combined event competition?

RULING: Yes. The athlete is not considered to have abandoned the combined event competition.

Rule 9-8 and Rule 4-1-2 Note 2

SITUATION: Is the athlete referred to in the situation immediately above permitted to compete in an open event in the same meet?

RULING: Yes. The honest effort rule does not apply to combined events.

Index to Rules

305